An Economic History of
the Middle East and North Africa

The Columbia Economic History of the Modern World
Stuart W. Bruchey, General Editor

AN
ECONOMIC HISTORY
OF THE
MIDDLE EAST *and* NORTH AFRICA

CHARLES ISSAWI

NEW YORK   COLUMBIA UNIVERSITY PRESS

Library of Congress Cataloging in Publication Data

Issawi, Charles Philip.
An economic history of the Middle East and North
Africa.

(The Columbia economic history of the modern world)
Bibliography: p.
Includes index.
1. Near East—Economic conditions.   2. Africa, North—
Economic conditions.   I. Title.   II. Series.
HC415.15.I84   330.956   81-19518
ISBN 0-231-03443-1   AACR2
ISBN 0-231-08377-7   (paper)

*Clothbound editions of Columbia University Press books are Smyth-sewn and
printed on permanent and durable acid-free paper.*

To the students
of Economics W4318 and W4337 at Columbia
and Near East Studies 350 and 351 at Princeton,
who heard much of it and improved it with
their questions, comments, and papers.

Contents

Abbreviations and Symbols

CC	France, Ministère des Affaires étrangères, Correspondance commerciale
FO	Great Britain, Public Record Office, Foreign Office
HHS	Austria, Haus-Hof und Staatsarchiv
IOC	Great Britain, India Office, Bombay, Commerce
IOPS	Great Britain, India Office, Bombay, Political and Secret
US GR 84	United States National Archives, Group 84, dispatches to Department of State
EHME	Charles Issawi, *Economic History of the Middle East* (Chicago, 1966)
EHI	Idem, *Economic History of Iran* (Chicago, 1971)
EHT	Idem, *Economic History of Turkey* (Chicago, 1980)
EHFC	Idem, *Economic History of the Fertile Crescent* (forthcoming)
CEHE	*Cambridge Economic History of Europe* (7 vols, 1942–78)
CSSH	*Comparative Studies in Society and History*
EDCC	*Economic Development and Cultural Change*
EI	*Encyclopaedia of Islam*
EI2	*Ibid.,* 2d edition
EJ	*Economic Journal*
IJMES	*International Journal of Middle East Studies*
JEEH	*Journal of European Economic History*
JEH	*Journal of Economic History*
JESHO	*Journal of the Economic and Social History of the Orient*
MEJ	*Middle East Journal*
BEM	*Bulletin économique du Maroc* (Rabat)
BESM	*Bulletin économique et social du Maroc* (Rabat)

EC	*L'Egypte Contemporaine* (Cairo)
Hesp.	*Hesperis* (Rabat)
MEEP	*Middle East Economic Papers* (Beirut)
RA	*La Revue Africaine* (Algiers)
RT	*La Revue Tunisienne* (Tunis)

. .	figure not available
—	nil or negligible
( )	figure estimated, e.g., (20)
/	between dates indicates fiscal or Muslim years, e.g., 1878/79
–	between dates indicates full period covered by the years, e.g., 1878–80

Preface

For over twenty years most of my research, and much of my teaching, has been on the economic history of the Middle East in the last two centuries. Given the state of scholarship in the field, I judged that the most useful service one could provide was a set of documentary histories of the main parts of the region, and wrote *The Economic History of the Middle East,* (Chicago, 1966), *The Economic History of Iran* (Chicago, 1971), *The Economic History of Turkey* (Chicago, 1980) and *The Economic History of the Fertile Crescent* (forthcoming). Although the topic is still not ready for synthesis, it now seems advisable to sketch the main patterns and trends of the development of the Middle East during the last two hundred years, a period that witnessed a fundamental transformation in its economy and society.

I am fully aware of the limitations of this study. In the first place, I have done little original research on North Africa; yet the evolution of that region is so interesting in itself, so unfamiliar to the English-speaking (and indeed to the Arab) world, and so germane to that of the Middle East—with which it is now increasingly involved—that I have tried, wherever possible, to refer to it in my narrative.

Second, the lack of monographs on by far the greater part of the subject means that the sketch map given here necessarily contains large blank areas and others that are marked only in outline. It will take several decades before the monographs are written, the blanks filled in, and the faint lines replaced by firm strokes. This will have to be done by the people of the region themselves, just as the groundwork for the economic historiography of the Far East has been laid by Japanese and Chinese scholars. But the enormous resources of the Ottoman archives and the far fewer but nonetheless valuable documents available in some Arab countries and Iran, and the excellent work being done in a few centers of the region, give great hope that this task will be undertaken in the near future.

Third, and most important, there is a fundamental and unavoidable bias in this book. The study is based mainly either on Western archival material or on secondary works by Westerners and Middle Easterners largely derived from those sources. It therefore tends both to over-emphasize the degree of Western influence and to dwell at much greater length on those sectors that were linked to the Western economy, rather than those that remained relatively unaffected. A similar bias tends to prevail in all historiography, since change attracts greater attention and receives more emphasis than continuity, just as a moving object is more visible than a still one.

This approach carries a major risk—that of regarding the Middle East as an inert body, stirring only in response to forces emanating from the West. Of course, that was not so; even at its weakest and most passive, the region had its own internal dynamic. In certain fields, such as the religious or social, the internal forces were far more powerful than the foreign; in politics they were probably preponderant—at least in the Middle Eastern half of the region. But in the economic field the main stimulus was external. To repeat a well-known, though much abused image, the Middle East was the "periphery" and subjected to impulses emanating from the "center." It was part of a world system, whose laws it obeyed and whose destiny it shared. However, several sectors of the region's economy remained, to a greater or lesser degree, unaffected by these developments and have received inadequate attention in this book.

Last, there is the question of chronological proportion. Once the decision had been made to carry the narrative down to the present, the balance between its various parts had to be determined. Developments since the First World War are more varied and better documented than those of the preceding period. But they have also received far more attention; the literature on this subject is voluminous and often of high quality. Hence, in this book, distinctly more emphasis has been placed on the earlier period. But throughout, an attempt has been made to view the last two centuries as a continuum, in which the earlier trends are related to the later, and to grasp the process as a whole.

A further explanation is necessary. The region of the Middle East and North Africa is undoubtedly a cultural unit, sharing the same Islamic historical heritage. The economies of its constituent parts are also sufficiently similar to warrant common treatment. But their political history was quite different. In 1800 the region consisted, juridically, of three states: Morocco, Iran, and the huge Ottoman Empire in between. In fact, however, the authority of the Ottoman sultan was restricted to a small area around Istanbul, and the rest of the empire was governed by autonomous pashas, notables, and tribal leaders. Much the same situation prevailed in Iran and Morocco. In the period ending with the First World War, the Ottomans gradually lost almost all their European possessions but reestablished their rule over Anatolia, Syria, Iraq, Libya, and most of Arabia. The remaining provinces—Egypt, Tunisia, and Yemen—became practically independent, though continuing to acknowledge the sultan's suzerainty. Algeria was occupied by the French in 1830 and was followed by Tunisia in 1881, and in 1907 Morocco was occupied by France and Spain. Libya was invaded by the Italians in 1911. The British occupied Aden and the surrounding territory in 1839 and Egypt in 1882; the Sudan, between 1821 and 1881 an Egyptian province, was reconquered in 1898 and administered by the British, ostensibly as an Anglo-Egyptian condominium. The British also established a de facto protectorate over the Arab sheikhdoms of the Gulf. After the First World War France was given a League of Nations Mandate over Lebanon and Syria, and Britain over Iraq and Palestine (including Transjordan). Between the 1920s and the early 1970s, all the Arab states achieved independence, as did Israel in 1948.

Finally, a word on sources. This book has several hundred notes and a fairly large bibliography. Since, however, the aim is to help rather than to impress the reader, almost all the references are to secondary sources, and wherever possible to my other books on the economic history of the region. The last incorporate much work based on British, French, Austrian, United States, and Ottoman archives.

I have endeavored, wherever possible, to use metric units, but some figures have been given in the local units commonly used, e.g., faddan, qintar. Values have been converted into pounds sterling for 1800–1914 and into dollars for subsequent years, since those two currencies were the stablest in the respective periods.

I am greatly indebted to Bernard Lewis, Sir W. A. Lewis, Ian Little, Lucette Valensi, Jean-Claude Vatin, and my wife, whose critical comments were most helpful, to Judy Gross and Dorothy Rothbard, who typed from a far from clear manuscript, and to Ralph Hattox and Michel LeGall, who helped to straighten out the bibliography. Stuart Bruchey's encouragement was invaluable, and Bernard Gronert and Karen Mitchell were exemplary editors. A grant from the Dodge Foundation has greatly assisted my research.

After this book was sent to the printer, Roger Owen's *The Middle East in the World Economy, 1800–1914* (London: Methuen, 1981) was published. It covers Egypt, Iraq, Syria, and Turkey and the reader is strongly urged to refer to it for a more extensive treatment of those countries in those years.

An Economic History of
the Middle East and North Africa

CHAPTER I

Challenge and Response, 1800–1980

The economic history of the Middle East* in the last two hundred years has a dominant theme: impact and reaction, or challenge and response. The impact, or challenge, was that of industrializing, capitalist Europe, expanding all over the globe in search of food, raw materials, markets, and outlets for its energy, capital, and population, quite determined to ensure that the rules of the economic system under which it operated were observed by the rest of the world—if necessary through annexation. The reaction, or response, of the Middle East was slow in coming and gathered momentum only in the present century. For hundreds of years the region had been stagnating, or even retrogressing,[1] and many decades passed before an awakening to contemporary realities, a growing strength, and a combination of favorable external circumstances enabled it to respond to the challenges posed by European economic and political dominance.

Impact

The Western impact was first felt through trade, which expanded, rapidly and continuously, until the First World War. Beginning with steamships in the 1830s, modern transport began to penetrate the region. The second half of the century witnessed the building of telegraphs, railways, and ports. The same period also saw the inflow of a considerable amount of European capital and, in North Africa, Egypt, and Palestine, the large-scale settlement of European immigrants. A rudimentary financial system was established, geared to foreign trade

*Unless otherwise specified, the term "Middle East" includes North Africa and designates the region stretching from Morocco to Iran. "North Africa" designates the area west of Egypt. When North Africa is distinguished from the "Middle East," the latter term includes the present-day countries of Iran, Turkey, Iraq, Syria, Lebanon, Israel, Jordan, Saudi Arabia, Kuwait, Bahrain, the United Arab Emirates, Qatar, Oman, North Yemen, South Yemen, Egypt, and Sudan.

1

and often requiring (e.g., in Egypt) the importation of a large amount of coin to finance the moving of crops. The gross domestic product of most parts of the region multiplied severalfold during the century, and although population also expanded it seems likely that per capita incomes rose; that does not necessarily mean, however, that levels of living advanced appreciably. And more than ever before the region was integrated in the network of world trade and finance.

The expansion of production took place mainly in agriculture (chapter 7). Handicrafts began to decline early in the 19th century or even before because of the competition of European machine-made goods; and after a false start in the 1830s and 40s, modern factories were built only in the two or three decades preceding the First World War (chapter 8). Mining was equally slow in developing, and was important only in a few spots in Turkey,* Tunisia, and Morocco; oil was discovered in Egypt and Iran in 1908, but its development came later. Services earning foreign exchange were insignificant except in a few small zones in Lebanon and Egypt.

Agricultural development was most marked in certain export crops: cotton, tobacco, silk, opium, wine, dried fruits, and cereals, where output expanded severalfold. Except for vines in North Africa, oranges in Palestine, and, after the First World War, cotton in the Sudan Gezira, these crops were not grown in plantations owned or managed by foreigners, as happened in parts of Latin America, Southeast Asia, and Africa. Rather, they were planted by native landlords or peasants in addition to, or instead of, the traditional subsistence crops of the region. As in other parts of the world where similar developments took place (for example, rice in Southeast Asia, or cocoa and oilseeds in West Africa), landlords and peasants were able to expand production because all the necessary inputs were readily available.[2] Little capital was required, and hardly any fixed investment other than irrigation works; working capital was supplied in the form of advances to the farmer and wage goods bought by him. Nor was any technological innovation or organizational change necessary: the same old methods continued to be used even when new crops were introduced, as with tobacco in Turkey and Syria† and cotton in Egypt, Turkey, and Iran. It was relatively late

*Throughout this book "Turkey" designates the area within the borders of the Republic. "Ottoman Empire" denotes the area subject to the authority of the sultan at the given date, excluding tributary states. (See EHT:passim.)

†Unless otherwise specified, for the period up to the First World War "Syria" designates geographical or "greater" Syria, i.e., the area consisting of present-day Syria, Lebanon, Israel, Jordan, and parts of southern Turkey. For the period after 1918 it designates the area under French Mandate (exclusive of Lebanon) and subsequently the Syrian Republic. (See EHFC: passim.)

that substantial investments and improvements were made in some high-value crops, like cotton in Egypt, oranges in Palestine, and fruit in Lebanon. Nor, with rare exceptions, was any outside labor needed; normally the peasant and his household could supply all that was wanted.

Output could expand rapidly because the two essential factors of production, land and labor, were available. In all the countries of the region cultivation had shrunk greatly compared with former times, and there were large reserves of unused land. This meant that cultivation could be extended easily until the margin set by current technology and economics had been reached, at which point expansion would slow down drastically. In Egypt and Algeria the turning point came before the First World War, in Turkey, Syria, and Morocco in the 1950s, and in Iran somewhat later. Today only two countries, Iraq and particularly Sudan, still have large reserves of cultivable land.

The other factor was labor. Generally speaking, the Middle East did not suffer from a labor shortage. A contrast is provided by tropical Africa, where, because of the sparseness of population and its uneven concentration, the long distances involved, the differences of climate, and the low level of consumption, coercive measures were taken to increase the labor supply, such as head taxes, forced labor, or inducement to run into debt.[3] In the Middle East reserves of unused rural labor were generally available, and more work could be supplied when inducements were provided. Moreover, quite early in the 19th century, population began growing almost everywhere, soon averaging close to 1 percent per annum, with corresponding increases in the labor force (chapter 6). Occasional shortages were felt that led to a rise in agricultural wages, e.g., in Egypt in the 1860s, in Turkey and Iraq at the beginning of this century, and in Morocco after the First World War. On such occasions there was always a foreigner to propose the importation of labor (Chinese to Egypt, Indians to Iraq, etc.), as had been done in Southeast Asia, Africa, and elsewhere, but fortunately these suggestions were not taken up.

Farmers responded to the increase in demand for crops by expanding output and marketing the surplus; this was done with grain in Turkey, North Africa, Syria, Iraq, and for some decades Egypt. They would then start producing a cash crop for the market but continue to meet their own needs by growing traditional food crops, e.g., cotton and wheat in Egypt, tobacco, cotton, and wheat in Turkey. Eventually some of them would switch completely to a cash crop, buying their food from adjacent regions or importing it from abroad. The Lebanese silk-growing districts began this development, which was accentuated by the extension of fruit and vegetable cultivation in that country. Palestine followed with the replacement of grain by oranges and other cash crops. Similarly, in Egypt—and much later in Syria—cotton replaced wheat in some districts, and so did cotton and tobacco in Turkey and cotton and opium in Iran. In all these countries, and the others, population growth greatly increased the need for food imports.

These developments in agriculture could not have taken place without some fundamental changes in other economic and social sectors. Foremost was the imposition of order. In Egypt this was established by Muhammad Ali (1805-1849). His contemporary Mahmud II (1808-1839) was able to extend his authority to Anatolia, but in Syria it took some decades more, and Iraq was not firmly subjected to government control until after the First World War. In Arabia, Ottoman authority prevailed in much of Hijaz but not in Yemen or other parts of the peninsula. Iran was not effectively brought under government control until the reign of Reza Shah (1925-1941). In Sudan, Egyptian rule (1820-81) was followed by great disruption and the imposition of British control after 1899. The French conquest of Algeria took seventeen years (1830-47) and was followed by several rebellions, culminating in 1871. The conquest of Morocco, begun in 1907, was not completed until 1926, but Tunisia was swiftly subjected in 1881. In Libya the Italians, who had landed in 1911, were not in effective control of the whole country until 1932.

Another necessary change took place in land tenure (chapter 7). The communal or tribal forms of tenure that prevailed in most of the region were slowly replaced by private ownership, and subsistence farming gradually gave way to production for the market. By and large, this transformation affected neither the actual scale of operation (as distinct from that of ownership), nor the methods employed, nor the peasant's way of life. But by tying farmers to the market it subjected them to fluctuations in demand and prices. When crops failed, the individual, who in the past would have starved with his village or tribe, was more likely to borrow money, after which compounding debt often led to alienation of his land. In Iraq and Syria the settlement of titles was carried out in conditions that transferred huge amounts of tribal and village lands to sheikhs and other notables; in Egypt Muhammad Ali laid the basis of a large landlord class; and in North Africa a large proportion of the land was acquired, mainly by expropriation or chicanery, by European settlers. This resulted in a different pattern of landlord-tenant relations and, with the growth of population, in the emergence of a new phenomenon: a large landless peasantry. As against these socially unfavorable effects, a positive economic one should be noted. The new system gave many farmers a far greater incentive to improve methods, switch to more valuable crops, and increase output. Of course, such opportunities were seized by the more ambitious, intelligent, and rapacious farmers, as well as by the luckier ones.

In the past, as today, the bulk of the region's crops were rain-fed, not irrigated. The major exceptions have always been Egypt and central and southern Iraq. In both countries agricultural expansion would have been severely limited without irrigation works. In Egypt increasingly large and expensive dikes, canals, diversion barrages, and storage dams were provided, as they had been in the past, by the government: first by Muhammad Ali and his successors, then by the British. In Iraq only minor works were built, the first large-scale project being the Hindiyya dam in 1913. Turkey also opened the Konya dam in 1913. In the other countries almost nothing was done until the First World War (chapter 7).

A fourth necessary change was the development of a transport system, to move the increasing agricultural products (chapter 3). In the 1830s and 40s, steamships began to converge on the region: on North Africa mainly from France and England; on Egypt, Syria, and Turkey from England, France, Trieste, and Italy; on Turkey from Russia and Austria, through the Black Sea; on the Red Sea and, in the 1860s, the Persian Gulf, from India. For some decades these ships remained small, about 100–500 tons, and did not require elaborate ports. The first ports to be improved, and subsequently greatly enlarged, were those of Alexandria and Algiers, and between 1860 and 1913 good ports were built in Izmir, Oran, Port Said, Suez, Tunis, Bizerta, Beirut, Aden, Sousse, Sfax, Port Sudan, Istanbul, and Casablanca. Minor installations were provided in other harbors.

Where navigable rivers existed, steam navigation soon penetrated inland: on the Nile in Egypt in 1841 and in the Sudan in the 1860s, on the Tigris in 1839, and on the Karun in 1888. But the rest of the region had to rely on land transport, which long continued to mean caravans of camels or mules using desert tracks and mountain trails. In Algeria an extensive road system had been built by 1860, mainly for military purposes but also serving economic needs. Between 1859 and 1914 Lebanon developed a relatively large network of good roads. In the 1890s Egypt began to improve its agricultural roads, and the Ottoman Empire started implementing a major program on the eve of the First World War. In northern Iran, in the 1890s, the Russians built a serviceable road system. But by and large the impact of roads on the region was small.

Railways were more significant. Thanks to the traffic between Europe and India and the Far East, Egypt began to build its first railway as early as 1851, before Sweden or Central Poland, and by 1914 had a remarkably extensive network covering the whole country. Asian-European trade was also responsible for the Suez Canal, opened in 1869, which had both favorable and adverse effects on Egypt, Sudan, Arabia, Syria, and Iraq. In Turkey, railway building started in 1857, in Algeria in 1858, in Tunisia in 1878, in Syria in 1894, in the Sudan during the British expedition of 1896–98, in Morocco in 1911, and in Arabia, in the form of the Hijaz railway, in 1900. The next fourteen years saw a flurry of construction centered on the Baghdad railway, which by 1914 had crossed Anatolia and included a small isolated stretch in Iraq. Other important lines were built in Syria and North Africa, and in several countries railways were carrying the greater part of inland traffic. However, because of the absence of roads and the costliness of pack transport, tens of thousands of villages remained unaffected by these railways, particularly in Iran, Iraq, Arabia, and Anatolia.

Telegraphs came to the region in the 1850s and spread rapidly, being connected with those of Europe and India by the 1860s and soon reaching every sizable town.

A fifth development was the growth of export-import firms that could handle and finance the outward flow of agricultural produce and the inward flow of manufactures and other consumer goods. These firms were almost wholly foreign: British in Egypt and Iraq, French in Syria and North Africa, British and Russian in Iran, British, French, Austrian, Italian, and others in Turkey. Except in North Africa, foreigners did not generally venture beyond the principal ports (Alexandria, Izmir, Istanbul, Beirut, Basra, Jidda), or large inland cities (Aleppo, Damascus, Cairo, Tabriz, Tehran, Baghdad). Their access to the farmers was through small merchants and moneylenders recruited chiefly from minority groups—Armenians, Greeks, Jews, Syro-Lebanese Christians—who advanced money, bought crops for resale to the exporters, and marketed the goods consumed in the countryside. Sometimes minority members established their own contacts with Britain, France, and other industrial countries, setting up branches of export firms, and successfully competed with the European firms; this phenomenon was much more widespread in the Middle East than in North Africa, where there was only one minority, the Jews. In one country, Lebanon, local merchants (mainly Christians but also including some Muslims) soon came to predominate in foreign trade. But generally speaking, the minorities occupied an intermediate role between the bigger European merchants and bankers and the Muslims (chapter 5).

The 1850s saw the beginnings of organized banking. The commercial banks, all of which were foreign, concentrated on financing export and import trade and the internal movement of crops, but also made loans to consumers. By 1914 some countries had a rather tight network, e.g., Egypt, Algeria, and Tunisia, while others had the bare rudiments, e.g., Iran, Iraq, and Arabia. Here again, small private banks owned by minority members played an important supplementary role, and in some places, such as Beirut and Baghdad, constituted the main source of finance.

Mortgage banks, catering mainly to large landowners, followed a few decades later in countries enjoying rapid agricultural expansion, such as Egypt and Algeria. Egypt also soon had a cotton exchange, dealing in spot and futures transactions, and a stock exchange. In most countries European insurance companies established agencies covering—with mixed success—various kinds of risk.

Banks accounted for only a small fraction of the capital flowing into the region. In Turkey, Egypt, and Tunisia about half the total represented government debt, and in Iran more than half. The private sector absorbed the bulk of investment in Algeria (much of whose public expenditure was borne by France), and the same was true, on a far smaller scale, of Syria. Foreign investment in Iraq, Palestine, Sudan, Libya and Morocco was negligible but was to assume large proportions after the First World War, and in Arabia after the Second. Most of the capital came from France and Britain, followed by Germany, Belgium, and Russia and, much later, by the United States. These countries also supplied the accompanying technology and technical personnel.

The bulk of the proceeds of the loans actually received by the governments—which were usually far smaller than the nominal debt contracted—was spent on arms, palaces, and other unproductive purposes, but a fraction was used for building railways, canals, and other public utilities (chapter 4). The servicing of the public debt was a heavy burden on many countries, absorbing at one time half the budget revenue or more in Turkey, Egypt, and Tunisia, and a sizable fraction in Iran, Morocco, and Algeria. Investment in the private sector was more productive, going mainly to public utilities (ports, railways, streetcars, water, gas, and electricity), mining (phosphates, coal, oil, etc.) and, to a very small extent, manufacturing. The servicing of foreign debt, public and private, absorbed a significant share of export proceeds, rising to about a quarter in Egypt and Turkey.

One more important process remains to be mentioned: immigration. Hundreds of thousands of Frenchmen, Italians, and Spaniards settled in Algeria and Tunisia in the course of the 19th century, and many tens of thousands of Europeans of various nationalities in Egypt. The interwar period saw large-scale French migration to Morocco, Italian to Libya, and Jewish to Palestine, the last accelerating after the establishment of Israel. The Gulf oil countries saw an explosive, and presumably temporary, immigration of Americans, Europeans, Asians, Africans, and Arabs in the 1960s and 70s. On the other hand, Turkey, Syria, Iraq, and—except for a brief moment in the 1970s—Iran received little immigration from outside the Middle East and its adjacent regions, i.e., the Balkans and Transcaucasia. Also important was the immigration of members of minority groups from inside or outside the region to such countries as Egypt and Sudan. This made possible the rapid development of certain sectors of the economy by means of a peculiar ethnic division of labor.

At the top came the Europeans, who supplied, directly or indirectly, the required capital and directed the economy along the path demanded by the international market, i.e., essentially the production of farm crops and of minerals where they were available. The European position was secured either by more or less direct rule, as in North Africa, or through the system of "capitulations" and "consular" or "mixed courts" which gave them immunity from taxation and from the jurisdiction of the governments of the region. Beneath them were the minority groups, who supplied the greater part of the commercial, professional, and administrative skills required, and who constituted the equivalent of a bourgeoisie and petty bourgeoisie. Still lower was the bulk of the population, the ethnic Turks, Egyptians, Arabs, and Iranians, who farmed the land and supplied unskilled urban labor. There were a few very rich minority members who performed the same economic role as the Europeans, though they did not have quite the same status, and who usually enjoyed foreign citizenship and protection. There were, of course, many large Muslim landlords, a few of whom took an active interest in their estates, though most just collected their rents. In Algeria, in the interwar period in Libya, and to a lesser extent in Tunisia and Morocco, the European layer went much deeper in the social scale, including not only a petty bourgeoisie but an urban working class and a few small farmers. Conversely, in Iran foreign penetration was far smaller, and although both Armenians and Jews played an important role in commerce and the professions, by far the greater part of the middle class and all the upper was Muslim. The pyramids of wealth in the diagram illustrate the position in various parts of the region.

The role of the state was either passive or obstructive. or at best consisted in the provision of infrastructure. The importation of a middle

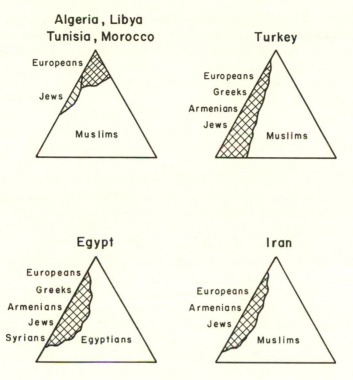

Pyramids of Wealth

class, *en bloc*, from abroad made it possible to exploit the natural resources of some countries with little development of their human resources. This was particularly true of Egypt.

Reaction

By 1914, Europeans held all the commanding heights of the economy except for landownership in the Middle East, and the minority groups occupied the middle and some of the lower slopes. But already forces were gathering to retake these positions. The clearest indications came from Turkey, where the Young Turk government that came to power after the 1908 revolution implemented several measures designed both to promote the development of some neglected sectors and to transfer control from foreigners to nationals, particularly Muslims. But in Egypt and Iran, along with increasing calls for political independence, there were also glimmerings of interest in achieving similar economic goals.

The reaction was against Western penetration and control, which not only subjected the peoples of the region to rulers alien in race, religion, and culture, but disrupted some of their most fundamental and cherished social and economic values and institutions.[4] The changes in land tenure undermined the basis of village and tribal solidarity, left farmers at the mercy of market fluctuations, and, combined with population growth, deprived many of their holdings. This process, of course, was greatly accentuated where foreigners acquired a large share of the land, as in French North Africa, to a much smaller extent in Egypt and Western Anatolia, and later in Libya and Palestine. The importation of foreign manufactured goods and the change in tastes and fashions ruined many handicrafts and threw tens of thousands of weavers and other craftsmen out of work—sometimes provoking riots like the one of the cotton ginners in Bergama in 1875—destroyed the guilds that had played an important role in town life, and swelled the underemployed urban proletariat, which was further augmented by the influx of displaced farmers from the countryside. Increasing use of mechanized transport displaced camel and mule drivers, sailors, boatmen, and other professions, also often organized in guilds; sometimes their protests were extremely violent, as in the ports of Istanbul and Beirut.[5] The introduction of Western legal codes, administrative practices, and educational systems rendered obsolete the painfully acquired skills of the ulama and other members of the traditional learned class. On the other hand, many displaced workers found employment in the new jobs created by the social changes. The modernization of the army and bureaucracy both opened new opportunities for certain groups and restricted the scope of the traditional beneficiaries; it also subjected the population to far tighter, if often less arbitrary, control than they had ever experienced before.[6]

Another powerful cause of discontent was the steady rise in prices. All foreign travelers in the early 19th century agree that the prices of foodstuffs and services were only a fraction of the corresponding ones in Europe, that those of many traditional manufactured goods were moderate, and that house rents were low. In the period 1780–1914, owing mainly to currency devaluation (chapter 9), the trend was upward, though there were some spells of stable or even falling prices, e.g., the 1840s in the Ottoman Empire and the years of the Great Depression (1873–95) in the whole region.[7] Although, on the whole, import prices were steady or declining until close to the end of the century, those of agricultural goods were pulled up by world demand until the onset of the depression. Both sets of prices rose sharply in the twenty years preceding the First World War (chapter 2). Apart from foreign trade and the rise in rents caused by the rapid growth of the principal cities (chapter 6), the main operative factor was the steady debasing of the currency, and, in Iran, the fall in world prices of silver (chapter 9).

No information is available regarding the impact of this price rise on such important matters as income distribution, capital formation, state revenues, and levels of living. Judging from the experience of other countries, one can only surmise that it must have been considerable and that various categories of fixed-income earners must have been gravely hurt.

The rise in prices was only one of many factors aggravating the financial difficulties of the various governments. Modernization, particularly of the army and navy,[8] is an expensive process. Modernization also whetted the appetite of the monarchs for luxury consumption, and access to Western credit enabled them to satisfy their desires by accumulating huge debts, entailing heavy service charges. But the revenue-raising capacity of governments increased relatively little. Customs duties were fixed by international treaties (chapter 2), and although their total yield increased in proportion to trade, it did not match the rise in expenditure. Receipts from traditional direct taxes rose much more slowly, and for various reasons no attempts were made to introduce more elastic income taxes (chapter 9). Decreased fiscal power must have caused serious discontent in both the ruling circles and the more conscious sections of the ruled.

Another disturbing process was the outflow of gold and silver from the Middle East to Europe in the first three-quarters of the 19th century, a phenomenon attested to by a large variety of British and French consular sources and caused by the failure of the region's exports to keep pace with its imports. The sums so dishoarded were, presumably, those accumulated in previous centuries, when the region's trade balance with Europe appears to have been positive and perhaps more than adequate to offset the simultaneous negative balance that seems to have prevailed in the Middle East's trade with India and the Far East. One can presume that the loss of gold, and the concomitant debasement of the currency, led many observers to conclude that the region was being impoverished.

Whether in fact this was so, in the sense that real per capita incomes and levels of living were falling, is doubtful. At some periods, in certain countries, and for some groups they clearly were, but as least as many examples of advance could be given (chapter 6). What is certain, however, is that distribution of the fruits of economic growth was highly unequal, and there is evidence that this fact was being realized and increasingly resented. Put at its simplest, the vast Muslim majority felt that it was getting very little compared with either the Europeans or the local minority groups. Indeed, in many places—most conspicuously French North Africa, Libya, and Palestine, but also western Anatolia, where Greeks were rapidly advancing in hitherto Turkish areas[9]—it must have felt thoroughly threatened. A modern scholar and a contemporary diplomat have described the situation well. Speaking of Egypt, Jacques Berque said, in terms that are somewhat flamboyant and economically inaccurate but are perceptive politically and psychologically:

> Who profited thereby, apart from the colonizers? Here and there we find partial indications: some middlemen—Jewish, Syro-Lebanese, Coptic, very occasionally Muslim, turning the import trade to their best advantage; some pashas, associated with the interests of those in power; an occasional landowner, acquiring mechanized pumps and setting himself up as a bourgeois lord of the manor; on a humbler level, the village *umdas* and shaikhs.[10]

In 1900, Sir Charles Eliot had put the matter even more strongly:

> But when force does not rule, when progress, commerce, finance and law give the mixed population of the Empire a chance of redistributing themselves according to their wits, the Turk and the Christian are not equal; the Christian is superior. He acquires the money and land of the Turk, and proves in a law-court that he is right in doing so. . . .
> One may criticize the Turkish character, but given their idiosyncrasies one must admit that they derive little profit from such blessings of civilization as are introduced into their country. Foreign syndicates profit most, and after them native Christians, but not the Osmanli, except in so far as he can make them disgorge their gains.[11]

For the Turks, Iranians, Syrians, Iraqis, Egyptians, Sudanese, Algerians, Libyans, Tunisians, and Moroccans, the economic history of the last sixty years has been mainly an attempt to make the beneficiaries "disgorge their gains."

In one important respect, however—that of population—the reaction against European domination had begun earlier. Unlike some of the peoples of Central America, tropical Africa, and the Pacific, the inhabitants of this region showed no inclination to die out. Around 1860, and even later, some European observers thought that the Turkish population of Western Anatolia was rapidly diminishing, and as late as

1880 a French demographer anticipated the disappearance of "the Arab race" in Algeria.[12] But on the contrary, almost everywhere growth was taking place, at annual rates varying between 0.5 and 1 percent (chapter 6). This demographic explosion, following several centuries of stagnation, was one of the most momentous results of the European impact, with its attendant security and hygiene, and ultimately one of the most disastrous. It provides an excellent illustration of Lord Cromer's statement: "Whatever impoverishment has taken place is much more due to good than to bad government."[13]

The Middle East scored its first economic victory in 1907 when, after nearly fifty years of fruitless negotiations and at the cost of valuable economic concessions to the Powers, the Ottoman government secured the right to modify its tariff (chapter 2). But it was the European Civil War of 1914–45 that, by fatally weakening European imperialism and stimulating Asian and African nationalism, allowed the region to regain both political and economic independence. Following the First World War and the nationalist movements, Turkey, Iran, Egypt, and Iraq, as well as Saudi Arabia and Yemen, achieved either complete or partial independence. The depression, by reducing their export earnings and causing a deterioration in their terms of trade, reinforced their desire to carry out fundamental economic changes, and shortly afterward the Second World War presented them with a unique opportunity of which they took advantage (chapters 8 and 9). The war also spawned innumerable controls on foreign exchange, trade, prices, and materials which greatly reinforced the power of the state. The oil crisis of 1973 opened the final act of this drama. Throughout, the governments of the region relied on political power, the weapon of the poor, to combat the foreigners' economic power. At first they worked in alliance with their own nascent bourgeoisies, and in some countries with their minority groups. Then the minorities were gradually squeezed out. Beginning in the 1950s, the native entrepreneurial bourgeoisies were, in turn, either eliminated or greatly restricted; the state emerged in virtual control of the economy; the prevailing ideology became that of Socialist Nationalism with a heavy Islamic tinge; and a new salaried bourgeoisie, employed by or dependent on the state, emerged. Needless to say, this process was greatly influenced by economic, political, and ideological developments in the world at large; by political events in the region, including both the struggles against Britain and France and the successive Arab-Israeli wars; and by internal upheavals and social changes in the various countries.[14]

The first step was the abolition of the "capitulations," which since the early Middle Ages had given foreigners and their protected subjects extraterritorial jurisdiction and immunity from local taxes. Turkey abolished them in 1914 on entering the war, saw them reimposed at the armistice, and finally did away with them in 1923; Iraq followed in 1922, Iran in 1928, and Egypt in 1937. The French and British Mandates for Syria, Lebanon, Palestine, and Transjordan did not include any extraterritorial privileges for foreigners.[15] These measures not only gave the governments greater control over the activity of aliens in their territory but allowed them to impose income and other direct taxes without having to exempt from their provisions the foreign subjects who controlled such a large portion of the economy.

Even more important was the lapse of the commercial treaties that had so severely restricted the governments' freedom in fiscal and development policies. In 1928–30, Tunisia, Iran, Turkey, and Egypt recovered full control, and in the Mandates this had come still earlier. They were now able to impose differentiated tariffs designed both to produce revenue and to encourage certain branches of industry and agriculture (chapter 2).

The governments also tried to help local industries by such measures as reduced railway rates, tax relief, and preference in government purchases. Another important act was the foundation of government-owned or sponsored banks to extend credit to sectors that had hitherto been neglected by the foreign-owned commercial banking system; this included both the establishment of new central banks, as in Turkey and Iran, or the strengthening of institutions that performed similar functions (like the National Bank of Egypt and the Banque de Syrie et du Liban), and the creation of various agricultural or industrial banks (chapter 9). Encouragement was also given to private banks designed both to increase national control of the economy and to promote industrial development, such as Misr Bank in Egypt (1920) and Ish Bank in Turkey (1924). Turkey and Iran intervened more directly by creating several state-owned and managed industries; in Turkey these were put under two government-owned holding companies, Sümer Bank (1933) for industry and Eti Bank (1935) for mining.

The governments also moved to promote political unification, extension of central control, and economic development by expanding their inadequate infrastructures. In the interwar period, Turkey doubled its railway network, Iraq and Morocco greatly extended their lines, which dated from just before the First World War, Iran built its first major railroads, and Sudan added new ones. After 1945, there was considerable construction in Iran, Saudi Arabia, Israel, and Syria. Port, airport, and road building was extensive throughout the region, and electric power generation, starting almost from nothing, expanded several hundredfold. In addition to building their own, the governments took over, by expropriation or purchase at low prices, the foreign utilities operating in their countries—such as railways, ports, streetcars, gas, water, and electric companies; in Turkey this was achieved in the 1920s and 30s and in the other states in the 1950s and 60s. Today, with insignificant exceptions, all transport and other utilities are government-owned and operated, as are telegraphs, radio broadcasting, and television.

The transfer of economic power from foreign to national hands was facilitated by—and in turn accelerated—a massive exodus of Europeans and minority groups. In the catastrophic events of 1915–23 Turkey eliminated its Armenian and Greek populations, and most of the Jews gradually emigrated. In Egypt the Second World War witnessed the sequestration of German and Italian property; the Arab-Israeli wars spelled the end of the Jewish community and the 1956 Suez War the expulsion of the British and French, while the other minorities (Greeks, Syro-Lebanese, and Armenians) left in the 1950s and 60s. In Iraq and Yemen the Jewish communities emigrated to Israel around 1950. Almost all the nearly 2 million Europeans in French North Africa and Libya emigrated in the 1950s and 60s, as did several hundred thousand Jews. The 1979 revolution in Iran resulted in the exodus of almost all the foreigners in that country. Thus, by 1960, the bulk of economic activity in the region, with the important exception of oil, had passed into the hands of the governments or the native bourgeoisies. The next two decades saw a powerful wave of socialization. Outside agriculture and housing, the national private sector was reduced to insignificance in Egypt, Syria, Iraq, Sudan, Algeria, Libya, South Yemen, and, most recently, Iran, and severely curtailed in the other countries. The takeover of the oil industry since 1973 has completed this process.

The Middle East has indeed come a long way since 1914. Its governments have achieved a large measure of control over the economy and society. Its infrastructure has been greatly expanded and is approaching adequacy, and the same may be said of its main financial institutions. Its energy resources are unmatched in the world, and it has a rapidly growing nucleus of industry and mining. Some attempts have been made to improve agriculture, but with little success. Taken as a whole, the region has enormous supplies of capital, which, however, is very unequally distributed between countries. Manpower resources have been developed, but almost every country in the region is still deficient in this respect. And, of course, problems are abundant: population explosion, urban hypertrophy, lagging food production, low industrial productivity, inadequately trained labor force, huge defense expenditures, increasing inequality, political instability, and social fragmentation.

Compared with the period before the First World War, the region's opportunities and potential have enormously increased and its political and economic importance to the world is far greater. But the difficulties it faces are also far more complex and intractable.

CHAPTER II

Expansion of Foreign Trade

Legislative and Administrative Framework

"The Ottomans, in their commercial regulations, adopted the extreme reverse of the Spanish fallacies for enriching and aggrandizing a nation. If Spain determined to admit nothing produced by any other country than her own colonies, Turkey seized upon the fanciful idea of becoming rich, prosperous and mighty, by letting nothing go out of, and to let everything come freely into, her dominions: a very acquisitive legislation, truly. . . . On the other hand, the Turkish Government, in tolerance and hospitality, opened her ports and dominions to the people and merchandise of all countries."[1] This quotation expresses very well the puzzlement of Europeans, whether protectionists or free traders, at the tariff policy of the governments of the Middle East. On the whole, the latter tended to encourage imports and discourage exports by levying low duties on both but subjecting many export items, especially foodstuffs, to prohibitions, monopolies, or high additional taxes.

The basic reason for this antimercantilist policy is to be sought in the balance of social forces in these countries. The dominant elements were bureaucrats and soldiers, whose interest in economic matters was limited to taxation and provisioning. As Carlo Cipolla put it so well: "The greatest concern of modern governments, in the field of economic policy, has been, in the last half-century, the 'business cycle.' The greatest bogey has been unemployment. Throughout the whole of the Middle Ages, the greatest concern of governments was the 'crop-cycle.' The greatest bogey was famine."[2] The governments were particularly concerned with the provisioning of cities, whose inhabitants could be troublesome in times of shortages. Hence efforts were made, by encouraging imports and discouraging or prohibiting exports, to ensure urban supplies. But whereas in Europe a counterweight was provided by the growing power

17

of merchants, craftsmen, and other producers, whose interests were more and more taken into account not only by the city states but also by the national monarchies,[3] in the Middle East their influence on policy was negligible—particularly since they were increasingly recruited from minority groups. This general factor was reinforced by other considerations. First, the lower level of prices in the region meant that it generally had an export surplus in its trade with Europe—though not with Asia. Second, customs duties and other levies on exports were an important source of income. Third, at least in North Africa and probably elsewhere, there was the belief that exports impoverished a country and that sales to infidels were immoral;[4] it may be recalled that, earlier, popes and emperors had banned the export of war materials (broadly interpreted) to Muslims, for much the same reasons. Finally, the Ottomans seem to have held that export taxes were fairer than import and that they could "make the pressure fall on the foreign consumer," which may sometimes have been true.[5]

Traditionally, the Ottoman Empire had levied duties of 3 percent on both imports and exports, rates that received international recognition in the treaties of capitulations, notably the one with England in 1675; Iran had similar arrangements. It should be noted, in passing, that these treaties provided for reciprocity: Ottoman and Persian traders in Europe were to enjoy privileges similar to those granted to European merchants in Turkey and Iran. Since in fact few Muslims went to Europe to trade—and those who did were not successful—the benefits became heavily one-sided.[6] But increasingly, from Anatolia to Tunisia, exports were subjected by the local rulers or governors to additional duties, monopolies, and prohibitions. In Morocco, imports generally paid 10 percent duty and exports more. Almost everywhere internal duties on goods transported from one town or region to another paid higher rates than imports.

The sharp depreciation of the Ottoman currency in the 18th century (chapter 9) greatly reduced the real yield of the customs duties. The government responded by multiplying prohibitions and monopolies, particularly on exports, and also requested the Powers to consent to an increase in rates. The Powers were naturally reluctant to accept a rise in the duties paid by their subjects, and were particularly apprehensive that any change might benefit their commercial and political rivals. But their trade—which was felt to have a great potential—was suffering from the multiplicity of restrictions and the haphazardness with which duties were levied and prohibitions applied; in particular they complained that their ships could not find return cargoes. Hence their merchants expressed willingness to accept a small rise in duties in return for less arbitrariness and capriciousness. This view was consonant with the belief that the interests of the industrialized countries were best served by the removal of all restrictions on commerce—the so-called "imperialism of free trade." In 1829, the Russians secured some commercial advantages under the Treaty of Adrianople. But the main thrust was that of Britain, by far the leading industrial power and the one that was to "open" such countries as China in 1842 and Morocco in 1856, and more generally to spearhead the Free Trade movement. The sultan's conflict with Muhammad Ali of Egypt made the Porte willing to accommodate Britain and, in return for that country's help, to grant its main demands, which were aimed even more at Egypt than at Turkey. The result was the Anglo-Turkish Commercial Convention of 1838.[7] This prohibited all monopolies, allowed British merchants to purchase goods anywhere in the empire without payment of any taxes other than import or export duty (or its equivalent in interior duty), and imposed duties of 3 percent on imports, 12 percent on exports, and 3 percent on transit. Besides the import duty, British merchants agreed to pay another 2 percent in lieu of other internal duties paid by importers. The convention was to apply to all parts of the empire, and specifically to Egypt. The other Powers soon acceded to it, and their consuls ensured its implementation.

In Iran Russia took the lead, with the 1813 and 1828 treaties, which imposed uniform duties of 5 percent on imports and exports, and in 1841 Britain, followed by the other Powers, obtained the same privileges.[8] In Morocco, the 1856 treaty with Britain subjected imports to a 10 percent duty and the main exports to specified rates.[9]

Between 1810 and the 1840s, Egypt pursued a very different policy. Muhammad Ali's aim was to build an independent state that was economically as well as militarily strong by improving and extending agriculture (chapter 7) and introducing factory industry (chapter 8). For this, control of foreign trade was essential; he used it both to raise revenue and to allocate resources and protect industry. Soon all the produce of Egypt, as well as that of Arabia and Sudan when sold for export, became a monopoly controlled by Muhammad Ali. Starting in 1812, he bought crops from farmers at low prices and resold them to Egyptian consumers at higher prices, and to foreign merchants at still higher ones—a system reminiscent of Soviet practice in the 1930's and of some underdeveloped countries after the Second World War. The following figures for 1833 (in French francs) are indicative:[10]

	Price paid to producers	Resale in country	Sale for export
Wheat (hectoliter)	3.34	6.40	7.60
Maize (hectoliter)	1.80	3.34	6.60
Beans (hectoliter)	2.00	3.60	5.00
Rice	10.00	. .	27.00
Cotton (metric quintal)	120.00	. .	250.00
Flax (metric quintal)	30.00	. .	72.00

Muhammad Ali soon controlled some 95 percent of Egypt's exports, and the profit of his foreign trade monopolies (half or more of which came from cotton) provided a quarter to a third of his budget receipts. On the import side, some 40 percent was on government account, and care was taken not to allow in goods that competed with his factories. Naturally, this system was resented by the Europeans, and the 1838 convention was, as noted, directed primarily against him. But, using every kind of pretext and administrative pressure, he continued to delay its application to Egypt even after his military defeat in 1840. By the end of his reign, however, and still more under his successors, the new Ottoman tariff was enforced.

By then the Turks were having second thoughts. By stimulating Ottoman exports, the new tariff undoubtedly benefited the agricultural interests that had helped to promote it. But it also exposed the handicrafts to the full blast of European competition, with disastrous consequences (chapter 8). Moreover, the government's need for funds was greater than ever. As early as 1843, it began negotiations with Britain for increasing import duties, and in 1861–62 new conventions were signed with the Powers, raising import duties from 3 to 8 percent, and reducing export duties from 12 to 8 percent with a further reduction of 1 percent a year until such time as they had reached 1 percent. Most internal duties were abolished by 1874, but an 8 percent duty continued to be levied on goods seaborne from one Ottoman town to another; in 1900 it was reduced to 2 percent and in 1909 abolished except for a few goods. The conventions of 1861–62 were also applied to Egypt and other Ottoman dependencies. In other words, by far the greater part of the Middle East became one of the lowest duty areas in the world, serving as a large market for European manufactures but with little protection for its own.

Starting in 1875, the Ottoman government repeatedly tried to raise import duties, mainly for revenue, but was as often rebuffed. Finally, in 1907, it was allowed to raise its import duty by 3 percent, the proceeds of the surtax to be allocated to the Public Debt Administration (chapter 4). And in 1914, as part of the overall settlement between the Powers (chapter 3), the duty was raised to 15 percent.[11]

The countries occupied by European states had a different tariff history. When the British took Aden in 1839, they applied to it the low Indian tariff rates. This, however, failed to divert to it trade from Hudayda and Mukha, so in 1850 it became a free port, with no duties.[12] Algeria, on the other hand, was by successive steps incorporated in the French customs zone. In 1835, goods from France were exempted from duty in Algeria. In 1851, duties on most Algerian goods imported to France were abolished, and in 1867 some remaining ones were also removed. In 1884, the French tariffs were applied to Algeria, with a few exceptions such as colonial goods, and in 1892 Algeria was included in the new French protectionist tariff.[13]

France's attempt to bring Tunisia into its customs zone was delayed by the treaties Tunisia had made with Britain and Italy, which would have enabled them to export their goods to France through Tunisia. In 1884 and 1885, various export and internal duties were abolished, and in 1890 the main Tunisian exports (cereals, oil, livestock) were exempt from import duty in France if carried on French ships. In 1898, following negotiations with the Powers, most French manufactured goods were exempt from import duties in Tunisia, while those of other countries paid high duties; and in 1904, 1915, and 1928 all the main Tunisian exports were, up to a certain quantity, allowed into France free of duty.[14]

France had a harder time in Morocco. The 1892 tariff reduced to 5 percent duties on certain goods that came mainly from France, such as silks, wines, and jewelry; but, because of German insistence and threats, the Act of Algeciras of 1906 laid down the principle of "economic liberty without any inequality." Under it, Morocco was allowed to add a surtax of 2½ percent, raising import duties to 12½ percent, and although after the occupation in 1912 certain French goods paid a lower rate, it has been well said that Germany prevented the "Tunisification of Morocco." After the First World War, Germany had to renounce its rights, but the United States took over its role, preventing France from obtaining favorable treatment for its goods though tariffs, and forcing France to resort to quotas and later exchange controls for that purpose. This, in turn, evoked a U.S. complaint which received a favorable decision from the International Court of Justice in 1952.[15]

In Libya the Ottoman tariff remained in force, with minor modifications, until 1921, after which duties on materials used in local industries were reduced, as were those on goods from Italy.[16]

On Turkey's entry into the war, import duties were doubled in 1915, and in 1916 replaced by a differentiated *ad valorem* tariff with rates of 8 percent for foodstuffs and raw materials, 12 percent for partly manufactured and 16 percent for wholly manufactured goods, with adjustments for currency depreciation. During the Allied occupation of Istanbul, a return to prewar conditions was decreed, but this decree was denounced by the revolutionary government. Under the Treaty of Lausanne of 1923 Turkey was allowed to maintain the 1916 tariff, with adjustment for currency changes, until 1929, at which time it would have full tariff autonomy.[17] Iran recovered tariff autonomy in 1928 and Egypt in 1930. All three countries immediately introduced highly differentiated tariffs intended both to increase revenue and to protect industry and certain branches of agriculture. Their example was followed by Iraq in 1933 and by almost all the other countries when they achieved independence after the Second World War.[18]

The breakup of the Ottoman Empire in 1918 had serious repercussions on its successor states in the Fertile Crescent—Iraq, Lebanon, Palestine, Syria, and Transjordan—which had played an important role in the commerce of Western Asia.[19] Instead of operating in a large duty-free zone, they were now confronted with rising tariffs in Egypt, Iran, and Turkey and with the threat of tariffs among themselves. The League of Nations Mandates therefore stipulated that, not withstanding the "open door" policy (which meant that any preferences granted, e.g., by Syria to France, would automatically apply to all League members), special customs arrangements could be made between contiguous states for duties below the "normal" tariff for League members (11 percent, raised in 1924 to 15 percent). Such arrangements were indeed made between the Mandates and Egypt, Saudi Arabia, and Turkey, but protectionist pressures soon raised duties. Of these the most powerful were the need for revenue and the desire to stimulate local industry. In Palestine, the tariffs were used to protect both Jewish industry and Arab agriculture.[20]

The 1930s also saw the introduction of quota systems, foreign exchange controls, and bilateral agreements with Germany, the Soviet Union, and other countries, particularly in Turkey and Iran. During the Second World War, foreign exchange control and import and export licensing became universal and were encouraged by the Allies acting through the Middle East Supply Centre.[21] Since then developments have been too diverse to allow of summarization. In those countries that have pushed socialization furthest, such as South Yemen, Algeria, Egypt, and Iraq, the state handles virtually all imports and exports. In a few others, notably Lebanon, Kuwait, and the Arabian oil countries, trade is practically free of restrictions, and duties are low; however, oil production and exports are now determined by the government. In a large number of intermediate countries, such as Turkey, Israel, Morocco, Tunisia, and until 1979 Iran, exports were free of restrictions, while imports paid relatively high, differentiated duties and many were subjected to licensing intended to protect national industry. Thus, taking the trade of the region as a whole, the laissez-faire period inaugurated in 1838 is over and gone. As in most parts of the world, governments are now firmly in control.

One last development may be mentioned: attempts at regional integration. The Regional Cooperation for Development (1965) between Iran, Pakistan, and Turkey has not achieved much, nor have various efforts to promote trade and other forms of integration in North Africa. In the Middle East the trend after the Second World War was at first toward disintegration: the cessation of economic relations between Israel and the Arab states in 1948, the breakup of the Syro-Lebanese customs and monetary union in 1950, the severance of the links binding some currencies (Egyptian, Iraqi, Palestinian, Transjordanian, and Sudanese) to sterling, the numerous boycotts between various pairs of Arab states in the 1950s and 60s. The Arab League's efforts to promote economic unity led to the creation, in 1964, of the Arab Common Market, in which the participating states (Egypt, Iraq, Jordan, Syria, and in 1977 Libya and Sudan) agreed to gradually remove customs duties between them, but the volume of trade is still small. The huge growth of oil revenues has greatly stimulated intraregional trade—which still, however, accounts for only about 5 percent of the total—and a far more potent factor for integration has been the movement of workers (chapter 5) and the flow of capital from the various oil-producing states and Arab funds (chapter 4).[22]

Expansion of Trade

Freed from its monopoly and tariff shackles, fed by growing industrial and agricultural production, carried by swifter and larger ships and trains, world trade expanded in the 19th century as never before. Whereas in the 18th century the growth rate of trade was a little over 1 percent per annum, in 1815–1913 it was over 3.5 percent. Trade multiplied 25 times in current values and about twice as much in real terms, since prices fell by more than half between 1820 and 1913.[23]

Table 2.1
Trade 1800–1914
(Exports plus Imports)
(£ million sterling and annual growth rates)[a]

	1830s		1870–73		1900		1910–12
Ottoman Empire	9	3.5%	41	−0.2%	38	2.7%	66
Turkey[b]	5	3.5%	26	−0.5%	20	2.4%	33
Iran	1800		1860		1901		1913
	2.5	1.2%	5	2.8%	15	2.6%	20
Egypt	1810		1850		1900		1910
	1.5	3.0%	5	4.0%	36	5.3%	60
Algeria	1835		1861–70		1891–1900		1913
	0.8	8.6%	9.6	2.4%	21	5.0%	47
Tunisia	1837–39		1861–65		1875–78		1913
	0.5	4.8%	1.6	−2.6%	1.1	7.1%	13
Morocco	1830s		1860s		1900		1913
	1	2.4%	2	2.0%	3.5	9.0%	9
Aden[c]	1843–50		1875		1903		1913
	0.2	10.2%	3.1	3.5%	6	4.2%	9
Iraq[c]	1845–46		1864–71		1880–87		1912–13
	0.2	3%	0.4	8.7%	1.8	4.6%	6.4
Syria[c]	1820s		1860s		1890		1913
	0.5	5.6%	4.5	2.8%	9	0.5%	10
World	1820		1860		1895–99		1913
	340	3.7%	1,450	2.7%	3,900	4.9%	8,360

[a] The percentages refer to growth rates between the relevant periods, i.e., the rate of growth in the Ottoman Empire between the 1830s and the period 1870–73 was 3.5 percent; that between 1870–73 and 1900 was −0.2 percent, etc.

[b] Trade of Istanbul, Izmir, Trabzon, Samsun, and Adana.

[c] Seaborne trade.

Notes: For details and sources: Egypt, EHME:363–64; Raymond 1973:107–305; Iran, EHI:130–32 which, according to Nowshirvani 1981:556, somewhat understates the increase; Turkey and Ottoman Empire, EHT:80–83 and Pamuk 1978; Iraq and Syria, Kalla 1969 and EHFC.

Aden's total seaborne trade in 1843–50 averaged 1.9 million rupees, and in 1851–58 6 million, to which should be added some 600,000 for land trade. By 1875–76 total sea and land trade stood at 35 million rupees, or about £3 million, and by 1903–4 £6 million (Hunter 1877:90; Great Britain, Admiralty 1916:190).

The trade of the whole Persian Gulf with Bombay, which was by far its largest overseas market and supplier, rose from an annual average of about £350,000 in 1801–5 to about £770,000 in 1825–29 and about £1,220,000 in 1854–58; IOC, 419 vols. 39–106, and table in EHFC.

For Algeria, Shaler 1826:79 puts imports at $1.2 million and exports at $273,000, the balance being made up by gold and silver. In 1831 total trade was 7 million francs, and in 1835 19.3 million (Demontès 1930a, Levasseur 1911). Other figures from trade returns.

Tunisia's exports in 1824 are put at 5.9 million francs and, in 1826 at over 8 million (Valensi 1969a:76). In 1837–39 trade averaged about 12–13 million francs, with imports somewhat exceeding exports (*Tunisie* 1900:2:66; MacGregor 1844:2:292). In 1861–65 imports averaged 19.6 million francs and exports 21.4 million—allowing for smuggling, the total was about 43 million, evenly balanced; in 1875–78 imports averaged 12 million francs and exports 15 million (Ganiage 1959:57–58, 465). In 1882–83 total trade was 44.5 million. Other figures from trade returns.

In Morocco sea trade in 1830–33 averaged 9 million francs, and by the early 1840s had risen to 23 million (Miège, 1961:2:123). The Saharan trade was much higher, and a contemporary estimate, probably exaggerated, put it at 60 million (*ibid*:2:151). The 1856 treaty stimulated sea trade, and by the mid 1860s it averaged 50 million, slowly rising to 55 million in the 1870s; the Saharan trade seems to have maintained its level (*ibid*:2:501, 3:237, 358). The Great Depression and droughts and epidemics in Morocco sent total sea trade down to an average of 37 million francs in 1878–84, and the Saharan trade also dwindled because of the decline of the slave trade and the diversion of other articles south, whence they were shipped to Europe (*ibid*:3:419, 371). But sea trade picked up again, averaging over 75 million francs in the early 1890s (*ibid*:4:364) and reaching 85 million in 1900 (Ayache 1956:53).

World figures taken from Imlah 1958:97–98, 189.

As table 2.1 shows, the volume of trade in the Middle East also expanded rapidly, though for most countries at a rate below the world average.

A few remarks may be made on this table. The greatest increase took place in Egypt, Algeria, and Tunisia, whose overall rate of growth about matched that of world trade.[24] In most countries there was one very rapid period of expansion, followed by slower and more "normal" growth: Turkey and Syria in the 1840s-60s, under the dual effect of the 1838 treaty and the world upswing; Egypt in the 1860s because of the rise in cotton prices and output due to the United States Civil War (chapter 7); Algeria, Tunisia, and Morocco following the establishment of French rule; and Iraq after the opening of the Suez Canal (chapter 3). All countries suffered from the Great Depression of the 1870s and benefited from the subsequent recovery. The percentage rates of growth suggest that, at least in the second half of the period, trade in the region grew much less rapidly than that of "temperate countries of settlement" and somewhat less than that of tropical countries.[25]

The trend of world trade in the next fifty years was very different. The upswing of 1926-29 compensated for the great drop during the First World War, giving an average annual rate of growth of 0.72 percent for 1913-29. The 1930s saw a sharp decline, the average rate for 1929-38 being −1.15 percent. The effects of the Second World War were exactly offset by the immediate postwar recovery, giving a rate of growth of zero in 1938-48. After that trade rose faster than ever before, at over 7 percent per annum.[26]

As table 2.2 shows, the main Middle Eastern countries followed world trends until the 1950s. More specifically, in real terms those countries that had grown fastest in the previous century—Aden, Algeria, Egypt, Syria, Tunisia, and Turkey—experienced sharp declines in the 1930s and little overall growth in 1913-46; the chief reason for this was, of course, the fall in world prices of agricultural produce. An increase was recorded in two groups of countries: oil producers, i.e., Iran and Iraq and in the 1940s and 50s the Arabian peninsula countries (chapter 10); and countries of heavy immigration—Libya, Morocco, and Palestine. Thanks to greatly increased cotton production from the Gezira scheme (chapter 7), the Sudan also had a surge similar to those of Egypt and the other countries in the previous century.

It is unnecessary to pursue this analysis further. By 1971, because of the great expansion of the volume of oil exports, total exports in the region amounted to nearly $21 billion and imports to over $13 billion, compared to $2.9 and $3.4 billion in 1948. After that the explosion of oil

Table 2.2
Value and Quantum of Trade, 1913–1955
($ millions)

		1913	1928	1933	1938	1948	1955
Algeria	M	129	198	160	143	482	696
	X	97	166	150	162	420	463
	T	226	364	310	305	902	1,159
	Q	89	98	115	100	168	189
Libya	M	8[a]	. .	15	47	22	40
	X	1[a]	. .	2	6	12	13
	T	9[a]	. .	17	53	34	53
	Q	22	. .	26	100	36	50
French	M	35	78	60	63	389	497
Morocco	X	8	50	26	43	178	328
	T	43	128	86	106	567	825
	Q	52	99	92	100	304	387
Tunisia	M	28	66	54	45	179	181
	X	34	48	27	39	61	106
	T	62	114	81	84	240	287
	Q	95	111	110	100	162	170
Egypt	M	135	245	88	188	674	538
	X	156	272	95	153	607	419
	T	291	517	183	341	1,281	957
	Q	150	124	61	100	214	140
Sudan	M	11	32	10	32	92	140
	X	6	29	9	30	99	145
	T	17	61	19	62	191	285
	Q	35	81	35	100	175	229
Aden	M	19	31	13	30	110	198
Colony	X	23	24	8	16	52	177
	T	42	55	21	46	162	375
	Q	117	98	52	100	200	406
Iran	M	55	76	26	71	170	565[b]
	X	38	153	69	134	589	735[b]
	T	93	229	95	205	759	1,300[b]
	Q	58	92	53	100	210	300
Iraq	M	(17)	35	19	46	184	272
	X	(15)	20	8	18	35	519
	T	(32)	55	27	64	219	791
	Q	(64)	70	48	100	194	615

Table 2.2 Continued

		1913	1928	1933	1938	1948	1955
Palestine/	M	. .	33	37	56	320	334
Israel	X	. .	7	9	29	38	89
	T	(5)	40	46	85	358	423
	Q	(7)	38	60	100	234	242
Lebanon and	M	(33)	52	28	37	214	394
Syria	X	(17)	21	6	17	36	159
	T	(50)	73	34	54	250	553
	Q	(119)	111	72	100	263	509
Turkey	M	114	114	35	119	348	498
	X	65	88	45	115	197	313
	T	179	202	80	234	545	811
	Q	98	71	39	100	132	172

[a] 1922
[b] 1958
M—Imports
X—Exports
T—Total
Q—Index of total (1938 = 100) deflated by average of United States consumer price index and wholesale price index, which was as follows (1938 = 100): 1913 78, 1928 122, 1933 88, 1948 176, 1955 201, 1958 213. The average of the United Kingdom import price index and export price index was (1938 = 100): 1913 83, 1928 122, 1933 85, 1948 265, 1955 343.

Sources: League of Nations, *Statistical Yearbook;* United Nations, *Statistical Yearbook;* United Kingdom, *Board of Trade Journal;* United States, *Statistical Abstracts.*

prices raised exports to $129 billion in 1977 and imports to $80 billion (see appendix table A.5). It should be noted that even the non-oil exporters (Egypt, Israel, Jordan, Morocco, Sudan, Tunisia, and Turkey) increased their imports (but not their exports) at a rate well above the world average.

Balance of Trade and Balance of Payments

The paucity and inaccuracy of data make it impossible to discuss this subject in detail. Until the end of the 18th century the region had an export surplus in its trade with Europe, and hence was receiving specie from Europe.[27] On the other hand, it almost certainly had a deficit in its trade with India, and therefore participated in the worldwide flow of bullion from America through Europe to the Far East.[28]

This situation changed radically after 1815. Rising demand for consumer goods (textiles and other manufactures and colonial goods— see below) does not seem to have been matched by increased exports. Fluctuations in crops and prices affected yearly totals, and no figures are available on the considerable overland trade; moreover, there was both contraband and underreporting. But, generally speaking, until the First World War the region seems to have had a clear deficit in both its merchandise and its current account. In a few areas like Lebanon and parts of Turkey, remittances from emigrants covered some of the deficit, and pilgrim and religious expenditures were important in Palestine and Hijaz.[29] Far larger was the capital inflow into Algeria, Tunisia, Egypt, Turkey, Syria, and Iran; but this in turn necessitated heavy service charges in the latter part of the period (chapter 4). Finally, many foreign observers report considerable dishoarding and export of specie—estimated at over 200 million francs in Morocco in 1860-95 and some 30 million in Beirut in 1838-57.[30]

As regards the main countries, Algerian statistics show a persistent trade deficit until 1913, presumably covered by capital inflow. Egyptian statistics show a steady surplus, which is anomalous considering the huge inflow of capital in the 1860s and 70s, and again in 1900-10. Ottoman trade figures record a constant deficit, and recent adjusted estimates by Pamuk also show an import surplus in every decade between 1830 and 1913. Tunisia's trade statistics are more or less in balance in 1880-1913, which again is puzzling in view of capital inflow. As for Iran, a rough balance until 1860 (a heavy deficit with India being offset by surpluses with Turkey, Russia, and Central Asia) seems to have been suceeded by a deficit until 1914. Returns for Syria's sea trade show a substantial import surplus and those on Iraq's sea trade show a small export surplus until 1904, after which importation of materials for irrigation and other works led to an import surplus; but lack of information on those two countries' land trade deprives such figures of significance.[31]

During the First World War, Algeria and Egypt had large export surpluses, owing to shipping shortages and the rise in the price of their products; and Britain's huge military expenditures in Egypt, Iraq, and Palestine greatly increased local holding of foreign exchange. Some of this was later used, e.g., by Egypt, to reduce foreign debt. In the interwar period the current account of Egypt, Turkey, Algeria, and—thanks to oil—Iran and Iraq was in rough balance. The rest of the region showed deficits which were covered by capital inflow in Libya, Morocco, Palestine, Sudan, Tunisia, and, to a small extent, Lebanon and Syria.

During the Second World War, shipping shortages once more reduced imports, and Allied military expenditures amounted to several billion dollars; hence almost all the countries came out with greatly increased sterling, franc, and other foreign exchange balances.[31] From 1946 to 1973, the region had a consistent pattern in its balance of payments. In every single country merchandise imports greatly exceeded exports (other than oil), sometimes severalfold. The region covered the gap by its exports of oil, men, and services, by drawing down its wartime balances, and by exploiting its strategic position to secure aid from a variety of sources. Oil revenues covered most of the deficit in current account in such countries as Iran, Iraq, Algeria, and Oman and more than covered it in Saudi Arabia, Kuwait, Libya, Qatar, and Abu Dhabi. Export of workers to Europe resulted in large remittances to Turkey, Algeria, Tunisia, and Morocco, while Arab workers in the Gulf countries and Libya sent huge sums to their countries of origin: Jordan, Lebanon, Egypt, Syria, and North and South Yemen (chapter 5). The services include religion (the holy places in Jerusalem, Mecca, Medina, Najaf, and Karbala), climate (tourism in Egypt, Israel, Lebanon, Morocco, Tunisia, and Turkey), antiquities (almost everywhere), and transport (Suez Canal, pipelines, airfields). The foreign exchange balances accumulated during the Second World War helped to cover deficits in Egypt, Iran, Iraq, Israel, Turkey, Lebanon, Syria, and North Africa. Finally, the aid received since 1945 has been enormous, far larger on a per capita basis than in any comparable region in the world (chapter 4).

Since 1973, with the explosion in oil revenues, the trends just described have been accentuated. Import surpluses have grown everywhere, but so have some offsetting items, notably remittances from the Gulf countries (but not from Europe) and aid from the various Arab funds. At the same time, some of the oil producers, notably Saudi Arabia, Kuwait, Libya, and the United Arab Emirates, have become the leading surplus area in international transactions and among the largest holders of foreign exchange reserves.

Composition of Trade

In the course of the 19th century the Middle East was integrated, as a producer of primary products and market for manufactured goods and colonial produce, in the international network of trade. The process had started much earlier. In the early Middle Ages, the region had exported to Europe and Africa such manufactured goods as paper, glass, metal ware, linen and silk fabrics, and to India linen, cotton, and woolen fabrics, rugs, and metal ware. It also exported certain colonial goods, notably sugar and cotton (and later on coffee), to Europe and re-exported spices. But by the 15th century, owing to the superiority of European production, the Middle East was importing such items as glass, paper, and silks, as well as clocks, spectacles, and other products of advanced European industry. As for the colonial crops, they were grown successively in southern Europe, the Azores and Madeira, and America, again causing the region to become a net importer of sugar and coffee. Most of the spice trade was diverted round the Cape in the 16th and 17th centuries. More and more, North African exports came to consist of cereals, hides, and wool, and those of the Middle East of raw silk, cotton, and cereals. Only in cotton did the Middle East continue to export manufactured goods, sending both yarn and cloth to England, France, and other countries. In the second half of the 18th century, however, these too disappeared, under the dual pressure of greater Indian competition and higher duties intended to protect French spinners and West Indian growers.[33] And European manufactured goods entered the region in increasing quantity and growing variety.[34] Exports of textiles and other manufactures to tropical Africa continued longer.

The 19th century saw an increase in these trends, resulting in both a far higher degree of specialization and a much greater orientation toward exports and dependence on foreign trade. On the one hand, the growth in foreign trade was many times as large as that in gross national product, greatly raising the ratio of imports and exports to GNP;[35] moreover, as never before, foreign goods penetrated the countryside, changing consumption patterns and disrupting old handicrafts, while exports drew on ever-widening areas of production, again deeply altering economic and social relations. And on the other hand, exports came to be concentrated on a few or even a single item. To these trends may be added three more recent ones. First, after the Second World War growing population, together with a rise in the level of living, have turned former food exporters like Egypt, Turkey, Algeria, Morocco, Syria, Iran, and Iraq into heavy net importers, and greatly increased imports in such traditional deficit areas as Lebanon and Arabia. Second, the huge expansion of petroleum production has caused it to overshadow all other exports put together. Finally, manufactures have come to constitute a still small but increasing fraction of exports, particularly in such countries as Israel, Lebanon, Egypt, Iran, and Turkey.

Exports should be examined country by country.

Egypt represents the most extreme example of specialization. Short-staple cotton had been grown for many centuries, but a new epoch opened in 1818 with the discovery of a high quality, long-staple plant by a French engineer employed by Muhammad Ali, who was anxious to develop cotton production for his textile mills (chapter 8). Samples sent to England were well received, and rapid expansion of output was made possible by large-scale irrigation works, which profoundly affected Egypt's social structure (chapter 7). From 1,000 *qantars* (100,000 lbs) in 1821 exports rose to 259,000 in 1823, and by the 1850s had leveled off at

500,000 *qantars* (50 million lbs). The American Civil War sent up cotton prices in Alexandria from an annual average of $12.25 per *qantar* in 1859 to $45 in 1863, and exports surged to 2.5 million *qantars* in 1865. After a postwar readjustment, the upward trend was resumed, and in 1910 a record 7.48 million *qantars* were exported. Since Egypt's other main export, wheat, was meeting increased international competition and losing acreage to cotton, the share of the latter in total exports rose to one-third in the 1840s–50s, over 80 percent in the 1880s and over 90 percent in 1910–14. In spite of stagnant production, attempts to diversify exports, and rapidly increasing domestic consumption, cotton remained predominant, its share being 70 percent in the 1930s and 80 in the 1950s. Even in the 1970s, cotton still accounted for one-half of exports, the other main items being cotton textiles, other manufactures, petroleum, and rice. (Until the Second World War, the figures include cottonseed, which constituted some 5 percent of exports.)[36]

Sudan also soon became a cotton-export economy. After the Anglo-Egyptian reconquest of 1896, its traditional exports—slaves, gold and ivory—dried up and were replaced by livestock and wild-growing gum arabic. By 1914 cotton had become an important item, and after the completion of the Gezira scheme in 1925 (chapter 7) dominated the picture. By the 1950s cotton and cottonseed were accounting for over 70 percent of total exports.[37]

In contrast to Egypt, Iraq did not develop any new export product in the nineteenth-century, but the structure of its exports changed significantly. Until oil started flowing out, in 1934, three agricultural items (dates, wheat, and barley) and three pastoral ones (wool, hides, and live animals) accounted for two-thirds to four-fifths of the total. In the 1850s and 60s a set of factors began to affect agriculture and exports: increasing government control of the countryside, the application of the Land Code of 1858, which facilitated settled agriculture (chapter 7), steam navigation on the Tigris, and the opening of the Suez Canal, which put Iraq within reach of European steamers (chapter 3). All this accelerated tribal settlement, and increased agricultural production far more rapidly than pastoral. In addition, world demand for such crops as dates and barley was rising, while domestic consumption of wheat was reducing the amount of that available for export. In 1912–13, dates accounted for 18 percent of total exports, barley for 24, wool for 9, and wheat for 5, a total of 56 percent; in 1933–39 the figures were: 23 for dates, 16 for barley, 12 for wool, and 6 for wheat, a total of 57 percent; and in 1946–51: 29 for dates, 41 for barley, 7 for wool, and 3 for wheat, a total of 80 percent. Soon after, because of greater consumption and stagnant production, exports of grain disappeared and petroleum, whose output greatly expanded, became practically the sole export.[38]

Syria's exports remained more diversified. The sharp decrease in cotton cultivation, owing to foreign competition and drastically declining demand from the local handicrafts which were being decimated by European competition (chapter 8), practically eliminated cotton exports. But raw silk exports increased rapidly and by 1913 constituted some 25 percent of the total. Another growing item was Jaffa oranges, developed by Arab farmers but greatly expanded by Jewish planters, both being helped by British traders who advanced funds; this provided nearly 10 percent of exports. Tobacco exports were held down by the action of the tobacco monopoly, and those of wheat and barley fluctuated widely. Traditional manufactures, such as silk cloth and soap, made up over 20 percent of the total.[39] As for the Syrian Republic, in the interwar period it exported cereals, but after 1951 cotton became the leading item, accounting for some 40 percent of the total; more recently petroleum has overshadowed other exports, and phosphates have been exported in significant quantities.

Palestine, after the First World War, increasingly specialized in citrus, which by 1938 formed 75 percent of exports. Citrus exports from Israel are still large, but they have been overshadowed by manufactured goods, notably diamonds and precision instruments. In Lebanon, mulberry trees were cut down during the World War I famine, and silk exports disappeared; but fruits and vegetables, because of the country's varied climate, abundant water, small-scale landownership, skilled labor, and access to capital, came to account for half the total. Another third came from textiles and other manufactures. Jordan also specialized in fruits and vegetables, especially early ripening varieties grown in the valleys, and more recently has exported phosphates.

Turkey experienced relatively little specialization. For the Ottoman Empire as a whole, in 1878–1913 "the share of any commodity in the total value of exports rarely exceeded 12 per cent . . . the shares of the more important commodities . . . did not change substantially . . . the eight largest exports, tobacco, wheat, barley, raisins, figs, raw silk, raw wool and opium" accounted for 51 percent of total exports in 1878–80 and 44 in 1913, wheat having declined sharply because of North American competition and tobacco risen to first place.[40]

In the first half of the century, Turkey had continued to export its traditional products—cotton, wool, silk, mohair, dried fruits, and grain. To these were added materials used by European industry for dyeing, such as madder, valonea, gallnuts, and saffron, but these disappeared in the 1860s with the advent of chemical dyes. Cotton showed a downward trend until 1860 because of foreign competition, surged up during the American Civil War, and then declined again until near the end of the century, after which it entered an expansive phase that still continues. Minerals, mostly copper and chrome, began to gain importance before the First World War and have continued to be significant. And in the last twenty years or so manufactured goods have been exported in increasing quantity.[41]

The structure of Iran's exports changed markedly. In the 1850s raw silk accounted for about one-third of exports, textiles for a quarter, and cereals for a tenth. In 1864 silk was blighted by disease, and its share fell steadily to 5 percent in 1911-13. Exports of textiles also disappeared owing to European competition. They were replaced by cotton (19 percent in 1911-13), fruit (13 percent), rice and other cereals (12 percent), and opium (7 percent). Helped by falling transport costs and rising world demand, exports of carpets expanded rapidly, accounting for 12 percent in 1911-13. In the interwar period oil became by far the largest item, followed by carpets, fruits, cotton, and opium; more recently some manufactured goods have been exported.[42]

Little need be said here about the Arabian peninsula. Except for Bahrain, whose pearls were world famous, and Yemen, which continued as in the past to export coffee and hides and more recently cotton, their exports were insignificant. After the discovery of oil, that item came to constitute almost 100 percent of exports.[43]

Passing on to North Africa, Algeria's export history is full of irony. The French government had hoped that it would replace Haiti as a supplier of tropical produce, and after 1830 completely unsuccessful attempts were made to grow sugarcane, coffee, tea, silk, and other items. Cotton enjoyed a brief prosperity during the American Civil War and was then abandoned, and flax, which showed promise, was wiped out by Indian competition following the opening of the Suez Canal. Tobacco proved more durable, but remained poor in quality and small in quantity. Hence Algeria concentrated on two items that competed with French production, wheat and wine. With the extension of French-owned farms, the improvement in transport, and the exemption of Algerian produce from French duties in 1851, wheat exports to France increased rapidly, but amounted to only 6 percent of total exports by 1938. Algerian wine was not exempt from French duties until 1867, but during the phylloxera ravages in French vineyards in the 1870s exports rose rapidly and remained high even after the French vineyards had recovered. By 1900 wine constituted one-third of Algeria's exports and by the 1930s one-half, a level maintained in the 1950s by which time exports of wheat had disappeared. Other minor exports included fruits and vegetables, iron ore, and phosphates. Since 1960 petroleum has dominated exports.[44]

Until the second half of the 19th century Tunisia had had five main export items: olive oil, which, when crops were good (in alternate years) led the list; woolen fezzes and cloth; raw wool; wheat; and hides.[45] Wool and woolen manufactures were gradually eliminated by foreign competition, but olive oil exports increased with the spread of groves, and, as in Algeria, exports of wheat and wine to France grew rapidly after the French occupation. At the beginning of this century exports of rock phosphates became prominent, and iron was also exported, but none of these or the older items accounted for more than about 15 percent of the total.[46] Since the 1960s small amounts of petroleum have been exported.

Morocco's traditional agricultural exports were similar to those of Tunisia. As in Tunisia exports of cereals increased, until growing population reduced the surplus available and phosphates became the leading export product, accounting for 20 percent or more of the total. Other significant items are metals (iron, manganese, cobalt, etc.) and fruits and vegetables.[47] Libya's exports were always small and limited to livestock products, cereals, and olive oil. At the end of the 19th century esparto grass, used for paper, assumed significance, and under the Italians many olive groves were planted which matured after independence.[48] Since 1960, petroleum has dwarfed all other exports.

One more general remark is in order. As Myint has pointed out, this specialization of the economy did not imply a corresponding specialization of the people of the region. The specialization was done by the Europeans, who supplied the equipment, working capital, technical skill, and management, whether in the mines or in plantations. Alternatively, new crops were grafted onto basically unchanged peasant economies: "here again one is tempted to say that much of the 'specialization' seems to have been done by nature and the complementary investments of transport and processing . . . thus, paradoxically enough, the process of 'specialization' of a backward economy for the export market seems to be most rapid and successful when it leaves the backward peoples in their unspecialized order as unskilled labour and peasant producers using traditional methods of production."[49]

But, when we turn to imports, we see a different picture. In sharp contrast to the Japanese, the people of the Middle East until very recently failed to learn European production methods but soon acquired new consumption habits. "It is only on the side of wants that disturbing changes seem to have been introduced, including a decline of skills in the domestic handicraft industries now no longer able to compete against the imported commodities."[50] The main trends are the large increase in imports of manufactured consumer goods, especially textiles; in traditional colonial goods; in building materials; in capital goods and fuels in the decades preceding the First World War; and, more recently, in capital goods, durable consmer goods, and industrial raw materials.

Textiles constituted the main item of 19th-century international trade and until the 1870s formed over half of Britain's exports.[51] Owing to the decline of the handicrafts and the change in tastes, they played a corresponding part in the imports of the Middle East, as of other underdeveloped regions (e.g., India, China, and Japan), sometimes amounting to half or more of the total. In Iran, textiles were put at two-thirds of total imports in the 1850s (cotton textiles alone being two-fifths) and again the same percentages in the 1880s and in 1910-11.[52] Judging from Pamuk's tables on Ottoman trade, cotton manufactures must have formed about half of Turkey's imports in the 1840s and some 30 percent in 1910-12. In Egypt, cloth accounted for a quarter to a third of imports from the 1830s to the First World War, and in Morocco a third to a half; in Iraq the figure rose to two-fifths, in Syria to over one-third, in Tunisia to two-fifths, and in Algeria to one-fifth.

In the interwar period, local production of textiles greatly increased and imports declined corresondingly, to a quarter to one-tenth of the total.[53] Since the Second World War their share has fallen much further. This corresponds to the shift in the composition of exports from industrial countries: thus by 1951 textiles formed less than 20 percent of U.K. exports, cotton's share being small, and since then they have become negligible or negative.

Building materials such as bricks, tiles, cement, and glass also increased sharply with the change in fashion toward Western-style housing, but never became a significant part of the total. They too have been replaced by local production.

Of the traditional colonial goods, coffee and sugar were imported in rapidly increasing quantities in the course of the 19th century. Tea-drinking was picked up by the Iranians and Turks from Russia, and came to the other countries mainly from India, through British traders. One set of figures is illustrative: in 1830-31, 3.5 tons of tea worth 65,000 francs and 250 tons of sugar, worth 400,000, were imported by Morocco, forming 6-9 percent of total imports. By 1890, 400 tons of tea worth 2 million francs and 10,000 tons of sugar worth 8 million were imported, amounting to 25 percent of imports.[54] In Iran in 1910–11, sugar constituted 25 percent of imports and tea 5 percent.[55] In Turkey, tea, coffee, and sugar were 10 percent of the total, and other countries showed similar figures. These items continued to be significant, but in many countries the bulk of sugar consumption is now met by local output.

As mentioned earlier, until the Second World War, the region was a net exporter or cereals, but since then growing population and a rise in the level of living have turned it into a large net importer. In 1978 imports of cereals amounted to nearly 23 million tons, costing over $4.2 billion; Turkey was the only significant exporter. More generally, the Middle East now has by far the highest per capita food imports among developing regions.

Fuels, first coal and then oil products (mostly kerosene, used for lighting and cooking) were imported in increasing quantities to meet the needs of railways, irrigation works, and factories, as well as for bunkering in Algiers, Port Said, Suez, Aden, and other ports. Even after the development of the Iranian oil fields, the vast majority of countries continued to import petroleum, as well as coal, from outside the region until the Second World War.

In view of the region's lack of industrialization until the First World War, imports of capital goods—best represented by metals and metal products—remained small. In Egypt under Muhammad Ali they amounted to 10–15 percent of total imports, but the proportion fell after that and rose again only at the end of the century, to reach 13 percent in 1905–9. In Turkey just before the First World War, capital goods were about 10 percent of the total, and in Iran about 3 percent, in Iraq (because of irrigation works and railways) some 8 percent, in Algeria and Tunisia about 10 percent, and in Morocco 1–2 percent.[56] In the interwar period the proportion of capital goods (metals and metal manufactures, machinery and appliances, and transport equipment) rose appreciably, to about 25 percent in Egypt, Iran, Iraq, and Israel, 20 percent or a little less in Lebanon, Syria, Sudan, Algeria, and Tunisia, and over 40 percent in Turkey.[57] After the Second World War, imports of capital goods increased enormously and now constitute one-third to one-half, or more, of the total.

With industrial development, imports of raw materials—rubber, metals, wood, fibers, minerals, and others—have greatly expanded, and the region's factories are still heavily dependent on foreign supplies (chapter 8). By the 1970s raw materials accounted for a third to nearly half of the imports of the more industrialized countries.

Direction of Trade

The direction of the region's trade shifted radically in the first half of the 19th century. Before that it had, for centuries or even millennia, been oriented eastward—toward India and the Far East—and to a much smaller extent southward, toward Africa. Available figures on Egypt and Iran around 1800 show this clearly, and there is also evidence that the land trade of Syria and Morocco was larger than their sea trade, and that Turkey's was considerable. Of course, there was also much re-exporting of Eastern and African products to Europe, and European products to Asia and Africa.[58] By around 1850, however, as a result of the specialization and changes in legislation and administration described earlier, Middle Eastern trade was overwhelmingly with the "industrial center." It has remained so to the present, but the center has greatly expanded to include, in addition to its original core in Western Europe, successively the United States, Russia, and Japan. Within this broad framework, there were some significant shifts, mainly determined by technology and economics, though political factors were also operative.

Before the French Revolution, France was the region's main trading partner, its share of Western-bound trade being about one-half; Britain, the Netherlands, and Venice accounted for about one-eighth each.[59] But French trade in the Mediterranean was wiped out during the revolutionary and Napoleonic wars, and France recovered its former level (but not its share) only in the late 1840s. Britain had taken its place and remained preponderant until the First World War, but in the last two or three decades before the war it lost ground to Germany and Italy. This was in line with Britain's overall performance: its share of world trade rose from about one-third in 1840 to a peak of 40 percent in 1870 and fell to 27 percent in 1913, while its share of world merchant shipping fell from 52 percent in 1850 to 46 in 1910. Austria usually came in third, after Britain and France, while Russia's share was rather small.

A breakdown by countries brings out more clearly the powerful political factors at work. After Italy conquered Libya, its share of the latter's trade rose to over 90 percent by 1938; previously, Britain had been Libya's leading partner. Similarly, by 1860 France accounted for 82 percent of Algeria's trade, a figure that showed no secular decline until 1938 and very little until the 1960s.[60] In Tunisia France, Britain, and Italy vied for first place from the 1830s to the 1870s but after the Protectorate France's share rose rapidly to some 60 percent in 1938 and somewhat more in 1955.[61] In Morocco, Britain accounted for some three-quarters of total trade in the 1830s and two-thirds in the 1870s.

Thereafter France increased its share (as did Germany); by the First World War it was supplying almost half the total and over half in 1955.[62] France was Syria's leading market until the First World War, taking one-third of exports, but Britain supplied over one-third of imports. Under the Mandate, France was the leading trade partner of Lebanon and Syria.[63]

In the Ottoman Empire, Britain remained the largest supplier until the First World War, but its share fell from 46 percent in 1884/85 to 19 in 1913/14; the shares of Austria and France showed a similar decline, while Germany and Italy advanced rapidly; in exports the picture was the same, France's share falling from 36 to 20 percent and Britain's from 35 to 22.[64] In the 1930s Germany became Turkey's main trading partner and is so once again, with the United States having increased its share. In Iran, Britain accounted for at least half of total trade in the 1850s and 60s, but by 1913 Russia was taking 70 percent of exports and supplying over 50 percent of imports; both proximity and a vigorous attempt to promote trade for political reasons explain this rise.[65] In the interwar period Germany and the Soviet Union predominated in Iran's non-oil trade, and since the Second World War trade with all the major industrial countries has been active.

In the other countries of the region, Britain remained predominant until the Second World War or shortly after. In Egypt, by 1885–89 it was supplying 39 percent of imports and taking 63 percent of exports; in 1913 the figures were 31 and 43, and in 1938 23 and 32; Britain remained the leading partner through 1955, after which it was overtaken by the United States and Soviet Union.[66] In Iraq Britain took some 30 percent of exports and supplied 49 percent of imports in 1909–11, and 17 and 30 respectively in 1937–38; by then, however, France had become the main market for Iraq's oil.[67] Britain remained Iraq's main supplier until the 1960s, but since then trade with various industrial countries, including the Soviet Union, has greatly increased. In Palestine, and later in Israel, Britain was the leading partner, and also in Sudan until the 1960s. The petroleum producing countries of the Gulf at first traded mainly with Britain, but in recent years more with the United States, Japan, Germany, and other industrial countries.

Terms of Trade

In view of the absence of import and export prices indices until quite recently and of the diversity of the region, a discussion of the Middle

East's terms of trade must necessarily be impressionistic. Since its exports consisted almost wholly of raw materials and its imports very largely of manufactured goods, a first approximation may be obtained by taking the reciprocal of the United Kingdom's net barter terms of trade. The latter shows a sharp deterioration between the Napoleonic Wars and the 1850s, from 138 in 1815 (1880 = 100) to 87 in 1857. Since the decline in freight costs (chapter 3) presumably affected the Middle East's bulky exports more than its lighter and more compact imports, one can infer that its terms of trade rose by at least as much. In the next fifty years the United Kingdom's terms of trade showed relatively little change, a rise to 117 in 1873 being followed by a drop to 97 in 1881 and a renewed rise to 116 in 1913. Between 1913 and 1938 the terms of trade fell by over one third.[68]

These general remarks may be supplemented by more specific ones. Pamuk's careful calculations suggest a rise in Ottoman terms of trade with France in 1840–55, due mainly to higher prices of raw materials — which is consonant with movements in the British general index. For 1855–1913 indices are available for Ottoman trade with the industrial center (the United Kingdom, France, Germany, Austria, and the United States). These show a decline from 136 in 1855 to 90 in 1876 (1880 = 100) because of the plunge in raw materials prices in the 1870s, followed by an irregular upward movement to 107 in 1913.[69] Over the whole period 1815–1913 it seems likely that there was an overall improvement.

For Egypt a longer series can be constructed. Average cotton prices in Alexandria (1880 = 100) fell from 114 in 1820–22 to 70 in 1850–52, rose sharply during the American Civil War and stood at 130 in 1870–72, fell to 86 in 1890–92, and rose again to 122 in 1908–12.[70] Using British export prices as a proxy for Egyptian import prices, a terms of trade index (1880 = 100) reads as follows: 1820–22 52; 1850–52 71; 1870–72 107; 1890–92 100; 1908–12 136. The upward trend is unmistakable. And since, as noted earlier, the quantum of exports expanded severalfold, Egypt's capacity to import rose even more; the same was probably true of Algeria and Tunisia and, to a lesser degree, of Turkey.

In the interwar period, Egypt's terms of trade improved in the 1920s and deteriorated sharply in the 1930s, falling by about two-thirds between 1925 and 1939. In the postwar period they rose rapidly to a peak of 131 (1958 = 100) during the Korean raw materials boom in 1951, fell to 85 in 1955, and recovered to an average of 130 in 1968–70.[71] Since then the rise in the price of cotton and, especially, petroleum may have offset the surge in import prices.

Turkey may not have benefited as much as Egypt from the relatively high raw materials prices of the 1920s, but probably suffered as much during the depression. After the Second World War, "the terms of trade improved gradually from 1950 to 1953 and remained fairly constant until about 1968, the latest year for which data are available."[72] Since then Turkey has, however, suffered greatly from the rise in the price of imported oil, food, and machinery, which has not been matched by the rise in its exports. For Syria, Aleppo's terms of trade rose by nearly 50 percent between the early 1890s and 1913. More generally, "Syria's net barter, and possibly its single factoral, terms of trade improved between the 1870s and 1913. The same cannot be said of the double factoral terms of trade." In the interwar period Syria's terms of trade probably deteriorated, owing to the drop in the price of agricultural produce. Some of Iran's main exports, such as opium, silk, and carpets, had a very different price trend from that of other raw materials.[73]

As regards the oil producers, three measures of the unit value of exports may be used: the posted price of oil; the actual price at which oil exports were made, which usually coincided with posted prices except when discounts were granted as in the early 1960s or during the 1973 and 1979 crises, when spot prices soared; and the government "take" per barrel of oil produced. No figures are available on oil export prices until 1945, when prices were first posted for the Gulf; they were raised by 117 percent in 1945–48, lowered by 12 percent in 1949, and thereafter showed only very small fluctuations until 1971. The 1945–48 rise led to a sharp improvement in the net barter terms of trade of exporters, but thereafter these fell steadily, since the prices of their imports were constantly rising. After 1971, the rise in the posted price of oil, which by 1980 had increased tenfold, far exceeded that of imports, and terms of trade showed a strong improvement.

The take per barrel is a more meaningful measure, since until the 1950s only a fraction of the value of oil exports remained in the producing country. Until the 1950s, the host governments received about 20–22 cents a barrel (chapter 10), an arrangement that implies improving terms of trade against the falling prices of imports in the 1930s and a sharp deterioration in the inflationary 1940s. In the early 1950s the average take rose to 75–80 cents, sharply improving terms of trade, in 1970 to 95 cents, and in 1973 to $2.12, more than keeping pace with world inflation. After the "price revolution" it went to $10 and then $30 or more per barrel. This meant a huge improvement in terms of trade in 1974—estimated by the International Monetary Fund at 137 percent— and, with fluctuations, a further improvement since then.[74] Thus, over all, the region's non-oil terms of trade improved up to 1913, deteriorated in the 1930s and 40s, and if anything rose thereafter until the 1970s. Its oil terms of trade have improved immensely. On the whole, it has no grounds for complaint on this score.

Finally, a few words may be said about the instability of export prices. The only available long-term series, for Egyptian cotton, shows that it closely followed world, and more particularly American, prices; and cotton was one of the more volatile commodities in international markets in the 19th century. As regards other commodities, one may, pending further research, presume that, like other primary producers, the Middle East experienced greater fluctuations in the price of its exports than did exporters of manufactured goods, and this has continued to the present.[75]

Trade, Growth, and Development

The fact that, as far as can be ascertained, the import capacity of the Middle Eastern countries expanded far more rapidly than their gross national products suggests, *prima facie*, that their foreign exchange receipts were adequate. To that extent, at least, trade was not a major constraint on growth and development. One may go further and say that trade was an engine of growth in those sectors supplying export goods— wheat and barley in most countries, cotton in Egypt, Turkey, and Iran, silk in Iran, Lebanon, and Turkey, wine in Algeria, olive oil in Tunisia, phosphates in North Africa, and later, petroleum. World demand for these goods was increasing, and the Middle East's output was only a fraction of total production. When exports of a particular good began to level off or decrease (e.g., cotton in Egypt and wheat in every country), the cause is to be sought on the side of supply: the inability of local agriculture to increase output significantly once a certain limit had been reached (chapter 7). This general statement is consistent with the fluctuations in the terms of trade discussed earlier and with the sharp cyclical changes in demand and price.

But foreign trade did not act as a nourisher of development, defined as follows by a wise but anonymous thinker quoted by Lord Acton: "it is the acquiring, not of greater bulk, but of forms and structures which are adapted to higher conditions of existence."[76] This was partly because of the weakness of linkages (forward and backward) between the export sector and the other sectors of the economy and to the low elasticity of supply of many domestic sectors. Partly it was due to the high demand for imports, which correspondingly reduced the size of the export multiplier. But it was also caused by a combination of factors that shaped all aspects of the region's development: the weakness of the governments, their ignorance of and lack of interest in economic problems, and their inability to pursue appropriate policies because of the capitulations and commercial treaties; a social structure that did not favor development; and the concentration of economic activity in the hands of foreigners or members of minorities—in other words, the absence of a national bougeoisie. All this meant that the export sector could not spontaneously exert a developmental effect, nor was it made to do so by a deliberate policy.

In the American colonies, merchants who were engaged in foreign trade also built or operated ships and established and managed the ancillary financial services—banking, insurance, brokerage, etc.—and later went into industry.[77] But in the Middle East shipping, banking, and insurance were carried out mainly by branches of foreign companies, and occasionally by companies domiciled in the respective countries but run entirely by foreigners, e.g., Ottoman Bank, National Bank of Egypt, etc.

In the late 19th century "Sweden developed by having valuable natural resources [iron and wood] which it industrialized for export," and Japan's silk industry was "transformed in scale, and to a lesser extent in production methods, by the opening of a foreign market. . . . [The latter] exerted steady pressure in favor of the application of science, machinery and modern business enterprise."[78] This too failed to happen in the Middle East. The industrialization of export products was confined to such processes as cotton ginning and pressing, silk reeling, and, much later, cotton spinning and weaving, copper refining, and the making of superphosphates—petroleum will be dealt with separately, in chapter 10. The branch that was most deeply transformed by foreign trade may well have been carpet making in Iran and especially in Turkey (chapter 8).

More generally, foreign trade has been described as Japan's "Highway of Learning,"[79] but it did not act as such in the Middle East. Unlike the Japanese, Middle Easterners did not carefully study the products they imported, with a view to imitating and adapting them for local production. And although some commercial, financial, accounting, and other skills were doubtless acquired in foreign trade, very few spilled over into other economic sectors, and it was not until the 1930s that local merchants began to turn their attention to industrialization. Perhaps most of the scanty technical skills available in the region were acquired not through foreign trade and its ancillary activities but by young men sent abroad by their governments to study such subjects.

The same is broadly true of the considerable amount of income generated in foreign trade. Some of it was drained abroad as payment of interest and profits (chapter 4), remittances by foreigners to their home countries, or purchase of luxury goods. The remainder tended to be reinvested in foreign trade, placed in local government securities or real estate, or invested abroad. Again it was only in the 1930s that an appreciable fraction was used for industrialization or other forms of development. Indeed, one can go further and say that, as in certain other parts of the world, it was only in the 1920s and 1930s, when the engine of growth represented by foreign trade began to falter, that a serious and sustained effort was made to pursue economic development.

CHAPTER III

Development of Transport

It can be argued that, of all economic activities in the Middle East, transport was the one most deeply revolutionized in the course of the 19th century. Around 1800 the means of transport, whether by land or water, were essentially the ones that had been used for hundreds or even thousands of years. By 1913, steam navigation had taken over almost all sea trade and the greater part of river trade, railways were carrying the bulk of land-borne goods, roads were beginning to play a significant part in a few countries, and motorcars were making their appearance. In the second half of the century a network of telegraphs covered the region, and in 1913 telephones were coming into general use.

Sea Transport

Transport by water is much cheaper than by land, and in the pre-industrial era the difference was far wider; thus in 1816 a United States Senate Committee estimated that it cost less to bring coal 3,000 miles from England by sailing ship than to carry it 30 miles overland.[1] Hence, until quite recently, large-scale trade was mainly confined to seaboards and the banks of navigable rivers, and "a Mediterranean economy was a possibility in a sense in which an Anatolian economy, for example, was not,"[2] although in the Middle East camels provided a relatively cheap mode of transport.

Compared with earlier times, Mediterranean shipping had shown only slight improvement. Sizes had hardly changed since the 15th century: "The use of iron made the construction of large hulls possible only in about 1840. A hull of 200 tons had until then been the general rule, one of 500 an exception, one of 1,000 to 2,000 an object of curiosity."[3] In 1787–89, the average size of European ships calling at Alexandria was 164 tons and of "Turkish and Greek" ships 125,[4] and these figures are representative of the region. Speeds had picked up, but only a little.[5] But winter sailings became more frequent and, more generally, a greater confidence prevailed. Thus in 1788 the British ambassador stated that the French government had decided to start a packet service between Marseilles and Izmir for letters, passengers, and a limited quantity of goods; the ships would sail every 15 days and take 18 days for the journey.[6] However, the main determinants continued to be the weather and security: the frequent European wars usually interrupted or greatly reduced navigation, and the Barbary, Maltese, and other corsairs took a heavy toll. Moreover, the level of trade was low. As a result, the volume of traffic was small. In 1787–89, an average of 528 ships, aggregating 77,500 tons, called at Alexandria.[7] In Tunis, by far the leading North African port, in 1820–26, an average of 176 ships departed each year for Europe and the Levant.[8] In Beirut in 1825, 178 ships entered the harbor, and in Istanbul in two months of 1802, 127 ships.[9] In Izmir in 1830, 1,125 ships aggregating 94,000 tons entered the harbor.[10]

In the other seas traffic was much smaller. At the end of the 18th century, some 50 to 60 ships of 200 tons or less sailed between Suez and Jidda.[11] In Basra in 1842–45, the average tonnage of ships entering the port was 11,000 tons and the average number of ships about 80.[12] As for the Black and Caspian seas, even as late as 1837, by which time traffic had increased considerably, only 131 ships aggregating 22,000 tons entered Trabzon, and the volume of ships calling at Persian ports on the Caspian was tiny.[13]

From the 11th century on, European shipping dominated the Mediterranean, and by the end of the 18th century it had taken over practically the whole traffic. The North African states had hardly any merchant ships at all; in Egypt, European ships accounted for all trade with Europe and North Africa and for half the traffic with the Ottoman Empire. The situation was not too different in Turkey, except that Greek, Ragusan, and Ionian ships played a larger part.[14] Even the coastal trade had largely passed into European hands, and a 1784 report stated that in addition to some 200 ships leaving Marseilles each year for "Barbary and Turkey, not including those of the Africa Company" and making an estimated 350 trips, some 150 vessels sailed from the southern French ports to carry on the coastal trade in the Levant.[15] In the Caspian, Russian shipping was overwhelmingly predominant. The Indian Ocean and Persian Gulf were dominated, successively, by the Arabs and Persians, Portuguese, Dutch, and finally the British, but until the 19th century few European ships sailed the Red Sea further north than Jidda. European supremacy was due to technical superiority, more efficient organization, greater availability of capital, economies of scale, and, above all, greater protection against corsairs. For the most part the Malta and Barbary corsairs preyed respectively on Muslim and Christian shipping; European ships, which had far greater military and political protection, benefited greatly from this situation. Various, generally half-hearted attempts by the sultans to reserve coastal traffic for Ottoman ships had failed.[16] But the great wars of 1740–1815 put European shipping under a heavy handicap and made possible the development of the Greek merchant marine, an event with far-reaching economic and political consequences. However, the Greek example was not followed by any Middle Easterners except, for a while, the Omanis.

The century after 1815 saw hardly any warfare in the Mediterranean, and piracy was gradually suppressed—first in Malta, then in North Africa, and last in the Greek islands. But the opportunities thus offered to the shippers of the region were more than offset by a new factor of which advantage was taken by shippers from the industrial countries: the development of steam navigation. Steamships, evolved on the rivers and lakes of the Unites States and Britain, were well suited to the narrow Mediterranean waters, and by 1825 there were a few British "experimental hulls" and a regular French Marseilles–Genoa line. In 1828, a British steamer reached Izmir and Istanbul, and in 1830 the British Admiralty sent steam packets to Gibraltar, Malta, and Corfu, reaching Alexandria in 1835. In 1833, the Russian Odessa Company inaugurated a run to Istanbul across the Black Sea, and in 1834 the steamers of the Austrian Danube Company reached Istanbul via Galatz. By 1837, the British (Peninsular and Oriental, and Oriental Steamship Companies), French (Messageries), and Austrians (Lloyd) had regular services in the eastern Mediterranean, calling at the main ports between Istanbul and Alexandria. The British packets were timed to connect with the East India Company's service to Suez, which had been started in 1830.[17] The effect of these and other lines may be judged by some examples.

By 1839, there were "eighteen regular opportunities to and fro every month from Alexandria to Europe by steam."[18] By 1844, passengers and mails between Istanbul and London had the choice of four steamship routes in the Mediterranean and one through the Black Sea and Danube.[19] And by 1862, "the mails leave London for Syria every Friday via Marseilles and every Monday via Trieste; while English steamers run regularly between Beirut and Liverpool,"[20] to which may be added the fact that Beirut was connected with Istanbul, Alexandria, and the intermediate ports by the Austrian, French, Russian, Turkish, and other lines. By 1870, there were 3 Egyptian, 3 British, 5 French, 4 Austrian, 2 Italian, 1 Russian, and 1 Turkish "lines of steamships maintaining regular services across the Mediterranean to Egypt, as well as a great number of merchant vessels, chiefly English, coming at irregular intervals."[21] The Suez Canal, opened in 1869, increased severalfold the volume of steam navigation in the eastern Mediterranean.

As regards North Africa, a French government-owned sailing packet was established in 1830, and steamers began connecting Toulon with Algiers in 1832, taking a few passengers. By 1842, Algiers had a weekly service to Toulon, one to Marseilles three times a month, and weekly services to Bône (Annaba) on the east and Oran (Wahran) on the west, stopping at intermediate ports. By 1847 the service had reached Tunis.[22] Other lines, for France and other countries, called at Algiers in the next decades, but in 1889 navigation between France and Algeria was declared to be coastal traffic and therefore reserved for the French flag; the result was much higher freight rates (see chapter 11). As for Tunisia, by the 1850s several steamship lines were calling regularly at Tunis from Algeria, Marseilles, Genoa, and Gibraltar.[23] Morocco continued to be linked with Gibraltar by sail until the 1850s, but a steam service from Marseilles started in 1853 and one from London in 1857. By 1862, Morocco had 18 monthly services to Gibraltar, 8 to France, and 1 to Britain.[24]

At the other end of the region, Russian steamers began to cross the Caspian to Iran around 1850 and greatly increased in numbers and size in the 1860s. In 1862, a British service was started between Karachi and various ports on the Gulf; here too the opening of the Suez Canal, by putting the Gulf within reach of steamers from Europe, multiplied their numbers.[25] In the Black Sea, in addition to the Russian and Austrian lines mentioned above, by 1836 the British and Austrians had regular services between Istanbul and Trabzon and were followed in 1839 by a Turkish line.[26]

Because of their regularity, the early steamers quickly attracted passengers and mails. But their freight rates were far higher than those of sailing ships (e.g., for wheat from Izmir to London 35 francs per ton compared to 3.30 francs); hence they were used only for very valuable merchandise, such as silk, where low insurance offset high freights.[27] Nonetheless, even in 1840 "it was estimated that steam did the work of about five sailing ships for equal tonnage,"[28] and steamers became steadily swifter and larger. Thus the Austrian Lloyd's original fleet in 1836 averaged 254 tons, but the figure rose to 397 in 1850, 526 in 1860, and passed the 1,000 mark in 1874; the other main lines in the Mediterranean show a parallel development.[29] Hence, from the 1840s on, steamers rapidly took over the region's trade in which local sailing ships had been important. By 1866, they accounted for 70 percent of Beirut's tonnage, and by 1871 it was reported from Izmir that sailing ships had almost disappeared except for the coastal trade, which was carried by Greek and Turkish ships, and for sailing ships bringing coal from England.[30] The expansion of traffic of the main ports in shown in table 3.1.[31]

More recent figures on these and other ports are available in the statistical yearbooks of the League of Nations and United Nations and of the individual countries.

When steamers first came to the region they could be handled in the same way as sailing ships, i.e., weather permitting, they anchored offshore, discharged their goods onto lighters, and left them in the open or under rudimentary sheds. But even then there were great difficulties. Except for Istanbul, the region has no noteworthy natural harbors, and none on river estuaries. There had been no port construction or improvement for many centuries; in fact, several ports had greatly deteriorated because of neglect (e.g., Alexandria), silting (e.g., Jaffa, Tyre, Salé-Rabat, and Suwaidieh, the port of Antioch), or even deliberate blocking (e.g., Beirut and Sidon by Fakhr al-Din in the 17th century, to keep out the Ottoman fleet). Consular reports are full of complaints about the dangers and difficulties and the deterioration of merchandise.

Alexandria was the first port to be improved. In 1818, with forced

Table 3.1
Approximate Tonnage of Shipping Entering Main Ports
(thousands of tons)

	1830	1860	1890	1913
Alexandria	140	1,250	1,500	3,500
Algiers	20		1,400	9,700
Basra	10		100	400
Beirut	40	400	600	1,700
Istanbul[a]			800	4,000
Izmir	100	600	1,600	2,200
Morocco	25	100		500[b]
Trabzon	15	120	500	
Tunis	20		400	1,400[c]

[a]Excluding shipping passing through straits, estimated at over 3 million tons in 1863–65 and 10–12 million in 1902–4.
[b]Casablanca only.
[c]1922.
Sources: British and French consular reports; MacGregor 1847; Miège 1961; *L'Algérie 1954;* Baeza 1924; Billiard 1930; Shaw and Shaw 1977:228. Figures are rounded and refer to nearest year or average of years available.

labor, work began on the 80 kilometer Mahmudiya canal, linking Alexandria with the Nile. The canal greatly facilitated communications between Alexandria and the interior and in addition provided irrigation and drinking water. The port itself was also deepened, permiting docking, and provided with a quay, warehouses, a lighthouse, an arsenal, and a drydock. In 1871–73, it was greatly widened and improved and provided with a floating dock, at a cost of £2.6 million. It thus became by far the best in the eastern Mediterranean, with an outer harbor of 566 hectares and an inner one of 188, the largest water area in the whole Mediterranean.[32] Further enlargements and improvements were made in 1906–7 and since. To cope with the increasing overland traffic to India (see below), a modern port was built at Suez in 1862–66, and deepened and improved in 1907–13. The Suez Canal Company also built a modern harbor at Port Said.

Algiers was slowly improved after the French conquest and by 1870 had a harbor of 70 hectares, extended by 35 hectares in 1880–1914. By 1906 a total of 55 million francs (£2.2 million) had been invested. Algiers became the second largest port of France for shipping (after Marseilles) and the fifth for merchandise. Further extensions (by 75 hectares) and improvements were made in 1931–45. Oran was provided with a small port in 1848–64, improved and enlarged to 106 hectares by 1914. By 1919 Oran was the fourth largest port of France for shipping and the seventh for merchandise. Similar developments took place in Bône (for minerals), Bougie, (Bejaya), Philippeville, (Skikda), Arzou, and other ports.[33] Investment in ports was put at 156 million francs (£6,240,000) by 1906. In all, Algeria had 21 improved ports, probably too many for the country's needs, but it should be remembered that coastal navagation was an important form of transport.[34]

Tunis has always had the advantage of a good natural harbor formed by its lake connected by a channel to the sea. In 1881, before the French conquest, the government began work on dredging the channel and building a basin, at a cost of 13.5 million francs (£540,000). In 1894, the Compagnie des Ports de Tunis, Sousse et Sfax was given a concession, and built good modern ports, those of Sousse and Sfax being designed mainly for phosphates; it was bought out by the state in 1938. Morocco had no improved port except Mazagan (al-Jadida), where some installations had been built by the Portuguese in 1509–1769. A small port at Casablanca was finished in 1917 and greatly extended in 1920–32, at a cost of 1,095 million 1926 francs ($44 million). Since then it has been further extended and improved. Safi was developed for phosphates and smaller ports were built at Qenitra, Agadir, Tangiers, and in the Spanish

Presidio of Ceuta.[35] In Libya the Italians built ports at Tripoli and Benghazi, investing £2.7 million between 1913 and 1941.[36]

In Turkey the first port to be improved was that of Izmir. In 1867 a British concessionary company began work, and after its liquidation a French company took over, opening the new port in 1875. Its area was 20 hectares and total cost £400,000. Unloading ships on the quay was four to five times quicker than by lighters, but the high dues charged by the company caused much friction with shippers. In Istanbul a French company, with a capital of £1 million, opened a modern port in 1901, but facilities continued to be inadequate. In 1902 the German Anatolian Railway Company built a port at the railway terminal of Haydarpasha[37] A modern port was built at Salonica in 1901. The only other Ottoman port developed was that of Beirut, in 1890–95, by a French concessionary company. A basin of 23 hectares was provided, at a cost of 11 million francs (£440,000); it was extended to 43 hectares and improved in 1924–38[38] and since. An ambitious program of Ottoman port construction launched in 1914 failed to materialize because of the First World War.

A careful study by Thobie shows that profits on investments in the Ottoman ports were generally low. In Izmir they averaged 12 percent on share and debenture capital, but for Beirut about 5 and for Istanbul apparently much less.[39]

As regards the other coasts, on the Black Sea simple installations were placed at the coal port of Zonguldak, and on the Caspian some improvements were made at Enzeli by the Russians. Nothing was done in the Gulf, except for some simple oil installations at Abadan. In the Red Sea a good port was built at Aden for bunkering, and a modern harbor at Port Sudan in 1906, and some improvements were made at the minor Egyptian ports: Qusair, Tur, etc.—mostly for export of minerals.

In the interwar period, new ports were built at Haifa, Basra, and Bandar Shahpur. After the Second World War, the main new ports were those of Latakia, Aqaba, Eilat, Jaffa–Tel Aviv, Jidda, Dammam, Hudaida, and the numerous oil ports in the Gulf and North Africa. By and large, capacity is adequate for the region's needs save in such highly exceptional circumstances as the huge influx of goods into the Gulf in 1974–76, following the rise in oil prices.[40]

The major construction work connected with sea navigation, the Suez Canal, can receive only cursory treatment here. Begun in 1859, opened in 1869, repeatedly widened and deepened, gaining added importance from the development of the oil fields of the Gulf, just before its nationalization in 1956 it was handling 13 percent of world shipping and 20 percent of tankers. As a private venture it was rather successful, yielding shareholders an average of 8–9 percent (depending on the currency used for calculations) per annum over the period 1859–1956[41] For world trade and shipping, it was of crucial importance. By cutting the distance from London to Bombay by half and to China by a third or a quarter, and by enabling ships to sail narrower and much more traveled seas than those on the journey around the Cape, the Canal gave a great stimulus to steam navigation.[42]

As a result, by 1870 the Bombay-Marseilles freight through the Canal had fallen to £3 per ton, or less, compared to £7 for the overland route and to £3.10.0 for the Cape route, and there were further sharp declines in the following decades; however, it was not until the 1880s that Canal traffic exceeded that around the Cape (almost all by sail) by value and volume[43] Although its government had strongly opposed the Canal, Britain, as the main shipping and trading nation, benefited most from it. By 1881, Britain accounted for over 80 percent of Canal traffic (declining slowly to 50 by 1938), and nearly two-thirds of its trade east of Suez passed through the Canal, as did half of India's *total* trade and a substantial and increasing share of that of Australia and New Zealand.[44] Moreover, as holder of 44 percent of the Canal stock after the purchase, in 1875, of the Khedive of Egypt's shares, the British government drew a substantial income. As *The Economist* farsightedly put it in 1869, the Canal had been "cut by French energy and Egyptian money for British advantage."

For the Middle East, the Canal had mixed results. Egypt not only lost the investment and labor it had put into the Canal (chapter 4) but also the substantial income generated by the overland route. Damascus, Aleppo, Mosul, Beirut and even Istanbul suffered from the diversion to the Canal of the pilgrim and caravan trade of Iraq, Arabia, and Iran. Local Red Sea shipping was also hurt by steamers passing through the Canal. On the other hand, Basra, and more generally Iraq, benefited from the great reduction in distance, time, and freight costs between it and Europe and its trade multiplied (chapter 2); Iran shifted much of its trade to its southern ports. As for Aden, it owed its whole development to the Canal, on which its prosperity continues to depend heavily.

The effect on the region of all those improvements in sea transport was momentous. Traveling time to and from Europe was reduced by a half or two-thirds, and regularity was assured. This not only greatly increased the flow of men and ideas but also facilitated foreign control—including Ottoman control over Arabia thanks to the Canal. Freights were also drastically reduced: e.g., between 1835–36 and 1876, Izmir to London freights fell by about a half, and the decline continued, with interruptions, until 1914.[45] This not only promoted the region's foreign trade but, since its exports were on the whole much bulkier than its imports, presumably helped to reduce the deficit in its balance of trade. The impact on agriculture and industry is discussed in chapters 7 and 8.

Inland Transport

The Middle East has fewer navigable rivers than any comparable region in the world, a fact that has always had an enormous influence on its economic and political life. The major exceptions, the Nile and Tigris-Euphrates, have, of course, been used since remotest antiquity. Moreover, for various reasons, wheeled vehicles passed away with the Romans, being replaced by the efficient camel.[46] Camel loads varied greatly, generally ranging between 250 and 300 kilograms, though higher and lower figures have been quoted; this is nearly twice and four times, respectively, the weight of the load of mules (and horses) and donkeys, the other animals used for pack transport.[47] The normal speed for a caravan was 4 to 5 kilometers an hour, and the usual daily stage 25 to 30 kilometers. Caravans varied greatly in size: in 1800 the annual Darfur caravan from the Sudan to Egypt averaged some 5,000 camels; around 1820 the Suez caravan had 500 camels and the Sennar caravan 500 to 600; in 1847 the Baghdad-Damascus caravan averaged 1,500 to 2,000 and the Damascus-Baghdad caravan 800 to 1,200, and there were 12–15 departures in either direction; in the 1870s on the Tabriz-Trabzon route, 15,000 pack animals made three round trips a year and carried 25,000 tons of merchandise.[48] Since "reasonable sized sailing ships of that period" carried 500–600 tons, [49] the Tabriz-Trabzon caravan represented the equivalent of 7 or 8 ships each way. The volume of goods thus carried was relatively large, but the cost of transport was high (see below). Moreover, camels and other pack animals were liable to be requisitioned by the government for military or other purposes.

Mechanical transport first penetrated the Middle East through its rivers. In the late 1830s steam tugs were employed for towing barges on the Nile and the Mahmudiya canal, and in 1841 the P & O Company ran steamboats as part of the overland route connecting Alexandria and Suez. The use of steamboats and tugs spread rapidly all over Egypt.[50] By the early 1860s a few river steamers were sailing on the Sudan Nile, and after 1900 steam navigation played a leading role in Sudan, aggregate services totaling over 3,300 kilometers.[51]

In Iraq, the Euphrates was surveyed by the Chesney expedition in 1836, and in 1839–42 four steamboats belonging to the East India

Company sailed up and down the Tigris, Euphrates, and Karun, surveying the rivers and carrying passengers and mails. In 1841, H.B Lynch took over those boats and in 1861 received a concession to run one boat—raised in 1864 to two and in 1907 to three; in 1855 a government line had started operations and was reorganized and expanded in 1867. This reduced sailing time from Baghdad to Basra to 52-60 hours, compared to 5-8 days by sailing ship, and the return journey to 4-5 days, compared to 40-60 days. Freights were also some 25 percent lower on the steamboats but were still high: "it costs as much or rather more to carry a ton of cargo from Basra to Baghdad by Messr. Lynch's steamers than it has to carry it from London to Basra by steamer through the Suez Canal", freights were twice as high as those of railways in India instead of being half as high. At times, according to a British merchant, "grain for export often paid in river freight . . . 50 percent of its cost in the market of Baghdad." The competition of the government-owned line, however, lowered freights after 1904.[52] In 1888, the Karun River in Iran was opened to foreign navigation, with similar results.[53] After the First World War, the development of road and rail reduced the share of water transport, but it still carried about a fifth of Egypt's total freight in the 1930s.

Only in Algeria, Tunisia, Lebanon, and Iran were roads significant before the First World War. In Algeria several highways were built to facilitate military operations and control, e.g., Algiers-Oran-Tlemcen, Algiers-Setif-Constantine, Setif-Bougie, Constantine-Philippeville, and deeper into the interior. By the 1860s Algeria had a good road system, totaling 3,000 kilometers and serving an economic as well as a military function, and there was further development by 1914. In Tunisia the French had built some 600 kilometers by 1892 and 4,000 by 1914.[54] In Lebanon, in 1859-63 a French concessionary company built a 111 kilometer road linking Beirut and Damascus. It was financially success-ful and for 30 years gave shareholders an average dividend of 11 percent. Under the regime of local autonomy established in 1861, local revenues were largely used for roads, and by 1900 Mount Lebanon had 415 kilometers (excluding the Beirut-Damascus road) with another 262 under construction, high figures for an area of 400 square kilometers and some 400,000 inhabitants. In Iran the Russians built, in 1890-1910, some 800 kilometers of very good roads in the northern part of the country: Tehran-Enzeli, Tabriz-Julfa, and Qazvin-Hamadan; the total cost was about 15 million rubles (£1.5 million). In Egypt, the building of rural roads started in 1890, and by 1907 there were 2,646 kilometers, mainly in lower Egypt. Turkey had an ambitious road-building program which was cut short by the First World War.[55]

Railways came to the region relatively early. To shorten travel time on the overland route from Alexandria to Suez, which took some 8 days, a railway was started in 1851, reaching Cairo in 1856 and Suez in 1858, for a total length of 353 kilometers. Muhammad Ali's earlier scheme, in 1834, for a Cairo-Suez railway was not carried out. The line was financed by the government, which provided materials and labor, and the construction and supervision were entrusted to Robert Stephenson, son of the famous inventor. By 1869, Egypt had 1,338 kilometers of railway, and by 1905 the state railways aggregated 3,000 kilometers, at an estimated total cost of £25 million. In addition, 1,400 kilometers of narrow-gauge rural railways had been built by private companies, with an aggregate capital of just over £3 million, and there were also some suburban lines; profits on the rural railways were very low. Relative to its inhabited area and population, Egypt was remarkably well provided with railways (table 3.2), and railways were carrying the bulk of the internal goods traffic.[56]

North Africa was also provided with fairly good railway networks. In

Table 3.2
Length of Railways (kilometers)

	1890	1914	1939	1948	1975
Algeria	3,056	3,316	4,877	4,478	3,837
Libya	—	230	387	357	—
Morocco	—	(427)	1,954	1,695	2,071
Tunisia	416	1,785	2,069	2,100	2,257
Subtotal	3,472	5,758	9,287	8,630	8,165
Egypt	1,797	4,314	5,606	6,092	4,856
Sudan	—	2,396	3,206	3,242	4,556
Subtotal	1,797	6,710	8,812	9,334	9,412
Arabia	—	(800)	—	—	612
Iran	—	200	1,700	3,180	4,944
Iraq	—	132	1,304	1,555	2,203
Jordan	—		332	332	(420)
Palestine/Israel	—		1,188	1,225[a]	902
Lebanon	—	(1,650)	232	423	417
Syria	—		854	867	1,761
Turkey	1,443	3,400	7,324	7,634	8,138
Subtotal	1,443	6,182	12,934	15,216	19,397
Grand total	6,712	18,650	31,033	33,180	36,974

[a] Palestine, 1947; in 1950 Israel had 416 kilometers.
Sources: EHME; EHT; EHI; Hecker 1914; League of Nations, Statistical Yearbook; United Nations 1951; Statesman's Yearbook, various issues; Guide Bleu, various countries.

Algeria construction began in 1858, and by 1880 there were 1,100 kilometers, belonging to six private companies, which were granted small subsidies and guaranteed a minimum return of 5 percent. Although they were supposed to work within an overall plan, there was in fact no coordination between them, and no less than five different gauges were used. In 1939, the state took over all railways. In Tunisia a small line was built in 1876 and, again with the aid of a 6 percent guarantee, by 1914 some 1,800 kilometers had been built. Coordination was somewhat better than in Algeria, and there was less variety of gauges. The state gradually took over the railways. In Morocco, a narrow-gauge railroad was built in 1911 from Casablanca to Rabat. After 1923 the railways developed rapidly under an overall plan, adequately serving the country's needs and run by two French companies.[57]

In Libya, the Italians built an 85-kilometer line south of Tripoli in 1911–13, and by 1939 there were 178 kilometers of line in Tripolitania and 164 in Cyrenaica, with a large gap in between.[58] These lines are no longer used. In the Sudan the British military expedition laid a railway from Wadi Halfa to Khartum, 931 kilometers long, at a cost of £1 million, and by 1913 this was linked to the new harbor of Port Sudan. By 1929 the state railways totaled 3,000 kilometers and their capital value was put at about £7 million. In addition, 750 kilometers had been built in the eastern part of the country by two companies whose capital of £4 million had been provided by the government.[59]

Much less was done in the Asian part of the Middle East. Iran did not have a railway until 1928, nor, except for the short-lived Hijaz railway, did Arabia until 1951, while Iraq in 1914 had only a 132 kilometer unconnected stretch of the Baghdad railway. Syria saw much more construction between 1889 and 1914. The 87 kilometer Jaffa-Jerusalem railway, which cost £400,000; the 147 kilometer Beirut-Damascus and 103 kilometer Damascus-Muzayrib lines tapping the Hauran wheat-fields—costing together £1.5 million; the 332 kilometer Rayak-Aleppo line, costing some £2.5 million; and the 103 kilometer Homs-Tripoli line, costing some £600,000. Except for the Jaffa-Jerusalem railway, all these lines were French, and some enjoyed a government guarantee of 15,000 francs (£600) for every kilometer of line operated; in 1902–14 a total of £900,000 was thus paid to the railways, an amount which was equal to their gross receipts and which ensured that they met their financial obligations. But the Beirut-Damascus-Muzayrib line, which did not have such guarantees, had to declare itself bankrupt in 1900 and to undergo reorganization.[60] Economically too the railways were unsatisfactory. Gauges were not uniform, and goods sent from Aleppo to either Damascus or Beirut had to be transshipped. Moreover, the Hijaz railway introduced an element of wasteful duplication. Started in Damascus in 1903, it reached Medina, 1,320 kilometers away, in 1908; branches were built to Haifa, Bosra, Lydda, and Awja, bringing the total in 1918 to some 1,650 kilometers. The railway was intended by Sultan Abd al-Hamid to serve mainly military and political purposes, and its economic results were negligible. It was financed by contributions from Muslims all over the world and cost, in all, about £4.5 million. By 1913, railways may have been carrying as much as one-half of Syria's internal traffic.[61]

Syria featured prominently in various grandiose plans, mainly British, to link Iraq—or even India—to the Mediterranean. Started in the 1830s, as an attempt to shorten the distance to India by a combination of steam navigation on the Tigris-Euphrates and a railway across the Syrian desert, such schemes were in fact rendered obsolete by the overland route through Egypt and the Suez Canal, but were periodically revived until the end of the century.[62] However, when the Baghdad Railway was finally built, it went through Turkey.

Turkey's first two railways, both British and both completed in 1866, tapped Izmir's fertile hinterland—the Izmir-Aydin line, which ultimately totaled 610 kilometers with a capital of £5.3 million, and the Izmir-Kasaba line, which eventually totaled 707 kilometers with a capital of £6.5 million. Both served a useful economic function, taking over the greater part of the camel trade, but paid low returns to shareholders in spite of government subsidies.[63] Other, very short, lines were built, but the government wanted a railway that would link Istanbul with the provincial capitals of Anatolia, Syria, and Iraq; in 1872 a master plan for a railway to the Gulf, with feeder lines, was drawn up by a German engineer. The completion of the Vienna-Istanbul line, in 1888, made such a railway more attractive to European capital, and in the same year a concession for a railway to Ankara, with kilometric guarantees, was granted to a German group, the Anatolian Railway Company. On completion of the Istanbul-Ankara stretch, in 1893, extensions to Kayseri and Konya were made, and in 1903 a concession for the 2,264 kilometer Konya-Basra line was given to the Baghdad Railway Company, controlled by the same German interests. Construction on this stretch was held up by shortage of capital (which necessitated recourse to the French market), Russian obstruction, and the opposition of the British government, whose consent was required if the Ottoman government was to increase its customs duties to raise the necessary revenue for the railway guarantees (chapter 2). By the outbreak of war, the Anatolian Railway (capital £9 million) totaled 1,032 kilometers, and the Baghdad Railway (capital £6 million) had 531 kilometers in Anatolia, Syria, and Iraq. The performance of the German companies was impressive: their alignment was sensible, construction cost low, and service good. The railways undoubtedly made possible a large increase in agricultural output in the districts they crossed—as witnessed by both the sharp increase in tithes collected and by observers' reports—and, furthermore, they tried more directly to stimulate development by providing various services. By 1913, railways were carrying a little over half Turkey's internal goods traffic.

Yahya Tezel has estimated total profits of the railway companies operating in the Ottoman Empire from 1899 to 1909, including government guarantees, at £T 26 million; i.e., £T 2.6 million per annum; this represents about 5 percent on the capital invested in the railways.[64] During the war the Turks, with German help, pushed the railway to Aleppo. Meanwhile, the British armies had built two railways—from Egypt to Haifa and from Basra to Baghdad, with branches. On the other hand, the Hijaz railway south of Maan was put out of commission, with technical assistance provided by T. E. Lawrence, and has remained so in spite of numerous projects to repair and rebuild it.

In the interwar period, the Iraqi and Syrian railways were extended and connected, providing through traffic to Istanbul. In 1938, the 1,394 kilometer Transiranian Railway, linking the Caspian to the Gulf, was completed at a cost of about $150 million. The Turkish network was also doubled. In 1951, the 560 kilometer Dammam-Riyadh line was opened, at a cost of $53 million. In recent years Iran and Iraq have considerably extended their railway systems.

A comparison with other regions shows that, in 1950, Middle Eastern countries (here excluding North Africa west of Egypt and Sudan) had "a lower 'density of railways' (length of railways divided by area of country) than pre-war eastern Europe or presentday India and Pakistan, but a slightly higher density than most of the countries of Latin America. The exclusion of desert areas in the Middle East does not greatly affect the comparison, except as regards Egypt. Relative to the size of the population in the Middle Eastern countries, the figures for railways are below those of eastern Europe and most of the Latin American countries, but slightly higher than for India and Pakistan."[65] This statement is still broadly true.

However, after the First World War, most countries put their main effort on roads, not railways, and the emphasis has been maintained. By 1950, relative to their area, the Middle Eastern countries had "fewer roads than eastern Europe but more than India. On the whole, the 'density of roads' is comparable with that of Latin America. Relative to their population, the countries of the Middle East fall well below the average for eastern Europe or Latin America, but somewhat above the figure for India. With regard to motor vehicles, the Middle Eastern countries have about as many, in relation to the population, as Latin America, and distinctly more than India or pre-war eastern Europe."[66] In the last thirty years there has been a great expansion and improvement of the region's roads, and the number of vehicles, both private and commercial, has multiplied many times.[67]

This development in transport has had profound and, on the whole, decidedly beneficial consequences by stimulating agricultural and mineral production and facilitating the formation of national markets and integrated societies and states.

The former compartmentalization of markets in the region—with the exception of Egypt, where cheap water transport has always been available—may be illustrated by the following examples. In Turkey, seasonal fluctuations were large; e.g., in Diyarbakir in 1860 the highest annual wheat price was 270 percent of the lowest, 148 percent in 1861, 182 in 1862, and 276 in 1863. So were annual fluctuations—in Kayseri wheat prices per imperial quarter moved as follows: 1843 7 shillings and 7 pence, 1844 10/7, and 1845 29/6. Finally, vastly different prices prevailed in localities that were quite close, e.g., in 1847, in the hinterland of Salonica flour was sold at 6 shillings per sack but at 31/- in places 130—160 kilometers distant; in 1867, wheat was selling at 18/- a quarter in Diyarbakir, 12/- in Erzurum 208 kilometers away, and 4/7 in Van 370 kilometers away. In Najd, a Maria Theresa dollar bought 3 *sa'* of wheat in 1805/6, 4 in 1807/8, 3-4 in 1808/9, 7-10 in 1809/10, and 13 in 1810/11; the corresponding figures for dates were 5-7 *wazna*, 11, 10, 30, and 37.* In the disastrous year 1819/20, during the Egyptian invasion, the dollar bought only 1.5 to 2 *sa'* of wheat and 2.5 to 4 *wazna* of dates. With the return of more normal conditions, prices fell sharply: in 1828/9 the dollar bought 18 *sa'*, in 1829/30 35 *sa'* and 70 *wazna* of dates, and in 1832/33 25 *sa'* and 70 *wazna*. Scattered figures for Mecca show similar fluctuations. In Syria, where transport of grain from Aleppo to Alexandretta, 110 kilometers away, cost £3 per ton—an amount almost

---

*The *sa'* varied between 2 and 6 pints, according to locality; the *wazna* was equivalent to 1 lb. 13 oz.

equal to the freight to England—during the drought of 1845 wheat prices rose 3.6 times, whereas on the coast they increased by only 50 percent. In 1875 a bushel of wheat sold for 1 shilling in Hauran but for 4 to 5 in Beirut, 225 kilometers away.[69]

In Iran in 1892 Lord Curzon reported: "At Damghan barley was recently selling for 8 krans per kharvar [290 kilograms] while in Tehran the current price is 50 krans. Meanwhile at Qum and Qasvin the price is 20 and 24 krans, but there is no means of transporting it."[70] In Sudan in 1900, grain at Gedaref cost 22 piastres per *ardeb* (150 kilograms) but at Khartum, some 350 kilometers away, 160; the excellent cotton grown at Gash could "hardly pay camel freight to the Red Sea."[71]

A few examples of reduction in costs of transport may be given. In Anatolia during the last decades of the 19th century, wheat sent by pack animal from Erzurum to Trabzon, 320 kilometers away, or from Ankara to Istanbul (360 kilometers), tripled in price, and barley, being less valuable, more than tripled. The rate per ton-mile on the latter route was about 10 cents. But the Anatolian railway charged only 1 cent per ton-mile, and gave discounts of up to 50 percent for bulk orders. Further east and south, rates by camel or mule ranged from 6 to 18 cents per ton-mile.[72] In Syria in 1883, "when goods are scarce and mule drivers available in large numbers, one can reckon the cost of transport on the basis of 4 francs for a mule load [say 125 kilograms] and 5 francs for a camel load [250 kilograms] for a day's journey [40–45 kilometers]. But in times of plenty two or three times as much may be paid. Sometimes the producers of Hauran, not knowing how to transport their cereals to Acre [about 125 kilometers away], give the camel drivers half the load in payment of freight." The various railways brought these costs down quite appreciably; the Damascus-Beirut railway reduced the freight from 0.56 francs per ton-kilometer to 0.20.[73] In Egypt, the cost of transport of one *qantar* (49 kilograms) of cotton from Delingat to Damanhur by pack animals was 12 piasters; the opening of an agricultural road in 1892, usable by carts, brought this figure down to 8, and the building of a light railway in 1902 to 4 piasters. In Iran the construction of rough motor roads in the 1920s and 30s brought down the cost of transport by three-quarters.[74] In Morocco a load of 175 kilograms cost, in normal years in the 1870s and 1880s, for the journey from Mogador (Essaouira) to Marrakesh, 201 kilometers, 10 francs; to Safi, 97 kilometers, 6 francs; and to Agadir, 129 kilometers, 10 francs. In 1901 the British consul estimated the average cost per ton-mile on the Fez-Tafilalet route at 6.86 d (0.70 franc) by camel and 13.72 d (1.45 francs) by mule, to which should be added tolls. Transport of dates from

Tafilalet to Tangiers, about 700 kilometers, added 146 percent to the purchase price.[75] These figures were reduced by the railways; by 1914 the tariff was 0.40 francs per ton-kilometer.

Still more spectacular was the reduction in travel time. In Iran, motor roads cut it by nine-tenths. In Syria in 1940, the Damascus-Baghdad journey took 18 hours by car, compared to 30–45 days by caravan, and the Damascus-Cairo journey 18 hours by car or train, compared to 20–25 days—and so forth.[76] This not only made for speed, comfort, and security but released much capital previously locked up in inventories.

Of course, the railways had grave defects. Some, particularly in European Turkey and Syria, were unnecessarily circuitous, in order to draw greater revenues from kilometric guarantees, and payments by the governments were correspondingly high. Others, especially in North Africa, have been criticized for running from a mineral deposit to a port, ignoring broader agricultural needs. Still more serious was the multiplicity of gauges, making transshipments necessary, especially in Syria, Algeria, and Tunisia. More generally, there was a failure to draw up a coordinated plan, except where the state built the railways, as in Egypt, Sudan, Iran, and Iraq. But the experience of Morocco shows that private lines could be fitted into an overall plan, and the Anatolian Railway is an example of excellent service provided by private capital. Finally, the railways failed to stimulate industrial growth in the region in the way they had done in Britain, Germany, the United States, and elsewhere by providing a market for coal, steel, and machinery, but here the fault clearly lies not with them but with the general state of the economy. Some technical skills were generated by the railways, but here too the effect was not great. Over all, there is little doubt that although the private return of railways was generally low, their social return was high.[77] And, except in Egypt and, to a lesser extent, in Iraq, where water transport was possible, there was no available alternative to railways.

Middle Eastern Transport
in the International Context

Since the Italians gained mastery of the Mediterranean in the 11th century and the Portuguese established control of the Indian Ocean in the 16th, the peoples of the Middle East have played a minor, essentially passive part in world transport. As noted above, even their own coastal trade largely passed into European hands, and the advent of steam navigation increased the European lead. However, around the middle of the 19th century, both the Egyptian and Ottoman governments established steamship lines, as did later some Greeks who were Ottoman subjects, and in the interwar period there were some private Egyptian and Moroccan lines.[78]

But it is only after the Second World War that the Middle East made a serious effort to enter the world transport system in both airlines and shipping. Practically all the governments in the region now run airlines, some of which stretch from the United States to the Far East. The enormous growth of oil production has turned attention to the advantages of owning tankers. Cargo shipping has also increased somewhat. The region's share in world tankers rose from less than 0.8 percent in 1969 to 3.1 in 1978, and in total shipping from 1.3 to over 2.6 percent (see appendix table A.10).[79] The region still plays a minor role in world transport, but one that may be expected to gain in importance in the coming decades.

Finally, there is the question of connections between the various parts of the region. A look at a vegetation map shows that it is in fact an "archipelago" of cultivated islands surrounded by seas of desert. In the past, caravans of camels plied between those islands, infrequently but adequately for the low volume of trade, and coastal navigation played a major part in some countries. Modern transport, on the other hand, linked the islands to the world market: railways ran to the sea, and sea lanes connected the ports with those of Europe. This is still largely true, but the flexibility of both road and air transport—not to mention oil pipelines—has made it possible to establish closer relations between the various countries. This is particularly true of the eastern half of the region, where communications between Iran, Turkey, and the Fertile Crescent have much improved. It is also true within the Maghreb. But the formidable geographical obstacle represented by the Libyan desert has not yet been overcome, and shipping, airline, and road services between North Africa and the rest of the region are still few and far between.

CHAPTER IV

The Influx of Foreign Capital

The history of foreign capital investment in the Middle East falls into quite clearly defined periods. The first half of the 19th century saw the dissolution of the old trading companies, such as the Levant Company and the Compagnie d'Afrique. They were replaced by private traders, engaged in import and export, whose capital consisted mainly of inventories and warehouses. Some of these merchants also financed small processing plants for export crops, e.g., in cotton ginning and silk reeling.

From the 1850s on, private and incorporated banks were established in Algeria, Turkey, Egypt, Lebanon, Tunisia, and elsewhere.[1] But the period 1850–80 is dominated by the huge debt accumulated by the governments or, more strictly, the monarchs of Turkey, Egypt, Tunisia, and somewhat later Iran and Morocco. This large flow ended abruptly in bankruptcy and either precipitated foreign occupation, as in Egypt, Tunisia, and Morocco, or resulted in foreign control over government finance, as in Turkey. Between the 1870s and 1914, there was a large amount of private investment in various public utilities such as railways, streetcars, water, gas, and electricity in most countries. A certain amount went to mining, notably in French North Africa, Turkey, and Egypt, and, just before the First World War, into oil in Egypt and Iran. There was little foreign investment in manufacturing or agriculture.

This stream was part of a torrent that poured out of Europe in 1815–1914 and that was broadened, in the 1850s and 60s, by banks like the Crédit Mobilier and others in France and Britain that drew on a much larger volume of savings. Long-term foreign investment outstanding in 1914 has been put at $44 billion, of which almost half came from Britain, one-fifth from France, and nearly one-sixth from Germany. This investment did not flow out at a steady rate but fluctuated violently, being periodically interrupted by financial crises that sent eddies all over the world, including the Middle East. Some of these, such as the crisis of

1837, merely resulted in local stringency and the bankruptcy of some firms. Others, like the 1873 crash, caused much wider tremors: as Leland Jenks noted, "The distrust it spread was one factor in the insolvency which ensued of Turkey, of Egypt and Peru."[2]

Like other governments, those of the Middle East borrowed through financiers and not directly from the public. Again to quote Jenks, "Great Britain and, at times, France and the United States, were the only countries that sold their securities by public subscription to the highest bidders. It was enough to blast the credit of any ordinary government for it to be known that it had shopped around London with its bonds in search of better prices. By control of maturing coupons or short term notes, by favorable position for making remittance, by some sort of preferential intimacy with powers authorized to borrow money for their government, one firm or group of bankers usually had the inside track in any loan negotiation. And if they were busy or disobliging, a government dealt somewhere else at even greater disadvantage."[3] These considerations help to explain why, once their credit began to deteriorate, the Middle Eastern governments had to accept such highly unfavorable terms for their loans.

By 1914 the Middle Eastern countries had a total debt of about $2 billion, of which a little over half was public and the rest private, or nearly one-twentieth of the world total. North Africa had a public debt of about $250 million and a much larger amount of foreign investment in the private sector. During the First World War, Turkey added greatly to its debt, but Egypt's sterling balances (chapter 2) enabled it to redeem a substantial amount. Something similar seems to have happened in Algeria.

In the interwar years, there was little public borrowing, Morocco and Libya being the main exceptions. But a large amount of private capital flowed into the oil industry and also to Morocco, Palestine, and Libya, which received many immigrants. During the Second World War the region accumulated huge amounts of sterling, franc, and other balances (chapter 2), but these were quickly drawn down in the early postwar period. Since then there has been little private investment, except in the oil industry and for a few years in Morocco, but Israel has received several billion dollars from Jewish communities in the United States and elsewhere. Public debt has, however, grown enormously. Relative to its population, the Middle East has received a greater amount of foreign aid, from a wider variety of sources, than any region in the world. Some of this was in grants, but in 1978 the aggregate public debt was about $61 billion. (Appendix table A.9)

Public Debt to 1914

The first foreign loan contracted was by the Ottoman government in 1854, during the Crimean War. The finances of all the governments had been under strain for at least two centuries, but budget deficits had been covered by various expedients, such as debasing the currency, borrowing from local bankers such as those of Galata, or issuing short-term annuities or treasury bonds such as the *esham* in the 18th century and the *kaime* in the 19th.[4] However, a combination of circumstances was raising government expenditures at a far higher rate than revenues, creating deficits much too large to be covered by the old methods. First, there were numerous wars involving particularly the Ottoman Empire but also Egypt (in Arabia, Syria, and Sudan), Iran, and Morocco; the direct costs to Turkey of the Crimean War alone were officially estimated at £11 to 13 million, to which should be added the opportunity costs.[5] When these wars ended in defeat, large indemnities were sometimes imposed by the victors, e.g., by Russia on Iran and Turkey and by Spain and France on Morocco (chapter 11). But even in peacetime, the military burden was heavy; the rising cost of armaments, particularly warships and artillery that now had to be purchased abroad, made military modernization a prohibitively expensive operation.[6] Administrative modernization and centralization, pursued in greater or lesser degree by all the governments, was also expensive. So was the provision by the governments of services which, in the past, had been supplied on a small scale by private charity, such as education and hospitals, or not at all, such as public health. And although expenditure on economic development, in the form of roads, railways, irrigation works, canals, factories, and other projects, constitued a small part of total government expenditure, it too helped to swell the deficit. Last, and second in importance only to military expenditure, there was the extravagance of the royal courts and higher officials, dazzled by European ways of life and enabled by apparently inexhaustible credit to satisfy their whims. As the British experts who wrote the Cave report in 1876 on Egypt's financial difficulties put it: "Egypt may be said to be in a transition state and she suffers from the defects of the system out of which she is passing, as well as from those of the system into which she is attempting to enter. She suffers from the ignorance, dishonesty, waste and extravagance of the East, such as have brought her Suzerein [The Ottoman sultan] to the verge of ruin, and at the same time from the vast expense caused by hasty and inconsiderate endeavours to adopt the civilization of the West."[7] To this may be added that the traditional system of financial administration was unable to handle the much larger sums involved.

Turkey's first loan, for £T 3.3 million in 1854, carried 6 percent interest and was issued at 80; its second for £T 5.5 million, was issued at 102 5/8 and carried 4 percent interest. Several loans followed, in quick succession and at increasingly adverse terms, as Turkey's credit deteriorated. Thus the £T 44 million, 5 percent loan of 1874 was issued at only 43.5. Including the 1877 loan, the total amount contracted was £T 268.8 million, of which just over half, £T 135 million, had been actually received.[8] Meanwhile, in 1875, the government had announced that it was suspending interest and amortization payments. After prolonged negotiations with the Great Powers the "Decree of Muharrem," of December 20, 1881, was issued. This set up the Public Debt Administration, consisting of representatives of the Powers and Turkey, to which certain revenues were assigned. It drastically reduced both the principal of the funded debt, to £T 141.5 million (about £128 million sterling), and the charges (interest at not less than 1 percent or more than 4 percent) to £T 3 million. Various conversions, and repayments, reduced the debt in subsequent years, but this was offset by new loans (£166 million, of which £T 147 million were actually received),[9] used mostly for military purposes or to cover budget deficits but also for railway construction. In 1914 the debt in circulation amounted to £T 139.1 million (about £126 million), with a service charge of £T 19 million, to which should be added £T 2.2 million in municipal debts guaranteed by the government, with a charge of £T 128,000.[10] This represents a debt of some £9 per capita, a high figure by contemporary standards.

Over the whole period 1854–1914, the gross amount borrowed has been put at £T 399.5 million. Of this £T 135.5 million, or 34 percent, represents commissions and the difference between nominal and issue price; £T 178.9 million, or 45 percent, was used to liquidate previous debts; £T 22.3 million, or 6 percent, for military expenditure; £T 20 million, or 5 percent, to cover budget deficits; £T 18.1 million, or 5 percent (10 percent of net receipts), was invested productively; and the balance was paid to the treasury or put to other uses.[11] Clearly Turkey derived little benefit from its huge debt. The burden of this debt, however, was great. At the beginning of this century, service charges equaled a little over 30 percent of government revenue and about the same proportion of export proceeds.

One last remark may be made regarding the nationality of the bondholders. Estimates vary, but all agree that France had by far the largest share, that Britain drastically reduced its share, and that Germany rapidly increased its holdings. In 1881, Britain and France owned a third each and Germany held very little stock; by 1895 France's share was 46 percent, Britain's 18, and Germany's 11; by 1914 these figures were 60, 14, and 20 respectively (but see Table 4.2).[12]

Egypt's experience ran parallel to that of Turkey. The first foreign loan, for £3.3 million at 7 percent, was issued at 82½, but by 1873 a £32 million loan, also at 7 percent, was issued at an effective price of 63. By 1876, the funded debt stood at £68.5 million, of which some £45 million had been actually received; in addition, there was a floating debt of £23 million.[13] In April of that year interest payments were suspended and, as in Turkey, an international body, the Caisse de la Dette, consisting of reprentatives of the Powers, was put in charge of finances. Since it lacked Turkey's international importance, however, Egypt was treated more harshly and its debt was not scaled down—the Law of Liquidation of 1880 fixed the consolidated debt at £98.4 million, bearing 4 percent interest, or about £14 per capita, one of the highest figures in the world. Of this some 40 percent was in French hands and a quarter or more in British.

It is impossible to estimate accurately how the proceeds of these loans were spent, but one can say with confidence that much was wasted or consumed unproductively. Perhaps the clearest picture is given by table 4.1.

Table 4.1
Revenue and Expenditure of Egyptian Government, 1863–1874
(£ millions)

Receipts		*Expenditures*	
Revenues	94.3	Administration	48.6
Loans (effective)	35.1[a]	Tribute to Turkey	7.6
Sale Suez Canal shares	4.0	Interest and sinking funds	29.6
Floating debt and interest (due 1876)	20.9	Interest and commissions on floating debt	11.9
Other	4.0	Wars, indemnities etc	7.8
		Suez indemnity, expenses, interest, etc.	16.1
		Public works	31.1[b]
		Other	5.6
Total	158.3		158.3

[a]Other sources give £45 million—see the text.
[b]Crabitès 1933: 128–33, quoting Mulhall, gives £46.3 million; Crouchley 1938:117 gives £52.6 million—see details in both sources. Both include expenditure on the Suez Canal. Owen 1969:141 gives two other estimates, totaling £14.3 million and £14.8 million, respectively, exclusive of the Suez Canal.
Source: Hamza 1944, appendix 4.

Under British rule, Egypt's debt received the highest priority, since any default would have led to intervention by France or other Powers. New loans, aggregating about £14 million, were issued in 1885–1903, and the 1890 conversion, reducing the interest on the preference debt from 5 to 3½ percent, also increased the capital.[14] But, thanks to uninterrupted redemption, the debt outstanding in 1914 had been reduced to £96.5 million, carrying an interest charge of £3.2 million compared with £4 million at the beginning of the British occupation. Moreover, all the money raised was used for development. But the burden on Egypt remained heavy. Interest and service charges absorbed some 40 percent of government revenues until the end of the century and over 25 percent in 1896–1914; as a proportion of export proceeds, the figure was almost 40 percent until around 1890, declining to about 12 by 1913.[15] What Lord Cromer called the "race against bankruptcy" had indeed been won, and in the process Egypt's administration had been vastly improved, its finances put in sound order, and its irrigation and railway systems greatly expanded. But the consequent neglect of other sectors, notably industry and education, was to have unfortunate consequences in subsequent decades.

Iran's first loan was contracted in 1892, when £500,000 was borrowed, at 6 percent, from the Imperial Bank of Persia to pay off the Tobacco Corporation, whose concession had been canceled under popular pressure. Other loans, from Britain and Russia, followed, at rates of 5–7 percent, and by 1914 Iran's debt stood at £6,754,000, with a service charge of £537,000. It may be safely stated that almost none of this was used productively. Although Iran's debt per capita (say 14 shillings) and as a proportion of GNP was far lower than those of Turkey and Egypt, it too was a heavy burden: service charges absorbed a quarter of government revenues and 6 to 7 percent of export proceeds.[16]

Tunisia began to incur a large floating debt in the mid 1850s and raised its first foreign loans in 1863 and 1865; both bore 7 percent interest but brought in only a small amount of cash. By 1867, the government was unable to meet its obligations, and in March 1870 an international commission reduced the outstanding debt from 160.2 million francs to 125 million (£5 million), at 5 percent interest; certain revenues were earmarked for servicing the debt and were to be collected by the commission. In 1884, a loan of 142.7 million francs, at 4 percent, was issued in France in conversion of all outstanding debt; France guaranteed payment, and the commission was dissolved. Further conversions in 1889–92 brought down the interest to 3 percent, and by the end of the century the service charge had fallen to 6.3 million francs, still a heavy burden compared to a government revenue of about 25 million francs and exports of 40 million. In 1902–12, three more loans, aggregating 205 million francs, were issued at 3 to 5 percent; the proceeds were used for railways, roads, and land reclamation. The amount outstanding in 1912 was 357 million francs.[17]

Morocco floated a loan of £426,000 in London in 1861, to meet the indemnity of 100 million francs (£4 million) imposed by Spain the previous year; this was repaid by 1882. Royal extravagance, combined with some modernization, necessitated another loan of 22.5 million francs, at 6 percent, in 1903, which actually brought in only 13.5 million, and still another, of 62.5 million at 5 percent—which brought in 48 million—in 1904 to pay off all other debts. Further indemnities of 135 million francs to Spain and France in 1909 led to the 1910 loan of 101 million francs, at 8 percent; France took control of the customs as security.[18]

Algeria fared better than its neighbors. In 1913, its public debt stood at about 750 million francs (£30 million),[19] but this amount had been raised at better terms and a greater part had been spent on development.

This brief survey suggests some conclusions. The credit of the independent governments, at first buoyed by such factors as the cotton boom in Egypt, quickly deteriorated, and the terms they had to meet soon became usurious. Moreover, the money raised was largely wasted. When, however, their finances passed under foreign control, they were able to raise new loans or convert old ones at more favorable rates, and the proceeds were put to much better use. The obligations taken earlier remained, however, as a burden for a long time to come.

Private Investment to 1914

The region did far better out of the capital that flowed to its private sector. Although some, e.g., mortgage credit in Egypt, was partly used to finance luxury consumption, and some was wasted in excessive costs or duplicated existing facilities, the bulk went to productive investment. By and large, returns on such capital were low: in most railway and port enterprises (which absorbed the bulk of foreign investment) profits were small. Those in the Suez Canal were moderate (chapter 3), and available figures on company profits in Egypt also suggest modest returns.

In the Ottoman Empire large-scale foreign investment began with the foundation of the Ottoman Bank in 1856. British railways and French ports and roads followed, but the biggest push came in the 1890s, with

German railways, ports, and other enterprises in Anatolia, French ports and railways in Syria, and various public utilities, mines, and banks. Shortly before the First World War there was some investment in manufacturing.[20] The most recent study estimates foreign investment (actual amount) in 1895 outside the public debt at 741 million francs (France 39 percent, Britain 24, Germany 19), increasing at a steady rate of about 15 million a year to 1,144 million in 1914 (France 45, Britain 16, Germany 25); if the amounts of government loans allocated to foreign-owned railways and other enterprises be added, the latter figure rises to 1,411 million (France 46, Britain 13, Germany 30).[21] Just as the British had gradually divested themselves of a large part of their holdings in the public debt in favor of the Germans, they sold part of their railways to the French. Table 4.2 gives slightly different figures on distribution.

Data on Egypt are more abundant and accurate, and have been thoroughly analyzed by Crouchley. Foreign banks and public utilities, mainly French, were founded in the 1850s and 60s, but large-scale investment followed the establishment of British rule. In 1883, the paid-up capital and debentures of companies operating in Egypt was

Table 4.2
Foreign Investment in Ottoman Empire around 1909–1912
(£T millions)

	French	German	British	Other[a]	Total	Of which within present borders of Turkey
Railways	23.7	22.7	5.8	1.1	53.3	33.7
Mining	2.9	0.2	0.5	0.1	3.6	3.3
Manufacturing	2.0	1.0	2.5	1.0	6.5	6.5
Banks and insurance	3.2	1.3	2.9	0.9	8.2	5.6
Ports and quays					4.7	2.9
Electricity, tramways, water, etc.	5.1	3.5	2.5	2.0	5.7	3.1
Commerce					2.7	2.1
Total	36.8	28.7	14.1	5.1	84.7	57.1
Percent	43.4	33.9	16.6	6.0	100	
Public debt	52.1	10.1	10.9	23.7	96.8	
Percent	53.8	10.4	11.3	24.5	100	
Grand total	89.0	38.8	25.1	28.8	181.5	
Percent	49.0	21.4	13.8	15.9	100	

[a]Belgian, United States, etc.
Source: Eldem 1970:190–91.

£E. 6.6 million, of which 6.0 million was foreign capital, but by 1902 the figures had risen to £E 26.3 million and 24.6 million, respectively; neither total includes the Suez Canal, the figure for which was around £E 19 million, all foreign. Then followed a boom, based on Egypt's economic advance, the feeling that British rule was now firmly established, and easy conditions in world money markets. Although the 1907 crash—part of the worldwide crisis of that year—witnessed large-scale liquidations, by 1914 the total capital had risen to £E 100.2 million (£102.4 million) of which £E 92 million was held by foreign interests.[22] A breakdown is given in table 4.3.

It will be seen that Britain did not use its political control to reserve Egypt for its own capital, since French and Belgian interests combined were twice as large as British.

Interest and dividends on this capital were low—somewhat below 5 percent in 1883–1914 and exceeding that figure only slightly in the boom years 1900–6. But the absolute value rose greatly, from about £E 300,000 in 1883 to 1,360,000 in 1902 and 3,184,000 in 1914; naturally, this added to Egypt's already heavy foreign exchange liabilities.[23]

Iran absorbed little foreign capital. The only important private British investments were the Anglo-Persian Oil Company, whose capital was raised from £2 million in 1909 to £4.2 million in 1914, and the Imperial Bank of Persia, with a capital of £1 million. Russian investment in banking and in roads, ports, and fisheries in the Caspian region aggregated about 40 million rubles (£4 million), and a substantial

Table 4.3
Egypt: Companies Containing Capital from Abroad, Grouped According to
Controlling Element, 1914
(£E millions)

	British	French	Belgian	Other	Total
Mortgage companies	13.5	39.1	2.0	—	54.6
Banks and financial companies	3.8	1.5	0.4	0.3	6.0
Agricultural and urban land companies	2.8	1.2	8.3	—	12.3
Transport and canals[a]	2.7	—	2.5	0.5	5.7
Manufacturing, commerce, and mining	7.5	4.4	1.1	0.4	13.4
Total	30.3	46.3	14.3	1.2	92.0

[a] Excluding Suez Canal.
Source: Crouchley, 1934:72.

amount was also advanced as mortgages and other loans by Russian subjects. Investments from other sources were negligible.[24]

There was even less foreign investment in Iraq—a 132 kilometer stretch of the Baghdad Railway between Baghdad and Samarra, the Tigris and Euphrates steamboats, some banks, and a few merchant houses.[25] Their capital has been included in the Ottoman figures. So have investments—almost wholly French—in Syria, in railways, roads, ports, public utilities, banks, silk reeling factories, and merchant houses—a total of some 500 million francs (£20 million).[26]

There was practically no foreign investment in Arabia or Sudan before the First World War. In Libya, before the Italian occupation of 1911, foreign investments—almost wholly Italian—amounted to some $5 million.[27] There was little addition before the First World War. The same was true of Morocco before the Protectorate: in 1902 French investments were officially estimated at only 6.5 million francs (but a private source gives a figure of 25 million), and there was some German investment also, both increasing until 1912. In 1913, the French invested another 25 million francs.[28] Tunisia absorbed more capital, almost wholly French: in 1902 French investments were officially estimated at 512 million francs (£20.5 million), about half of which was in the private sector; in 1912 French capital invested in the purchase or improvement of real estate was put at 300 million francs and that in various companies at 110 million.[29]

For Algeria even a rough estimate is impossible, since so much of the investment consisted of capital raised by Frenchmen domiciled in the country and reinvestment of profits. In 1912, Piquet estimated the "wealth of the colony"—by which he seems to refer exclusively to French holdings—at 2.6 billion francs (£104 million). This was broken down into: agriculture 1 billion (land 500 million, agricultural buildings 180 million, equipment and livestock 113 million); urban real estate 1.3 billion; movable capital (bank deposits, shares, etc.) 340 million.[30]

The Flow of
Foreign Capital Since 1914

During the First World War, Turkey received extensive aid from Germany and Austria, and by 1918 its debt had risen to £T 465.7 million.[31] But at the Lausanne Conference these wartime debts were canceled and the debt was fixed at £T 129.4 million (gold) with a service charge of £T 8.7 million (gold). This was divided among the successor states as follows: Turkey 67 percent, Syria and Lebanon 8.4, Iraq 5.2, Palestine 2.5, Saudi Arabia 1.3, Yemen 0.9, Transjordan 0.7; the balance was shared between the European successor states. Thus Turkey's share was £T 84.6 million, with a service charge of £T 5.8 million. But in 1928 Turkey succeeded in scaling down its share considerably and, after it had defaulted in 1930 because of balance of payments difficulties, in 1933 a new agreement was reached, reducing the debt to only £T 8 million (gold) and the service charge to £T 700,000. Even so, debt servicing absorbed some 15 percent of government expenditures. In 1936, a Franco-Turkish agreement gave Turkey further concessions; by 1944 the bulk, and by 1954 the whole, of the old debt had been paid off. On the other hand, a few loans aggregating some $70 million (gold) were contracted, for development, in 1930–38.[32]

Turkey also drastically reduced its private debt. In 1928–35 the remaining foreign railways were nationalized; compensation of about $80 million was to be paid in the form of long-term loans. So were the coal mines in 1936, and the foreign shares of the copper mines were acquired by the Eti Bank that same year. Various other firms went bankrupt during the depression and were taken over. As a result, foreign investment fell from £ 63 million in 1923 to £18 million in 1933.[33]

During the Second World War Turkey, which was the only country in the region that could trade with both sides, built up substantial foreign exchange balances.[34] These were, however, quickly exhausted, and it soon began to accumulate huge foreign debts—at first through the Marshall Plan and U.S. aid, then from the World Bank and various European countries, and more recently, from the Soviet bloc as well. For recent figures on the indebtedness of Turkey and other countries and the ratio of servicing to total foreign exchange receipts see appendix table A.9.

Egypt was by no means as successful in getting rid of its debt until much later. During the First World War, thanks to British military spending and the restriction of imports, it accumulated about £100 million in sterling balances. This was used to repatriate half the public debt (£47 million), to reduce drastically mortgage and other debts due to foreign companies, and to invest in foreign securities. Only one small public loan was contracted in the interwar period, and the debt, which had been steadily reduced, was converted in 1943, the sterling bonds being replaced by Egyptian. By 1938, the servicing of the debt—of which more than half was held by residents in Egypt—absorbed only one-tenth of government expenditure and a little more of export proceeds. During the Second World War, Egypt again accumulated large sterling balances, totaling over £400 million, but these were drawn down in the early postwar period. Starting in 1955 Egypt, like Turkey, contracted a huge foreign debt, from the Soviet bloc, the United States, the Arab countries and funds, and the World Bank.

Little private capital flowed to Egypt after 1914. In 1933, total foreign investments (excluding the Suez Canal) were put at £E 81 million ($400 million). Of this French investments, mainly in mortgage banking and public utilities, accounted for £E 39 million; British interests, mainly in industrial companies and mortgage banks, £E 32 million; and Belgian capital, mainly in land companies, £E 7 million. In 1948, foreign capital in Egypt was estimated at approximately £E 100 million at current stock exchange quotations, representing a considerable decrease in real terms from the prewar figures; of this £E 45 million was French and an approximately equal amount British. Starting in 1956, after the Suez War, Egypt successively nationalized practically all foreign capital in Egypt, paying very little compensation.[35]

As long as it was under British administration, the Sudan accumulated relatively little debt, and used the capital mainly for railways and irrigation. For several decades, the Sudan budget was supported by Egypt which, between 1898 and 1940, gave an estimated £20 million in grants and £5.5 million in non-interest-bearing loans, a large figure considering that only in 1919 did the total Sudanese budget reach the figure of £3 million.[36] Several loans were floated in London, at low interest rates, and the foreign capital cumulatively invested in 1898–36 was estimated at: public loans £25.4 million; Egyptian grants-in-aid £10.8 million; private listed £5.1 million; estimated unlisted £2.1 million; total £43.4 million.[37] Private investment was largely accounted for by the Gezira scheme (chapter 7), the capital of the two British companies participating in it rising gradually to £2.5 million in 1935. In 1934–39 their dividends ranged from £150,000 to £300,000 per annum, which may be compared with the value of exports from the Gezira of £1 to £3 million; in 1950 their concession lapsed and was not renewed.[38] However, the public debt charge of nearly £1 million was high compared to government revenues of £4 million and exports of £3 to £6 million.

In 1938–46 Sudan had a surplus of £16 million in its balance of payments, and in 1947–51 another £53 million. This was used to reduce the public debt and accumulate balances.[39] But, starting in 1958, it took loans first from the World Bank, then from the United States and the Soviet bloc, and finally from other Arab countries and funds.

Iran's debt was drastically reduced during the First World War, since the Soviet government canceled its loans and the decline in sterling halved the value of British loans. No further obligations were contracted

until after the Second World War, the large development program being
financed from domestic sources. There was also almost no private
investment, except in petroleum. The same was true of Iraq, except for a
£1 million loan at 4 1/2 percent interest in 1937, and the Arabian
Peninsula, where Aden Protectorate contracted loans of £5.3 million,
also at 4 1/2 percent, for the 1955-60 development plan; in addition Aden
had received grants totaling £2 million from the British Colonial and
Welfare Fund.[40]

In the postwar period Iraq borrowed sparingly, but Iran received
rather large amounts from the United States, the Soviet Union, and other
sources, and it also attracted a small amount of private capital; but the
rapid increase in oil revenues after 1973 made it a net creditor. Iraq also
became a substantial creditor, and the Arabian countries—first Kuwait,
then Saudi Arabia, the United Arab Emirates, and Qatar—accumulated
huge investments abroad (chapter 9).

Petroleum is discussed more fully in chapter 10. Here it may be noted
that gross fixed assets, at historical costs, in the Gulf region amounted in
1925 to some $100 million, all in Iran; in 1935 to $350 million, the bulk
being in Iran; and in 1947 $900 million, some two-fifths in Iran. An
ownership breakdown by nationality at that date shows: United
Kingdom 44 percent, United States 40, France 8, and Netherlands 8.[41] By
1970, gross investments in fixed assets were put at $7,450 million and net
investments at $3,685 million. Investments in the refinery and tanker
harbor at Aden amounted to nearly $150 million.[42] During the 1970s,
all these investments were gradually taken over by the respective
governments.

Syria and Lebanon did not contract any debt until after the Second
World War and failed to attract any significant private capital: one
source puts the total inflow in 1922-41 at £S 21 million, or about $10-15
million.[43] In the postwar period Syria received considerable aid, mainly
from the Soviet Union and the Arab countries, while a large amount of
Arab private capital flowed into Lebanese banks and real estate. The
foreign-owned public utilities, railways, port of Beirut, electricity, and
water were nationalized in the 1950s.[44]

Palestine floated only one loan, for £4.8 million, in 1927 and attracted
a few million pounds of private capital. But in 1919-39 it received well
over $500 million in Jewish national funds, and another $100 million
in 1939-44.[45] Since 1948, Israel has received, in economic and military
aid, some $15 billion, mainly from the United States.[46] Jordan has also
been heavily dependent on foreign aid, first from the United Kingdom
then from the United States and in recent years from Arab countries.

The Italian government invested lavishly in Libya. In 1913–42 a total of $159 million was spent on roads, ports, railways, public buildings, and agriculture; indirect state investment amounted to $71 million; and state loans to $35 million—a total of $265 million. Private investment amounted to $109 million.[47] After independence Libya for many years was deeply dependent on international aid, receiving large amounts from the United Kingdom, the United States, and other sources. In 1956–59 foreign aid averaged one-third of gross domestic product. The situation was completely transformed by the discovery of oil, which converted Libya into a large creditor.

In Tunisia, public loans aggregating a little over 300 million francs were contracted in 1914–39 for railways, roads, and land reclamation, but the devaluation of the franc, and amortization, greatly reduced the burden of the debt; the outstanding debt stood at only 1,049 million francs ($30 million) in 1938 and the same amount in 1945. In 1947–55 the French government advanced loans totaling 81 billion francs ($230 million) to Tunisia, at 1.5 percent interest.[48] After independence Tunisia received considerable aid from the United States and contracted a relatively large debt. There was also a large amount of private investment. In 1934, the paid-up capital of the 146 companies working exclusively in Tunisia was 1,164 million francs ($79 million) a figure that understates considerably the real value of their properties. In 1947–55 private investment totaled 65 billion "francs actuels," or about $200 million.[49] Altogether, the value of French property in Tunisia in 1955 was probably well over $1 billion. Following independence, public utilities, phosphate mines, and other enterprises were nationalized.

Morocco received much more foreign capital, again almost wholly French. In 1912–56, it raised 388 billion 1959 francs ($920 million) in loans in the French market or in advances from the French government; this accounted for nearly one-half of public and semipublic (phosphates, railways, electricity, etc.) investments undertaken in Morocco; over half the total was received after the Second World War. A huge amount of private capital also flowed in: an estimated 720 billion 1959 francs ($1.7 billion) in 1912–56; well over half of this came in 1946–56, when French investors felt more secure in Morocco than at home. An estimated 40 percent went to industry and mining, 35 to buildings, and 10 to agriculture.[50] A small portion of this was nationalized after independence. Morocco has received considerable aid from the United States and Soviet Union, and has contracted a large foreign debt.

For Algeria again only the roughest approximation is possible. In 1914–39, loans aggregating 4.2 billion francs (say, roughly $400 million) were contracted, and in 1947–55 the French government advanced 208 billion, i.e., some $600. As regards private investments, the capital of companies operating in Algeria in 1940 was 131.6 billion francs, or about $3,300 million.[51] The bulk of private capital in mining, industry, water, electricity, banks, commerce, and transport, worth about 35–40 billion francs or $1 billion, was stated to be "in the hands of French metropolitan capital."[52] According to the agency representing the ex-*colons*, French assets in 1961 amounted to 14 billion francs, or $2.8 billion; of these 5 billion francs were in factories, 2 billion in businesses, and 7 billion in agriculture.[53] All this was taken over by the Algerians after independence. In spite of its relatively large oil revenues, Algeria has contracted a large foreign debt, used mainly for industrialization.

The above account brings out a fairly clear pattern. In the 19th century the Middle Eastern governments contracted huge loans, at unfavorable terms, which were not invested productively. The result was both total or partial loss of sovereignty and the shouldering of heavy service charges. A partial compensation for foreign control was that subsequent loans were less burdensome and were spent more wisely. In the interwar period, little further debt was incurred, and what was got was spent productively; in fact, outstanding debt was drastically reduced by devaluation of currencies (Turkey, Iran, and North Africa), by negotiated reduction (Turkey, Iran), or by repatriation and redemption (Egypt, Syria, Iraq). In the postwar period, the governments rapidly accumulated a debt which is enormous whether measured by former standards or in terms of their economic capacity. Clearly this debt cannot be repaid; yet, unless the international balance of power changes drastically and in a quite unforeseen direction, it is not likely to lead to foreign control. Instead the International Monetary Fund is frequently called in to assist in rolling back debts and prescribing unpopular measures—such as devaluation or reduction of government expenditures—which sometimes result in riots.

The experience of foreign private capital in the region has been disappointing. Profits on investments before 1914 were rather low. After the First World War devaluations, or nationalization with low compensation as in Turkey, led to substantial investor losses. The oil industry was, of course, a conspicuous exception, its profits being very large indeed (chapter 10). Starting in the 1950s, in almost all countries foreign property has been taken over, usually with little compensation. Once again oil has been an exception, for although control and an overwhelming proportion of profits have passed to the governments, the industry is still earning a handsome return on its capital.

CHAPTER V

Migration and Minorities

In the 19th and 20th centuries the Middle East witnessed migration flows far larger than ever before in its history. Some of these were part of worldwide currents, e.g., the influx and subsequent outflow of Europeans; the emigration of Greeks, Armenians, and Syro-Lebanese to the New World, and the emigration of South Arabians to Indonesia. Others were due to causes originating in or around the region, like the inflow of Muslims from the Caucasus and Balkans; the migration of Syro-Lebanese, Armenians, Greeks, and Jews to Egypt and Sudan; the exodus of Palestinians and influx of Jews from Arab countries into Israel; the Greco—Turkish exchange of population in the 1920s; and the massive movement of labor to the oil countries. The status of minorities also changed radically during this period; first they came to enjoy affluence and power on an unprecedented scale, and then they were gradually squeezed out of the favorable economic and social positions they had succeeded in occupying.

Migration Within the Region

There has always been a certain amount of migration within the region, mainly from the Arabian Peninsula to the Fertile Crescent and Nile Valley, but sometimes into North Africa as well, as with the notorious Banu Hilal and Banu Sulaym in the 11th century. Starting in the 9th century, various Turkic peoples settled in Iran, northern Syria, and northern Iraq, as well as Anatolia.

In the 19th century there were some new streams, small in numbers but of cultural and economic significance. The French—and later Italian—occupation of North Africa sent several thousands of Algerians, Libyans, Tunisians, and Moroccans to the surrounding countries or to Syria and Egypt, depriving these peoples of a large part of their social and cultural leadership. On the other hand, economic development attracted tens of thousands from neighboring countries: in 1952 there were some 60,000 Moroccans and Tunisians in Algeria and 32,000 Algerians in Morocco.[1] All these immigrants were easily assimilated, both in the Middle East and North Africa.

In the 1820s, to escape Muhammad Ali's conscription and forced labor, thousands of Egyptians fled to Palestine and beyond, and in the following decades a much larger number of Lebanese, Syrians, Armenians, Jews, and Greeks were attracted to Egypt by its rapid development. The economic and social contributions of these minorities are discussed below; however, they remained unassimilated, and practically all their descendants have left the country.

During and immediately after the First World War some 150,000 Armenians fled from Turkey to Syria and Lebanon, of whom 120,000 were still resident in 1927.[2] They made a significant contribution in industry, handicrafts, and trade, but after Syria obtained independence, most of them left the country, and now a large number is emigrating from Lebanon. Some 25,000 "Assyrians" (Nestorian Christians) also fled to Iraq at the end of the First World War but, after the 1933 clashes, most gradually moved out.[3]

The next major conflict in the region, the Palestine war, set in motion two tidal waves of refugees. In 1948–49, some 726,000 Arabs fled to the surrounding countries. This number grew rapidly, mainly by natural increase of around 3 percent but also by further emigration, particularly after the 1967 war.[4] By the end of the 1970s the Palestinians were estimated at some 3.5 million, of whom about half were in Israel, Gaza, and the West Bank. The heaviest concentrations were in Jordan, Lebanon, and Syria, but there were substantial numbers in the oil countries of the Gulf and Libya and also in the United States and Europe. Thanks to better education in Palestine under the Mandate, the shock effects of exile, and the substantial help provided by the United Nations and private philanthropy, the Palestinians today represent the most highly educated and skilled Arab community, with an estimated 50,000 holders of college or university degrees in 1969. This massive outflow was matched by one almost as large of Jews into Israel: some 586,000 in 1948–72, of whom 330,000 were from French North Africa, 130,000 from Iraq, and 50,000 from Yemen and Aden.[5] By and large, these immigrants have been assimilated with the usual degree of friction accompanying such processes.

The last flow to be mentioned is purely economic in character. By 1977 there were an estimated 3 million foreign workers in the oil-producing countries of the Gulf and North Africa, of whom about one-third came from outside the region (Pakistan, India, Afghanistan, Korea, Bangladesh, etc.) and the rest from North and South Yemen, Egypt, Jordan, Sudan, Syria, Turkey, Tunisia, and Morocco. The impact on the countries of emigration has been, on balance, favorable: unemployment has been brought down, and in 1977 remittances from these workers were: to Egypt $1,425 million; North Yemen $1,000 million; Jordan $425 million; South Yemen $180 million; and Sudan $40 million.[6] However, the emigration of skilled workers has caused some shortages, and the influx of remittances has, in certain areas, had disturbing economic and social effects, particularly by inflating land values.[7]

The impact on the host countries has been immense. In 1975 immigrants formed either a majority (85 percent in the UAE, 81 in Qatar, and 69 in Kuwait) or a large proportion (Saudi Arabia 43 percent, Libya 42, Oman 34) of the total labor force. The vast majority consists of unskilled workers in construction or service industries, but the number of both highly skilled workers and technicians and administrators is also large, and their role in the economy and education is crucial. Without them, the remarkable economic and social advances of the last decade would have been impossible, but their presence has had two negative effects. First, the influx of so many foreigners—including, of course, the conspicuous Americans and Europeans discussed below—has created a deep feeling of revulsion and resentment that recently exploded in Iran and will no doubt do so elsewhere. Second, it has had a profoundly demoralizing influence on the inhabitants of these countries, who are increasingly confirmed in their attitude that any work—from installing antimissile systems to garbage collection—can be handed over to foreigners, leaving the fortunate owners of oil wealth to spend and enjoy the revenues. A further disturbing effect must be the resentment of foreign workers at the contrast between their condition—much improved though it has been by emigration—and the surrounding affluence.

Immigration

The Russian conquest of the Caucasus and the achievement of independence by the Balkan countries sent large waves of Muslim refugees to the Ottoman Empire. Karpat estimates that in 1859–79 over one million Caucasians, mostly Circassians, entered Ottoman territory. About half were settled in the European provinces and most of the rest in Anatolia, but some were also sent to Syria and Transjordan. The same author states that one million Turks were expelled from Bulgaria in

1878, and also settled in the European provinces and Anatolia. A British consul estimates that, following the 1913 war, over 300,000 persons fled from the Balkans to Turkey.[8] And after the First World War, 1.2 million Greeks living in Turkey were exchanged for 600,000 Turks in Greece; subsequent emigration by Turks in Europe, especially from Bulgaria in 1950–52, brought the latter total up to around one million. These Muslim immigrants, and also the tens of thousands who fled the Bolshevik revolution to Iran, have been gradually assimilated in their new homes. So were the many thousands who, over numerous decades, came to the Red Sea and Gulf ports from Somalia, Central Africa, India, and Indonesia, as slaves, pilgrims, or merchants.

That did not happen to the equally numerous and far more influential European immigrants and colonists. Egypt was the first country to receive them: in addition to the many thousands of Greeks deported by Muhammad Ali,[9] by 1836 there were some 3,000 Europeans who served the pasha in various military or technical capacities or who had come to trade. In 1872 Europeans were put at 80,000, of whom 30,000 were Greeks and 15,000 Italians. By 1907 they reached a peak of 221,000, or 2 percent of the total population.[10] They were concentrated in the cities, forming, in 1907, 16 percent of the population of Cairo, 25 percent of Alexandria, and 28 percent of Port Said.

The power of this group was, however, disproportionate to its size. The Europeans owned an appreciable proportion of the cultivated area—12 percent in 1909—though much of it consisted of land being reclaimed by foreign-owned development companies. Until the Second World War, they constituted the bulk of the professional class, supplying most of Egypt's doctors, engineers, and to a lesser degree lawyers, and many high civil servants. Finally, and most important, until the 1950s they owned and managed the main financial, commercial, and industrial enterprises. Their occupational structure differed sharply from that of Egyptians: in 1937 only 1 percent of foreigners worked in agriculture, compared with 59 percent of Egyptians, and 42 percent in commerce, finance, and services against 11 percent—and the divergence between incomes in the primary and tertiary sectors was far higher than elsewhere, since it reflected the gap between two coexisting cultures as well as the usual economic factors. Thus in the 1930s a rural laborer earned £E 1 ($5) a month, while a bank clerk started at £E 8. Altogether, foreigners may have owned a tenth or more of Egypt's total wealth. In addition, they enjoyed political privileges under the capitulations which exempted them from taxation and put them under the jurisdiction of the consular and mixed courts, not the Egyptian ones.

The change in their position began with the achievement of partial independence in 1922. The number of foreigners declined slowly to 150,000 in 1947 and precipitously thereafter, only to a small degree by naturalization. The government began to squeeze them (and also the minorities), out of the civil service and private employment. In 1937 the capitulations and consular courts were abolished, and in 1949 the mixed courts. During the Second World War Italian and German property was sequestrated, in 1956 British, French, and Jewish, and in 1960 Belgian, practically eliminating foreign ownership (chapter 4).[11] One is reminded of the pioneering role played by, and the subsequent fate of, Jews and Italians in the Commercial Revolution in northwestern Europe in the 13th–14th centuries.

In the eastern Arab countries the number of foreigners never exceeded a few thousand except in Lebanon, which in the 1940s–60s became the center of American and European enterprise in the region.[12] For the resources of these countries were few, they attracted small amounts of foreign investment, and, until the 1950s, their development was slow. Moreover, they had a relatively large middle class, consisting mainly of Christians and Jews. In Iran the number of Europeans in 1914 may have been around 1,000. The development of Gulf petroleum drew a few thousands of Europeans and Americans to the industry or related jobs.[13] The 1970s saw an "oil rush," and the number of Europeans and Americans rose to some 150,000, of whom an estimated 85,000 left Iran in 1979.[14]

Except for Hellenes, there were also few foreigners in Turkey—under 20,000 toward the end of the 19th century. Of these some 5,000 were French (excluding Algerians and protected subjects), 2,000 British, and 8,000 Austrians; these numbers rose slowly until the First World War. There was little foreign land ownership, except for some British holdings in the Izmir area, and ambitious plans to settle German farmers along the Anatolian railway did not materialize. A few foreigners were engaged in trade and finance. They supplied professional skills, and an increasing number of skilled workers was employed in industry and transport. But the great economic and political influence enjoyed by the European countries in Turkey was not accompanied by any commensurate settlement.[15]

North Africa presents a complete different picture, since it was the scene of "demographic" as well as "economic" colonization, in which foreigners provided not only the bourgeoisie but workers and farmers as well.

In the 1940s there were nearly 2 million European settlers, mainly

French, many of whom represented the third or fourth generation. Algeria saw the earliest and most thoroughgoing attempt to settle a large colony and make it part of the metropolis. The enterprise was, however, given a peculiar twist by the fact that the French birthrate was exceptionally low, France did not suffer from population pressure, and its beauty and resources have, quite rightly, always made its inhabitants reluctant to emigrate. Hence the bulk of the colonists came not from France but from the coastlands of other Mediterranean countries: Spain, Italy, Malta, as well as Corsica and Provence; in 1912 it was estimated that only one European settler in five was "pure French." Four periods of settlement are usually distinguished.[16] In 1830–51 the military conquest was completed, and an attempt was made to build up the town of Algiers and to plant farmer-colonists, on the Roman model. By 1841 there were 37,000 Europeans and by 1845 over 100,000; since death rates were high, the bulk of the increase came from immigration. In 1851–72 another 100,000 immigrated from France and elsewhere, the death rate was reduced, and some 25,000 Jews were granted French citizenship in 1870–71; this raised the European population to over 250,000. In 1872–1901 immigration accelerated, including both Frenchmen from Alsace-Lorraine, attracted by land grants and the development of viticulture following the phylloxera epidemic in France (chapter 7), and Spaniards . fleeing the civil wars; there was also some natural increase, bringing the total to 634,000 by 1901. During the present century, immigration slowed, but a natural increase of 1 percent a year was maintained, raising the number of Europeans to 833,000 by 1926, a peak of 14 percent of Algeria's total population, and 1,054,000 in 1954, 11 percent of the total.

In spite of various attempts to settle the countryside, by 1926 80 percent of this population lived in towns, and the cities had become predominantly European. There were, however, some 25,000 European farms, mostly large, that held nearly two-fifths of the privately owned cultivated land (chapter 7). Practically all industry, large-scale commerce, and finance was owned and run by Europeans, who also staffed the professions and civil service and provided the skilled and semiskilled workers.[17] An official estimate put the Muslim share of the country's wealth in 1900 at only 37 percent.[18] Income disparities were also great, on the order of at least 6:1.[19] So were social: whereas all European children of school age went to school, only 15 percent of Muslim children did so. Attempts in the 1950s to raise the Muslim level were overtaken by the War of Independence, which was followed by a mass exodus of Europeans and the seizure of their property. By 1966 there were only 82,000 Frenchmen in Algeria.

Tunisia repeated Algeria's experience, but on a somewhat reduced scale. The European population grew from about 8,000 in the 1830s and 12,000 in 1881 to about 135,000 in 1911, of whom the greater part retained Italian nationality. By 1936 the total had risen to 214,000 (8.2 percent of the total population) and by 1946 to 240,000 (7.5 percent). After independence, in 1955, there was a large outflow, the European population dropping to 100,000 by 1959 and diminishing further since; however, much less property was taken over than in Algeria. Europeans, 85 percent of whom lived in towns, held one-fifth of the cultivated land and owned the large industrial, commercial, and financial enterprises, but the Tunisian middle class, both entrepreneurial and salaried, was much bigger than the Algerian; it was also helped by the fact that Tunisia, being a protectorate and not a French department like Algeria, gave more scope to its own people in administration. Nevertheless, a United Nations study indicates that in 1957 in Tunisia European per capita income was eight times as high as Tunisian and consumption six times as high; European income was also higher than that of France.[20]

In Morocco immigration began much later and remained smaller. The number of Europeans went up from about 130 at the beginning of the 19th century, 1,400 in 1867,[21] and 20,000 in 1913 to about 150,000 in 1931 and some 350,000 in 1952; of these some 70 percent were French, a large number drawn from Algeria and Tunisia by Morocco's economic upsurge. They formed 5 percent of the population and held only 9 percent of the cultivated land, but owned practically the whole of the private modern sector; but, like Tunisia, Morocco retained a relatively large bourgeoisie. The income gap between Europeans and Muslims may well have been larger than in Algeria or Tunisia, and the Europeans probably had a higher real per capita income than that of France.[22] After independence, most Europeans left, their number dropping to around 100,000 by 1965, but a much smaller proportion of their property was taken over by Morocco.

In Spanish Morocco, the Spanish population grew to 85,000, or 8.5 percent of the total by 1950. It too was highly urbanized, only 7 percent being rural, and included a large working class as well as a far-from-affluent middle class.[23] Here too there has been large-scale emigration since independence. Tangiers had an estimated foreign population of 60,000, out of a total of 100,000 in 1958.

Libya had only some 5,000 foreigners in 1908, of whom 3,000 were Maltese and 1,000 Italians.[24] Since one of the purposes of Italian expansion was to find alternative outlets for the surplus population that was emigrating to the New World—an objective which was met only to a small degree[25]—vigorous and costly attempts were made to settle farmers in Tripolitania in the 1920s and Cyrenaica in the 1930s. By 1939 there were about 18,000 farmers (including families) in the former[26] and some 7,000 in the latter. The total Italian population reached 110,000 in 1941, of whom 70,000 were in Tripolitania. During the Second World War the Italians were evacuated from Cyrenaica, but some 35,000 to 40,000 remained in Tripolitania; however, after the overthrow of the monarchy in 1969, there was a general exodus, and by 1980 the number was down to 20,000. The Italians had held over half the land of Tripolitania, and at least as large a share of Cyrenaica's, and provided not only the whole middle class but a significant proportion of the working class as well.

The last large wave of immigration was of Jews to Palestine and Israel, which started at the same time as European migration but gained amplitude several decades later. In 1839 there were an estimated 10,000, of whom 5,000 were in Jerusalem, and by 1880 about 25,000. Systematic immigration and settlement then began, and by 1914 some 40,000 persons had come in, raising the total number to a little over 80,000, of whom 60,000 were in Jerusalem; the bulk were from Eastern Europe, but there were also some 10,000 oriental Jews.[27] During the First World War some 12,000–15,000 left the country, bringing the total down to about 67,000; under the Mandate immigration totaled 452,000, of whom some four-fifths were from Europe. At the beginning of 1947 Jews numbered 610,000 and formed 32 percent of the population of Palestine. Between the establishment of the State of Israel in 1948 and the end of 1978, immigration amounted to 1,637,000, of whom 761,000 were from Asia and Africa.

Some of the early settlers had used Arab labor on their farms but this was rejected, as leading to an incipient "planter class," by the socialist groups who came at the end of the century and later by the trade union movement, the Histadruth. The urge to employ only Jews, both to provide employment for new settlers and to change the traditional Jewish occupational distribution, reinforced by growing hostility between Arabs and Jews, resulted in two almost insulated economies. In 1936, "total sales of final and intermediate products and services between the two sectors amounted to a sum equal to only 7 percent of Palestine's national income."[28] In agriculture, where Jews owned a fifth of the cultivated land (chapter 7), "there is a clear division between the two communities except in the case of citriculture," where the planted area was almost equally divided between Arabs and Jews and where there was joint marketing and export;[29] however, Arab farms sold an estimated 33–40 percent of their agricultural produce, mainly cereals, to the Jews.[30]

In industry the vast majority of modern enterprises were Jewish. A survey of 12 industries showed that capital per worker in Jewish enterprises was 70 percent higher than in Arab and net output per worker 87 percent, but because of high wages, labor costs were also 107 percent higher.[31] In a unified labor market Jewish wages would have fallen and Arab risen; this was prevented by the Histadruth and other institutional factors, but there is some evidence that under the Mandate the threat of Arab competition kept wages for unskilled Jewish labor lower than they would have been.[32] In 1945 the government statistician put the per capita income of Jews at £P 141 ($560) and that of Arabs and others at £P 50 ($200), a ratio of almost 3:1. Incomes per worker were much closer—£P 333 and £P 205—but, because of large families and an unfavorable age composition, the dependency ratio was much higher among Arabs.[33] In the early years of the State of Israel, Jewish wage rates were some five times as high as Arab, but since then the two communities have become much more integrated economically, and by the early 1970s the gap had narrowed to between 1.5:1 and 2:1; the occupational distribution of the two communities is, however, still markedly different, the proportion of Arabs in agriculture and construction being far higher and in industry, finance, and professions much lower.[34]

Emigration

In antiquity the Phoenicians colonized the western Mediterranean, the Jews began their long Diaspora, and Syrians settled in large numbers first in Rome, evoking some uncomplimentary remarks from Juvenal, and then in Gaul. The Arab conquest of Spain was accompanied by a relatively large migration of Syrians, Berbers, and others. From about the 10th century to the 19th—with an interval of some two centuries when the Portuguese dominated the region—Omanis and other Arabs emigrated to and controlled the East African coast, engaging extensively in the slave trade; their rule in Zanzibar ended only with the massacre of 1963. The Ottoman conquest of the Balkans was followed by a large-scale settlement of Turks. Otherwise, there seems to have been little emigration from the region.

In the second half of the 19th century two new streams emerged. The Netherlands East Indies were opened to private enterprise, and Hadramis from South Arabia, who had started coming in half a century earlier, entered in large numbers. By 1860 there were some 9,000, by 1900 27,000, and by 1952 85,000, of whom 65,000 were in Java. Most were engaged in export and import trade and moneylending. Another 30,000 Hadramis, or more, settled in Malaysia, Hyderabad, and East Africa. Their remittances of about £600,000 a year played an important part in the economy of the Aden Protectorate.[35]

Syrian Christians, mostly from Lebanon, started emigrating to the New World in large numbers in the 1880s and were later followed by Muslims and Druzes. Several factors were at work: population pressure in the mountains, social and religious unrest culminating in the 1860 massacres, the desire to avoid military service, and the opening of new horizons by the foreign schools established in Lebanon and Palestine— as well as the usual forces operating elsewhere. Between 1860 and 1900, some 120,000 persons emigrated, and in 1900–14 annual emigration was about 15,000; by 1914, some 300,000 to 350,000 had left, two-thirds to the United States and most of the rest to Brazil and other parts of Latin America. Most of these emigrants were from Lebanon, and the number of Lebanese abroad must have equaled at least a quarter, and probably more, of the population of the Mountain, and nearly half in some districts.[36] In the 1920s emigration resumed, at a slightly higher level, to Latin America and West Africa, but was soon greatly reduced by restrictions in the countries of settlement. A rough estimate in 1960 put the number of Lebanese emigrants *and their descendants* at 1.2 million, of whom 400,000 were in the United States, 350,000 in Brazil, 200,000 in Argentina, 150,000 in other Latin American countries, and 40,000 in sub-Saharan Africa. In the New World the emigrants have been easily assimilated and have made a noteworthy contribution to the economic and political life of the leading Latin American countries.[37]

Their impact on Lebanon, and parts of Palestine and Syria, has been great. The remittances they sent formed an important part of the balance of payments and, in Mount Lebanon, of the national income. In 1914, remittances to geographical Syria were put at nearly $8 million, in 1924 at $19 million (exeeding commodity exports), and, for Lebanon alone, at $20 million in 1952 (compared to exports of $22 million) or 4 percent of national income. Some of this money was used to buy land, helping to break up large estates, and much for building houses in villages. In addition, returning emigrants brought back capital and skills, founding industries and other businesses and improving agriculture. Finally, Lebanese emigrants in the New World, of whom the most celebrated was Khalil Jibran, were important literary innovators and introduced new political and social ideas in the Arab world.

Greek emigration from Turkey may have been somewhat greater than

Syro-Lebanese, and Armenian distinctly smaller. Both had broadly comparable causes and effects. There was also a large amount of Armenian emigration to Russia.[38]

After the Second World War two powerful currents of emigration flowed to Europe: from Algeria and other North African countries, mainly to France, and from Turkey, principally to Germany but also to Austria, the Netherlands, and Scandinavia. (Mention may also be made of two smaller streams: from Lebanon and Jordan to Europe and the United States, and from Israel to the United States.) During the First World War 150,000 North Africans, of whom 60 percent were Algerians, were recruited to work in France, but almost all had been repatriated by 1919. In the 1920s over 100,000 came in, and the number in the country was only slightly smaller by 1938. During the Second World War many North Africans were recruited for work in German labor organizations.[39] But it was after the war that Algerian emigration assumed large proportions, reaching a level of 150,000 a year by 1951. By 1962 there were 509,000 North African workers in France and by 1972 1,136,000; of the latter 799,000 were Algerians, 218,000 Moroccans, and 120,000 Tunisians.[40] Perhaps another 200,000 to 300,000 worked in Germany and other European countries. After that immigration was sharply curtailed by the Franco-Algerian Agreement of 1964 and subsequent measures. The main *pull* factors were France's economic expansion and its labor shortage, which drew in well over 3 million foreigners, and the lack of restrictions on immigration from Algeria. But, unlike the Italians, Spaniards, and Portuguese, North Africans have not proved assimilable in French society. The *push* factor was the high population density of Algeria, particularly Kabylia, which had long been a center of emigration, and the high unemployment rate. A large majority of North African workers are unskilled or semiskilled, and are employed in construction, low-grade services, metallurgy, and mining. But their relatively high wages and low standard of living have enabled them to save a large proportion of their earnings. In 1965 emigrant remittances to Algeria were put at $200 million—or 31 percent of merchandise exports—and it was reckoned that each Algerian worker in France supported 5 people at home. By 1975 Algerian remittances had risen to $466 million, which, because of the increase of oil exports, represented only 11 percent of exports. In 1973, an OECD study put total transfers by migrant workers to Algeria at about $300 million, or 20 percent of earnings of foreign exchange; to Morocco at about $400 million, or 25 percent, and to Tunisia at about $60 million, or 12 percent.[41]

One can also surmise that returning emigrants are bringing back skills, attitudes, and capital that may make a significant impact on the economic and social development of North Africa. Until the late 1960s, however, this had not taken place, since most of the returnees had not found jobs where they could utilize the experience they had gained in Europe, and since the mix of skills acquired did not correspond to Algeria's needs.[42] But, with increasing industrialization, Algeria may be in a better position to absorb its workers. Their political influence has, of course, been immense, since they were the seedbed of the Algerian Independence Movement.

The impact of emigration on Turkey has been much more thoroughly studied than that of Algeria. Starting in the 1960s, it grew rapidly and by the end of 1973 there were 786,000 legal workers in Europe, of whom 616,000 were in Germany; in addition, there were over 100,000 illegal immigrants.[43] After that, the economic recession led the German and other governments to restrict immigration and offer inducements to foreign workers to return home. The push and pull factors were essentially the same as for Algerians in France, but there were some significant differences: a quarter of the workers were women; only 20 percent of emigrants were unemployed when they left Turkey; about 70 percent had received at least primary education; and some 30–40 percent were classified as "skilled."[44] Their wages in Europe represent an appreciable increase over their hypothetical earnings in Turkey, and their savings rate has been high.[45] As a result their remittances have been very large, peaking at $1,425 million in 1974, or 93 percent of commodity exports, and passing the $2 billion mark in 1980.[46]

Although the evidence is not conclusive, it strongly suggests that emigration has had favorable effects on growth of GNP and per capita income, on the balance of payments, on capital formation, on employment, and on labor productivity in Turkey.[47] There are, however, some indications that the positive effects have not been as great as might have been expected. Although the increase in the productivity of the emigrants, through on-the-job training, has been impressive, it does not seem that the skills acquired were put to full use on their return; this is because half or more of the returnees preferred to work in services rather than in industry, and invested the bulk of their savings in housing and relatively little in industrial enterprises.[48] On the other hand, the skills and experience of the returnees seem to be highly valued by Turkish employers;[49] here too one can surmise that the attitudes and aptitudes acquired in Europe will have a deep and, on balance, beneficial, even if initially disturbing, impact on Turkish society.

Minorities

The rise, and subsequent downfall, of the minorities in the Middle East is part of a worldwide process.[50] The creation of a world market facilitated the emergence of intermediaries between the Europeans, who controlled the large enterprises, and the local population: in Southeast Asia these were the Chinese, in East Africa the Indians, and so on. In the Middle East this role was filled by the local minorities or *millets* — Greeks, Armenians, Jews, and Christian Arabs; in North Africa the presence of a large body of colonists obviated the need for intermediaries, but the Jews performed a similar function. The minorities also acted as transmission belts between the modernizing governments and their subjects. The ending of European political and economic preponderance meant the downfall of these groups in various parts of the world, including the Middle East.

The ascent of the *millets* is explained by a set of factors. First, from the late 18th century on, they participated actively in the expanding sectors of the economy, notably foreign trade with the West, finance, mechanized transport, modern industry, and export-oriented agriculture. Second, they enjoyed foreign protection; this exempted them from certain taxes and, more important, secured them against the arbitrary and oppressive tendencies of local officials. Third, the Tanzimat (Ottoman reforms of the 1840s) and other reforms removed many of the disabilities with which the *millets* had been burdened for centuries; and since they continued to be exempted (or excluded) from military service, they were in a much better position to compete with Muslims.[51] Fourth, they took much fuller advantage of educational opportunities than did Muslims; in particular, they acquired both foreign languages and technical skills, which made them more employable in government departments and foreign enterprises. Finally, they received much help, especially in education, from coreligionists in Europe and America. To this should be added the usual clannishness of minorities, their habit of helping and promoting each other, and, since they were excluded from certain fields, their incentive to excel in others. A few examples are illustrative.

In Turkey, the Greeks, Armenians, and Jews, in that order, dominated the urban sector and controlled a considerable part of the rural. The Galata bankers, consisting of Levantines and minority members, had controlled finance, and their replacement by modern banks only enlarged the field; in 1912, of 112 bankers and bank managers in the Ottoman Empire only one was a Muslim Turk. In industry, it has been estimated that only 15 percent of capital belonged to Turks. In commerce, Armenians and Greeks established themselves in Europe early in the 19th century and handled most of its trade with Turkey. In agriculture, *millets* were particularly active in such important cash crops as silk and cotton.[52] As for other activities, a Soviet scholar gives the following percentage breakdown for 1912.[53]

	Turks	Greeks	Armenians	Others
Internal trade	15	43	23	19
Industry and crafts	12	49	30	10
Professions	14	44	22	20

In Iran minorities played a far smaller part, but Armenians were important in industry and trade and Jews in trade.[54]

In Egypt, Copts held a substantial amount of land and were well represented in government service and the professions. The Greeks, Jews, Syro-Lebanese, and Armenians ranged over a wide spectrum of activities: industry, trade, finance, transport, professions. They supplied a large proportion of skilled workmen, craftsmen, and petty traders; some Armenians, Lebanese, Syrians, and Jews reached high positions in government service; and all played a certain role in agriculture, particularly the Greeks in cotton growing. An overall picture, at the highest level, is shown by the following breakdown of company directors as late as 1951, after great efforts had been made to Egyptianize business: 31 percent were Muslims, 4 Copts, 30 Europeans, 18 Jews, 11 Lebanese or Syrians, 6 Greeks, and 2 Armenians. In addition, the Lebanese founded and owned most of Egypt's leading newspapers and journals.[55]

The same groups largely controlled Sudan's trade, and Lebanese and Syrians formed an indispensable link between the highest British officials and the lower-rank Sudanese.

In Lebanon, from the 1830s on, Christians began to take over the country's two leading activities: foreign trade and silk growing.[56] They became equally prominent in branches that developed later, such as tourism, finance, and industry, and were predominant in government. In Syria at the beginning of the 19th century Jews were influential in trade and finance, but their power gradually declined and that of Christians increased correspondingly. In Iraq, however, Jews remained predominant in both branches until after the Second World War.[57]

The minorities reached their zenith at the beginning of this century. After that, increasing national awareness among Turks, Egyptians, and

Table 5.1
Approximate Number of Religious Minorities around 1900
(thousands)

	Armenians	Greeks	Arab Christians	Copts	Jews
Algeria	—	—	—	—	60
Libya	—	—	—	—	20
Morocco	—	—	—	—	100
Tunisia	—	—	—	—	40
Egypt	20	60	50	700	40
Sudan	—	—	—	—	—
Iraq	—	—	100	—	80
Lebanon[a]	30	—	300	—	3
Syria[a]	. .	—	200	—	10
Palestine[a]	—	—	70	—	80
Yemen	—	—	—	—	50
Other Arabia	—	—	—	—	—
Turkey	1,100	2,600	—	—	220
Iran	60	—	—	10[b]	50

[a] Around 1922.
[b] Zoroastrians; there were about 200,000 Bahais.
Sources: Estimates vary considerably. The ones in the table were derived from the following, in which further references are given:
Algeria—1906 census.
Libya—*Encyclopaedia Judaica*, s.v. "Libya."
Morocco—based on 1936 census; Chouraqui 1952:163.
Tunisia—based on 1921 census; *Initiation* 1950:135.
Egypt—1907 census: Issawi 1947:35, 165–66.
Iraq—Batatu 1978:40, 248.
Lebanon and Syria—Himadeh 1936:405–7.
Palestine—*Survey* 1946:1:141.
Yemen—EHME:235.
Turkey—EHT:18, 69; Shaw and Shaw 1977:2:238–41.
Iran—EHI:6.

others, and their growing capacity to take over functions that had hitherto been confined to members of the *millets*, made the position of the latter more and more precarious. In Turkey the terrible communal conflicts of 1895–1923 eliminated almost all Armenians and Greeks. After that, many Jews emigrated, and the remaining minority members were adversely affected by the Varlik Vergisi tax (capital levy) of 1942, which was applied in a discriminatory manner. In Egypt, from the 1930s the government tried to squeeze minority members, as well as foreigners, out of their privileged position and to encourage the growth of a native bourgeoisie to replace them.[58] After the Second World War minority members began leaving the country, and their position, undermined by the Suez War of 1956, was destroyed by the nationalizations and sequestrations of 1961. A similar process took place in Syria after 1949 and in Sudan after independence. In Iraq, the position of Jews became increasingly difficult with the development of Zionism in Palestine; there were anti-Jewish outbursts, and the 1948 Arab-Israeli war was followed by a mass exodus. In Lebanon the civil war which started in 1975 destroyed a large part of the wealth, and the predominant position, of the Christians. The 1979 revolution in Iran rapidly began eliminating the minorities in that country. As in so many parts of the world, the decline has been far swifter than the rise.

CHAPTER VI

Population, Level of Living, and Social Development

Population Growth

Statistics on the population of the region before the 19th century are completely lacking, except for the 16th-century Ottoman Empire and some Roman provinces, but it is possible to hazard educated guesses about magnitudes and trends. In the 2nd century A.D. the Middle East may have had something like 40 to 45 million inhabitants, accounting for perhaps a fifth of the world total. The plagues of the 2nd and 6th centuries greatly reduced the population, but a recovery took place in the 8th–11th centuries, raising the total to a new peak of perhaps 35 to 40 million. The Black Death of 1346–48 may have carried off a quarter or a third of the inhabitants of some countries.[1] Thereafter, population seems to have fluctuated, without showing any clear trends, except for an upsurge in the 16th century associated with the establishment of order by the Ottomans. Table 6.1 gives some estimates for the 19th and early 20th centuries. (For more recent figures see appendix table A.1.)

The estimates and guesses in the table suggest almost a doubling of the population in 1830–1914, or a growth rate of just under 1 percent per annum. This is about twice the world rate of growth during the 19th century[2] and may indicate that the earlier figures are too low, but the world total is weighted downward by India and China, both of which experienced severe famines. The same rate prevailed in 1914–30, and was also somewhat above the world rate. In the 1930s and 1940s growth accelerated to nearly 2 percent, and in recent years it has been running at around 3 percent.

A few additional remarks, based mainly on the sources mentioned in the table, may be made. For Algeria it is generally agreed that, because of the French invasion and other causes, the Muslim population decreased and did not regain its former level until the 1870s.[3] After that it grew at

Table 6.1
Population 1800-1930[a]
(millions)

	1800	1830	1860	1900	1914	1930
Algeria	(3.0)	(3.0)	(2.5)	4.7	5.7	6.6
Libya	(0.5)				0.7	0.7
Morocco	(3.0)				4.0	5.7
Tunisia	(1.0)		(1.1)		2.0	2.4
Egypt	3.9	4.7	5.5	10.2	12.3	14.7
Sudan			(4.0)	(3.5)		6.0
Iraq				(1.2)	(3.2)	3.5
Lebanon		(1.5)	(2.5)	(3.5)	(4.0)	0.8
Palestine						1.0
Syria						2.1
Transjordan						0.3
Arabia		(5.0)			(7.0)	(8.0)
Iran	(5.0)	(5.8)	(6.5)	9.9	10.9	12.6
Turkey	(6.5)	(6.7)		12.5	14.7	14.7
Estimated total[b]		(34)			68	79

[a] Figures in parentheses are educated guesses.
[b] Including guesses for figures missing in table.

Sources

Algeria—Valensi 1969a:21; *Initiation* 1957:141-43; Chevalier 1947; first census 1856.

Libya—Evans-Pritchard 1949:39; Despois 1935; Nuss 1955; first census 1911.

Morocco—Noin 1970 1:21-43; Valensi 1969a; Chevalier 1947; Figueras and de Roda Jimenez 1955: 1:66; first census, French Morocco 1931 and Spanish 1940.

Tunisia—Valensi 1977:11-14; Ganiage 1959:130-32; Brown 1974:375-78; *Initiation* 1950:136; partial census 1911, first census 1921.

Egypt—McCarthy 1977; incomplete census 1882, first census 1897.

Sudan—Cromer 1908:2:545; Henderson 1946:13; first census 1956.

Iraq—Hasan n.d.:39-40; Cuinet 1892; McCarthy 1980; first census 1947.

Lebanon, Palestine, Syria, Transjordan—Bowring 1973:3-4; Cuinet 1892; Ruppin 1916:185; McCarthy 1980; first census 1921-22.

Arabia—Palgrave 1865:1:84, 2:381; EI2, s.v. "Djazirat al-Arab"; McCarthy 1976; Great Britain, Admiralty 1916:18; censuses in 1960s and 1970s.

Iran—EHI:20-21; Gilbar 1976; Robert Hill, unpublished paper cited by Abrahamian 1974; Bharier 1971:23-28; first census 1956.

Turkey—EHT:17-22; McCarthy 1981; Karal 1943; Eldem 1970; first census 1927.

nearly 1 percent per annum, and European immigration raised the total further. Tunisia's population may have been in slow decline from the 1780s until after 1860, because of plagues and famines, after which it rose at a little over 1 percent, including immigration.[4] Libya's Muslim population fell sharply during the fighting against the Italians in 1911-15; and in Cyrenaica in 1921-32, "The beduin population was probably reduced by one-half to two-thirds by death and emigration between 1911 and 1932," no less than 80,000 being deported to concentration camps in the desert and some 20,000 emigrating to Egypt.[5] Italian immigration probably just offset this decrease. Almost the only statement that can be made about Morocco's population is that it declined following the famines and epidemics of 1878-81 and probably rose after that.[6]

Egypt's population has risen almost uninterruptedly from the time Muhammad Ali established his rule, in 1805, to the present. McCarthy's series has only one sharp decline, caused by the plague of 1835, to which may be added the influenza epidemic of 1918; his estimates show an annual rate of growth of 0.7 percent in 1800-45, accelerating to over 1.5 until 1907.[7] For the Sudan, there is general agreement that the Mahdist period saw a sharp drop in population due to wars, social disorganization, pestilence, and famine.[7] But Lord Cromer's estimate of 8-8.5 million in the 1870s and a loss of over 6 million is surely greatly exaggerated, and when the "Khalifa's apologists deny that the pre-Mahdist population can have been more than 4 to 4 1/2 million" they may well be closer to the mark.[8] Since 1900 the population seems to have grown steadily. The demographic history of the Fertile Crescent is so uncertain that the only landmark that stands out is the famine in Syria in 1916-18; an estimated 300,000 people, or more, died of starvation, of whom perhaps half were in Lebanon; there is also evidence that growth began in Lebanon rather earlier than elsewhere.[9]

Iran's population had declined in the 18th century and seems to have recovered in the first third of the 19th. But the 1871/72 famine was disastrous; a British observer estimated that deaths had not exceeded half a million, "though, from the disproportionate mortality of women and children, the ultimate loss to the country will be far higher." However, soon after that, population began to grow rather fast.[10] Turkey's population too declined quite considerably sometime in the 17th or 18th century. The beginning of the 19th century saw epidemics and much disruption, but after about 1830 population began a rapid growth, at over 0.8 percent per annum, which seems to have been interrupted only by the famine of 1873-74. Immigration seems to have exceeded emigration, contributing to the rate of increase.[11]

The region's experience during the last two centuries is explainable by the theory of demographic transition, which, in essence, attributes modern population growth to the reduction in death rates while birthrates maintain, for some generations, their previous level, near the biological maximum. However, certain qualifications and amplifications are necessary. First, as regards the birthrate, there are a few indications that the population of the Middle East did not always breed to capacity. Thus Musallam has shown that in the 14th-15th centuries

Cairo's middle class practiced some form of birth control, though its quantitative impact cannot be determined.[12] Second, there is much evidence that in the late 18th and 19th centuries many Turks in Western Anatolia and the Morea practiced abortion.[13] Finally, one can ask oneself whether in 19th-century Egypt the large and sustained increase in the demand for labor, caused by such factors as the spread of cotton cultivation and the expansion of public works, may not have broken down any restraints that had formerly operated and led to a rise in birthrates. Or whether the improvement in food supplies and the reduction in epidemics did not result in a higher proportion of live births. The same questions may be applicable to other countries—after all, in both Russia and Japan the birthrate seems to have risen in the second half of the 19th century. At any rate, when accurate statistics become available, i.e., in the course of this century, they show birthrates of around 4.5 percent. At present, demographers believe that "Moslem populations invariably experience higher fertility than neighboring communities of other religious persuasions . . . owing to pro-natalist social forces common to the Moslem World, in which marriage of women is early and universal and their subordination general, and matrimony and fecundity are fundamental virtues of the family. Moreover sexuality is emphasized rather than criticized, while celibacy is abnormal and rare. Some have considered polygamy a pro-natalist force is Moslem societies, but there are contrary views." However, more recent data, particularly on Lebanon, seem to indicate that the religious factor is less important than the economic and social.[14] Only in the last few years has there been convincing evidence that, excluding Israel, contraception has spread beyond the middle class and is beginning to affect birthrates significantly in such countries as Egypt, Iran, Lebanon, Tunisia, and Turkey.

The Malthusian checks—war, pestilence, and famine—were very active, and their gradual reduction brought down death rates from, presumably, some 4–4.5 percent to their present level of 1.5–2 percent. The Ottoman Empire throughout its existence was involved in wars, and this was true of the 18th and first half of the 19th century.[15] But the period between the Crimean War and the eve of the First World War was relatively peaceful. Iran did not engage in any major wars after those with Russia in 1813 and 1828, nor did Egypt after Muhammad Ali's defeat in 1840, nor did North Africa, except for the European invasions and subsequent "pacification." After the devastating Mahdist revolt and the British reconquest, Sudan was at peace. Arabia continued to be the scene of tribal warfare but, except in Yemen, which the Turks attempted to subdue, this involved small numbers and caused little destruction. But perhaps even more effective than the reduction of international warfare in lowering death rates was the elimination of local fighting and the establishment of order; indeed, this may be the most important single cause of the initial population growth of most of the countries, e.g., Egypt under Muhammad Ali, Turkey after about 1840, Algeria after 1870, etc.

The plague and cholera seem to have been particularly virulent in the late 18th and early 19th centuries. For the area of Libya, Tunisia, and eastern Algeria, Valensi reports five outbreaks in the 17th century and others in 1701, 1740, 1755, 1767, and 1780. Then follows a series of severe plagues in 1784, 1794, 1800, 1818, and 1826. Cholera struck in 1827, 1836, 1849, 1856, and in the 1860s. After that pestilence was much less frequent and devastating, but Nouschi mentions outbreaks of cholera in eastern Algeria in 1865 and 1893. Morocco had plagues in 1742-44, 1747-51, 1799-1800, and 1818 (which was estimated to have killed a quarter of the population), 1834-35, 1856-58, 1860, 1868-69, 1878, and 1895; and famines in 1719-24, 1736-37, 1776-82, 1816-22, 1825-26, 1847-51, 1858, and 1878-82.[16]

Many of the epidemics had come from Egypt. Raymond mentions the following outbreaks: 1718, 1723 (with victims estimated at 200,000 to 300,000 by foreign observers), 1736, 1759, 1785, and 1791, the last two causing many deaths.[17] C. F. Volney, who visited Cairo at that time, states that in the winter of 1783/84 up to 1,500 dead were carried out of that city each day.[18] These epidemics continued throughout the 19th century, but their incidence diminished. McCarthy puts deaths during the 1835 plague at 500,000; Lane's estimate had been "not less than 80,000 in Cairo, that is a third of the population; and far more, I believe, than 200,000 in all Egypt"; and Jomard put deaths in Alexandria at 14,000 out of 52,000 inhabitants. McCarthy also lists the following cholera epidemics: 1831, with 180,000 deaths; 1850 39,000; 1855 116,000; 1865 122,000; 1883 59,000 (however, according to Lord Cromer "it is certain that the real number was far in excess of this figure"), 1896 16,000, and 1902 35,000.[19] The next cholera attack was in 1947 and was quickly contained, but the influenza epidemic of 1918 was severe.

Iraq also suffered greatly from plagues. Longrigg and Batatu mention the following major ones in Baghdad: 1689, 1719, 1799, 1802, 1822, and, most terrible, 1831: "by the 10th of April, 7,000 had died in fifteen days. On the 11th, 1,200 perished. From that day until the 27th the daily roll of dead stood at 1,500 to 3,000. Not one patient in twenty recovered." The plague was followed by a flood which swept away whole quarters because not enough people were left to man the dikes. Deaths in Hilla,

Hindiya and other areas were also extremely high. Epidemics recurred throughout the 19th century, e.g., in 1877, but their incidence was lower.[20] In Iran, the British consuls at Tabriz listed cholera outbreaks in 1835, 1846, 1847, 1853, 1856, 1857, 1860, 1861, 1866, and 1872; for other parts of the country D. Behnam listed nine in 1851–61, and there were also attacks of plagues. After that the incidence of epidemics seems to have decreased, but the cholera epidemic of 1892 killed some 10,000 persons in Gilan and was also severe in Khurasan and Tehran.[21] In Turkey, plagues were also frequent in the 18th century[22] and continued to be so in the first two-thirds of the 19th. That of 1812 was particularly devastating, carrying off an estimated 321,000 persons in the Istanbul area—the British ambassador saw "no reason to suppose that this calculation is much exaggerated." Attacks of cholera were also frequent, but the number of their victims was not great.[23]

After the First World War, modern medicine began to penetrate beyond the cities; and after the Second it spread to large sections of the countryside. This resulted in the elimination of many endemic diseases, like smallpox and malaria, and the reduction of others, such as tuberculosis. Hygienic conditions in the region still leave much to be desired, but the improvement during the last fifty or sixty years has been immense.

Mention has already been made of some of the major famines. Valensi discusses the famine of 1805 in Tunisia and states that "during the whole of the first third of the 19th century, only two years of good crops may be noted." Morocco had famines in 1798, 1815, 1825, and 1878, and Algeria in 1815, 1845–47, and 1866–70.[24] Raymond lists the following famines in Egypt: 1687, 1694–96, 1705, 1718, 1721, 1731, and then, after a period of prosperity interrupted only by the famine of 1759, a series of very bad years between 1783 and 1792.[25] However, by the 19th century famines are no longer recorded. For Iraq, Haider shows the following local or general famines: 1689, 1690, 1700, 1719, 1733, 1756, 1786, 1801, 1827, and 1831.[26]

The gradual elimination of the Malthusian checks was part of a worldwide process. The 19th century was peaceful and saw the establishment of order over the greater part of the globe, the conspicuous exception being China. The setting up of quarantine posts in major ports and the improvement of public health in many areas helped to reduce the incidence and spread of plagues. Quarantines were established in most ports of the Middle East in the first half of the 19th century, but other health measures became significant only toward its close.[27] One contemporary through probably overoptimistic testimony may be cited:

in a well-informed report on the rather sleepy and out-of-the-way province of Menteshe in 1850, the British vice-consul attributed the sparseness of the population to the plagues that had formerly ravaged Anatolia, adding that "Quarantines have exterminated this scourge." Famines were avoided thanks to the increase in agricultural production (chapter 7) and the marked improvement in transport; the latter meant that food could now be brought into areas of shortage both from other parts of the country, where crops were adequate but hitherto unavailable because of prohibitive transport costs (chapter 3), and from abroad. In the past such shipments had been small in amount and confined to areas accessible by water transport—for example, Raymond cites imports of grain from Anatolia or Syria to Egypt in times of scarcity in 1723, 1732, and 1792, and Valensi notes imports from Gibraltar to Morocco and from Naples to Tunisia in 1818.[28] To take only one dramatic example, Louis Chevalier estimated that in North Africa in 1945 one million people would have died if imports had not been available.[29]

In all likelihood, the growth in population was initially beneficial. With the exception of a few regions like Lebanon and Kabylia, the Middle East had a sparse population, and it is probable that higher density enabled it to achieve economies of scale in such matters as transport, trade, and government. At various times a labor shortage was felt, and usually evoked suggestions for mass immigration from elsewhere: Chinese to Egypt and Africans to Turkey in the 1860s, American blacks to Sudan and Indians to Iraq before the First World War, and Algerians and others to Morocco,in the 1920s; fortunately, such schemes did not materialize.[30] Today it is almost certain that, except for parts of Sudan, the region is overpopulated, in the sense that smaller numbers would mean higher per capita incomes; this is particularly true of Egypt and Algeria. In these two countries the turning point probably came just before the First World War, and in the others two or three decades later.

The Middle East shares two other adverse consequences of rapid population growth with the rest of the Third World. First, in most countries, the greater part of investment is absorbed by population increase and is not available for raising per capita income; this applies particularly to such services as education, health, and housing, where merely keeping up with growing numbers—let alone widening coverage or improving quality—presents great difficulties. Second, the prevailing age pyramid results in a high dependency ratio, i.e., the number of persons under 15 or over 65 who are supported by the population between those ages; in many countries this ratio is over 1.0, as compared to under 0.6 in advanced countries. Moreover, in spite of the sharp drop in infant and juvenile mortality, the combination of very high birthrates and moderately high death rates still means that a sizable investment is being made in children who will not live long enough to repay society by engaging in productive work for a sufficient number of years. Because of the age structure, and the very low rate of female participation in urban economic activities, the labor force is small. Almost everywhere it is little over 30 percent of the total population, compared to 40–45 in developed countries.

Like other parts of the world, the Middle East has undergone much urbanization, but its pattern has been distinctive.[31] In 1800, it was one of the most urbanized regions of the world, as it had been for the preceding two thousand years and more (see table 6.2). In Egypt, towns with 10,000 inhabitants or more accounted for nearly 10 percent of the population, in Syria for nearly 20, and in Iraq for over 15. Iran's six largest cities had some 10 percent of the population, and in Turkey about 20 percent lived in towns of over 10,000. North Africa was less urbanized: in Tunisia the ratio was about 15 percent, probably less in Morocco, and much less in Algeria. Arabia and Sudan had few large towns.[32] These ratios compare with the following ones for towns of over 5,000 in 1800: England and Wales 25 percent, the Netherlands about the same, France under 10 percent, other European countries distinctly less, and the United States under 5.

Many factors explain this high degree of urbanization in a period of economic decline. Except in Lebanon and Palestine, there was the absence of a strong rural-based feudal system: military leaders and landlords lived in the cities, increasing urban purchasing power and inducing a concentration of craftsmen and merchants; in North Africa, however, conditions were different. The insecurity of the countryside caused many farmers to flee to towns and others to live in towns and cultivate adjacent lands; this concentration was reinforced by the fact that the urban population was taxed more lightly and that, in periods of famine, the authorities made sure that its grain supplies were adequate even if the peasants starved. Finally, pilgrim and transit traffic continued to be active even when agriculture and industry declined.

The most striking trend during the 19th and early 20th centuries was the growth of "heterogenetic" seaports. In North Africa this was brought about by the immigration of Europeans, who until the 1920s constituted a majority or a large minority of the population of such cities as Algiers, Oran, Casablanca, Tunis, Tripoli, Benghazi, and also of Jaffa–Tel Aviv, Alexandria, and Port Said. In the other Mediterranean seaports,

Table 6.2
Approximate Population of Cities[a]
(thousands)

	1800	*1860*	*1914*	*1930*	*1975*
Fez	50–100	50–100	100	140	450
Casablanca	1	5	40	250	1,800
Algiers	50	50	170	250	1,200
Oran	10	20	120	160	280
Tunis	100	80		200	900
Tripoli			40	91	600
Cairo	250	300	700	1,200	6,400
Alexandria	15	200	350	600	2,400
Aleppo		100	120	230	770
Damascus		100	220	210	1,100
Beirut	6	50	150	180	1,500
Jerusalem	10	20	80	90	240
Baghdad	50–100	60	150	300	3,800
Basra	4	10	20	60	680
Aden	1	20	50	48	300
Mecca	12	(50)		80	370
Tehran	50	70	280	500	4,300
Tabriz	40	150	200	200	580
Istanbul	400	500	1,100	700	3,900
Izmir	100	150	300	150	600
Ankara	20	30	40	80	1,700

[a] In the 18th and early 19th centuries the population of towns fluctuated sharply because of epidemics and other disasters, and figures are approximate.

Sources

Morocco—Noin 1970:1:26; Miege 1961:3:13–15, 4:397–400; Le Tourneau 1949:153–59.

Algeria—Valensi 1969a:50–51; *Initiation* 1957:178–80; Masson 1911:579.

Tunisia—Valensi 1969a:50–51; Brown 1974:375–78; Ganiage 1959:130–32.

Libya—Rushdy 1953:104; *Statesman's Yearbook, 1935*.

Egypt—McCarthy 1977; Abu-Lughod 1971:115–21, 174–76.

Syria, Lebanon, Palestine—EHFC; Gibb and Bowen 1950:1:282; Ruppin 1916:187–88; Ben-Arieh 1970:passim; Fawwaz 1979; Himadeh 1935:7; Baer 1981.

Iraq—EHFC; EI2, s.v. "Baghdad"; Batatu 1978:35.

Aden—Apelt 1929; *Statesman's Yearbook, 1935*.

Mecca—Burckhardt 1829:132; Great Britain, Naval Intelligence 1946:557; *Encyclopaedia Britannica*, s.v. "Mecca."

Iran—EHI:26–32 and sources cited; Bémont 1969:66–71; Gilbar 1976.

Turkey—EHT:33–36 and sources cited.

1975 figures are from United Nations, *Pattern of Urban and Rural Population Growth* (New York, 1980), and refer to urban agglomerations.

Istanbul, Izmir, Mersin, Beirut, and Tripoli (Lebanon), there were few foreigners but minority groups formed a large fraction of the population, as they also did in the Egyptian ports. Except for Aden, no large ports developed in the Red Sea or Gulf before the First World War.

Since the Arab conquest, the region's main cities had been located in the interior: Cairo, Aleppo, Damascus, Baghdad, Mosul, Mecca, Tehran, Isfahan, Tabriz, Konya, Bursa, Qayrawan, Constantine, Fez, Marrakesh, etc; the only exceptions were Istanbul and Tunis, with their magnificent harbors and long history. In the 19th century, these cities grew slowly, partly because some of their activities were diverted to the seaports and partly because their handicrafts declined under foreign competition (chapter 8). As a result, the total town population grew only about as fast as the total population, and the urbanization ratio showed little or no increase.[33] Here, again, the region's experience diverges from that of advanced and many developing countries.

Since the 1920, however, and more particularly since the Second World War, urban growth has been explosive. At present about half the population of the region is urbanized (appendix table A.1), and in 1975 there were 11 urban areas with over a million inhabitants out of a world total of under 200. Urban population is growing at 5 to 10 percent a year, or 2 to 3 times the overall rate. It has been suggested that the Middle East is "overurbanized," i.e., urbanization has proceeded far more rapidly than industrialization.[34] It is certain that the rapid growth of cities is presenting the governments of the region with intractable economic, social, and political problems.

This growth has come about partly by natural increase within the cities but mainly by migration, propelled by powerful push and pull forces. Incomes in agriculture are far below per capita incomes, partly for the reasons prevailing elsewhere and partly because of government policies keeping farm prices low and favoring the urban population. The much more rapid growth of rural population than of cultivated area has also created a surplus labor force that migrates to the cities. The multiplication of oil revenues has greatly increased government receipts, and these are spent primarily in the cities, especially the capitals, and have helped to swell bureaucracies. Foreign aid, which has been received in such large quantities (chapter 4), has played the same role. The region's traditional transit, tourist, and pilgrimage services are still, as in the past, centered on cities—or else the revenue derived from them, e.g., from the Suez Canal and the oil pipelines through Syria, Jordan, Lebanon, and Egypt, accrues to the government. So far, industrialization has been—as in most of the Third World and in contrast to advanced countries—heavily concentrated in one or two major cities, and so has other business, partly because of the size of the urban market and the unavailability of skills and infrastructure outside the towns and partly because business prefers to be close to the government, which plays an important role (chapters 8 and 9). The social amenities have also been concentrated in major cities. Only in the last few years have education, health services, clean water, and electricity reached the villages. It is also only recently that the governments have made a deliberate, and so far only partially successful, effort to decentralize industry and other activities. As a result, not only is the region heavily urbanized, but, like preindustrial Europe, it is marked by one or two huge cities towering over the rest. The only country that seems to follow the "rank-size" rule (which states that the population of a city multiplied by its rank equals the population of the largest city) characteristic of advanced societies is Turkey.[35] All projections point to a huge growth in the main cities, and this prospect cannot but arouse serious forebodings.

Levels of Living

This is a subject about which we know little and where, in all likelihood, our knowledge will not grow greatly. Generalization about such a large area and long period is impossible, but the following observations may be made. First, starting at different times, all the peoples of the region benefited from the gradual elimination of epidemic, and more recently the reduction of endemic, diseases, and from the consequent decline in death rates and rise in life expectation from perhaps 30 years or less to some 50–60 years (see appendix table A.1). Second, even if it be assumed that per capita food consumption did not increase over the whole period—which is improbable—at least the population is no longer subjected to periodic famines.

Third, greater security has helped to improve the living conditions of the masses—though it has usually been accompanied by firmer government control and higher and less evadable taxes. Fourth, per capita incomes have certainly risen; however, since a large part of the increment was absorbed by the privileged sections of society—foreigners, minorities, wealthy Muslims, army, and bureaucrats—this does not necessarily imply that the levels of living of the masses rose correspondingly. Fifth, there is no doubt that the condition of the great majority of city dwellers—who, of course, include almost all the privileged groups—has improved, economically, socially, and culturally, and that they have come to enjoy amenities undreamt of by earlier generations. Sixth, not only the towns but the countryside has been provided, in varying degrees, with electricity and drinking water—for example, in Egypt the government claims that 94 percent of the urban population, and 56 percent of the rural, has access to clean water, and in Syria 90 and 55. Finally, the spread of education, cinemas, radio, and television should, presumably, count as an improvement in the quality of life, as should the great increase in ability to travel made possible by the spread of motorbuses and trucks to the countryside.

One more remark may be made: from the mid-1950s to the late 1970s levels of living rose significantly over the greater part of the region. This is shown by the increase in such articles of mass consumption as cereals, sugar, textiles, radios, and bicycles, as well as by the much greater rise in luxury consumption.[36] It was made possible largely by the huge increase in oil revenues and the vast amount of foreign aid. Whether the advance can be sustained remains to be seen.

A distinction is in order before we discuss individual countries. The following analysis deals with *levels* of living, i.e., actual living conditions as measured by certain indices, and not with *standards* of living, which measure aspirations and expectations at any given time. Standards always manage to keep ahead of levels, producing dissatisfaction and frustration.

More information is available on Egypt than on other countries. Under Muhammad Ali, agricultural and industrial expansion must have significantly raised per capita incomes. But military expenditure and high investment—much of it wasted—may well have absorbed most of the increment, and the only evidence that mass consumption rose during his reign is that between 1821 and 1844 production of the six basic cereals and pulses (minus exports) rose faster than population. As against that must be set the burden of conscription and forced labor. An average of 100,000 or 3 percent of the whole population—a very high level by the standards of that time—served in the armed forces, and as for forced labor, "in the course of one year as many as 400,000 men could be called." The condition of peasants was, of course, deplorable, but so had it been under the Mamluks; and the flight of thousands of men to Palestine and beyond was probably caused by fear of conscription rather than by a fall in levels of living.[37]

Under Muhammad Ali's successors, peasants benefited from the drastic reduction in conscription and, until the 1870s, in taxes. During the Crimean War boom in cereals, a well-informed observer stated that "the peasants have been receiving, during the past two years, fabulous prices for all commodities," and imports of cotton textiles increased

greatly. The expansion of cotton cultivation also benefited small
farmers, although the greater part of the crop, and the finer grades of
cotton, were produced by large landowners. The cotton boom of 1861–66
led to a great rise in rural consumption, at all levels.[38] In the late 1860s
and 70s, the peasant was squeezed by a combination of falling prices and
rising taxes, and conditions probably deteriorated. On the other hand, it
should be noted that agricultural output per head of total population
showed a continuous rise from the 1820s to around 1900.[39]

The British occupation saw a sharp increase in national income until
the turn of the century and a leveling off until 1913; in all, per capita
income rose by nearly 50 percent.[40] Again one can assume that the
greater part of the increase was absorbed by the richer groups, but there is
also clear evidence of improvement at the mass level, such as the rise in
per capita consumption of staples like coffee, tobacco, sugar, and
textiles. On the other hand, consumption of cereals and pulses showed a
slight decline. Farmers also benefited from the drop in conscription and
the abolition of corvée labor. During the First World War consumption
was cut, but it more than recovered in the 1920s. The depression caused a
marked decrease in both income and consumption;[41] this was accentuated during the Second World War, but after that there was a slow
recovery, and in the 1950s and 60s consumption of staples as well as
luxury goods rose markedly.[42]

Much less is known about Turkey. Until 1840 the country was almost
continuously at war, and conditions were hard. Indeed, British consular
dispatches from Izmir in 1838 and Bursa in 1845 state that the peasants
were selling their copper utensils, a sure sign of increasing misery; some
foreign observers attribute this to the destruction of the Janissaries,
"who had been the born guardians of the interest of the people" and
whose disappearance removed the only check on government extortion.
But already in the 1840s an increase in the consumption of coffee in Izmir
and improvement in Bursa are noted. After the Crimean War, conditions
seem to have improved, and consular reports become more cheerful.
Scattered data point to an increase in agricultural output and income,
and in view of the relatively equal distribution of land, one may assume
that a large part of the benefit accrued to small farmers. From about 1870
on the evidence is much clearer. Eldem reckons that real per capita
income rose at about 1 percent a year in 1889–1914. Real wages of both
skilled and unskilled labor also rose from about 1850 to 1914, although
some handicraftsmen must have experienced a drop in income. There
are also indications of an increase in the demand for various semiluxury
items, such as watches and bicycles.[43]

The First World War and its aftermath were catastrophic, but Turkey recovered swiftly in the 1920s. Farmers benefited from peace, the reduction of taxes, and some social services, but per capita consumption of such staples as wheat and sugar showed little change through the 1930s or the Second World War.[44] Since then, there has been a marked increase in per capita consumption of both food and manufactured goods.[45]

Data on Iran are even scantier, and the great variety of conditions prevailing in the different regions (e.g., Gilan is far above the average and Baluchistan far below) make generalization even more difficult than for other countries. A study of wages up to the First World War tentatively concluded that craftsmen must have suffered badly, and on the whole, the wages of unskilled labor failed to keep pace with rising prices.[46] Keddie states: "although the periods of anarchy and war were hard on the peasants, in periods of peace before the mid-nineteenth century the peasants were apparently better off than they are today," i.e., in 1950; Keddie attributes this to greater exploitation under the Western impact.[47] Lambton seems to imply that the tax burden increased in the course of the 19th century. As against that Ansari and Nowshirvani give data suggesting a distinct improvement in Khuzistan between 1890 and 1913.[48]

Conditions were certainly bad; perhaps the best commentary is that of a Russian in 1908: "compared to it the mournful Russian picture pales completely." This may be contrasted with Chardin's often quoted remark of 1686 that peasants "are quite well off, and I can assert that there are, in the most fertile countries of Europe, people who are incomparably more wretched." The intervening period had seen Iran's collapse at the beginning of the 18th century and a recovery under the Qajars in the first third of the 19th, and it does not seem as if one can be more specific than that.[49]

Iran suffered great hardships during the First World War. In the interwar period GNP must have increased considerably but, in view of heavy taxes, increased military expenditure, and high rates of investment, there is no reason to believe that levels of living rose. Following another period of disruption in 1941–53, Iran experienced over twenty years of rapid economic growth, accompanied by a rise in consumption at all levels. The same years also witnessed impressive social advance.[50]

On the Fertile Crescent only two statements may be made with confidence. First, conditions in Mount Lebanon and a few places in Palestine improved appreciably in the 19th century, probably after 1860; by 1914 these regions stood at an economic and social level far above that of their neighbors. Secondly, although handicraft output may have recovered after the 1870s (chapter 8), craftsmen in such cities as Aleppo, Damascus, Mosul, and Baghdad, and also in some smaller towns such as Hama and Nablus, must have suffered a sharp reduction in earnings.[51] Some scholars, such as Smilianskaya,[52] Chevallier, and Schatkowski-Schilcher,[53] hint at a more general impoverishment of Syria, adducing the drain of specie caused by an adverse balance of trade (chapter 2). But in fact we know too little about the major determinants of the level of living—production, population, income distribution, taxation, and even foreign trade—to hazard a guess. One can point out that the period 1860–1914 was peaceful and relatively orderly and that food crops increased markedly, but this too is insufficient evidence. Following the great disruption of the First World War, conditions continued to improve in Lebanon, in Palestine, and perhaps in Syria. Since the early 1940s, Lebanon and Syria have had a large increase in GNP and a marked rise in levels of living, and both have risen still more sharply in Israel.[54] Of course, the condition of the Palestinians who became refugees plummeted.

Still less is known about Iraq. Judging from exports and from the extension of the cultivated area, grain output increased considerably in 1870–1914, but given the structure of landownership (chapter 7), it is conceivable—though not very likely—that all the increment was absorbed by the landlords. After the disruption caused by the First World War, the same was true of the 1920s–40s, which also saw a large increase in agricultural output and the beginnings of the oil industry. By 1950, rising oil revenues made it possible both to expand social services greatly and to raise mass consumption, and this trend was accentuated in the next two decades.[55] The huge increase in oil revenues has also greatly raised living standards and improved social conditions in the producing countries of the Arabian Peninsula. For Sudan, all that can be said is that the inhabitants of the Gezira (chapter 7) and the population of the main towns raised their level of living.

As regards North Africa, one can be more definite about Algeria, thanks to the excellent studies by Ageron and Nouschi. The initial hardships of the conquest were followed by the steady appropriation of land by the colonists (chapter 7), and between the 1870s and the First World War per capita output of the major cereals in the Muslim sector shows a definite decline. Concurrently, livestock numbers decreased. At the same time the handicrafts—which had played a smaller part in the economy than in other parts of the region—suffered greatly from foreign competition. It is difficult to see what other factors could have offset this decline. These general conclusions are confirmed by Nouschi's detailed monograph on eastern Algeria.[56] The downward trend, accentuated both by the acceleration of population growth and by general world conditions, continued until the 1950s,[57] and was followed by the intense disruption caused by the War of Independence and the subsequent exodus of the Europeans. It was only in the late 1960s, thanks largely to oil, that levels of living began to rise.

As for Tunisia, Valensi's exhaustive study shows that, after an expansion in 1700–75, the economy deteriorated until around 1860; this is shown by such indicators as the shrinkage of cultivation, the fall in tax yields, and the rise in prices.[58] At the same time the handicrafts, which were an important element of the traditional economy, began to feel the full blast of European competition (chapter 8). The financial difficulties of the next twenty years probably had adverse repercussions on the level of living. Colonization may not have affected Tunisia as adversely as Algeria. Between 1885 and 1950–54, the area planted to cereals doubled, but a fifth had passed into European hands, implying that in the Muslim sector the amount of land per capita had declined markedly. No breakdown of output is available for the earlier years of the French occupation, but wheat production in the Muslim sectors is put as follows: 1914–18 1.3 million quintals, 1921–25 1.4 million, 1931–35 1.8 million, 1950–54 4.3 million—an increase well above population growth. Production of olive oil, of which three-quarters came from Muslim farms, kept pace with population, the number of trees increasing from 8.3 million in 1882 to 27 million in 1949.[59] There were relatively more Tunisians than Algerians employed in the urban sector. Since independence the level of living has shown some improvement, and there has been great social progress.

Much less can be said about Morocco. The years 1877–84 seem to have been particularly difficult because of poor crops and low export prices, and this was also true, to a lesser degree, of 1901–5, but no clear trends emerge.[60] After the initial disruptions of the French occupation and "pacification," agricultural and other production increased rapidly, and may have raised levels of living in the countryside, but the period between the early 1930s and independence saw a decline in per capita cereals output and livestock holdings. Consumption of sugar and tea increased. There has been little progress since independence.[61]

For Libya, on the other hand, the trend is only too clear. The Italians took half the cultivable land of Tripolitania and most of that of Cyrenaica. In addition, the "pacification" of Cyrenaica resulted not only in the loss of thousands of lives but also in the reduction of livestock to a fraction of its former numbers.[62] The Second World War also caused much hardship. Since the discovery of oil, Libya's level of living has risen very fast.

A tentative conclusion may be suggested. In most parts of the Middle East, the period until the Second World War saw either a constant or, more generally, a slightly rising level of living. In North Africa colonization seems to have produced a definite decline. In the last twenty to thirty years, the trend has been almost everywhere distinctly upward. In addition, social mobility has greatly increased, and in all the countries it is now common to find children of working class people and peasants doing well in the professions, the civil service, the army, the government-run enterprises, and other occupations. This mobility does not, of course, show in the figures on income distribution and Gini coefficients (see appendix table A.4).[63] These and other available data indicate an improvement in the 1960s and early 70s. However, there seems little doubt that in the previous 100 to 150 years income inequality widened. This applies to both sectors that experienced rapid growth, such as cotton in Egypt, and those where the impact of the world market was much more restricted, e.g., livestock among the pastoral tribes of Iraq and Arabia.[64] Moreover, it seems likely that the huge rise in oil revenues in the 1970s increased inequality in the producing countries, and inflation and other factors seem to have had a similar effect on the remainder of the region. Causes of the discrepancy, in addition to unequal distribution of property, include the coexistence of a small capital-intensive modern sector with a traditional one, especially in the oil-producing countries; the wide gap between incomes of the educated and the uneducated; the large difference between wages of the skilled and the unskilled and between those working in large and in small enterprises; the high urban-rural ratio and "Kuznets coefficient" between agricultural and nonagricultural incomes; and wide regional differences. All of these may be expected to diminish with increasing national economic and social integration.

Social Development

This subject may be, very cursorily, studied under three headings: education of the elite, instruction of the masses, and formation of new social classes. The change in the condition of women, an important topic, cannot be adequately covered here; the reader is referred to the study by Beck and Keddie (1978) and the sources given therein.

When one paints a picture of intellectual conditions in the Middle

East in the 18th century only the darkest colors are appropriate. The curriculum of the leading Islamic university, al-Azhar, shows that the great medieval thinkers and scientists—al-Biruni, Ibn al-Haytham, Ibn Sina, Ibn Rushd, and even the philosophical works of al-Ghazali—were no longer studied. Conditions outside the university were no better: when Muhammad Ali started introducing Western science he was unable to find a single Egyptian who knew a European language.[65] Except in Turkey, where some modernizing efforts had begun in the 18th century, and in Lebanon, where contact with Rome had started earlier, things were at least as bad. Even in Turkey, when in 1821 the Greek dragoman was executed it proved difficult to replace him.[66] A clear idea of the complacency of the peoples of the region and their complete ignorance of the outside world is given by the writings of two historians, the Ottoman Naima and the Egyptian al-Jabarti.[67] Some scholars have discerned the "first sign of a spontaneous cultural revival" which was a purely internal phenomenon and included all the traditional branches of study,[68] but the results were hardly impressive, and it was soon overtaken by and absorbed in the general movement caused by the introduction of Western learning.

The latter was, at first, sought for purely utilitarian reasons: the desire to modernize the armed forces and the supporting civilian sectors. Three overlapping methods were used. First, young men were sent to Europe (mainly France) for training in technology, science, and languages: in 1813–48 the total from Egypt was 339, in 1849–82 279, and in 1883–1919 289.[69] Turkey soon followed, but the numbers seem to have been smaller, and in Iran far smaller.[70] Second, technical schools were established: in Egypt medicine in 1827, pharmacy and veterinary in 1829, engineering in 1834, translation in 1836, and other military and civilian schools; in Turkey, medicine in 1827 and military sciences in 1834, in addition to the naval and military engineering schools that had been opened in 1773 and 1793:[71] Instruction was initially provided by foreigners, with local interpreters, and then increasingly by Egyptians or Turks who had either been to Europe or otherwise acquired some knowledge of the particular subject. Third, an intensive effort was made to translate European books in the various disciplines, again using students who had been abroad; here Turkey had begun earlier, around 1750.[72] These rough and ready but effective methods carried Egypt and Turkey through the first stage of modernization, the one imposed by enlightened despots. Around 1860 a new phase began, one that was both spontaneous and more broadly based. Modern secondary schools for civilians were founded, including Dar al-Funun in Tehran in 1851, Galatasaray in

Istanbul in 1868, the Sadiqi College in Tunis in 1875, and several schools in Egypt. Many foreign schools had been opened, catering mainly to minorities but also attended by Muslims, and the minorities had also opened their own schools. Young men from Egypt, Turkey, Iran, and also Lebanon and Syria were going to Europe on their own to study or travel—by 1918 some 500 Iranians were studying in Europe.[73]

Journalism made its appearance, and books were being published in increasing quantities, including many Muslim classics that had been ignored for centuries. In Turkey, two institutes of learning were founded, *Enjümen-i danish* in 1851 and *Jemiyyeti ilmiyye* in 1860, and in Egypt the *Institut d'Egypte* in 1859 and *Jam'iyyat al-ma'arif* in 1868.[74] There were interesting developments in Arabic, Persian, and Turkish literature, which cannot be discussed here. The foundation of Robert College in Istanbul in 1863, the Syrian Protestant College in 1867, and the Jesuit University in 1875 in Beirut was followed by the development of Istanbul, Cairo, and Tehran universities around 1900.

By the First World War, the more advanced countries of the Middle East had a very small but incommensurately important nucleus of engineers, physicians, agronomists, and administrators who could provide many of the essential services needed by modern society; however, a large proportion came from minorities. In addition there were a few solid thinkers who were applying themselves to the human and social sciences—the Lebanese Shibli Shumayyil, Farah Antun, and Amin Rihani, the Egyptians Ali Mubarak, Lutfi al-Sayyed, Qasim Amin, and Salama Musa, the Turks Midhat pasha, Namik Kemal, and Ziya Gök Alp, the Iranians Malkom Khan and Muhammad Jamal Zadeh, and others.[75] But most of the region had shared in this progress only slightly, and Longrigg's description of Iraq in 1900 is not overdrawn: "Of publishing, book production, or generally readable literary output there was nothing save the dull official newspaper. . . . The professional classes—lawyers, doctors, military officers—had acquired from Turkish sources a modicum of specialized knowledge reaching no standard admissible in Europe; in other branches of applied knowledge— agriculture, engineering, economics—there was nothing, or almost nothing to show." To which may be added that in Mosul, a town of well over 50,000, there was only one Muslim who knew a foreign language.[76] As for North Africa, the University of Algiers was founded in 1879, but as late as 1914 only 12 Muslim lawyers, one physician, and one pharmacist graduated, and the number from universities in France was about 15 lawyers and 8–10 physicians; in 1945 only 150 out of 5,000 students were Muslims. The other North African countries were certainly no better off.

Nor, except for Tunisia, was this compensated for by large numbers of students in France; in 1934 there were 83 Algerians, 37 Moroccans, and 317 Tunisians, compared to 560 Egyptians, 449 Iranians, and 207 Turks.[77] As regards Libya, a United Nations report has claimed that after the Second World War it had exactly two men with university degrees.

In the interwar period the Middle Eastern universities grew in number and size and greatly improved in quality, particularly in Egypt, which made good use of Italian, French, and British scholars, and Turkey, which benefited from the influx of Jewish and other refugees from Germany and Austria.

After the Second World War there was an explosive growth in higher education. Two sets of figures are illustrative: first, the number of Iranian students in the United States in 1979 was over 50,000, and of Arab students in 1981 nearly 100,000; the number of students in higher education in the Arab countries rose from 20,000 in 1945 to some 400,000 in 1971 and was expected to double again by 1980. Second, to take a matter more closely related to economic development, in 1945 there were only 5 engineering colleges in the whole Arab world, but by 1973 there were 34. In 1968, 5,500 engineers graduated in the Arab countries, or 50 for every million inhabitants; for Egypt the ratio was 125, for Israel 271, for Turkey 42, and for Iran 25. This compares with 265 per million in the United States, 20 in India, and 12 in Pakistan.[78] These figures undoubtedly give an overly favorable picture. Quality has not matched quantity, and in several of the older universities standards have fallen. Moreover, like other parts of the world, the region is suffering from a "brain drain" of many of its ablest people to both the West and the Gulf. But there is equally no doubt that, by now, it has built up a large and in many fields impressive stock of skills in science, technology, the social sciences, and the humanities. For the first time in nearly six centuries a few of its sons and daughters have begun to make a significant contribution to world science and literature; for example, in 1965 about 1,000 papers in the natural sciences were published by Arabs in journals appearing abroad[79] (although this is only 0.1 percent of all the scientific papers published that year; on a per capita basis, the Arab share was only 3 percent).

The early modernization of the Middle East was achieved largely by importing from Europe not only the entrepreneurs and technicians but most of the skilled workers required. A large proportion of the balance was met by the minorities, which made it possible to develop the region's natural resources while tapping its human resources lightly, and removed one of the main incentives for popular education.[80] In addition, its rulers, both native and foreign had no particular desire to enlighten the masses, as distinct from producing a small elite of army officers, technicians, and bureaucrats. "In a private instruction to his son Ibrahim [in 1836] Muhammad Ali strongly advised against spreading education beyond the recruits for state service"; and in fact of those who graduated in 1865–75, 63 percent were absorbed in the army and 19 in the civil service.[81] His British successors, alarmed by the growth of Indian nationalism, echoed his views; thus in his annual report for 1901 Lord Cromer noted that the aim of the government had been: "to spread as widely as possible, amongst both the male and female population, a simple form of education, consisting of an elementary knowledge of the Arabic language and of arithmetic. In the second place it has worked to form a highly educated class suitable for the requirements of government service." The Ottoman government was hardly more enlightened than the Egyptian and the Iranian far less. As for North Africa, the French too had no wish to repeat Britain's experience in India. Following the conquest of Algeria, the old religious schools—whose value was small but not entirely negligible—were dismantled, leading Tocqueville, clear-sighted and forthright as ever, to say: "we have made Muslim society much more . . . ignorant and barbarous than it had been before knowing us." A brief attempt to open schools under Napoleon III was succeeded by a most restrictive policy by the *colon*-dominated Third Republic.[82] The Italians did next to nothing for Muslim education in Libya.

A few figures illustrate this process. First as regards budgets, in 1860/61 Ottoman expenditure on civilian education was 0.2 percent of total expenditures, and in 1911/12 2.1 percent. In Egypt, in 1882–91, education and health, combined, absorbed 1.5 percent of government expenditure, and education reached a peak of 3 percent just before the First World War. In Algeria, expenditure on Muslim education was under 2 percent of the civilian budget in 1890–1914, and in Iran probably smaller still.[83] As for numbers in the Ottoman Empire there were 3,400 pupils in government primary (*rüshdiye*) schools in 1858, 7,800 in 1867, and 31,400 in 1895; at the last date there were 5,400 pupils in government secondary (*idadi*) schools. The number attending minority and foreign schools was far greater (83,000 and 19,000, respectively) and that in elementary schools—whose educational value was slight—1,189,000.[84] In Egypt in 1875 there were 1,400 pupils in government civil schools, 9,000 in foreign, and 130,000 in traditional religious schools (*kuttab*). By 1913 numbers were: 15,000, 48,000, and 231,000, in addition to 99,000 in Egyptian private schools.[85] In Algeria, 10,600 Muslims received a modern education in 1890.[86] In Tunisia, in 1904 there were 2,800 Muslims in French and Franco-Arab schools, 49,000 in 1914, and 35,000 in 1930; in Libya 9,600 Muslims attended modern schools in 1939.[87] In Iran, until the First World War, the number was very small. Only in Lebanon, and to a much lesser extent in Syria, did a sizable proportion of children of school age attend modern schools.

The result was a high illiteracy rate: 93 percent in Egypt in 1907 (and higher among Muslims), and probably more in the other countries. In Mount Lebanon perhaps half, or more, of the population was literate and in Syria possibly a quarter.[88]

Thus, when the Middle Eastern countries gained a full or partial measure of independence, and control over their educational policy, after the First World War, they had to start almost from scratch. In the early 1920s the total school population of Iran was 75,000, or about 0.6 percent of the total population, in Iraq 10,000, or about 0.3 percent, in Syria 50,000 or 2.5 percent, in Turkey 400,000 or 3 percent, and in Egypt 600,000 or 4 percent. By 1950, Iraq's school population had risen twenty-fourfold, to 240,000, Iran's almost tenfold to 740,000, Syria's sixfold to 300,000, Turkey's more than fourfold to 1,800,000 and Egypt's nearly threefold to 1,600,000. Expansion continued in the next twenty years: by 1970, Iraq's school population stood at 1,470,000, representing 16 percent of the total population, Iran's 4,150,000 or 14 percent, Syria's 1,320,000 or 21 percent, Turkey's 6,500,000 or 18 percent, and Egypt's 5,400,000, or 16 percent. In the Arabian peninsula countries, which started expanding their school systems only in the 1950s or 60s, and in the North African countries that obtained independence in the same decades, the rate of increase in the school population has been higher, and some of them have reached the level of the older countries, e.g., 15 percent in Algeria, 21 in Tunisia, 10 in Morocco, and about 10 in Saudi Arabia, but far less in the southern and eastern parts of Arabia. On the other hand, some of the small countries—Israel, Jordan, Kuwait, and Lebanon—stand well above the regional average. The same is true of adult literacy rates (see appendix table A.1). In other words, in the last few years the Middle East has reached the level of primary education which some economists regard as the most important single factor in the absorption of technology and, consequently, in economic development—the level attained by Western Europe and the United States in the first half of the 19th century, by Japan at the close of that century, and by the larger Latin American countries in the 1920s or 30s.[89]

A few words may be added about on-the-job training. Until the 1920s, the number of people who acquired mechanical skills—on the railroads, riverboats, and industrial installations—was very small, since foreign technicians were generally used. After that, the development of manufacturing and the oil industry and the mechanization of transport and agriculture immensely expanded employment, and the number of persons with industrial skills now runs into the hundreds of thousands.

Traditional Middle Eastern society consisted of the rulers—the Men of the Sword and the Men of the Pen—and the ruled: merchants, craftsmen, and peasants. The Men of the Pen staffed the bureaucracy and the religious establishment, receiving salaries or income derived from *waqfs* (endowments). The Men of the Sword were assigned lands—*iqta's* under the Caliphate, *timars* in the Ottoman Empire, *tuyuls* in Iran—part of whose income they could retain in return for service in the cavalry (chapter 7).[90] The ruled pursued their occupations and paid taxes.

The position of the Men of the Sword was the first to be undermined. Changing methods of warfare increased the importance of the artillery and infantry at the expense of the cavalry and necessitated the tapping of new sources of revenue with which to pay them; at the same time inflation was intensifying budgetary pressure. Hence there was a tendency to replace the *timar* system by *iltizam*, or tax-farming, a change that was generally detrimental to the peasants, since the supervision and restraint exercised by the central government usually diminished. More and more the tax-farms tended to become life term or even hereditary, and the tax-farmers landowners; this process was accentuated by the increasing value and profitability of land, arising from the expansion of exports to Europe.[91] Some of the beneficiaries of this change—the notables, i.e., *ayans* or *derebeys*—even achieved autonomy or independence before being resubjected to central government control in the first decades of the 19th century. Large landownership meanwhile gained strength from the expansion of production and trade and the introduction of private ownership under the various land codes (chapter 7), and landlords became, until the land reforms of the 1950s, the most powerful class in soceity.

The traditional army virtually disappeared with the massacre of the Mamluks in Egypt (1812) and Janissaries in Turkey (1826). The new, Western-type army was subordinated to civilian control and remained almost inactive until the beginning of this century. It was only in the 1950s that it became the dominant single factor in Middle Eastern politics.

The Men of the Pen suffered a drastic decline. On the one hand, many of their sources of income, such as *waqfs*, were taken over by the government. More important, with the modernization of education and administration and the introduction of Western law, their traditional skills lost their value. However, conditions vary between countries, and it would be premature to proclaim the demise of the *ulama*. In Shi'i countries, notably Iran and Iraq, their hold on the population and government is strong, and the same seems true of Wahhabi Saudi Arabia. Moreover, in several countries, notably in North Africa, a new breed of influential Western-educated *ulama* has emerged. The position of the old Men of the Pen was taken by a new intelligentsia—often consisting of their own sons—trained in modern schools, acquainted with a European language, usually French, and earning its livelihood in the bureaucracy, law, and, later, journalism. And whereas the old pen-wielders had been deeply committed to Islamic values and therefore conservative, the new ones, like their Western models, were radical or revolutionary even when they did retain their attachment to Islam. Their power has increased immensely in the last decades.

The merchants suffered from the shifts in the direction and composition of trade (chapter 2) and the craftsmen from the decline of the handicrafts (chapter 8), and their guilds dissolved. However, in both groups many individuals, or their sons, entered new occupations and did well. The position of peasants changed significantly. With increasing production for the market, the introduction of private property, the rise in indebtedness, and population growth, the relatively undifferentiated village, held together by kinship and other traditional bonds, saw the emergence of a small, relatively prosperous class of medium farmers; the growth of a huge number of small and poor peasant proprietors; and a landless peasantry, earning its living by wage labor or by renting land.

Until recently, there was practically no Muslim entrepreneurial bourgeoisie. The functions performed by such a class in trade, finance, industry, and to a large extent even the professions were taken over by foreigners or members of minority groups (chapter 5). The 1920s saw the beginnings of a Muslim bourgeoisie, which grew rapidly in the next three decades before being overwhelmed by the nationalizations and upheavals of the 1960s and 70s (chapter 9).[92] Owing to tardy and limited industrial development, a working class began to take shape only at the turn of the century, and did not attain a significant size until the 1940s. The first unions were formed, and the first strikes launched, by foreign or minority workers, and it was only in the 1920s that the labor movement passed into Muslim hands.[93] The power of the working class is still small, and it remains very much under the control of the government.

Finally, there is the bureaucracy, which from ancient times has enjoyed great influence in many countries. In the 19th century it gradually became modernized by drawing on the graduates of the new schools and foreign universities. In the last few decades, with the huge expansion in the revenues and functions of the state, the elimination of the foreign and minority bourgeoisies, and the subordination of the indigenous entrepreneurial class, its size and power have immensely increased. Today it forms the new middle class of the region.

CHAPTER VII

Agricultural Expansion

In many respects agriculture is still the largest economic sector in the Middle East, and until quite recently it was overwhelmingly so. Up to the First World War, and even later, some four-fifths of the population lived on the land, the vast majority of crafts and industries processed agricultural raw materials, agricultural produce formed the bulk of export, and agriculture and livestock raising probably accounted for at least two-thirds of GNP. Although these proportions have sharply decreased (see appendix tables A.2 and A.3), and although oil now dwarfs agricultural produce in foreign trade, this still holds true. It is also true that agriculture has changed far less than other sectors. Nevertheless, there have been some significant shifts in crop patterns, innovations in agricultural techniques, an extension of the cultivated area and expansion of output, and a fundamental transformation of land tenure.

Crop Patterns

Because of the abundance of land and the scarcity and precariousness of rain, practically all the cultivated area in the region, since time immemorial, has been planted to cereals. Wheat occupied the greater part, while barley was used in marginal areas with less rainfall. Farming methods have always been extensive, with one-half to nearly two-thirds of the land being left fallow each year, to recover moisture. This is still largely true: in the mid-1960s, cereals occupied 80 to 90 percent of the cropped area in Morocco, Algeria, Tunisia, Libya, Syria, North Yemen, Turkey, Iraq, and Iran, and even in Israel, Egypt, and Lebanon their share was close to half. Similarly, only in Egypt, Israel, Lebanon, and Turkey was substantially less than half the land left fallow.[1] If figures were available for 1800 they would show at least as high percentages on both counts. Except in Egypt, yields were very low, probably on the order of 500 kilograms of wheat per hectare (about 7 bushels per acre), compared to about 1,000 in France and Germany. Capital inputs into land, and perhaps labor inputs, were much lower than in Europe.[2] Most of the output was consumed locally, though a significant proportion was sent to the towns in payment of taxes or rent, and in good years a certain amount was exported.

But there were, in addition, some valuable crops grown primarily for the market, under irrigation or in the more humid coastal zones. Of these the most important were fibers: silk in the Caspian provinces of Iran and the Bursa region of Turkey and Lebanon; cotton in the Izmir region of Turkey, various parts of Syria, and elsewhere; and flax in Egypt. Tree crops were also important: olives in Tunisia, Syria, and Turkey, dates in Arabia, Iraq, southern Iran, and North Africa, figs in the mountainous areas, apricots, plums, pistachios, and other fruits and nuts in small spots all over the region (e.g., the Damascus Ghouta, Azerbaijan and elsewhere in Iran, various parts of Turkey, etc.), coffee in Yemen, and dyestuffs in Turkey. Vineyards, which in classical times had been widespread, had largely disappeared—presumably because of Islamic prohibitions on wine—but already in the 18th century Turkey was exporting raisins to England and elsewhere. Rice was grown in the wetlands of the northern Delta in Egypt, along the lower Tigris and Euphrates, and in Iran's Caspian provinces. Maize, introduced from the New World, had established itself in Egypt and elsewhere, and tobacco was grown in many areas, notably the Latakia district in Syria, the Black Sea coast from Sinop to Trabzon, and the Kurdish areas of Iran. Livestock breeding was widespread and in many parts of the region was more important than crop cultivation. Even today it typically accounts for about one-third of gross agricultural production. Such products as live animals (horses, camels, sheep, and goats), wool, and hides formed the leading export items in Arabia, Iraq, and Libya and significant ones in the other North African countries. Except in Egypt, there was no "mixed farming" (i.e., animals were not fed with fodder crops grown by farmers, as in Europe and North America), a condition that still prevails. Most of the flocks were tended by nomads, and the others by shepherds who took their sheep and goats to graze outside the cultivated areas of the village.[3]

In the 19th century some valuable cash crops were developed for export. Most of them established themselves when disaster struck the major producers in the industrial core: the American Civil War for cotton, the pebrine and muscardine diseases for silk, and phylloxera for vines. The most important single change was the expansion of cotton cultivation, first in Egypt, then in Turkey and Iran, and more recently in Sudan, Syria, and Israel. Attempts to grow cotton on a large scale in the other countries have been unsuccessful. An inferior kind of cotton had been grown for many centuries in Egypt, but the discovery of a new variety by a French engineer employed in Muhammad Ali's textile factories started a new era. By 1823, with strong encouragement from the pasha, output had risen to around 13,000 metric tons, and small quantities were exported to Europe. They were well received by spinners, and Muhammad Ali was quick to see that cotton formed an ideal crop for his monopolies (chapter 2) because of its high value and profitability—two or three times as high as wheat[4]—the fact that it could not be eaten by the peasants, and the ease with which it could be fitted into the prevailing systems of cultivation and rotation. Quality was improved through crosses with American Sea Island cotton, but production showed little change until Muhammad Ali's death. However, by the mid-1820s cotton not only supplied the raw material needed by the textile factories (chapter 8) but had become the leading export and the main source of government revenue.[5] It survived the abolition of the monopolies in 1841 (chapter 2), and by the end of the 1850s exports had risen to some 500,000 *qantars* (23,000 metric tons). The outbreak of the American Civil War and the ensuing "cotton famine" sent prices up sharply (chapter 2). The response was immediate: by 1864, about 1 million *faddans* (420,000 hectares) were planted to cotton in the Delta, and a further small area in Upper Egypt: in 1865 exports amounted to 2.5 million *qantars*, worth over £15.5 million, or more than 90 percent of the country's total exports. The collapse of prices after the Civil War caused a sharp contraction in acreage, and output and exports fell by about half, but the upward trend was soon resumed; by 1875 the previous peaks had been surpassed. On the eve of the First World War cotton occupied 1.7 million *faddans*, or some 23 percent of the *cropped* area, and accounted for about half of agricultural production. Output equaled 7.5 million *qantars* (340,000 tons), and exports amounted to 7 million; together with cottonseed, cotton constituted well over 90 percent of total exports.[6] After the First World War output showed little growth, and cotton exports began to decline because of increased domestic consumption, but still accounted for 80 percent of exports as late as the 1950s.

In contrast to Egypt, in some countries, notably Turkey and Syria, cotton production decreased during most of the 19th century. This was partly because of the decline in handicrafts (chapter 8) and the consequent loss of the domestic market and partly because of the competition of American, Indian, and Egyptian cotton in world markets. The rise in prices during the American Civil War and the desperate attempts of the British Cotton Supply Association to develop alternative sources led to a flurry in production in Turkey, Iran, Syria, Morocco, and Algeria, but this soon ended with the fall of prices. However, the opening of the Russian market for Persian cotton, thanks to steamships on the Caspian and Russian railways, resulted in a sharp increase in Iran's output and exports, beginning in the late 1850s; around 1852 Sea Island cotton had been introduced in the Urumiya region by American missionaries. By 1913, the area planted to cotton was put at 110,000 hectares, output at 33,000 metric tons, and exports, almost all to Russia, at 25,000 tons. Thus cotton occupied little over 5 percent of Iran's cropped land but contributed a much larger fraction of agricultural output and accounted for one-fifth of total exports.[7]

In Turkey, the Izmir and Salonica regions—as well as Adana, Morea, and Cyprus—were until the end of the 18th century important sources of cotton for Europe; in 1780 they produced some 12,000 and 9,000 metric tons, respectively. By 1860, total Ottoman production had fallen to around 2,000 tons, being unable to compete in world markets because of its poor quality. The American Civil War greatly stimulated production, but after that the decline was resumed in response to falling prices. At the turn of the century, however, prices recovered and output increased rapidly. By 1912 the Izmir region was producing 10,000 tons on some 100,000 hectares and the newly developed Adana region over 20,000 tons on some 200,000 hectares, and cotton exports had become significant. In addition to higher prices, cotton cultivation in Adana was stimulated by improved transport and by the efforts of the Deutsche Levantinische Baumwolle Gesellschaft, founded by the Baghdad Railway Company in 1904. Rapid expansion resumed in the 1950s, because of higher income per acre—about three times that from cereals—and the introduction of improved strains.[8]

In Syria, also an important supplier until the end of the 18th century, the course of events was similar but recovery came much later, increases in the 1900s, 20s, and 30s proving short-lived. The Korean raw materials boom, however, started a more durable expansion, and in the 1950s cotton became Syria's leading crop.[9] There was a similar decline in Palestine, but in Israel cotton expanded in the 1960s.

Immediately after the reconquest of the Sudan, its British rulers set about developing long-staple cotton to provide an export product and a source of government revenue. Careful experiments at Zaydab, Tayiba and Barakat, using pump irrigation, demonstrated the suitability of the crop, and in 1925, with the completion of the Sennar Dam, the Gezira scheme, based on cotton, was lanched (see below). Cotton immediately became the Sudan's main cash and export crop and an important source of government revenue. Having survived the successive stresses of disease, the depression, and the Second World War, it expanded still further. In 1956 cotton occupied over 200,000 hectares, output reached 130,000 metric tons, and cotton accounted for about one-tenth of acreage and over half of production outside the subsistence sector.[10]

Table 7.1 presents recent figures on area and production; the Middle East now accounts for some 12 percent of world cotton output, but in the extra long staples its share is about 65 percent.

In contrast to cotton, the main forces influencing the output of silk after the First World War were connected with supply, not demand. Middle Eastern silk was, of course, affected by competition from China and Japan, accentuated by the opening of the Suez Canal and reduction

Table 7.1
Area and Production of Cotton, Tobacco, Sugar, and Oranges
(Average 1976–78, thousands of hectares and metric tons)

| | Cotton lint | | Tobacco | | Sugarcane and beet | | Oranges |
	Area	Output	Area	Output	Area	Output (raw sugar)	Output
Algeria	—	—	1	2	3	8	327
Libya	—	—	1	1	—	—	32
Morocco	18	8	5	6	63	307	606
Tunisia	—	—	7	5	4	10	99
Egypt	543	413	—	—	108	657	709
Sudan	415	166	—	—	17	168	43
Iran	298	162	17	19	183	650	68
Iraq	22	10	14	9	6	36	46
Israel	55	65	1	1	6	30	929
Jordan	1	1	3	1	—	—	6
Lebanon	—	—	5	6	3	13	188
Syria	182	150	16	13	11	30	16
Turkey	670	522	283	281	258	1,187	628
North Yemen	9	3	5	5	—	—	—
South Yemen	12	4	1	2	—	—	—
Total for region	2,225	1,504	359	351	662	3,096	3,697
World	32,040	12,937	4,426	5,656	22,452	89,422	34,137
Region as percent of world	7.0	11.6	8.0	6.2	2.9	3.5	10.8

Source: Food and Agricultural Organization of the United Nations, FAO Production Yearbook 1978.

in freights, but the increase in world consumption assured a market, at reasonable prices, for all its output. In the main producing centers, the Caspian provinces of Iran, Macedonia and Bursa, and Mount Lebanon, output increased until around 1860. Iran's production, which had fallen drastically in the 18th century, rose steadily and rapidly in the first half of the 19th. For the 1840s most estimates put the Gilan crop, which accounted for about five-sixths of total output, at some 400 metric tons of raw silk, and for 1864 at 1,000 tons. An important factor was the activity of Greek and Armenian firms that advanced funds to growers. In 1864, the muscardine disease, which had been ravaging European silk, reached Iran, and by 1873 production had dropped to 100 tons. The introduction of Japanese and Turkish eggs immune to the disease permitted a recovery starting in the mid-70s, but as of 1910 the 1864 peak does not seem to have been regained. Nevertheless, silk remained by far the most valuable cash crop. There was some expansion in the interwar period, but after the Second World War silk dropped to insignificance.[11]

The important Ottoman silk industry had been largely dependent on Persian silk, and the Turkish-Persian wars of the 16–17th centuries and the collapse of Iranian production in the 18th century stimulated expansion in Macedonia, Morea, Lebanon, and especially in the Bursa region; by the end of the 18th century both production and exports were large. After 1815 rising world demand led to a further increase. The introduction of improved reeling machinery, which by the 1860s was almost wholly steam-driven, raised quality considerably. In the 1840s the Bursa district was producing 100–200 tons of raw silk, and the inclusion of adjacent districts raised the total to 300–400. By the 1850s Bursa district was producing 300–400 tons. But the pébrine disease struck the Ottoman European provinces in the 1850s and Bursa in 1860, reducing the latter's production to around 100 tons by 1880 and leading many growers to cut down their mulberry trees and shift to other crops. Here again relief was afforded by the use of Japanese and other eggs, and the government and the Public Debt Administration (to whom the silk tithes had been ceded in 1881–88—see chapter 4) made great efforts to revive silk growing. Some 60 million mulberry trees were planted on 50,000 hectares, and output surpassed its previous peak; that of fresh cocoons in the whole empire, including Lebanon, rose from 7,000 tons in 1888 to 20,000 in 1910–12, and exports of raw silk from 300 to 1,400 tons. But during the First World War and the Greco-Turkish War, silk production was greatly disrupted and never recovered.[12]

Lebanon shifted to a cash crop, and dependence on grain from other areas, far earlier than any other part of the region. The adequacy of rainfall and the relative security and abundance of labor in the Mountain had resulted in the development of silk cultivation by the 18th century. By the 1840s production of raw silk averaged 300 metric tons, and it accounted for over half the gross value of the main crops.[13] Disease took its toll in Lebanon too, in the 1850s, but here also, helped by favorable prices, output recovered, from an annual average of 1,756 tons of cocoons (equal to about 170 tons of raw silk) in the 1860s to 1,978 in the 70s, 3,310 in the 80s, and 4,855 in the 90s, and 5,360 in 1900–13. By the beginning of this century 60 percent of the cultivated area of Mount Lebanon, as well as parts of the coastal plain, was planted to mulberries, and silk accounted for two-thirds of agricultural output. The rearing of silkworms and reeling of silk were financed at first by French but increasingly by Lebanese merchants and bankers. During the famine of the First World War, however, most mulberry trees were cut down, and thereafter silk became a minor item, being replaced by fruits and vegetables.[13]

Another set of cash crops that developed was stimulants: tobacco, opium, wine in North Africa, and tea in Iran and Turkey. High-quality coffee continued to be grown in Yemen, as it had been for a thousand years, but the amount was small and in recent years has declined sharply, being replaced by another stimulant, qat.[14]

Both the smoking and the planting of tobacco came to the Ottoman Empire at the beginning of the 17th century. As in other countries, smoking was prohibited, and "many thousands of men were sent to the abode of nothingness"; capital punishment, however, failed to stop smoking and was replaced with taxation. By the end of the 17th century cultivation had established itself in Macedonia, Syria, and the Black Sea region, which exported small quantities. Expansion continued, and by 1850 the Ottoman Empire had become a large exporter. The American Civil War greatly increased demand for Turkish tobacco, mechanization of cigarette making stimulated consumption, and Greek and Jewish emigrants helped to familiarize American and European consumers with Turkish tobacco, which was increasingly used for blending. Cultivation spread to the Izmir region which, after 1900, was dominated by the American Tobacco Company; by 1912 the latter was spending $10 million a year in buying and preparing tobacco. A setback occurred when, in 1883 as part of the settlement of the financial crisis (chapter 4), a tobacco monopoly was conceded to a European consortium, the Régie des Tabacs. In addition to much smuggling, this led at first to a fall in output, but expansion was soon resumed and production rose from an estimated 10,000–13,000 tons in the 1870s to 31,000 in 1900 and 64,000 in 1911. Tobacco became Turkey's leading export. Cultivation was greatly disrupted during the First World War and Greco-Turkish War by the emigration of Greek growers from the Black Sea region, but after that it spread in the Bursa and Izmit regions, to replace destroyed mulberry trees. Table 7.1 shows present area and output; today tobacco is Turkey's second leading export, after cotton.[15]

The course of events was similar in Syria, where Latakia tobacco was exported for blending. Here too the establishment of the Régie led to a decline, which, however, was not reversed; on the eve of the First World War output was only 1,500 tons. After the war output expanded again.[16]

Iran took up both smoking and tobacco planting at the same time as Turkey, and "by 1622 the Persians had already invented the art of smoking through water." Cultivation spread in many parts of the country and, output increased to perhaps 20,000 tons by the end of the 19th century, but exports remained small. The attempt, in 1890, to set up a Tobacco Monopoly similar to the Ottoman Régie provoked a major political crisis and was not renewed.[17]

It may be added that in Egypt, where a good deal of tobacco had been grown, cultivation was forbidden in 1890, partly to stamp out hashish, which was grown in tobacco fields, and partly to increase government revenue. The excellent Egyptian cigarettes were made with Turkish and other tobacco.[18]

In the Middle East opium has been grown and used, for medicinal and other purposes, since ancient times, but its cultivation greatly expanded in the 19th century in response to rapidly rising world demand. Europeans and Americans bought increasing quantities, partly for use in their own countries but mainly for reexport to China. By 1824 Iranians were also shipping directly to China. Opium was a profitable crop—about three times as much as wheat—and both output and exports multiplied severalfold. In Turkey the main growing areas were Bursa and Konya provinces and Macedonia, and in Iran Yazd, Isfahan, and other regions. Attempts have been made in Iran and Turkey, at various times, to prohibit opium cultivation, but with little success.[19]

During the present century, tea plantations were established in the Caspian provinces of Iran and in the eastern Black Sea region of Turkey. Both countries meet a substantial proportion of their consumption needs.

Sugar cane has been grown on a large scale in Egypt since the introduction of perennial irrigation, and is now also raised in Sudan and southern Iran. Beets have been planted in most countries, beginning in the 1920s, and now supply sugar for the bulk of the region's consumption (see table 7.1).

Vineyards are found in Iran, Lebanon, Syria, and more recently Egypt.

In Turkey vineyards have been much more extensive, especially near Bursa; in the course of the 19th century area and output expanded severalfold, especially in the period between the 1860s, when European vineyards were attacked by phylloxera, and the 1880s, when the disease reached Turkey. Raisins, along with figs and other dried fruits, have been and remain among Turkey's leading exports.[20]

But it is in North Africa, more specifically Algeria, that wine making reached substantial proportions. In the first decades of the French occupation various unsuccessful attempts were made to raise colonial crops in Algeria (chapter 2). Little attention was paid to vines, which by 1878 occupied an area of only 18,000 hectares (compared with 2,000 in 1854). Nearly 90 percent of this area belonged to Europeans, almost all of them small farmers; production of wine was 338,000 hectoliters. Vineyards demanded large investments, and costs of production per hectare were twice those of wheat, but net income was more than 6 times higher than from wheat and still further above income from cotton and tobacco.[21] The ravages caused by the phylloxera in French vineyards stimulated expansion in Algeria, and abundant credit was furnished to vine growers. By 1888 the area of vineyards had expanded to 103,000 hectares (almost wholly European) and output averaged 2.5 million hectoliters. Systematic and largely successful attempts were made to improve both vine growing and wine making. These attempts were aided by the immigration of French and Spanish peasants with experience in viticulture, but the bulk of the labor was supplied by Algerians.[22] The 1890s, however, were a difficult period. Phylloxera spread to Algeria and was overcome only with the diffusion of American vines, after 1900. The price of wine fell sharply with the recovery of French production. And the burden of debt on vine growers had become very heavy: in 1878–1912 the cost of a hectare of vines (including land purchase, preparation of the soil, cultivation for three years, and wine installations) varied between 2,000 and over 4,000 francs (£80–160), and the total debt of wine growers may have been around 150 million francs.[23] Algerian wine was saved by protection in the French market, and expansion resumed to 177,000 hectares and 10 million hectoliters in 1914. But in the process the number of European growers fell from 17,000 in the 1890s to 11,000 in 1914, and the average size of their farms went up from 2.5 hectares in 1879 to 14.2 in 1914. By then vineyards represented over 40 percent of the capital of Europeans in Algerian agriculture, a figure larger than that for cereals.[24]

In the interwar period expansion resumed to over 200,000 hectares and 8 million hectoliters in 1930 and an average of 400,000 and 17.5 million in the late 1930s. There was some disruption in the Second World War, and by the early 1950s the area had shrunk to 370,000 hectares, but this was offset by a rise in yields. By then viticulture accounted for one-third of agricultural income.[25] During the Algerian War of Independence many vineyards were destroyed, and more recently many more were planted to other crops. In 1977, the area of vineyards was only 206,000 hectares and production about 4 million hectoliters.

In the other North African countries viticulture made much less progress. In Tunisia, by 1914 European vineyards covered an area of 18,000 hectares and produced 400,000 hectoliters. After the First World War expansion was rapid but was halted in the 1930s by the fall in prices and the difficulty of selling in the French market, where Tunisian wine enjoyed only partial protection. From a peak of 50,000 hectares, producing nearly 2 million hectoliters, in 1935, the area was reduced to 43,000 in 1938 and, by wartime disruption and postwar phylloxera, to 27,000 hectares, producing 500,000 hectoliters, in the late 1940s.[26] In 1977, Tunisia's vineyards had an area of 40,000 hectares and produced about 1 million hectoliters. For Morocco the figures were 75,000 and a little under 1 million, respectively.

Olives and olive oil have supplied the bulk of the fat consumed in Mediterranean countries for thousands of years, but such oilseeds as sesame and peanuts have also been important in the Middle East. In the 19th century olive growing spread in Turkey,[27] Syria, and especially Tunisia. Cottonseed oil production expanded with the development of cotton. These developments took place in spite of increasing competition from the tropical regions of Asia and, subsequently, Africa. The Tunisian olive groves developed after the French occupation, the number of trees increasing from some 8 million in 1881 to 17.5 million in 1938 and 23 million in 1948. Over two-thirds of the trees are in the dryer central and southern regions. In normal years, Tunisia is a major exporter of olive oil.

Oranges and other citrus plants came to Europe from the Middle East, into which they had been introduced during the early Middle Ages.[28] In the 19th century, Arab farmers in Palestine evolved a new variety, the "Jaffa" orange, which was taken up by Jewish immigrants. By the 1850s exports to Europe are mentioned in British consular reports. In 1881, 171,000 boxes were exported, for a value of £50,000; in 1909 the figures were 774,000 and £200,000 and in 1913 1,609,000 and £300,000.[29] In the interwar period orange groves, half of which were owned by Arabs and half by Jews, spread rapidly; in 1939 their area was 30,000 hectares and their output some 15 million crates, and oranges had become by far the leading Palestinian crop and article of export. Recent figures on output of oranges in Israel and other countries are shown in table 7.1.

Other fruits that are widely grown and exported from the region include dates, figs, and apples. Vegetables, of which a wide variety are grown, have always formed an important item in Middle Eastern and North African diets. Recently their output has greatly increased, both to meet growing urban consumption and for export to the markets of Europe and the Gulf; in some countries the low prices fixed by the government for cereals and other crops have also caused farmers to shift to vegetables. As table 7.2 shows, in several countries fruits and vegetables form the leading, or second, item in agricultural production.

It should be mentioned that in the first half of the 19th century the Middle East, particularly Turkey, was an important supplier of such dyestuffs as madder, gall nuts, and yellow berries. The development of synthetic dyes, however, eliminated trade in these articles, and their output contracted sharply.[30]

By now, the bulk of agricultural production is marketed. The main exception is in cereals, of which a large part—for some crops and places over half—is consumed on the farm. Thus in Morocco in the early 1960s, whereas most of the wheat was marketed, some three-quarters of the

Table 7.2
Gross Value of Crop Production[a]
(percent)

	Cereals[b]	Cotton	Other industrial[c]	Fruits and vegetables
Egypt	37	(43)	(2)	18
Iraq	(50)	—	. .	47[d]
Israel	6	8	. .	79
Jordan	40	—	. .	59
Lebanon	7	—	. .	67
Syria	32	(40)	. .	18
Turkey, 1968	34	7	10	28
North Yemen	(60–70)	. .	. .	(20–30)[e]
Algeria, 1967–69	47	1	8	32[f]
Tunisia, 1966	36	—	2	62[g]

[a] Circa 1965, unless otherwise specified.
[b] Including wheat, barley, millet, maize, rice, and minor crops.
[c] Mainly tobacco and sugar beets or cane.
[d] Including dates.
[e] Including cotton.
[f] Of which wine 21 percentage points.
[g] Including olives and olive oil.
Sources: Clawson et al. 1971:81 and appendices; Issawi 1963:139; World Bank 1979a; unpublished data in reports of World Bank.

much larger barley crop was consumed by the farmers.[31] In Turkey in the 1950s only some 60 percent of the wheat grown by small farmers—those averaging 10 hectares—reached the market,[32] and in Iran, Iraq, and parts of Syria and North Africa the proportion was probably smaller. In Sudan the subsistence sector occupies some two-thirds of the farm population and accounts for about half of agricultural output. In Algeria in the interwar period, some 500,000 families, or about two-thirds of the rural population, did not market any of their produce.[33] But the shift away from cereals, the improvement of transport, the large growth of the urban market, and, in a few countries, the small increase in output per farmer, have resulted in a much greater monetization of agriculture in the region.

Techniques

The shift to cash crops did not necessitate any great changes in technique. For the most part, these crops could be fitted into prevailing agricultural patterns and be grown with traditional methods and tools. The major exception was cotton in Egypt and Sudan, which required major irrigation works. Since cotton is a summer crop, it could not be raised under the "flood" or "basin" system of irrigation, which had prevailed since time immemorial and in which the whole cultivated land was submerged during the summer flood. Egypt, therefore, had to shift to perennial irrigation, which required dikes to keep the river off the land in summer, canals to bring the water to the fields and drains to carry it away, barrages to raise the level of the river so as to fill the canals when the river was low, and, eventually, storage dams to provide additional water in winter. The advantage of perennial irrigation was that it made possible not only the growing of such valuable summer crops as cotton and sugarcane but also the raising of more than one crop a year on the same patch of land. Its drawbacks were that it deprived the land of the annual deposit of silt left by the flood and also facilitated the spread of *bilharzia*, a debilitating disease from which Egypt had always suffered but which now greatly increased. It also required huge amounts of labor, to build the works, keep up the dikes, and clean the canals and drains. Under Muhammad Ali and his immediate successors this was supplied by *corvée* labor, which was eventually abolished during the British occupation. By 1833 some 400 kilometers of canals had been dug. Ismail (1863–79) added another 13,500 kilometers, spending some £12.6 million on irrigation. Under British rule (1882–1922) many dams and barrages were built, including the Aswan dam in 1902, at that time the largest in the world; expenditure on irrigation was well over £20 million. After independence Egypt continued to expand and improve its irrigation system and in 1966, with Soviet help, inaugurated the High Dam at Aswan, at a cost of over $1 billion. These successive measures resulted in a considerable expansion of the cultivated area and the conversion of the whole country to perennial irrigation (see below) but have also caused serious problems such as waterlogging, erosion, and loss of soil fertility.[34]

Until the First World War, no other country underwent a remotely similar change. In Iraq, because of political instability, irrigation seems actually to have deteriorated until the opening of the Hindiya dam in 1913, at a cost of £600,000; the outbreak of war prevented the implementation of further schemes.[35] In Algeria, in the second half of the 19th century, seven small dams were built at a cost of 6.3 million francs. In Turkey the Konya dam, irrigating some 50,000 hectares at an estimated cost of £1 million, was also opened in 1913. Otherwise, nothing noteworthy was achieved in the field of irrigation.[36]

In the interwar period several large works were built in Sudan, Iraq, and Algeria, and after the Second World War almost every country built one or more major dams.[37] There has also been much pump irrigation, in Iraq, Sudan, Syria, and elsewhere. The present extent of irrigation is shown in appendix table A.6. In the Middle East irrigation usually makes land 3–8 times as productive—for example, in Syrian cotton the ratio is 4.5:1[38]—since not only is yield much higher and double cropping possible but many crops can be grown only under irrigation. Incremental costs vary widely: thus in 1967 they stood at $70 per hectare in the Gezira scheme in Sudan but in Egypt in 1960–71 at about $1,500 and in 1977 at $1,700–2,500 near the Nile and $3,700 in the New Valley, other countries falling within this range.[39]

But by far the greater part of the region is still rain fed, and agricultural output continues to show wild fluctuations in response to changes in precipitation. Thus in Syria the index of production of cereals (1956 = 100) was 42 in 1955, 132 in 1957, 53 in 1958, 57 in 1959, and 48 in 1960. In Jordan the oscillations of wheat production are even sharper (1961–62 = 100): 50 in 1963, 225 in both 1964 and 1965, and 72 in 1966; for 1961–74 the correlation between production and rainfall was 0.944 and between yield and rainfall 0.928, both being significant at the 0.999 level.[40] For barley the fluctuations are still greater, since it is grown on marginal land enjoying less rainfall than wheat.

Apart from irrigation, the most important technical change has been greater use of fertilizers, especially nitrogen fertilizers. Here too Egypt pioneered, starting on a small scale shortly before the First World War to combat falling cotton yields and greatly expanding in the interwar period. As appendix table A.7 shows, until the 1960s only Israel and Lebanon had followed Egypt's lead, but since then there has been a large expansion in Turkey, and to a lesser extent in Iran, Syria, and elsewhere. Whereas in 1950/51 the Near East (as defined by the FAO and excluding former French North Africa, which used insignificant amounts), used 86,000 tons of fertilizer (net content) and in 1960/61 343,000 tons, by 1975/76 the figure had risen to 2,015,000 or 2.3 percent of world consumption.[41] Use of fertilizers per hectare of agricultural land, at 25 kilograms, was equal to that of other developing countries but less than half the world average. A favorable factor has been the great increase in output of chemical fertilizers, usually from a gas base, in most countries.

The use of fertilizers in the region is quite advantageous. Calculations by the FAO in the mid-1960s show that the value-cost ratio in Turkey was: for cotton 2.9 : 1, for wheat 3.2, for maize 3.5, and for potatoes 5.5; in Syria it was 2.0 for wheat and 3.6 for cotton. In the mid-70s the figures for Turkey were: cotton 11, rice 10, beets 4, and cereals 3.[42] In the 1970s the price of fertilizers rose sharply, because of the increase in oil prices, and use was temporarily reduced, but the upward trend has been resumed in most countries.

Tools used in agriculture have hardly changed. As an example, in 1950 in Turkey, the most advanced country in this respect, only 24 percent of farms had iron plows, the rest using the traditional wooden plows with iron tips.[43] Mechanization was introduced to Turkey under the Marshall Plan and then spread to other countries, the total in the Near East (as defined above) rising from 97,000 tractors in 1950/51 to 362,000 in 1975/76, again giving a figure per hectare of a little under half the world average.

Egypt also pioneered the use of improved seeds, care being taken from the beginnings of cotton cultivation to select seeds and evolve superior strains; eventually this necessitated strict government control and much research. Serious attention was given to wheat only after the Second World War, and as late as 1972/73 only in Egypt, Israel, and Lebanon was over 30 percent of the planted area given to high-yielding varieties, compared to over 50 percent in India and Pakistan.[44]

Area and Production

Except for Egypt, Algeria, and Tunisia, figures on area, yields, and output are scanty and unreliable until after the First World War. Nevertheless, two statements may be made with confidence regarding the period 1800–1914. First, in view of the growth of total internal food consumption (and in some countries and periods even of per capita consumption) and exports of agricultural produce, overall output must at least have kept pace with population. Second, except for that part of the growth which was due to the shift to more valuable crops and increasing irrigation, the expansion in production outside Egypt was almost wholly due to extension of the cultivated area, and not to greater output per acre. One more point should be observed: this expansion was greatly stimulated by the growth of foreign demand and the more favorable prices received by the farmer for his produce. The latter, in turn, may be traced to two factors: the abolition of monopolies by the 1838 Anglo-Turkish Treaty (chapter 2), which by stimulating competition raised farm prices,[45] and the improvement in both sea and internal transport, which lowered delivery costs to domestic and foreign markets (chapter 3). Of course, the establishment of greater security was everywhere favorable to, and in many areas an indispensable condition for, agricultural expansion.

For Egypt, data are far more abundant than for any other country and have been skillfully analyzed by O'Brien, whose results are summarized in table 7.3, which links three of his tables.

The trends are clear: an extension of area until the 1870s and a severalfold increase in output due to the spread of perennial irrigation, the shift to cotton, the rise in yields, and the growth in farm population (it may be noted that O'Brien assumes a population of only 2,489,000 in 1821, and so overestimates the increase); a slowdown until the First World War, and a marked slowdown thereafter. In the period since 1895–99, output per worker declined slightly and output per acre rose by a third thanks to more double cropping and intensive use of fertilizers.

Table 7.3
Egypt: Indices of Agricultural Development (1821 = 100)

	Agricultural output	Rural population	Cultivated area	Cropped area
1830–35	164	118	109	
1872–78	1,208	206	156	178
1895–99	2,247	(327)	162	206
1910–14	2,719	409	173	235
1930–34	3,033	491	180	260
1960–62	4,584	697	193	313

Source: O'Brien 1968. In the absence of a figure in the source, an estimate has been made for rural population in 1895–99. See also Hansen and Wattleworth 1978, who calculate that between 1886–87 and 1912–13 real output about doubled.

For the other Middle Eastern countries no comparable data are available. The grain output of the Ottoman Empire, the bulk of which came from Anatolia, rose by about one-third between 1888 and 1913 (an average year), in spite of the shrinkage of the empire's borders, and it may be assumed that practically all of this increase was due to extension of area and not rise in yields.[46] One can also presume that a substantial extension of cultivated area took place in Anatolia in the 1840s–80s. In Syria, there was a temporary expansion under the Egyptian occupation (1831–40). For 1850–1950, "the following conservative estimates may be hazarded. In the area of the present Republic of Syria, excluding the Jezireh . . . . about 10,000 square miles of new land was ploughed up and about 2,000 villages established on this land; in Transjordan, perhaps 1,500 square miles and 300 villages. During the same hundred-year period an enormous amount of land must have been brought into regular cultivation, having in the past been at best infrequently used."[47] Although the figures seem distinctly too high, the trend described is indubitable, and there was also a small expansion in Lebanon and Palestine. For Iraq, the large increase in grain exports suggests a considerable extension of cultivation.[48] Even less information is available on Iran, but it would seem that the increase in the output of rice, cotton, silk, opium, and fruits in the second half of the 19th century more than offset the decrease in wheat and barley, and it is probable that output per head of agricultural population rose. New land was brought under cultivation in Gilan by clearing the jungle and in Khurasan, Kirman-shah, and Sistan by reoccupying abandoned areas. There was some extension of *qanat* (underground channels) irrigation. In Khuzistan, in 1890–1914, the cultivated area was extended and output grew fairly rapidly.[49]

As regards Algeria, the area planted to cereals by Muslims declined slightly, from 2.5 million hectares in the 1870s to 2.2 million in 1909–13, and the area under other crops was negligible; but this decrease was more than offset by the increase in European-owned lands to 1.8 million hectares, of which well over 1 million were cultivated. In Tunisia, the period 1775–1858 witnessed a marked shrinkage of cultivation and a fall in output. After the French conquest there was rapid expansion, and the area under cereals, olives, and minor crops rose from 600,000 hectares in 1881 to over 1.5 million in 1909–13.[50]

Tables 7.4 to 7.6 summarize available data on the main crops since the First World War. They indicate that, in the interwar period, substantial extension occurred in Iraq, Turkey, Sudan, Morocco, and probably Iran. After the Second World War this process continued in these countries

Table 7.4
Area of Wheat, Barley, and Cotton
(thousands of hectares)

	1909–13	1934–38	1948–52	1961–65	1976–78
Algeria	2,799	2,932	2,768	2,779	2,958
Libya	. .	169	(300)	499	584
Morocco	1,327[a]	3,096	3,301	3,217	4,186
Tunisia	1,027	1,201	1,506	1,503	1,509
Egypt[b]	2,098	2,096	2,090	2,025	1,927
Sudan	32	184	221	467	709
Iran	. .	2,348	2,970	4,942	7,252
Iraq	(500)	1,420	1,899	2,758	1,742
Israel/Palestine	(300)	450	86	138	182
Jordan	. .	. .	244	359	175
Lebanon	(100)	101	93	81	55
Syria	(700)	780	1,469	2,420	2,815
Turkey	(5,500)	5,471	6,216	11,410	12,633

[a] French Morocco only.
[b] Including maize.
Source: League of Nations, *International Statistical Yearbook*, 1927, 1928; Food and Agricultural Organization, *Yearbook of Food and Agricultural Statistics, Production*, 1952, 1957, 1970, 1978; Eldem 1970: pp. 73–75; Mears 1924:284; Huvelin 1921:8.

and also in Syria and Libya. Since the 1960s there has been almost no increase in cultivated area. An FAO study shows that in the Near East (as defined above) between the prewar period and 1953–55, area increased by 42 percent but yield increased by only 1 percent; between 1953–55 and 1962–63, however, area expanded by only 20 percent and yield by 14.[51] Yields have risen most markedly in cotton and other cash crops, but those of wheat are more indicative of the general state of agriculture, and, as shown in table 7.5, they are low except in Egypt and Israel and extremely low in North Africa. However, in recent years they have risen perceptibly. The scope for improvement is indicated by experiments recently carried out in Iraq which show that, by retaining existing varieties of wheat but using suitable doses of fertilizers, pest control, and irrigation, yields could be raised 3.4 times, and that by introducing Mexipac ("miracle wheat") varieties the increase would be sixfold.[52]

Land Tenure

Land tenure is a complex subject, and nowhere more so than in the Middle East, a region that has given birth to and been influenced by

Table 7.5
Wheat Yield
(kilograms per hectare)

	1934–38	1948–52	1961–65	1976–78
Algeria	560	620	637	654
Libya	470	90	245	400
Morocco	490	610	847	949
Tunisia	510	490	494	671
Egypt	2,010	1,840	2,651	3,332
Sudan	760	1,180	1,308	1,012
Iran	1,200	900	802	1,425
Iraq	720	480	532	1,031
Israel/Palestine	400	660	1,544	1,953
Jordan	. .	700	671	465
Lebanon	520	730	939	1,097
Saudi Arabia	. .	1,370	1,300	1,752
Syria	970	770	783	995
Turkey	990	1,000	1,079	1,624
North Yemen	. .	1,040	1,000	882
South Yemen	. .	1,640	2,025	1,653
Near East[a] average	(1,000)	920	972	1,415
World average	1,010	990	1,206	1,780

[a] As defined by FAO; excludes Algeria, Libya, Morocco, and Tunisia; includes Afghanistan, Cyprus, Ethiopia, and Somalia.
Source: Food and Agricultural Organization, *Yearbook of Food and Agricultural Statistics, Production,* 1970, 1973, 1978.

many civilizations, each with its peculiar legal system. Nevertheless, underlying the great diversity, a basic pattern has usually prevailed, involving the state, the farmer, and an intermediary. The ownership of the land (*raqaba*) was vested in the state or ruler, with minor exceptions such as *milk*, or freehold land (which prevailed in towns), and *waqf*, or mortmain, where ownership was regarded as transferred to God, its income being earmarked for specified religious or charitable purposes; or entailed within the family, the religious or charitable beneficiary having only a reversionary right. The farmer who tilled the land enjoyed usufructuary rights (*tasarruf*). In between came various intermediaries, who collected rent or taxes from the farmers and transferred part of the proceeds to the central treasury, keeping the balance as payment for the military or administrative services they performed. In Egypt they were the Mamluks and later the *multazims* (tax farmers); in Turkey the *sipahis*, followed by *mültezims*; in Iran the *tuyuldars* and holders of *soyurghals*. In addition to collecting taxes or rent, these intermediaries

Table 7.6
Output of Wheat and Barley, 1913–1978
(thousands of metric tons)

	1909–13	1925–29	1934–38	1948–52	1961–65	1976–78
Algeria	1,958	1,563	1,656	1,804	1,730	1,905
Libya	. .	74	54	66	124	269
Morocco	1,207[a]	1,583[a]	1,834	2,268	2,652	3,945
Tunisia	339	511	552	670	557	935
Egypt[b]	2,468	3,059	2,800	2,491	3,372	4,855
Sudan[c]	. .	. .	. .	195	339	800
Iran	. .	. .	1,662	2,627	3,665	6,993
Iraq	. .	(800)	1,053	1,170	1,700	1,521
Jordan	. .	51	118	179	242	75
Lebanon			64	76	77	60
	1,177	650	.			
Syria			749	1,083	1,742	2,261
Palestine/Israel	70[d]	141	154	68	156	217
Saudi Arabia	. .	. .	. .	28	165	145
Turkey	(4,500)	2,957	5,366	7,041	12,032	21,383
North Yemen	. .	. .	. .	16	16	107
South Yemen	. .	. .	. .	6	18	25

[a] French Morocco only.
[b] Wheat and maize.
[c] Wheat and millet.
[d] 1921–23.
Sources: League of Nations, *Statistical Yearbook*, various issues; Food and Agricultural Organization, *Statistical Yearbook, Production;* Mears 1924:282–86; Eldem 1970:74–77; Himadeh 1936:76–78, 1938a:125.

were also usually assigned a portion of the village land, which was cultivated for them by the peasants as part of the latter's labor obligations, or which was leased to the peasants. The nomads lived outside this system, raising their herds and cultivating their traditional tribal area (*dira*) with little outside interference. They paid a tax on livestock whose amount was determined mainly by their power relative to the nearest center of authority.

This system differed in many important respects from European feudalism, largely because the Middle Eastern states were more centralized (chapter 9) and their economies more monetized. In Europe the homage paid by the vassal to his liege was more elaborate, and the mutual rights and obligations of each party were more clearly defined. In the Middle East, there was little or no subinfeudation—each vassal held his land directly from the king. In the Middle East, again in contrast to Europe, the lord had no right of jurisdiction over the peasants in his "fief," who were under the authority of a *qadi* (judge) appointed by the king. European feudalism rested on status, was hereditary, and referred to a specific territory. Buyid, Seljuk, Mamluk, and other Middle Eastern lords were granted estates (or, more correctly, revenue from estates) for services rendered; their lands could be taken back by the king, who could transfer his vassals to other parts of the country, and in most places and periods their heirs had no claim on the estate. Two differences followed: European fiefs tended to be consolidated, whereas Middle Eastern lords usually drew their incomes from widely scattered pieces of land; and whereas the Europeans built castles and resided in their fiefs, Middle Eastern lords generally preferred to dwell in cities. Both these differences weakened the link binding the Middle Eastern lord to his land and reduced his political power. In the Middle East, unlike Europe, peasants were not serfs, i.e., they were not legally tied to the land, though various forms of pressure usually kept them there.[53]

In the 15th–16th centuries, Ottoman feudalism, perhaps influenced by Crusader practice in Greece, was closer to the European than its predecessors had been. Outside cities, land was divided into two categories: *has*, the private property of the sultan or members of the imperial family, or land the revenues of which were assigned to holders of certain offices; and *timar*, or fiefs, assigned to Sipahis who collected revenue (rent or taxes) from the farmers. The Sipahis, or *Timariots*, lived on their estates and had a certain jurisdiction over their peasants, including the right to compel those who left to return—but they were under much stricter supervision from the central government than was the case in Europe, and their land was subjected to periodic surveys for tax purposes. The *timars* tended to stay in the family to a much greater degree than had the earlier Middle Eastern "fiefs" (*iqta'*, *soyurghal*), being generally inherited by a son or brother or even by a widow who remarried and could thus ensure the performance of obligations. From the 17th century on, the government's growing need for cash, which was connected with the change in the structure and weaponry of the army and was aggravated by inflation, led to increasing conversion of *timar* land to *has* when its owner died. This land was then assigned to tax farmers, who acquired the right to collect taxes from a specified area. By the 18th century such tax farms (*malikane, iltizam*) had become both salable and hereditary. Another factor working in the same direction was the growth of a lucrative trade in agricultural produce with Europe. A new landed gentry, the *a'yans* and *derebeys*, emerged with large estates known as *chiftliks*.[54]

The land tenure system of the Middle East underwent drastic change in the 19th and 20th centuries. The rise in the value of agricultural produce greatly strengthened the desire to own land outright. The governments, anxious to increase their revenues from taxes on such produce—and occasionally also wishing to promote agricultural development by giving the cultivators a greater incentive—abolished the *timars*, *iltizams*, and other intermediary institutions. At the same time, the bonds tying the peasant to the land were snapped and those binding the village community together—in some areas common holding and periodic redistribution of land, collective responsibility for taxes, and, in Egypt, village responsibility for the maintenance of irrigation works— were loosened; among the causes were greater security, increasing government centralization, growing population, and, above all, integration in the market with the accompanying economic differentiation, indebtedness, sale and alienation of land.[55] The result, all over the region, was the development of a land tenure characterized by: large estates, accounting for a quarter to four-fifths of privately owned land and in the main tilled by sharecroppers; a huge number of very small peasant proprietors, often with highly fragmented holdings; short and precarious leases; high rents (mostly one- to two-thirds of gross output); large debts; rising land values; and a growing landless proletariat earning very low wages. The relative magnitudes were determined by a variety of geographic, economic, social, and political factors. Both units of ownership and units of operation were larger where rainfall was low, population scarce, and distance from the nearest city great, and rents tended to be lower on such lands. Lands irrigated by flow were owned and operated in smaller units than rain-fed lands, but where pumps or other lifting machinery had to be used, as in Iraq and southern Iran, the position of the small farmer became much weaker than that of the owner of the machine; rents were higher on irrigated than on rain-fed lands both in absolute terms and as a fraction of gross output. Similarly, holdings of land planted to trees were smaller than those planted to annual crops, and rents were higher. Where the government provided security, small farmers could survive more easily than in areas where they needed the protection of a large landlord or tribal chief. And high-value cash crops such as cotton, tobacco, or vegetables both absorbed more labor than did cereals and made it possible for a farm family to subsist on a much smaller area. Thus in Egypt a plot of 1–1.5 hectares, and in Saudi Arabia 1 irrigated hectare, can support a family, whereas in Mandatory Palestine the "lot viable" for an Arab family was put at 12 hectares of unirrigated, mainly cereal-growing land, in Algeria at 10 hectares of cereal land, and in Syria and Iraq at 10 to 30 hectares. Similarly, in Turkey in the second half of the 19th century, silk-raising farms near Bursa and tobacco farms near Trabzon averaged about 2 hectares, whereas cereal farms around Ankara ranged from 10 to 100 hectares.[56]

One further distinction is necessary. In countries of settlement—Algeria, Tunisia, Morocco, Libya, and Palestine—large estates were owned mainly by immigrants, but in the rest of the region the large landowners were indigenous.

At the time of the French conquest of Algeria, the Tell (Mediterranean zone of about 14 million hectares, enjoying 40–60 or more centimeters of rainfall a year) was divided as follows according to the French authorities, who were not fully aware of the intricacies of North African land tenure: 4.5 million of *milk* (alodial) land in the coastal plains, oases, and mountains; 5 million of *'arsh* or *sabiqa* lands administered by the tribal chiefs or *jama'as* (village councils) on payment of land tax and tithe; 1.5 million of state domain (*'azl, makhzan, beylik*), given to friendly tribes in return for military service; and 3 million of "dead" lands (*mawat*), consisting of forests and grazing lands owned by the state but used by the villages or tribes for grazing or passage.[57] French policy, which was based on the assumption that "the flood of emigration, which for long was directed to America, now flows to Algeria,"[58] sought to facilitate the transfer of land for both official and individual colonization. Private land purchases began immediately and were regulated and stimulated by the ordinances of 1844 and 1846 and the law of 1851, which declared that French law applied to all transactions between Muslims and Christians; that the state could expropriate all uncultivated land; that *habus* (*waqf*, mortmain) land could be sold; that in zones under civilian rule *'arsh* land could be sold to individuals and in military zones to the state; and that all forests belonged to the state. Meanwhile, in 1830, the state had taken over *beylik* lands, lands sequestrated from the Turks, and many charitable *habus*. This, together with some 250,000 hectares of tribal and forest land taken under the law of 1851, provided a fund for distribution of free land to official colonists, who by 1852 numbered 10,450, at a cost to the state of 28 million francs.[59]

Napoleon III, by the *Senatus consulte* of 1863, tried to reassure the Muslims regarding their land. *Milk* land was to continue to be freely alienable, but tribal lands were to be delimited and converted to collective property, vested in the *duwar* (clan) and inalienable outside it, even to the state; afterward such land was to be divided among the clan members as *milk*. During his reign there was little private colonization, but the state established 21 villages with 4,500 colonists and conceded some 150,000 hectares to large land development companies.[60]

The establishment of the Third Republic, giving more power to the *colons*, the Kabyle insurrection of 1871, the influx of refugees from Alsace-Lorraine (chapter 5) and the development of viticulture created great pressure for speeding land transfers. This was achieved by the law of 1873, modified and supplemented by those of 1887, 1897, and 1926, which facilitated individual appropriation of *'arsh* land and its sale to the French. In 1877 through 1890, individual French settlers acquired 378,000 hectares, for which they paid 37.4 million francs. Meanwhile, in 1871, 100,000 hectares had been put at the disposal of immigrants from Alsace-Lorraine, and in the next few years 356,000 hectares of cultivable land were sequestrated from the Kabyles; this was used for official colonization, amounting to 577,000 hectares in 1871–90. In the overlapping period 1880–1917, official colonization amounted to 192,000 hectares and *net* private purchases to 844,000; in addition 3,115,000 hectares of *'arsh* land had been converted to "state domains."[61] By 1930, official colonization amounted to a little under 1.5 million hectares and private to 1 million. By 1954 Europeans held 2.7 million hectares, i.e., a little under a quarter of the area of the Tell. Of the land actually under cultivation, some 25,000 Europeans owned 2,073,000 hectares or 37.9 percent; the rest was owned by 530,000 Muslims, and supported some 6 million persons; about 60 percent of Arab owners held less than 10 hectares and 1 percent over 100 hectares. Europeans owned almost all the vineyards, and, partly because their land was better but mainly because they used modern methods (around 1910 the value of the equipment used by an Arab farmer was put at 3.70 francs per hectare, that of a *colon* at 30–300 francs), their cereal yields were twice as high as those of the Muslims. Over all, output per hectare on European farms was 7 times as high as on Arab, and income per owner 10 times as high. Europeans received about 50 percent of net agricultural income. They employed, on a permanent or seasonal basis, many Arabs in their vineyards, citrus groves, vegetable gardens, and other labor-intensive farms.[62]

During the War of Independence European farms were occupied by Muslims, and in 1962–63 the government tried to regularize the situation by instituting self-management, on the Yugoslav model, on 2,646,000 hectares tilled by 150,000 workers; the results have been disappointing, and the wide gap between incomes on such farms and those in the traditional sector (9 or 10:1) creates much tension. In 1972 a land reform law was passed, expropriating land in excess of 50 hectares, and by 1978 1.9 million hectares had been taken and 1,350,000 had been distributed to 83,000 families grouped in cooperatives. But Algeria's total agricultural output has stagnated.[63]

In Tunisia foreign colonization was much less extensive. Already by

1881 Frenchmen owned over 100,000 hectares, and after the conquest both individual and official colonization were encouraged. The Decree of 1885 registered titles, facilitating sales. The large and usually neglected *habus* lands were affected by the decrees of 1888, 1898, 1902, and 1905, and by 1938 nearly 200,000 hectares had passed to the colonists by sale, exchange, or payment of *enzel*, perpetual rent. In 1881 350,000–400,000 hectares were confiscated, mainly from tribes, and by 1939 some 90,000 had been transferred to colonists. By then private French holdings amounted to 400,000 hectares and Italian to 140,000 hectares. In addition, official colonization included 267,000 hectares of cereal, vines, and other field crops and 203,000 hectares planted to olives and other trees. Around 1950 some 8,000 European families and companies owned 800,000 hectares, or about one-fifth of the arable area, while the rest supported 350,000–400,000 Muslim families. The French owned most of the vineyards and a quarter of the land under cereals, citrus, or other fruits; their cereals yields were about three times as high as the Tunisians'. The latter owned 80–85 percent of olives and 90 percent of the livestock; Europeans accounted for about one-third of gross agricultural output.[64]

After independence Tunisia bought back some French-owned land and took over about half the total area under the nationalization law of 1964. The government has given much attention to agriculture, reclamation schemes have been implemented, and output has risen. Service cooperatives, were developed to help small farmers, and an attempt was made in 1969 to extend production cooperatives to the bulk of farmers. It caused much disruption and was soon stopped.

Morocco's traditional land tenure was broadly similar to that of Algeria and, especially in the 1920s, it was subjected to similar strong pressures for transferring land to Europeans. But the outcome was very different, partly because France did not have the same freedom of action in Morocco and partly because Marshal Lyautey secured greater protection for tribal lands under the *dahir* (decree) of 1914, which was only slightly relaxed by the *dahir* of 1919; moreover, in contrast to Algeria, no land was distributed free to colonists. By 1913, 524 Europeans owned almost 100,000 hectares of fertile land, by 1935 the numbers were 2,070 and 569,000. By 1953 there were 4,270 private colonists owning 728,000 hectares, three-quarters in the Casablanca-Rabat region. Official colonization transferred land mainly to large companies; in 1923–32 some 200,000 hectares were sold, and by 1953 there were 1,600 owners of 289,000 hectares, over half in the Casablanca-Rabat region. Thus 6,000 Europeans held 1 million hectares and 800,000

to 900,000 Muslim families owned some 6.5 million. As in Algeria and
Tunisia, European farms were more productive, the value of their gross
output per acre being about twice as high as that of Muslim farms.
Muslim landownership was highly unequal, about half the area being
held by some 10 percent of landowners, while over half the rural
population worked as wage laborers. Since independence much French
land has been bought back, but little has been done to change the
structure or improve the performance of agriculture. In 1957-72 181,000
hectares were redistributed, and further redistribution was planned for
1973-77.[65] In Spanish Morocco, the total area occupied by Europeans
was some 40,000 hectares, on land confiscated after the Rif War of
1921-26 or bought from the original owners.[66]

Like France in Algeria, Italy aimed at settling a large population in
Libya, but the results in terms of numbers were meager, though causing
much suffering to the Libyans. A series of decrees in 1922-28 declared all
land to be state property unless proof to the contrary were produced;
confiscated rebel land; allowed expropriation of uncultivated land for
reasons of public utility; and urged owners of land considered useful to
the state to renounce their claims, receiving compensation in proportion
to their *tasarruf* (usufructuary) rights. In Tripolitania, by 1925 67,000
hectares had been nationalized or purchased, by 1933 203,000, and by
1940 250,000. In Cyrenaica—where resistance was much stronger and
was met with drastic measures, including the expulsion of whole
villages to the desert—120,000 hectares had been acquired by 1932, and
by 1940 629,000 hectares of registered land were owned by the state.[67] As
regards settlement, in 1922-28 Italian capital and technicians, employing local labor, were encouraged to buy large holdings by concessionary
prices, tax exemptions, and generous credit. By 1933 there were over 500
private large farms with 1,500 colonists in Tripolitania, holding over
100,000 hectares, and 90 farms in Cyrenaica. Starting in 1928, and more
particularly after 1938, an attempt at mass settlement was made. By 1940,
4,000 families (over 30,000 persons) in Tripolitania and over 2,000
families (15,000 persons) in Cyrenaica lived on some 550,000 hectares, of
which 228,000 were cultivated (148,000 in Tripolitania and 80,000 in
Cyrenaica) and plans were under way to settle another 300,000 persons.
All expenses were borne by the state or by government institutes; the
estimated total was 728 million lire (about $45 million), to which should
be added the cost of infrastructure, and the farms were far from being
self-supporting. The Italians farmed over half the land in Tripolitania
and the greater part of that of Cyrenaica.[68] During the Second World War
the Italians evacuated Cyrenaica. After independence some land in

nts; of the net proceeds of cotton growth on the tenants' plots,
went to the government, 40 to the tenants, and 20 to the
s. A high technical level was maintained, and the scheme
ts objectives, contributing in the mid-50s some 40 percent of
xports, supplying a quarter or more of government revenue,
iding the tenants with a per capita income three times the
average. In 1950 the companies' concession lapsed and was
er by the Gezira Board, the tenants' share of income being
y raised. Successive extensions have brought the total area of the
to 800,000 hectares, with some 100,000 tenant families.[76]

egal evolution of the Ottoman Empire was like that of Egypt:
were abolished in 1831 (after the massacre of the Janissaries), and
d Code of 1858 was similar to the Egyptian law of that year. But
nt geographic, political, and social situations produced very
nt outcomes. The central provisions of the code were that all land
be registered in individual and not collective ownership (thus
ating direct taxation) and that usufructuary title would be granted
se who could prove continuous occupation.[77] In Turkey, the result
hat the bulk of the land passed into the hands of peasants. Scattered
or 1863 show that small ownership was predominant. In 1910 only
ndful of peasants were landless, and small holdings (under 5
ares) numbered over 1 million or 75 percent of landowners.
eover, the abundance of land—title to much of which could be
ained at a nominal cost—and the shortage of labor meant that rents
e relatively low and wages high; thus in the 1860s an average annual
ge could have bought several acres of land and 2 to 4 draft animals.
ter, however, land values rose sharply, and, especially in such areas of
velopment as Adana and Izmir, estates tended to grow.[78] In 1867
reigners were allowed to own land, but except in the Izmir area, where
ey had about 250,000 hectares, their holdings remained small. Most of
e larger properties were rented out to sharecroppers, but, particularly
here cash crops were grown, some were directly managed by owners.

Under the republic the only significant attempt to improve land
enure was the 1945 Land Reform Law, which by 1965 had distributed
ome 1.8 millon hectares of unowned land, or unused state or community land, to 360,000 families, with good results. In 1963 there were
4,300 owners of over 100 hectares (not a large size in Turkey) holding
2,146,000 hectares, or 10 percent of the area; 110,000 medium owners (20
to 100 hectares) held 4,932,000 hectares, or 23 percent; 853,000 small
owners (5 to 20) held 8,775,000, or 42 percent; and 2,132,000 very small
owners (under 5 hectares) held 5,219,000, or 25 percent. Rapid popula-

Tripolitania was sold to Libyans and the rest expropriated. More recently, Libya has used part of its vast oil resources for agricultural development and its output has risen sharply.

The original Zionist settlers in Palestine, in the 1880s, had no previous experience with agriculture and therefore tended to follow existing methods, grow cereals, and employ Arab labor. This emergence of an incipient planter class ran counter to Zionist nationalist and socialist ideology, and by 1914 most of the labor was Jewish, irrigation and other intensive methods were used, and a variety of valuable cash crops were raised. By then some 12,000 settlers tilled about 42,000 hectares, mostly provided by the Palestine Jewish Colonization Association. In 1920 Jewish holdings were put at 65,000 hectares, and by the end of 1946 purchases had raised the figure to 162,000, or more than a sixth of the cultivable area of Palestine; of this some two-thirds belonged to the various funds, of which the Jewish National Fund was the most important.[69] In December 1948 land abandoned by Arabs who had left Israel (estimated at some 450,000 cultivable hectares) was put under custody and eventually leased or sold to the funds. Within the 1966 borders of Israel, 75 percent of the land belonged to the state and 17 percent to the funds; 2 percent was in private Jewish ownership and 6 percent in Arab. Communal (*kibbutz*) farms—of which the first was founded in 1909—and cooperatives (*moshav*) accounted for some three-quarters of agricultural output. Already under the Mandate Jewish farming had reached a high level; wheat yields were twice as high as on Arab farms, and a much larger proportion of valuable vegetables, fruits, dairy and poultry products were grown.[70] But this was achieved at a high capital cost. An expert put the cost of settling a Jewish family of three, exclusive of the land, at £P2,500 in 1922, declining to £P525 (about $2,500) by the late 1930s, and costs of production on Jewish farms were well above those of Arab farms or adjacent countries.[71] Citrus was evenly divided between Arab and Jewish groves, and yields were equal. Since independence, Israel has made remarkable progress in agriculture; production has greatly increased, yields per acre are the highest in the region except for Egypt, and output per worker is far above the regional level (see table 7.5 and appendix table A.7).

In Egypt the transformation of land tenure began earlier than anywhere in the region and was carried out most thoroughly. Some changes were under way in the latter half of the 18th century. Napoleon's invasion and reorganization of land taxation shook the bases of the old system, and in 1811–16 Muhammad Ali massacred the Mamluks and took over their *iltizam* (tax farms) and the *rizaq* (*waqf*, mortmains). He thus became in effect the sole owner of the country, gave out land to peasants in plots of 3–5 *faddans* (acres), and collected taxes directly from them. Legally the farmers were tenants at will, but in fact enjoyed much security because of the labor shortage; indeed, they were forbidden to leave and were collectively as well as individually responsible for taxes. Between 1829 and 1842 large tracts of uncultivated land were granted, wholly or partly tax free, to notables (*ib'adiya, rizqa bila mal*) or to members of the royal family (*chiftlik*), and in 1840, because of the pasha's financial difficulties, officials who had become rich were forced to take over certain villages and be responsible for their taxes (*'uhda*). This laid the basis for Egypt's land system: a substantial proportion of land in big farms and a very large number of very small farms. Coupled with cotton and perennial irrigation, this led to a rapid growth in output and large tax and monopoly revenues (chapter 2).

In the 1840s restrictions on the disposal of land were greatly eased. In 1855 collective responsibility for taxes was abolished, and the 1858 Land Law gave holders practically complete rights to sell, mortgage, and transfer land and recognized the rights of both male and female heirs. Foreigners were also allowed to acquire land and eventually held 12 percent of Egypt's acreage; but the greater part belonged to companies engaged in the reclamation of waste land for sale. However, a large amount of foreign capital flowed to the countryside in the form of mortgages and loans. A few remaining anomalies were abolished by the *Muqabala* law of 1871 and by the British in 1891 and 1899. Thus, by the end of the century, Egypt's land had been converted to freehold.[72] In 1913 it was distributed as follows: 13,000 large landlords (50 *faddans* and over) held 42 percent, 133,000 medium landowners (5–50 *faddans*) held 31 percent, and 1,411,000 small owners held 27 percent; of the last 942,000 had dwarf holdings of less than 1 *faddan*. The figures show little change compared to the earliest ones, those for 1896. Some estates were worked by hired labor, or by peasants who were allowed a small plot in return for their services; others were rented to sharecroppers or, increasingly, to cash-rent tenants.[73]

No data are available on distribution of agricultural income in the 19th century. Labor was scarce and real wages rose, but one may presume that most of the increment in agricultural income (see above) went to landowners. Hansen's careful calculations suggest that in 1895–1913, although daily wages lagged behind the growth of agricultural output, the share of wage income almost kept pace with output, because of greater labor input per acre, while rents rose somewhat faster.[74] After that, however, population growth far outstripped the expansion of the

cultivated area, and a large class o
very little land developed. The
illustration. Between the 1870s
remained constant. In 1912–29 dail
expressed in terms of the price of m
wages rose by some 30 percent but
index they fell by about 35 percent.
sharply; money wages by some 50 p
tenth more, and in terms of the index
Second World War money wages follo
a lag, and the downward trend in rea
land reforms. On the other hand, ren
1.00–1.50 *per faddan* in 1890 and 3.595 i
and 18.400 in 1945–46; this movement, h
reforms. In 1976 the number of landless a
or one-third of the agricultural labor forc

The Egyptian Land Reform Law of 19
Middle East, being closely copied by the
ceiling of 200 *faddans* (with additional exem
which by 1969 was reduced to 50. Land wa
(2–3 *faddans*) to peasants who had to join a c
provided with various services and technical
to receive compensation, which was more
stallments paid to the government by the new
payments were eventually discontinued. By 197
expropriated land and nearly 200,000 of state la
Egypt's area) had been distributed to some 400,0
percent of Egypt's rural population, with a
income. The economic as well as the social effec
are generally acknowledged to have been bene
reduced rents, attempted unsuccessfully to raise ag
abolished *waqfs*.

Little has been done to alter land tenure in Sudan
scheme, a British attempt to grow cotton for export a
escape Egyptian-type landlordism. After prolonged
ments, a tripartite scheme was devised. The governme
Dam in 1925 and the main canals; two British co
management and working capital; and the original o
forced to lease the land for a long term at a nominal rent
option of becoming tenants of the scheme and working
them. Output was shared as follows: all grain and fodder

by the ten
40 percen
companie
fulfilled
Sudan's
and pro
national
taken o
gradual
scheme
The
timars
the La
differe
differe
was t
facili
to the
was t
data
a ha
hect
Mo
obt
wer
wa
La
de
fo
th
th
w

tion growth has produced a large landless proletariat which has emigrated to the cities. In spite of this, landless households among the rural population rose from 9 percent in 1963 to 22 in 1973.[79]

In the Arab provinces the application of the Land Code was impeded by bad records and poor administration, and, moreover, ran counter to prevailing communal (*musha'*) or tribal ownership, which in turn was well adapted to the lack of security, the precarious rainfall, and the consequent instability of crop yields. One most unfortunate consequence was that a large amount of land was registered in the name of tribal chiefs or village or city notables, depriving hundreds of thousands of peasants of any title. The urge on the part of the big men to grab land was intensified by the growth of foreign trade and the development of transport, which greatly increased the value of land and its produce.

In Iraq the attempt, in 1869–71, by the reforming governor Midhat Pasha to apply the code led to confusion and land alienation. Hence the 1880 and 1891 decrees suspended the application of article 78 of the code in the irrigated zones and created a new, extralegal class of land—about 80 percent of the cultivable area—in which both ownership and usufruct belonged to the state and which was held by the occupiers as tax-paying tenants at will. Under the Mandate the British introduced minor improvements, but did not attempt to alter the system for fear of antagonizing the landlords and tribal leaders, on whose support they were dependent. Following the Dowson Report of 1932, a commission for settlement of titles—the uncertainty of which was holding up agricultural development and denying landless farmers access to the available land—was set up. By 1958 most of the land had been settled, the main categories being *miri tapu* and *miri lazma* (land held in permanent tenure from the state), aggregating 6,300,000 hectares, and *miri sirf* (state land unencumbered by occupancy rights), 12,750,000 hectares. Except in the northern provinces, where peasant farms prevailed, the bulk of the registered area was held by landlords: 3,400 owners of 250 or more hectares had 68 percent of the area, and the total registered landowners were only 168,000, which means that the mass of the rural population was landless. Rents were very high: in flow-irrigated lands three-fifths of the crop, and in pump-irrigated areas five-sevenths. In its last decade the monarchy attempted to improve conditions by providing irrigation, credit, and storage and by distributing some *miri-sirf* land through the Dujaila and other schemes.[80]

The 1958 Land Reform Law was closely modeled on the Egyptian but had much higher ceilings, which were drastically lowered in 1970. However, unlike the Egyptian, it encountered many difficulties: acute political instability, administrative inability to handle the large areas involved, absence of records, and strong tribalism; in addition, Iraq's fragile ecology was more easily disrupted, and a series of droughts added to the damage. By 1975, 2.3 million hectares had been taken over, or 46 percent of the agricultural area. Of this 1.6 million hectares had been distributed, and 1.3 million of expropriated land and *miri sirf* were cultivated by farmers on very short leases; some collective farms were also established. All this has both kept production down and caused a large amount of land to go out of cultivation, and Iraq's agricultural record in the last twenty years has been poor, in spite of large investments in irrigation.[81]

The same process took place in Syria, but on a smaller and less disruptive scale. Uncertainty and insecurity of tenure continued to affect both private and state land, the latter being much smaller than in Iraq, but it was not until 1952 that half the agricultural land had been covered by a cadastral survey started in 1926. This showed that, in the registered areas, 49 percent of privately owned land was in holdings of over 100 hectares, 38 in holdings of 10–99 hectares, and 13 percent in those under 10 hectares; scattered data indicate a roughly similar distribution at the beginning of this century. Some 250,000 families owned land, and about half that number were landless. Rents were high: in dry-farming areas the landlord took 15 to 40 percent of the crop if he provided the land, 50 to 60 if he provided seed as well, and 75 if he supplied land, seed, and equipment. Under pump irrigation half the crop went to the pump owner.[82]

Like the Iraqi, the Syrian Land Reform Law of 1958 was closely modeled on the Egyptian, and it too had higher ceilings, which were reduced in 1963. It too ran into political and administrative difficulties and, like the Iraqi law, was not well adapted to the country's natural conditions and failed to provide a substitute for the active role played by many Syrian landlords, who had pioneered a large expansion of area and production in 1943–57. As a result Syria's agricultural output has grown very slowly. By 1966 all the land subject to requisition—1,250,000 hectares, representing almost a quarter of the cultivated area—had been taken over, and 450,000 hectares distributed to 22,000 families. Production cooperatives have been set up in some areas.[83]

In the coastal areas of geographical Syria, which are mountainous and receive adequate rain, small property was much more widespread. In Mount Lebanon this was helped by the agrarian revolt of 1858 directed against the "feudal" *muqata'jis*—the only one of its kind in the region— and by land purchases by peasants receiving remittances from relatives in America. Another factor was the widespread use of *mugharasa*, a practice known in other parts of the Middle East, under which a landlord provides uncultivated land (and if necessary water) on which a tenant grows trees; when these reach maturity the tenant keeps either half the land and trees or only half the trees. Some large properties exist in the Biqa' and southern Lebanon, but the bulk of the arable land is held by 275,000 small owners averaging 1.2 hectares apiece.[84] In Palestine many large estates were sold to Zionist organizations, and the 1944 Village Survey showed that 27 percent of the Arab-owned area was in holdings of over 100 hectares, 36 in those of 10–100 hectares, and 37 in those under 10 hectares; a great deal of fragmentation prevailed.[85] In Jordan too small properties are predominant; in East Jordan in the 1950s 53 percent of private land was in holdings of 20 hectares or less, 33 in holdings of 20–100 hectares, and 14 percent in holdings of 100 hectares.[86]

The evolution of Iran's land tenure is obscure, but two trends may be observed in the 19th century and up to the Second World War, caused by the economic and political factors mentioned earlier in this section. First, crown and state lands (*khaliseh*) were extended by purchase, confiscation, and seizure for abandonment or failure to pay taxes. Second, much *khaliseh* land was sold or transferred to large land-owners.[87] As a result, Iran presented, with Iraq, the darkest picture in the region. A tenth of the cultivable land belonged to the state or crown, a fifth was *vakf* (*waqf*), a half was owned by large landowners and tribal leaders, and only a fifth was in medium or small holdings. It has been estimated that 90 percent of the rural population was landless.[88] The Land Reform of 1963, limiting ownership to one village, had by 1975 redistributed 17,000 out of Iran's 55,000 villages to about a third of the rural population. In the second phase of the reform those landlords who had kept a village were given various choices, such as buying out the tenants, selling the land to them, or dividing it; 80 percent chose to lease it to their tenants for a 30-year term. Thus landlordism was drastically reduced, and the economic effects of the reform seem to have been favorable. Unfortunately, much of the good effect was undone by a misguided attempt to spread modern farming by introducing agro-businesses, whose record seems to have been dismal.[89]

Thus, in the last thirty years major efforts have been made to improve Middle Eastern land tenure. However, it continues to constitute a serious obstacle to the economic and social development of the region.

CHAPTER VIII

Deindustrialization and Reindustrialization

Deindustrialization

Like many parts of the world in the last two hundred years or so the Middle East has gone through a process of deindustrialization followed by reindustrialization. The decline of the handicrafts continued until well after the First World War. By then another development was under way: the growth of a modern factory industry, which started around the 1890s, gathered momentum in the 1920s and 30s, and since the Second World War has proceeded at a rapid pace. However, it was probably not until the 1920s or 30s that rising employment in factories offset the decline of the handicrafts, and that the proportion of the population employed in industry began to grow instead of decreasing.

The craftsmen were organized in guilds, which tended to be conservative and restrictive, used rather primitive tools, and had little access to capital. Most crafts had been in decline since the late Middle Ages,[1] and there is much evidence that, by the 18th century if not earlier, some were suffering from the competition of Indian textiles and still more from that of European goods. Thus Tunisian fezzes began to lose some of their export markets to the French in that century, and Algerian crafts were in a steep decline.[2] In Egypt and Syria, exports of linen and cotton cloth and cotton yarn to France and England fell off in the second half of the 18th century, partly because of protective duties in the importing countries, partly because of technological progress in Europe, and partly because of a deterioration in quality. They were increasingly replaced by exports of raw cotton, flax, and wool. Conversely, imports of European woolens, as well as paper, glass, hardware, and other manufactured goods, rose sharply.[3] There is some evidence of a decrease

Part of this chapter appeared, under the same title, in IJMES (December 1980); the petroleum industry is not discussed in this chapter, being covered in chapter 10.

in output and exports of silk cloth in Bursa toward the end of the 18th century, accompanied by a large increase in exports of raw silk.[4] In the European parts of the Ottoman Empire, e.g., Istanbul, Salonica, and Edirne, textile manufacturing also declined.[5] And European observers were with few exceptions, highly critical of the quality of Middle Eastern handicrafts.[6]

However, the picture must not be overdrawn. The region's cities contained hundreds of thousands of handicraftsmen, who supplied the bulk of its requirements of manufactured goods. Particularly noteworthy were those of Istanbul, Bursa, Salonica, Izmir, Ankara, and Tokat in Turkey; of Aleppo and Damascus in Syria; of Baghdad and Mosul in Iraq; of Isfahan, Tabriz, Yazd, Kashan, Shiraz, and Hamadan in Iran; of Cairo, Mahalla, Asyut, and Fayyum in Egypt; and of Tunis, Fez, and Marrakesh in North Africa. In many branches there was an elaborate division of labor between towns, each specializing in one particular process. Thus in 1839 a Russian source stated: *"Kindiak* or *Bogaz* . . . is woven in Amasya and Malatya, dyed in Aleppo and Tokat, and glazed in Mosul; . . . *Astar* and *Borla* are mostly made in the town of Zile and neighboring places in the pashalik; merchants buy the cloth there and take it to Amasya and Tokat for finishing."[7] Many, or perhaps most, villages also had their own simple handicrafts, which met some of their basic needs.

The Revolutionary and Napoleonic wars gave the region a respite, but in the 1820s and 30s it was hit by the full blast of European competition. Factories were pouring out cheap goods, and peace and increased security in the Mediterranean and improvement in shipping made it possible to land them at low costs (chapter 3). To this should be added the effects of the various commercial treaties, which froze import duties at low levels and opened up the region's markets (chapter 2). As a result in Turkey and Iran the internal duties paid by native producers were higher than the import and other duties paid by foreigners.

At first, the impact was confined to the ports and coastal areas, but with the development of railways and improvement of road transport in the latter decades of the 19th century, it gradually spread inland. The effect on many crafts was catastrophic. In 1845 a French consul reported that the number of looms in Aleppo had fallen to 1,500 and in Damascus to 1,000, from a combined total of 12,000. In 1862 the British consul in Aleppo stated that in the preceding ten years the number of looms in that city had fallen from 10,000 to 2,800 and output from 4 million pieces to 1.5 million.[8] In 1868, a government commission reported that, during the preceding 30–40 years, the number of cloth-making looms in

Istanbul had fallen from 2,750 to 25; of brocade looms from 350 to 4; and of upholstery silk looms from 60 to 8. In Bursa, already in 1838 manufactures of cotton and silk were "on the decline"; in 1843 some 20,000 pieces of cloth were produced, but by 1846 output had fallen to 13,000, and by 1863 to 3,000.[9] No figures are available for Iran, but British consular reports in the 1840s show that a similar process was under way.[10] In Iraq, scattered data also show a sharp decline in handlooms after the Suez Canal had reduced the cost of importing textiles.[11] In Tunisia, fezzes, cotton and silk fabrics and clothing, hardware, leather, pottery, and ceramics increasingly suffered from foreign competition, losing first their remaining export markets and then a large part of the domestic one.[12] In the 1870s Morocco's handicrafts—textiles, fezzes, pottery, hardware, glassware, firearms, and others—began to be severely hurt by foreign competition at least in the coastal zones; the price of a yard of British cotton cloth fell from 7 francs in 1800 to 3 in 1830, and 60 centimes in 1860.[13]

Nevertheless, neither the speed nor the extent of the devastation should be exaggerated. Thanks to poor transport, handicrafts survived for longer in the interior and distant parts than in the coastal areas. Thus in Turkey, British consular reports for the period 1885–1914 show that handlooms, as well as handicraft copper, leather, and woodwork, remained active in such towns as Mardin, Diyarbakir, Malatya, and even Konya; on the eve of the First World War, there were some 10,000 handlooms in western Anatolia (e.g., Manisa, Burdur, Denizli) and several thousand in the northeastern parts.[14] It should be added that, in Turkey as elsewhere, weavers were able to cut their costs greatly by using imported yarn; thus the Industrial Revolution, which had wiped out the spinners, gave the weavers a precarious reprieve. The same happened in Egypt: according to the 1873 statistics some 30,000 persons, and to the 1907 census over 300,000 persons, were employed in handicrafts and small workshops; of the latter, 45,500 were weavers, showing an increase of 27 percent over 1897, a figure confirmed by the 53 percent rise in the value of imports of cotton, woolen, silk, and other yarns during the same period.[15] Many crafts survived beyond the Second World War.

In Syria, in 1880 it was "estimated that nearly five million yards of stuffs of all kinds are made annually, the greater part of which is exported to Egypt, Rumelia, Rumania, etc."[16] Imports of cotton yarn rose from £60–70,000 a year in the 1890s to £650,000 in 1908–12 and imports of silk thread increased almost as much. In 1909 the number of looms in Syria was put at about 20,000. The number of craftsmen active just before the First World War was put at 110,000 (in Lebanon at

10,000), and as late as in the 1930s there were some 40,000 handweavers and many other craftsmen.[17] In the early 1900s, Damascus was still supplying Egypt with silk fabrics, using Chinese raw silk.[18] In Iraq there also seems to have been some revival, and in Baghdad in 1907, there were 900 handlooms producing some 5 million yards of cotton cloth and 500,000 of silk.[19] In Iran, as late as 1950, there were about 20,000 handloom weavers and a somewhat larger number of workers in the other crafts.[20] Many craftsmen also survived in Tunisia (e.g., 25,000 weavers in 1946) and Morocco until the Second World War and well beyond.[21]

Indeed, certain handicrafts were actually stimulated by a rise in world demand for their products. Some of these processed a raw material that was exported, e.g., raw silk in Turkey, Iran, and Lebanon and opium, henna, and leather in Iran.[22] Some catered to tourists, or to demand outside their countries for such goods as copperware, inlaid woodwork, and embroidery. But the outstanding example was carpets. A small number of luxury carpets had been exported to Europe from Turkey and Iran for hundreds of years. But it was only around 1870 that large-scale export began, thanks to a rise in demand in Europe, falling transport costs, and the investment of European capital in the Iranian and Turkish carpet industries. In Turkey, British merchants in Izmir entered the industry in the 1860s, and in 1908 British merchants founded the Oriental Carpet Manufacturers Ltd., with a capital of £400,000, subsequently raised to £1 million. Output increased severalfold, and in 1913 Turkey's exports amounted to 1,584 metric tons, worth £600,000, compared to £300,000 in 1889. However, the First World War and War of Independence shattered the carpet industry. Although exports recovered in the late 1920s, they declined steadily thereafter.[23] In Iran, there was also a small investment of British capital in carpet making, and exports rose rapidly to about £100,000 in 1900 and £1 million in 1914, accounting for almost one-eighth of Iran's exports. Carpet making held up better in Iran than in Turkey and in the early 1950s still employed some 130,000 persons; exports, at some 5,000 metric tons, accounted for one-sixth of Iran's non-oil exports.[24] Exports of *kilims* (woven rugs) from Egypt, Syria, Tunisia, and Morocco were also fairly substantial, and on the eve of the First World War 11,000 persons in Algeria were employed in making carpets and cloth.[25] In Lebanon the handicrafts textiles of Zouq, Dayr al-Qamar, and other villages began to revive and by the 1880s were supplying markets in "Syria, Europe and even America."[26]

It need hardly be added that in all these and the other surviving crafts wages were squeezed down to—or kept at—very low levels. In Damascus in 1873 the wages of a craftsman averaged "45 to 60 cents per day, according to the nature of his work."[27] In Turkey, a figure of 7 piasters a day (about 32 cents) for weavers was quoted for Rhodes in 1851 and 1854 and 12 piasters (54 cents) in 1858; for Alexandretta, 7 piasters in 1854 and 12 in 1858; for Trabzon 11-16 piasters in 1878; for Istanbul 7-13 piasters in 1896 and 9-18 (40-80 cents) in 1906. In Erzinjan in 1886 owners of looms earned about £20 ($100) a year and apprentices £5 to £10. And in the carpet industry in 1914 the average wage was 5 1/2 piasters, but skilled workers could earn more than 14.[28] In Cairo in 1933 weavers and shoemakers earned 6-8 piasters (30-40 cents), and the figures for 1913 were probably slightly higher.[29] In Rasht, in Iran, shortly before the First World War, men weavers earned around 1 1/2 krans a day (15 cents), women 1 kran, and children half a kran; in silk-reeling factories the wage for men was 1 1/2 to 3 krans and for women 1/2 to 3/4 kran; in Baghdad, in 1870, weavers earned 5 to 10 piasters (23-46 cents) a day, with some making more, shoemakers 3 to 7, and potters 2 1/2 to 7.[30]

Reindustrialization

The deindustrialization of the Middle East—the decline of its handicrafts—was a slow process; so was reindustrialization—the rise of modern factories. An early and vigorous attempt to establish modern industry was made by Muhammad Ali in Egypt in the 1820s. By 1838, investment in industrial establishments amounted to about £12 million, and employment to some 30,000 persons, an impressive figure in a total population of about 4 million. The industries covered a wide range, including cotton, woolen, silk, and linen textiles; dyeing; foundries; sugar refining; glassware; tanning; paper; chemicals; arms and ammunition; shipyards. But Muhammad Ali's factories, largely designed to meet military needs, were kept going only by his enormous energy and constant supervision, and suffered from great inefficiencies, including lack of fuel and metallic raw materials and the total absence of skilled labor, which meant that not only foreign engineers and supervisors but also foreign workmen had to be brought in.[31] Production was generally well below capacity, and spoilage was considerable. Moreover, the factories survived only thanks to the high protection provided by the monopolies (chapter 2). When, therefore, following his defeat in 1841, his army was reduced and he was forced to implement the 1838 Anglo-Turkish Treaty, the industries began to decline rapidly and under his

two successors were either liquidated, sold, or leased to private individuals.[32] It may be added that Muhammad Ali contributed greatly to
the ruin of Egyptian craftsmen by direct competition, by drafting some
into his factories, and by forcing others to return to their villages to
supply the labor so badly needed in cotton growing.

In Turkey, a similar but more limited attempt was made to establish
state factories—textiles, boot making, a sawmill, a copper-sheet rolling
mill, arms, ammunition, a machine shop, and a small shipyard—also
mainly designed to meet military needs. At their peak, they employed
5,000 men, but they too were highly inefficient, and by 1849 most had
been abandoned.[33] Still feebler efforts were made in Iran in 1850-51, in
Tunisia in the 1840s, and in Morocco in the 1880s, all of which ended in
failure.[34]

After that there was a long pause, and in the second half of the century
the region experienced far less industrialization than Latin America or
the Far East.[35] Except for a few sugar refineries set up in the 1860s and 70s
there was practically no industry in Egypt until the turn of the century,
after which a few textile, cement, cigarette, food processing, and other
plants were built by foreign private capital. In 1916, some 30-35,000
persons were employed in modern factories.[36] In Iran the ambitious
schemes of a Belgian company in the 1890s to set up glass and sugar
factories and gas works failed completely, and so did those of various
Iranian capitalists to establish small factories making textiles, matches,
paper, porcelain, and other products; in 1913, less than 2,000 persons
worked in modern factories.[37]

Turkey too, in spite of much more favorable conditions, made very
little headway. In 1863 a Prussian report on Istanbul stated: "only one
branch of industry has, strictly speaking, passed beyond the handicraft
stage: [flour] milling. There are six steam mills. . . ." And in a 1872
British report on the textile industry we read: "There is no progressive
increase of production in these factories in Turkey. The Imperial
household has some few factories for spinning and weaving cotton, silk
and woolen fabrics, and there are a few factories on a limited scale
belonging to private individuals. The amount produced is incon-
siderable." But, after a slow beginning in the 1870s, foreigners and
members of minority groups (Greeks, Armenians, and to a lesser extent
Jews) began to take increasing interest in industrialization, and a textile
and vegetable oils industry began to develop in the cotton-growing areas
of Izmir and Adana. Other industries—food processing, paper, wood,
ceramics, etc.—grew in Istanbul and elsewhere, and mechanized silk
reeling was widespread. After the 1908 Revolution, industry received

much encouragement from the government, including exemption of
machinery from customs duties. However, a partial census in 1913,
which included the two main centers of Istanbul and Izmir, showed only
17,000 workers in factories using power. In Syria there were only some
silk reeling and tobacco factories, and in Iraq, Arabia, and Sudan none at
all; in Palestine, however, there were a few Jewish factories and
workshops.[38]

North Africa made even less progress. In Algeria, on the eve of the First
World War, there were in addition to wineries some modern flour mills,
tobacco factories, and fish canneries. In Tunisia, there were four steam-
powered factories for pressing olive oil as well as numerous smaller
establishments, some flour mills and dough product factories, building
materials industries, and fish canneries. A few modern installations had
been set up in Morocco, including flour mills and canning plants. All
these factories belonged to Europeans.[39]

Mining developed more rapidly than manufacturing and included
coal, lead, copper, boracite, and chromium in Turkey; oil and ochre in
Iran; oil, phosphates, and manganese in Egypt; and phosphates, iron,
coal, zinc, and lead in North Africa. Here again almost all the capital
engaged was foreign, as were the managers and technicians.

The basic reasons for this lack of industrial development were those
prevailing in most of the world outside Europe and North America:
neither markets nor input supplies were attractive, and therefore it was
more profitable to supply manufactured goods from outside than to
make them in the country concerned. Moreover, demand was shifting
from local to foreign products. The governments were either un-
interested or unable to help.

As regards markets, population was rather small, Turkey having some
15 million inhabitants in 1914, Egypt 12 million, Iran about 10 million,
and the other countries much less. Per capita incomes were low and were
kept down by failure to raise agricultural productivity—those of Egypt
and Turkey being about $50 and most of the others distinctly less.
Incomes were also distributed unequally, which meant that the mass
of the population had little purchasing power. And the markets
had almost no protection against foreign competition. Moreover, it
should again be stressed that, in sharp contrast to the Japanese, who
took over Western production methods while retaining their traditional
consumption pattern, the Middle Eastern upper and middle classes
rushed to adopt European ways of dress and build European-style
houses, while failing to learn European methods of production. This
shift affected primarily the handicrafts, which gradually lost their

markets for old-style shoes, headgear, clothing, window screens, etc.[40] But the fashion for things European also meant that foreign factory goods would always be preferred to indigenous ones, whose quality often left much to be desired. All the early industrializers complained bitterly of this fact.

As regards inputs, there was a shortage of cheap fuel. Only in Turkey was much coal produced, and only in Damascus was there hydroelectricity until the late 1920s. The oil industry started on the eve of the First World War; until the Second World War the region continued to import most of its oil products. Aside from cotton, raw materials were also scarce. Few minerals were extracted, wood was expensive, and agricultural produce was neither adequate in quality, e.g., wool and hides, nor dependable in quantity and grade, e.g., fruits and vegetables. Except in the coastal zones and in Egypt, which had both Nile navigation and excellent railways, transport was slow and expensive. In Iran a British Indian commercial mission reported in 1905: "The cost of transporting machinery is prohibitive and at present no heavy machinery could be got up [to Tehran] at all." Matters were not much better in Turkey until railways started to penetrate the interior, at the turn of the century (see chapter 3).

In Egypt labor was cheap and docile; just before the First World War an unskilled worker earned 5–7 piasters a day (25–35 cents), a mason 17–18, and an engine driver 17–20. But in Iran, according to the same mission, labor, "while fairly cheap (though dearer than Indian) is inefficient and undisciplined to a degree hard to conceive." In both countries skilled workers were scarce and were often foreign, usually Italians or Greeks. In Turkey, thanks to the presence of the minority groups, skills were somewhat more abundant, but wages were also distinctly higher; the 1913 industrial census shows that the average wage was about 12 piasters a day (55 cents). And all over the region, foremen, engineers, and managers were nonexistent and had to be imported, at high salaries, from abroad; most of the latter either did not desire or failed to transmit their skills to local assistants.[41]

Local capital was scarce and, not unreasonably, afraid to get tied up in large, long-term ventures; alternative outlets such as trade, money-lending, or agriculture were safer and not less remunerative. The only available estimate is for Egypt, where, in 1904–13, investment in industry averaged 14 percent of gross fixed capital formation and 2 percent of gross domestic product. One can state with confidence that these figures represented a peak for Egypt and were well above the corresponding ones for other countries.[42] As for foreign capital, with few exceptions it flowed to such fields as government loans, railways, utilities, or mining, rather than manufacturing (chapter 4). Industrial credit was scarce, since the banks concentrated on trade and mortgages.

Finally, a large share of the blame rests with the governments, which were corrupt, inefficient, and often obstructive. They were dominated by bureaucrats, soldiers, and occasionally landlords for whom fiscal preoccupations came far ahead of considerations of development (chapter 9). They were also massively ignorant of economics, and, insofar as they had an economic policy, it was one of *laissez-faire* which had no room for the protection and fostering of industry. In this they were encouraged by foreign well-wishers, as well as interested parties, who told the Middle Easterners that they were fit only for agriculture. In 1873, the distinguished Orientalist Armin Vambery stated that the spirit of application and hard work which had made possible Europe's factories "never have been nor ever will be conceivable amongst Muslims of Asia." A few years earlier, the Iranophile Jakob Polak had given several good reasons, including labor shortage, transport difficulties, and the corruption and inefficiency inherent in state enterprise, why "a factory industry suddenly imported to Persia could not thrive." In Egypt, Lord Cromer's opinion was that "it would be detrimental to both English and Egyptian interests to afford any encouragement to the growth of a protected cotton industry in Egypt," and he backed it by imposing an 8 percent excise duty on local cotton goods, to offset the 8 percent import duty.[43] Moreover, there was the feeling in government circles that industrial development would be carried out mainly by, and for the benefit of, foreigners or members of minority groups, which considerably diminished its attraction. The subjects, for their part, reciprocated with well-founded distrust. The voices calling for industrialization were few and far between—Talat Harb in Egypt, Muhammad Jamalzadeh in Iran, and a few influential Young Turks.[44]

But even if they had wanted to, the governments could not have given much help. The commercial treaties they had concluded with the Powers prevented them from either raising or differentiating customs duties—it was only after several decades of negotiations that the Turks were able to modify their tariff slightly in 1907. The capitulations forbade them to impose direct taxes on foreigners, and their fiscal difficulties made it impossible to provide subsidies or extend any kind of financial aid, let alone carry out large-scale industrial investment. And the great influence of the Powers was often used to block development projects that could have benefited industry, e.g., railways in the Ottoman Empire and Iran. It is significant that the only Middle Eastern government that was in a position to help industry before the First World War, the Young Turk government, made sustained efforts to do so.[45]

It remains to mention the main landmarks in the industrialization of the Middle East. The First World War, by cutting off supplies, made people realize their complete dependence on the outside world for manufactured goods. The achievement of some measure of political independence after the war, the heightening of nationalism, and dawning awareness of the importance of economic matters led to systematic private and public efforts to promote industry. Campaigns were launched to persuade the public to buy indigenous rather than foreign goods, and the governments gave preference to native products in their purchases, granted industrialists rebates on state railways, and reduced some of the taxes paid by them. In Egypt, Bank Misr, the first bank financed and managed by Egyptians, was founded in 1920, and it soon established a large cotton textile plant and other industrial enterprises. In 1922 the Federation of Industries was founded; by 1925 its 90 members (less than a quarter of whom were Egyptian) had an estimated capital of over £E 30 million and employed about 150,000 workers.[46] In Turkey, the private Ish Bank was founded in 1924 and the state Bank for Industry and Mining in 1925 to manage the few state enterprises and extend credit to private industry. In 1927 the Law for the Encouragement of Industry was passed, granting various substantial benefits to enterprises that met specified criteria; in that year firms with some 27,000 employees were covered by it.[47] In Iran industry benefited from tax exemptions, rebates, and preference in government purchases, and there was some response on the part of the private sector.

But it was only in the 1930s that industrialization began to move fast. The abolition of the capitulations in Turkey and in the mandates in 1923, Iran in 1928, and Egypt in 1937; the latitude allowed to the mandatory authorities, which enabled Iraq, Palestine, Lebanon, and Syria to grant some exemptions and protection to industry as early as 1927–28; and the lapse of the commercial treaties in 1928–32—all this gave the Middle Eastern governments full tariff and fiscal autonomy. The concurrent fall in the prices of raw material exports, with the consequent deterioration of terms of trade and difficulties with balance of payments, convinced them of the need to develop alternative sources of income and foreign exchange. High tariff protection was granted, as well as other benefits such as rebates, tax exemptions, and preference.[48] Efforts were made to provide industrial credit, hitherto almost completely lacking, by setting up such banks as Sümer and Eti in Turkey, the

Agricultural and Industrial Bank of Iraq in 1936, and the Industrial and Agricultural Bank of Iran in 1937. In Egypt, the government advanced funds through Bank Misr, and in Palestine the Industrial and Financial Corporation of Palestine, a private Jewish organization, also supplied industrial credit. Attempts were made, usually with little success, to provide technical education and develop industrial skills. More important was the substantial improvement in infrastructure—and general education—which provided significant external economies.

Under this protection, much import substitution took place, and manufacturing advanced at a far faster rate than ever before. In Egypt, this was achieved mainly by the Misr and 'Abbud groups, which received government encouragement; most of these enterprises entered into some form of partnership with foreign capital.[49] In Palestine, Jewish immigrants with funds and skills established a wide range of industries, and in Iraq, Lebanon, and Syria a few modern factories were founded.[50] In Iran, there was more industrialization, both in the private sector and on the part of the state, which established and operated several factories, and mines.[51] In Turkey, state intervention—influenced by the examples of the Soviet Union and Germany—went further: the Sümer Bank was founded in 1933 for the promotion and management of industry, and the Eti Bank in 1935 for mining. In 1934 Turkey launched an industrial Five Year Plan, the first of its kind in the region, and followed it in 1938 with a more ambitious Second Five Year Plan. The first plan invested some $100 million, but the war prevented the implementation of much of the second.[52]

By 1939, there was a wide range of light industries (food processing, textiles, building materials, and simple chemicals) in Egypt, Turkey, Iran, Palestine, Iraq, and Lebanon and the beginnings of heavy industry (coal, iron, steel) in Turkey. Petroleum was also making a significant contribution in Iran and Iraq (chapter 10).

North Africa also witnessed some industrialization in the interwar period—in 1918 there were 25,000 workers in industry in Algeria and 70,000 in 1939—though without benefit or tariff protection; the most that could be done for local industry was the granting of rebates on railways, tax exemptions, and small subsidies in Morocco, but in Morocco the government played a major part in mining.[53] Three groups of industries developed: cement and building materials; food processing, including flour milling, wine, beer, olive oil, fish and vegetable canning, tobacco, and dough products; and chemicals, usually connected with phosphates, e.g., acids, superphosphates, fertilizers, and also soap and matches. Interestingly, there were no factories for textiles until 1939, when a small one was opened in Algeria. Nor, except in Morocco, were there glassware factories or sugar refineries.[54]

It is difficult to estimate the amount of industrial growth. In Turkey the net value of manufacturing production at constant prices almost doubled between 1929 and 1938, i.e., it grew at a compound rate of about 7.5 percent a year, and mining advanced at a roughly equal pace.[55] In Egypt, which started at a slightly higher level, the rate of growth was almost certainly smaller. In Palestine, the value added (in current prices) by Jewish industry and handicrafts tripled between 1929 and 1936, but the rate of growth slowed down in the next two or three years.[56] In Iran, between 1926 and 1940, about 150 factories with 10 or more workers, employing some 35,000 persons and with a paid up capital of about 2.5 billion rials (about $125 million) were established; total investment in industry up to 1941 has been put at $260 million.[57]

Nevertheless, industry continued to play a minor role in the economy. In 1939 employment in manufacturing and mining was everywhere well under 10 percent, and in most parts of the region was nearer to 5. Industry's contribution to Net Domestic Product was put at 8 percent in Egypt, 12 in Turkey, and 20 in the Jewish sector of Palestine.[58] Industry was still heavily dependent on imports of machinery, spare parts, raw materials, and technicians. There were no industrial exports of any significance. And even in such a relatively advanced country as Egypt, local production met only a small part of demand in many important branches.[59]

But this industrial nucleus served the Middle East well during the Second World War. The Allied blockade of Europe and the shortage of shipping reduced imports drastically, while the enormous Allied troop expenditure (which at its peak equaled 25–30 percent of national income in Egypt, Palestine, and Lebanon—see chapter 2) greatly increased the demand for manufactured goods. In the Middle East over 300,000 persons were employed by the military authorities, including 90,000 skilled and 20,000 semiskilled workers. Help was also provided by the Anglo-American Middle East Supply Centre, established in 1941 and designed to reduce the strain on Allied shipping. It greatly assisted Middle Eastern industry by supplying spares, materials, and technical assistance.[60] As a result, by 1946 industrial output in the Middle East had risen by some 50 percent, and it more than doubled again in 1946–53.[61] In North Africa, however, the rate of industrial expansion was much smaller until the 1950s. Since then growth has been rapid, and in the last fifteen years or so output in the region has risen faster than in almost any other part of the world. A recent study, based on the figures in the United

Nations *Yearbook of National Income Statistics*, puts the annual rate of growth in manufacturing in the Middle East, excluding North Africa, at 13.5 percent in 1950–59 and 10.6 in 1960–73; these figures compare with 6.9 and 7.5 percent, respectively, for "All Developing Market Economies"[62] and are also higher than the rates for either developed market economies or socialist economies. In North Africa the rate of growth was distinctly lower. Table 8.1 shows that in the period 1970–76 rapid expansion was maintained in the whole region, but since 1978 Iran has experienced a sharp decline.

At present, in the more advanced countries, industry (including mining and power but excluding petroleum) contributes 20 to 25 percent of GNP and employs 10 to 15 percent of the labor force (see appendix tables A.2 and A.3). Nevertheless, it should be noted that in 1976 the region's total value added in manufacturing (in 1970 dollars) amounted to only some $15 billion; this compared with $9 billion for India but was just about equal to Spain ($15.7 billion), lower than Brazil ($19.1 billion), and less than half the figure for Italy ($35.6 billion). The region's industrial output represents about 1.5 percent of the world total (a figure slightly below its share of world population); only in a few branches, notably textiles and petrochemicals, is the figures significantly higher. In mining—excluding petroleum—the region's contribution is far smaller; only in chromium and phosphates is its share significant (table 8.2).

This upsurge reflects the high priority assigned by governments to industrial development, for the reasons given earlier: because industry is regarded as the most dynamic sector of the economy, the one which embodies the most up-to-date technology and the one in which the most rapid rates of growth can be attained; because rapidly growing urban populations need to be absorbed; because of the mistaken belief that industrialization reduces import dependence; and for a variety of good and bad military, political, and social considerations. As Sir Oliver Franks put it some years ago: "nowadays part of the definition of nationhood is industrial development." In several countries manufacturing, mining, and electric power have received 40 percent or more of total investment. Thus in the late 1970s, the share of manufacturing, mining, and energy (including oil) in total investment was about: Algeria 45 percent, Morocco 20, Egypt 42, Syria 46, Iraq 42, Turkey 23, and Iran over 30.[63] In addition, a substantial proportion of investment in infrastructure is often related to industry. It may be added that this development has been partly achieved at the cost of agriculture, with unfortunate consequences which are only beginning to be understood.

Table 8.1
Structure of Manufacturing Industry, 1976

	Gross output per capita (1970 dollars)		Value added (millions of 1970 dollars)		Distribution of value added, 1976 (percent)				
	1970	1976	1970	1976	Food	Textiles & Clothing	Machinery & Equipment	Chemicals	Other
Algeria	..	..	735	1,117	29	18	11	6	36
Libya	88	142[a]	..	..	..	..	..	..	..
Morocco	..	..	599	879	41	14	6	7	32
Tunisia	90	163	115	234	65	10	..	22	3
Egypt	146	..	1,326	1,882	17	34	11	13	25
Sudan	51	..	252	368	41	36	3	11	9
Iran	140	..	1,501	3,720	14	34	34	5	13
Iraq	77	144	325	652	37	23	..	2	38
Israel	833	..	1,101	..	11	17	26	7	39
Lebanon	..	..	202	..	..	..	..	..	..
Kuwait	199	..	106	486	..	..	..	..	..
Saudi Arabia	..	..	372	458	..	..	..	..	..
Syria	117	..	238	3,294	50	33	..	3	14
Turkey	106	217	1,930	..	55	23	..	..	22
North Yemen	..	..	12	23	..	..	..	..	..
Kenya	55	116	174	357	18	13	19	8	42
India	51	62	7,093	8,973	15	29	13	12	31
Brazil	229	..	9,972	19,147	15	10	30	12	33
Italy	1,251	1,578	29,059	35,586	13	14	27	11	30

[a] 1975
Source: World Bank 1980.

Table 8.2
Share of World Mining and Manufacturing Production, 1977
(millions of metric tons)

Mining	World	Middle East	Percent of world	Main producers
Hard coal	2,529	6	0.2	Turkey, Iran
Lignite	903	9	1.0	Turkey
Iron ore	483	4.7	1.0	Algeria, Turkey, Egypt
Antimony ore	69	3.7	5.0	Turkey, Morocco
Chromium	4.2	0.4	10	Turkey
Phosphate Rock	116	24	21	Morocco, Tunisia, Jordan
Potash	27	0.6	2.2	Israel
Manufacturing				
Refined sugar	57	3.4	6.0	Turkey, Iran, Egypt
Cotton yarn	10.4	0.5	5.2	Egypt, Turkey, Iran
Cotton fabrics (million square meters)	52,656	2,640	5.0	Egypt, Iran, Syria
Cement	784	40	5.1	Turkey, Iran, Egypt
Crude steel	658	(2.5)	0.4	Turkey, Egypt, Algeria
Nitrogenous fertilizers	48	1.1	2.2	Kuwait, Turkey, Egypt
Sulphuric acid	118	1.5	1.3	Turkey, Morocco, Iran
Caustic soda	29	0.1	0.4	Egypt, Israel, Turkey
Paper and newsprint	59	0.4	0.6	Turkey, Israel, Egypt

Source: United Nations, *Yearbook of Industrial Statistics, 1977.*

As regards the sectoral distribution of industry, table 8.1 shows that, except in Israel, food processing and textiles and clothing account for a half or more of output. The region shares this characteristic of early industrialization with most developing countries. It reflects the fact that these industries—together with building materials—cater to basic human needs, require little capital per worker and relatively simple skills, and lend themselves easily to import substitution through protection. But by now import substitution in these and a few other branches has reached its limits, and in several countries local industry is capable of meeting present and immediately foreseeable local demand, which is leading to a change in the industrial strategy. Some countries have begun to look outward, to regional or foreign markets, for some products like textiles, cement, and assembled consumer durables. In this the Middle East has been much less successful than other Third World regions, such as Latin America and Southeast Asia. On the one hand. attempts at regional economic integration have so far been rather disappointing. Inter-Arab cooperation has resulted in the establishment of joint funds for chaneling capital from the oil-rich countries to the others and in joint enterprises like the Arab Maritime Petroleum Transport Company and the Arab Shipbuilding and Repair Yard Company, but all the countries are still reluctant to give preference to each other's manufactures. Other attempts at regional integration, e.g., in the Maghreb or between Turkey, Iran, and Pakistan, have had even less success. Hence only a small fraction of total Arab exports have gone to other Arab countries—an average of 5 percent in 1965-73[64]—and for the whole region the proportion is distinctly lower. As for international markets, with few exceptions manufactured goods have been competitive in neither price nor quality; perhaps the region's best hopes lie in the Soviet and East European markets, where consumers are not choosey and price considerations are secondary.

In view of all this, and for other reasons such as the desire to strengthen the tenuous backward and forward linkages among their industries,[65] the governments have put increasing emphasis on the production of intermediate and capital goods. The percentages for machinery and equipment and chemicals in table 8.1 are far higher than they were a few years earlier; to them should be added basic metals and metal fabrication. Iron and steel mills have been established in Turkey, Egypt, Iran, Algeria, and on a small scale in other countries, and a wide range of engineering industries—from simple assembly to the manufacture of most or all the components—has evolved. A rapidly growing chemical industry has also developed, based on the region's enormous supply of oil and gas, especially in such countries as Iran, Iraq, Saudi Arabia, Algeria and Kuwait. The region is becoming one of the world's leading centers for the production of fertilizers, plastics, basic petrochemicals, and other products, and its exports will soon be weighing heavily in international markets. These countries and Algeria, Bahrain, Libya, Qatar, and the United Arab Emirates are also setting up energy-intensive industries, such as aluminum and steel, to take advantage of their surplus natural gas.[66]

Two further features may be noted. First, industry is still heavily dependent on outside sources for machines, spare parts, chemicals, raw materials, and, in a few countries, even fuels. Many of the technicians are still foreign. One of many examples may be given: in Algeria in 1969 nationally produced inputs equaled only 39 percent of value added, a slight improvement over the 1966 figure of 35 percent. As in so many other regions, industrialization has not, so far, reduced import dependence.

Another characteristic of Middle Eastern industry is its heavy concentration in one or two cities—the capital and main seaport. This started early, when industry was established by foreigners or members of minority groups who lived there and when those cities alone offered a modicum of transport facilities, power, water, skills, and repair shops. Moreover, they constituted by far the largest markets, since landowners as well as merchants, professional people, government officials, and other relatively affluent groups lived in them. A further attraction, which has grown with increasing intervention in industry, has been proximity to the government, so useful for obtaining licenses, contracts, and foreign exchange. In 1967, 67 percent of Egyptian industrial workers (and 59 percent of value added) were in Cairo and Alexandria. In the early 1960s, 70 percent of Iraq's factory employment was in Baghdad; in Tunisia 60 percent was in Tunis; and half of the Algerian establishments with 20 or more workers, and 47 percent of employment, were in Algiers. There was a similar concentration in Tehran. As early as the 1930s the Turkish government deliberately established new industries in the provinces, mainly for political and social reasons—though private industry tended to settle in Istanbul, Ankara, and Izmir—and more recently other countries have made efforts to create new industrial poles outside the capital: Isfahan, Shiraz, Tabriz, and Arak in Iran; Suez and Aswan in Egypt; Annaba in Algeria; Basra, Mosul, and Kirkuk in Iraq.

A close look at industry reveals serious economic shortcomings. First, the capital-intensive factories favored in recent years all over the region have provided relatively few jobs and done little to absorb the heavy unemployment prevalent in all but the smaller oil countries. Hardly any effort has been made to evolve more labor-intensive methods or to improve and modernize the surviving handicrafts and cottage industries that could have provided work for many more people. For a long time capital investment per worker was low, but recently it has risen sharply, especially in the oil-producing states which have invested in large and up-to-date plants. In the 1950s, the figure for Egypt, Turkey, and Iran was around $1,000, for Lebanon $2,500, and for Israel $5,000, compared with $12,500 for the United States. By the 1960s investment per worker in Egypt was about $2,000, and for establishments of 10 or more persons $3,500. In Iraq in 1964 government industries averaged $8,000, private industries (large and small) $1,700, and those employing less than 10 persons $300. In the 1970s investment per worker in new industries in such countries as Algeria, Libya, Iraq, Iran, Kuwait, and Saudi Arabia has been well above $10,000, and sometimes even $20,000. Yet at the same time, the factories are grossly overstaffed, several persons doing work

which, in Europe or the United States, would have been done by one
man or woman using similar equipment; this is particularly noticeable
in state enterprises, where for political reasons firms are forced to take on
several times as many workers as they need, but it is not uncommon in
the private sector.

A few examples from the 1950s may be given: In Egypt: "in many
factories . . . 6–8 workers were employed to produce what one, with
comparable machinery and equipment, would turn out in the U.S." In
Turkey, a United Nations expert stated that a cotton mill he had visited,
with 150 managerial staff and 3,000 workmen, could have done with 50
and 800–1,000 respectively. In Iran a group of consultants judged that in
both government and private textile mills 20 to 50 percent more persons
were employed than was needed for efficient operations. Of course the
fact that labor is—or was—cheap encourages its overuse. And some
countries are deliberately using factories as a means of relieving
unemployment. For example, in Egypt in 1961 the work week was cut
from 48 to 42 hours and enterprises were urged to hire more workers. As a
result the cement industry's labor force rose from 3,600 employees in
1961 to 5,900 in 1966 and the value added per worker fell from £E 907 to
£E 546.[67]

Hence output per man is low, and although wages are far lower than
in more advanced countries (in the 1960s they were about 15–25 cents an
hour, except in Israel and the oil industry, compared to 10–15 cents in
India, $1.00 in Western Europe, and $3.00 in the United States), unit
labor costs are often high. Thus a 1961 study showed that although
Sudanese unskilled workers earned 70 cents *a day* and skilled workers
$1.50–3.00, and German workers 75 cents *an hour* (plus social security
and other costs) the output of German riveters was so much greater that
unit labor costs in the Sudan were 40 percent higher. In 1960 an
American consulting firm found that in cement, textile, and metal-
working plants in Morocco output was only one-third that in comparable European factories, and, in spite of low wages, labor costs were up
to 50 percent higher.[68]

This low output is reflected in various measures of physical productivity, e.g., production of cement or sugar per worker, or number of
spindles or looms tended by each worker.[69] Another, more comprehensive, measure is value added per employee. Around 1972, the figure for
Egypt was $1,400 per annum, for Iran and Jordan $2,500, for Iraq $2,600,
and for Tunisia $3,100. For Turkey it was $6,500, but this was largely the
result of an artificially high exchange rate. For Israel it was $7,200 and
for Kuwait $19,500, a figure that reflects the newness and very high

capital intensity of the Kuwaiti petrochemical industry. Comparable figures were: India $900, Colombia $5,000, Italy $10,400, and the United States $21.500.[70]

A second serious shortcoming of Middle Eastern industry is the small size of local markets, which often prevents the installation of large plants. This is especially true of such industries as steel mills, motorcar plants, and others where economies of scale are important. This too raises unit costs, sometimes considerably.[71] In addition, many plants operate far below capacity, sometimes by 30–40 percent or more.[72] This is sometimes a result of bad planning (e.g., building too large a plant or locating it where it does not get an adequate supply of raw materials, or only materials of unsuitable quality); sometimes of faulty management (and in the Middle East, as in most parts of the world, there is a tremendous shortage of competent managers) and the inability to organize a smooth flow of production; and sometimes of external causes such as power failures or shortages of raw materials or spare parts due to lack of foreign exchange. These too raise unit costs. The steel mill built for the Turkish government at Karabuk by a German firm in 1939 exemplifies many of these difficulties. Coal has to be carried to it 100 kilometers and iron ore more than 1,000, and its products have to be sent back 100 kilometers to the coast. Moreover, the plant was unbalanced: its two blast furnaces had an annual capacity of 350,000 tons of pig iron, but its steel furnace only 150,000 tons, and its rolling mill 60,000; it took about ten years and much expenditure to rectify this mistake.[73]

More generally, the region's industry has been grossly overprotected and therefore tends to enjoy a monopoly position in the domestic market, a condition almost guaranteed to remove any incentive for efficiency. The effect tends to be cumulative, since the high-cost products of one industry—e.g., sugar, steel, chemicals—are often the inputs of another, which therefore starts with a handicap. To make matters worse, industry is either largely in the hands of the state, as in Iran before the Revolution, Turkey, Tunisia, Morocco, Saudi Arabia, Sudan, and Kuwait, or almost wholly so, as in Egypt, Algeria, Libya, Syria, Iraq, and South Yemen. It is difficult to imagine a more cumbersome and inefficient instrument of industrial management than Middle Eastern bureaucracy. The decline in efficiency in Egypt's industries following their nationalization and the somewhat better performance of the private than the public sector in Turkey are illustrative.

But even if all the factories operated efficiently, Middle Eastern industry would still be subject to four major constraints. First, the region is not particularly well endowed with raw materials, a handicap that can be borne but is still a burden. Second, the labor force, although far better in every way than when industrialization started some fifty years ago—and much less plagued by the absenteeism and rapid turnover characteristic of the early stages of industrialization[74]—is still suffering from poor health, inadequate nutrition, overcrowded housing, and lack of the education and training required of industrial workers. Third, industry has not yet developed or diversified itself sufficiently to enjoy the full benefits of cumulative growth, including linkages, learning processes, and external economies. Finally, industry suffers from the backwardness of other sectors of the economy—transport, power, agriculture, etc.—which often supply it with insufficient or deficient inputs, raising its cost and lowering the quality of its products.

All this is certainly true. It is also true that many industries are ill advised, and far from increasing national product have "negative value added," i.e., the value of their output is smaller than the value of the resources which they use and which could have made an important contribution elsewhere—good examples are the airplane, motorcar, and steel industries in almost all countries.[75] Corrective action is urgently needed. But, when all reservations have been made, there seems little doubt either that the reindustrialization of the region is well under way or that, in the long run, when it begins to enjoy the cumulative economies of scale, complementarity, and experience, the region will greatly benefit from the process.

CHAPTER IX

Institutions and Policy, Money and Prices, Savings and Investment

Institutions and Policy

Perhaps the most important single fact shaping Middle Eastern society was that, in the early Middle Ages, the Byzantine and Sasanian states did not break down—in contrast to the Western Roman Empire—and that the Arabs soon succeeded in setting up a strong and fairly centralized government. Thus whereas in Western Europe the ground was cleared for the growth of numerous and vigorous independent centers of power and activity—Church, city states, feudal principalities, universities, guilds, and other associations—in the Middle East the continued power of the state stifled such developments. The social and political consequences were numerous and momentous. The main economic consequence was that the state and its bureaucracy made it almost impossible for groups of producers to enjoy sufficient autonomy to set up institutions that could further their interests and expand their economic base, thereby enlarging the productive capacity of the economy. Thus in European towns the merchants and craftsmen were able to form independent guilds and city states that pursued industrial and commercial policies favorable to themselves; even in some national monarchies, notably England and France, their needs were taken into account. But in the Middle East, as indeed in most parts of the world, there were no city states and municipal autonomy was limited; guilds may or may not have existed before the Ottoman period, but they too were controlled by the government.[1]

In the European countryside first the monasteries played a pioneering role in improving methods and later progressive landlords found it worth their while to introduce new and better techniques. Neither of these two groups had a counterpart in the Middle East. The closest approximations to monasteries were the religious brotherhoods, which were urban; and landowners, with few exceptions, either held their estates through a government grant or resided in cities (chapter 7)—very few felt they had enough security of tenure and interest in their locality to wish to invest and improve. The state apparatus remained in the hands of soldiers and bureaucrats (with some assistance from the ulama), whose main concerns were fiscal and provisioning: to raise enough taxes to meet their salaries and other expenses such as war, regardless of the effect on production, and to ensure that the cities were adequately provided with foodstuffs, again irrespective of the broader economic consequences (chapter 2). In Cook's words: "The interests which rulers represented were those of a ruling segment to which merchants did not belong. Equally, the only group outside this ruling segment which exercised any systematic constraint on the economic policies of governments was not the merchants but, curiously enough, the poor in the great cities. Most governments preferred to expend some of their resources on seeing that the populations of their capital cities were fed, rather than face the threat of riot from a hungry mob."[2] In 1805, speaking of Europe, David MacPherson stated: "No judicious commercial regulations could be drawn up by ecclesiastical or military men (the only classes who possessed any authority or influence) who despised trade and consequently could know nothing of it." His remarks apply much more strongly to the Middle East.

The power of the state also helps to explain another feature of Middle Eastern and North African society: the precariousness of property. From the early caliphate on, the history of the region is replete with accounts of the confiscation of the property of merchants, officials, and others; similarly, with few exceptions, landed estates did not remain in the same family for many generations. No student of European history can doubt the importance of security of property in the rise of capitalism, and its absence goes a long way to explain the lack of a parallel development in the Middle East. Perhaps the most striking contrast is between the Hansa and their contemporaries and counterparts, the Karimi merchants.[3] The latter operated over a far larger and richer area—centered on the Red Sea and Indian Ocean but stretching from China to North Africa—and, considering the high price of the spices and other articles in which they traded, may have had a turnover equal to or larger than that of the Hansa. Yet their weakness as against the Muslim states is apparent, and they vanished leaving no records and only scattered references in contemporary histories. As many observers have noted, the strength and permanence of property are closely connected, as both cause and effect, with those of family structure. In Schumpeter's words: "The bourgeoisie worked primarily in order to invest, and it was not so much a standard of consumption as a standard of accumulation that the bourgeoisie struggled for and tried to defend against governments that took the short-run view."[4] Now whether because of the general fluidity of society, the ease and frequency of divorce, polygamy accompanied by absence of discrimination between children of wives and those of slaves, the retention of property rights by women after marriage, the inability of the father to change inheritance laws and disinherit his children, or for other reasons, Muslim families—with some exceptions in the more "feudal" or tribal regions such as Lebanon, Kurdistan, and Anatolia, with its Derebeys, and some families of ulama or merchants in the cities—do not show the durability and continuity of European families or their preoccupation with preserving and increasing the family fortune. This does not negate the fact that, at any given point of time, family feeling and solidarity in the Middle East were very strong indeed.

This phenomenon became even more marked when the ruling class, in Mamluk Egypt, the Ottoman Empire, and Safavi Iran, came to consist primarily of foreign converted slaves, whose children, being freeborn and Muslim, could not succeed them; this development took place at the expense of, and was strongly opposed by, the old Turkish, Turkoman, and other "feudal" families. Hence although one does hear of some dynasties of Karimi, Cairene, Fasi, Tunisian, and other merchants, they were few in number and of short duration.[5] And one cannot help surmising that this factor further weakened the incentive to accumulate and invest, as did the fact that any wealthy and successful person had to assume a "host of responsibilities towards relatives and co-religionists."[6]

Middle Eastern institutions generally were weak compared with European. This has often been remarked on as regards politics, administration, and law, but it also holds for economics. In the medieval period Middle Eastern guilds, banks, and shipping convoys were less structured than their European counterparts, and methods of accountancy and insurance less developed. With the passage of time the gap widened greatly.[7]

Another striking feature is the lack of mechanical inventiveness. In the Islamic period the Middle East originated, adapted, and diffused many important technological changes, particularly in agriculture and irrigation. But even here it would seem that, after reaching a peak in the 11th or 12th century, agriculture both shrank in area and declined in quality.[8] And in many important fields, notably shipbuilding, the use of inanimate sources of energy, the development of such machines as watermills, windmills, and clocks, and to a lesser extent metallurgy, the region lagged well behind both China and Europe. In this context, it may be noted that, as late as 1860, 60 percent of total horsepower in French industry was provided by watermills (and 8 percent by windmills) and only slightly less in the United States. High rates also prevailed in Britain, Switzerland, and elsewhere. Of course, it should be remembered that, compared to China and Europe, the Middle East was far poorer in such basic resources of the preindustrial era as forests, minerals, navigable rivers, and swift streams. These factors may help to explain the region's loss of seapower and maritime carrying trade, first in the Mediterranean and later in the Indian Ocean, which had adverse effects on its economy.[9]

At this point we may briefly consider the influence of Islam on the economy, which most observers have tended both to exaggerate and to misinterpret. Thus it is stated that Islam is an egalitarian religion, and this is certainly true as regards free Muslim males. Islam had neither the castes of India nor the social estates of Europe, no consecrated priesthood, and with minor exceptions such as the *ashraf* (descendants of the Prophet), no hereditary nobility. It was also a fluid society, with much upward and downward social mobility. But no serious, sustained attempt was made to translate the Brotherhood of Believers into economic terms. Vast inequalities of wealth and income prevailed, were recognized by the religious establishment and other scholars, and were generally regarded as having socially desirable consequences.

Again, Islam lays great stress on the right to property, and indeed assimilates many social relations, such as marriage, to property contracts. Yet, as noted earlier, property has in fact been precarious and subject to confiscation. On the other hand, Muslim laws of inheritance, which excluded primogeniture, strictly prescribed the shares of the various heirs, and allowed for very limited bequest, undoubtedly helped to break up large properties. By doing so they made it more difficult to accumulate large blocks of capital, and thus may have hindered investment. To circumvent inheritance laws, and ensure against confiscation, much property was converted into *waqf* (mortmain), with an ostensibly charitable purpose. But here again the economic effect was usually adverse, since *waqfs* were notoriously mismanaged. And, as noted earlier, divorce, polygamy, and inheritance laws, by weakening the family's economic structure, may also have diminished the urge to accumulate. It should be added that in many rural areas women were by custom deprived of the share of land to which they were entitled under Muslim law.

Islam's strictures against usury have often been held responsible for lack of capital accumulation, investment, and progress. But in fact there has always been a great deal of moneylending in the region, at rates not too different from those prevailing in Europe. Much of this was undertaken by Christians, Jews, and Zoroastrians, but Muslims played their part.[10] And since returns on risk-sharing were not regarded as usurious, a wide variety of legal fictions and devices were used, from early Islamic times, to invest money in commercial and to a lesser extent industrial partnerships. This undoubtedly facilitated the large expansion of trade that took place in the Islamic period.[11] In certain other important respects Islam was favorable to economic activity. First, trade was regarded much more highly than in many other civilizations, including early medieval Europe;[12] it has been said that Islam is the only major religion to have been founded by a successful businessman, and the Prophet's example was often cited. Second, the political unification of the vast area formerly separated by the hostile borders between Rome and Iran, and Iran and northern India, greatly facilitated economic intercourse. This advantage was retained even after political unity broke down, since the region kept a common legal system, a shared culture, and an Arabic *lingua franca*. The essentially urban character of Islam also probably encouraged industry and trade, just as, by incorporating and spreading beduin attitudes, Islam may have discouraged agriculture.[13]

Finally, Islam has often been blamed for the intellectual rigidity of the Middle East, and for its stagnation over several centuries. The argument in this form is untenable, since the region demonstrated great receptivity, adaptability, and creativity during the first four centuries of Islam. But all religions based on holy books tend to be conservative, and Islam's astounding early military successes made it even more so; therefore it may well have reinforced the dangerous complacency and lack of interest in Europe or other civilizations that the region showed in the late Middle Ages and early modern period.[14] And Islam, like other religious and secular ideologies of the majority, justified and supported existing governments and the status quo, and therefore may have helped to stifle the emergence of other creative intellectual, social, political, and economic forces.

As regards economic policy one has to be tentative, but it seems that a marked deterioration occurred in the 11–14th centuries, when the primarily civilian authorities were replaced by military regimes. Goitein agrees with Claude Cahen that during the High Middle Ages the Egyptian government "had neither the wish, nor the machinery, to impose strict control over a burgeoning economy"; this also seems to have been true of Abbasid Iraq.[15] After that, however, at the time when the region was suffering from the Crusades, Mongol invasions, beduin infiltration, epidemics, including the Black Death, loss of sea trade in the Mediterranean, and other shocks, government policy became more restrictive. In Ashtor's words: "In the age of the Seldjukids and the Ayyubids the princes curtailed freedom of enterprise, established monopolies and imposed taxes on the workshops"; and conditions deteriorated under the Mongols and Mamluks.[16] The debasement of the currency in Egypt and the Mongols' issue of paper money made the situation still worse.

Matters improved somewhat in the early Ottoman period, when the state's responsibilities to its subjects seem to have been taken more seriously. The prevalent view, taken over from ancient Middle Eastern thought, was that society consisted of four classes, Men of the Pen, Men of the Sword, Men of Negotiations, and Men of Husbandry, the wealth produced by the last two supporting the intellectuals, bureaucrats, and soldiers. Farmers benefited from the greater security imposed by the government, from its much stricter control over the "feudal" landlords (chapter 7), and from a reduction in taxation. Trade was helped by the upkeep of a few strategic roads, the building of caravanserais, the protection of some sea lanes, and low customs duties and by the granting of capitulatory privileges to European merchants.[17] But at their best the Ottomans—and Safavis—fell far behind contemporary Europeans in their interest in and grasp of economic questions. This is brought out, on the one hand, by the low level of economic thought,[18] and on the other by the continued and accelerated debasement of the currency—a process that started in the Ottoman Empire in the 15th century, well before the influx of bullion from America, and in Iran not much later—by the lack of serious attempts to develop the country's productive powers, and by the absence of mercantilist policies. By the late 17th and 18th centuries order had broken down in large areas. Peasants were being oppressed by their landlords, who at least in the Balkans had become more profit conscious and were increasingly producing for export to Europe.[19] The tax burden was heavier and monopolies were multiplying, causing an indignant Englishman in the mid-19th century to complain that "everything was made a monopoly, from the Governor-Generalship of Syria and Mesopotamia to the privilege of selling a handful of salt."

The provisioning of the towns still received a large amount of attention,[20] but nothing was done for either urban or rural producers. And, if the governments had been inclined to use tariffs for protection, they would have been thwarted by the European Powers, which by then were in a position to insist on their capitulatory rights to payment of very low import duties and access to the large Middle Eastern markets.

Many of these attitudes, tendencies, and policies have survived to the present: the power of the army and bureaucracy, the suspicion and stifling overregulation of producers, the pursuit of fiscal objectives at the cost of economic, the insecurity of private property, the subsidization of urban consumers at the expense of farmers, and so on. But the prevailing institutions were profoundly transformed in the course of the 19th and 20th centuries by two powerful forces: the foreign hold over the economy and attempt to reshape it so as to serve the broader European objectives and the efforts of Middle Eastern governments to reform their structures in order to preserve their independence and modernize their societies.

The chief foreign concern, after the provision of physical security, was immunity against the Middle Eastern governments. This was furnished by the capitulations, which exempted foreigners from taxation other than specified customs duties and stipulated that they should be tried in their own consular courts, not the local ones. This secured them against arbitrary action and subjected them to low taxation, thus giving them— and the few members of the minority groups who enjoyed foreign protection—a great advantage over Middle Eastern nationals, who were entirely at the mercy of their governments and bureaucracies.[21] Of course, where there was direct foreign rule, as in Algeria, Aden, and Sudan, such arrangements were not necessary.

The second concern was freedom of trade, which was secured by the treaties of 1838–56 and strictly enforced by the foreign consuls (chapter 2). Third, a rudimentary internal transport system was required, and this was either directly provided by foreigners, who ran the river boats and built the ports, railways, and roads, or was supplied by the local governments at their behest, as with Egyptian railways and the Suez Canal (chapter 3).

Foreigners also laid down the commercial and financial network required to move imports and exports to and from the region. Their trading houses advanced the necessary funds to farmers, often using minority groups as intermediaries, and where necessary set up processing plants for ginning cotton, reeling silk, crushing oilseeds, and so on. In the second half of the 19th century, several joint-stock commercial banks—most of them branches of leading French or British banks— started operating in the region.[22] They supplied adequate short-term credit, at reasonable rates, to meet the needs of foreign and large-scale internal trade. But their advances to agriculture—mainly to large or medium-sized owners—consisted entirely of seasonal loans, secured by crops. The very small amount of credit they supplied to industry was also on a short-term basis. The other needs of trade and finance were met by setting up stock exchanges in Egypt and Turkey, cotton exchanges in Egypt, and insurance companies. The last were entirely foreign, and almost all agents and operators on the stock exchanges were foreigners or members of minority groups. In North Africa foreigners took over much of the agricultural land, but in the rest of the region this did not occur. However, the change in the land laws of the 1850s (chapter 7) made it possible to seize land for debt, and facilitated a large flow of foreign credit into agriculture. In most places this was provided by individuals, but in Egypt, Algeria, and Tunisia foreign mortgage banks advanced large sums. Foreigners also set up the public utilities—water, gas, electricity, streetcars—in the main cities, exploited the mineral resources, and built almost all the few large factories that were operating by 1914.

Two more foreign concerns must be noted. First, the unstable currency greatly impeded their business, and they used all their influence to make the governments stabilize it. This was achieved in North Africa, Egypt, and Sudan, but in the Ottoman Empire and Iran the situation remained unsatisfactory until the First World War (see below). Second, means had to be taken to make the governments pay the large debts they had contracted; this was achieved, in the 1870s and 80s, by the establishment of international bodies in the Ottoman Empire, Egypt, and Tunisia charged with servicing the debt, to which certain important revenues were assigned (chapter 4). In Egypt the Caisse de la Dette played a passive and often obstructive role, owing to Anglo-French rivalry, but in Turkey the Public Debt Administration took an active part in developing certain branches of agriculture (chapter 7).

Until the First World War, or even after, the Middle Eastern governments had far less influence on economic institutions and policies than did the foreigners. For one thing, the fact that the most dynamic and accessible sector of the economy was in foreign hands, and protected by the capitulations and commercial treaties, severely limited the scope of the governments. For another, with the important exception of Muhammad Ali, they had neither the desire, the knowledge, nor the machinery to enforce an active policy, as was done, for example, by Japan. The numerous wars in which they were engaged absorbed much of the investible surplus of both government and society. Moreover, the fact that the economically most active part of their population consisted of unassimilable minorities, who would presumably be the main beneficiaries of development, must have further reduced their inclination. Faced with increasing European encroachment, their main concern was to modernize their armies and bureaucracies and establish control over all their territories; with the help of better rifles, telegraphs, and foreign experts they slowly succeeded, providing in the process a large degree of security, which was an indispensable precondition of development.

For all this they needed more revenue, but that was difficult to obtain because of the low elasticity of the tax system. As with all preindustrial governments, their main sources were taxes on farm produce, excise taxes, and customs duties. The last-named could not be raised (chapter 2), but the expansion of foreign trade increased total receipts severalfold and raised their share to between a fifth and a quarter of total revenue. Many excise taxes were abolished, but the total collected grew because of greater consumption of sugar, tobacco, spirits, and other such items. Taxes paid by farmers kept pace with the increase in output, but central government receipts rose more than proportionally, partly because tax-farming was replaced by direct collection (in Egypt from 1813; in Turkey on and off), partly because the share of the central government grew at the expense of that of the provinces. However, the share of tithes (taxes on farm produce) in total revenue fell from one-half or two-thirds to about one-third. In addition, some light taxes were imposed on urban incomes, like the Ottoman *temettu*, a 3 percent tax on profits introduced in 1860 and raised to 5 percent in 1886, when it was extended to salaries and wages. A few figures are illustrative: Egypt's total revenues rose from £E 1.2 million in 1798 to £E 1.5 million in 1818, £E 3.1 million in 1836, £E 5.1 million in 1861, £E 9.6 million in 1881, and £E 17.7 million in 1913. In spite of the shrinkage of territory, Ottoman central revenues rose from £T 3 million in 1830 to £T 6 million in 1840, £T 15 million in 1863, £T 24.5 million in 1907, and £T 29.2 million in 1913. Iran's central revenues rose much less, from 2.5 million tomans (about £ 1,250,000) in 1836 to 4.9 million (£ 2 million) in 1867 and 10–11 million (£ 4 million) in 1913. In Tunisia government revenues ranged between 6 and 12 million piasters (4 to 8 million francs) in 1800–30, stood at 5 to 10 million in 1841–45, and were about 15 to 20 million (10 to 12.5 million francs) in the early 1870s. Under the Protectorate they rose from 19 million francs in 1884 to 43 million in 1907.[23]

Taxes were a heavy burden. In Egypt, just before the First World War, they equaled about 15 percent of national income and in Turkey about 10, but in Iran a much smaller fraction. Still more serious was their unequal incidence: they bore more heavily on farmers than on the urban population and more on the poor than on the rich.[24]

As for government expenditure, almost all was absorbed by four items: debt servicing (chapter 4), defense, administration, and civil list. In Egypt, in 1882–1901, health and education between them accounted for only 1.5 percent of total expenditure. In Turkey the proportion was still lower, and in Iran the amount spent for such purposes was negligible.[25] In Algeria greater sums were allocated to social services, but the beneficiaries were overwhelmingly the Europeans. In the decade preceding the First World War, however, these figures rose sharply and the amount spent on public works also increased considerably. This shows the increased interest of the Turks and Egyptians in economic and social development, an interest that in Turkey may be traced back to the 1870s and 80s, when industry was granted tax exemptions and efforts were made to provide agricultural credit. By then both countries had tiny nuclei of technocrats—in irrigation and railways in Egypt and in civil engineering and agriculture in Turkey.[26] And the Young Turks made sustained attempts to develop some branches of the economy, particularly transport and industry, using tariff protection, exemption from taxes, and other measures, and increasing the capital of the Agricultural Bank, which had been founded in 1888. They also took various steps to stimulate the development of an indigenous bourgeoisie and, where possible, used political pressure to help it at the expense of foreign interests.[27]

The shortages experienced during the First World War, growing nationalism, and a much greater degree of independence impelled the governments to increase their economic action and enabled them to do so, while the world depression of the 1930s made such action more urgent. Political pressure was used to transfer economic power from foreigners and minorities to Muslims (chapters 1 and 5). The lapse of the commercial treaties around 1930 was followed by active use of the tariff for revenue and protection and bilateral agreements (chapter 2). Railways were extended, particularly in Iran and Turkey (chapter 3), and large irrigation works were built in Egypt, Iraq, and Sudan (chapter 7). After the abolition of the capitulations, new taxes, including income taxes and death duties, were introduced, tapping more abundant sources of revenue. Central banks were established in Turkey and Iran, and the powers of the National Bank of Egypt were extended. In Turkey, Egypt, Iran, and Iraq, government-owned or sponsored agricultural banks began to meet some of the farmers' credit needs, and a small amount of long- and medium-term credit was also made available to industry. Private banks set up by the national bourgeoisie, notably Bank Misr in Egypt and Ish Bank in Turkey, received active encouragement and assistance, and nationally owned insurance companies were also helped. Industry, whether owned by national or foreign capital, was aided by protection, preference in purchases, rebates on railways, and other measures, and in Iran and Turkey the state itself established several industries (chapter 8). The rise in the educational level enabled the governments to improve their bureaucracies, which played a much more active role than before in education, health, labor laws, and some other social fields, as well as in agriculture, industry, transport, and trade.

During the Second World War inflation necessitated the imposition of price controls, rationing, and the allocation of basic foodstuffs and materials, all of which increased the power of the governments and expanded the bureaucracies. Exchange controls were also imposed, at the insistence of the Allied authorities; this enabled the Middle Eastern governments, after the war, to cut their links with sterling and the franc and to manage their currencies. And some attempts were made to increase and coordinate the region's production through the Anglo-American Middle Eastern Supply Centre,[28] further expanding government intervention in the economy. So did the sequestration of Axis property in Egypt and elsewhere and the Turkish Varlik Vergisi (capital levy) tax of 1942, which bore heavily on minorities. The civil services grew accordingly: for example, in Iran from 60,000 in the prewar period to 130,000 in 1950, 260,000 in 1961, and over 500,000 in the 1970s; in Egypt from 240,000 in 1940 to 310,000 in 1947, nearly 770,000 in 1960, and 1,035,000 in 1967; and in Lebanon from 6,600 in 1943 to 16,000 in 1958. In 1947 it was estimated that one-third of Egyptian holders of primary certificates or higher degrees worked for the government, and in 1958 some 90 percent of Iraqi physicians were in government employ.

The armies expanded even more. In the turmoil caused by inflation, shortages, the struggles against external forces (independence movements against the British and French, the Arab-Israeli conflict, the oil nationalization crisis in Iran, etc.) and the rising tide of nationalism and radicalism they overthrew both the monarchies (in Egypt, Iraq, Yemen, and Libya—while those of Tunisia and, more, recently Iran, were also abolished) and the post-independence civilian governments (Syria, Turkey, Algeria, and Sudan). The army regimes became increasingly radical, especially in Egypt, Iraq, Syria, Algeria, Libya, South Yemen, and Sudan. Usually they first carried out land reforms (chapter 7) that broke the power of the only class that could oppose them, the landlords, and then introduced wholesale socialization, occasionally supplemented by sequestration, which transferred the banks, insurance companies, shipping lines, airlines, public utilities, firms engaged in foreign trade, the leading hotels, department stores, and practically all large or medium industry to government ownership. Thus, except for construction, residential buildings, small-scale trade, tourism, workshops, and handicrafts, practically all urban activities are run by the government. Agricultural land everywhere is still privately held, but here too the government exercises a large measure of control through irrigation, credit, cooperatives, and the pricing of crops.

Three other factors have contributed to enlarge the public sector. In the oil-producing countries the huge increase in revenues has forced even such conservative governments as those of Saudi Arabia or Kuwait not only to encourage the private sector by generous loans but to engage in a wide variety of economic activities, including industry. And the large-scale foreign aid received by almost all the governments of the region has, naturally, increased their scope and activity. Thus, ironically, among the main agents of socialization in the region must be counted the oil companies and the Western governments.

The third factor is huge, and rapidly rising, military expenditures. Until the Second World War the only countries that had a large defense budget were Turkey, Iran, and Iraq. Since then, however, and more particularly in the 1970s, military expenditures have greatly expanded: an official United States publication put the total for the Middle East (excluding North Africa) at $6.2 billion in 1969 and $32 billion in 1978. In some countries in the mid-1970s such expenditures represented extraordinarily high percentages of GNP: Israel 38, Egypt 34, Iraq 33, Jordan 31, Saudi Arabia 22, Syria 17, Iran 14, and South Yemen 13 (compared to 5 percent in the United States and less in Western Europe), but these percentages dropped slightly thereafter. In the oil-producing countries this was because of the sharp rise in GNP. In the other countries the high expenditures were made possible by the fact that the greater part was borne by outside donors: the United States, the Soviet Union, and oil-producing Arab countries. In Turkey, Lebanon, and the North African countries, military expenditures remained moderate.[29]

The growth of the public sector may be seen from figures on employment, investment, government expenditure, and taxation. Since half, or more, of the region's population is rural, the public sector's share in *total* employment is low; however, in the mid-60s the figures were 40 percent in Kuwait, about 30 in Saudi Arabia, and 27 in Israel.[30] With agriculture excluded, the share of government civilian employees rises to about half in Egypt (in 1974 there were 1,250,000 persons in the civil service and another 1 million in public-sector enterprises; for 1980 the total seems well over 3 million) and is probably even higher in such countries as Algeria and South Yemen. The addition of the military would raise the figures appreciably.

As regards investment, until the 1950s—with a few exceptions,

Table 9.1

Public and Private Consumption and Investment

Year	Country	Consumption			Investment			
		Government	Private	Total	Government	Private	Total	Share of government (percent)
Oil Countries								
1973	Algeria	4.9	16.8	21.7	..	..	14.2	..
1976	(billions of dinars)	9.8	31.3	41.1	..	..	31.5	(50)
1960	Iran	34	230	264	..	..	58	..
1976	(billions of riyals)	978	1,800	2,778	784	619	1,403	42
1960	Iraq	107	(275)	382	..	..	120	..
1971	(millions of dinars)	309	633	942	..	..	195	(40)
1963	Kuwait	89	192	281	..	..	92	..
1975	(millions of dinars)	519	592	1,111	140	106	246	49
1963	Libya	34	150	184	..	..	75	..
	(millions of dinars)	1,110	1,475	2,585	..	..	1,170	(50)
1970	Oman	14	21	35	..	..	15	..
1976	(millions of rials)	244	132	376	..	..	321	..
1963	Saudi Arabia	1.4	2.8	4.2	..	..	1.2	..
1976	(billions of riyals)	41.1	34.1	75.2	27.4	16.7	51.4[a]	58[a]
Non-Oil Countries								
1960	Egypt	256	996	1,252	..	..	226	..
1976	(millions of pounds)	1,361	3,800	5,161	1,105	239	1,344	(38)

Israel (billions of pounds)	1960	0.8	3.1	3.9	..	..	1.1	..
	1976	41.1	62.9	104.0	..	..	25.7	(40)
Jordan (millions of dinars)	1960	27	89	116	..	..	18	..
	1976	156	326	482	..	..	138	..
Lebanon (millions of pounds)	1965	335	3,111	3,446	..	..	779	..
	1972	571	5,543	6,114	..	..	1,268	..
Morocco (billions of dirhems)	1960	1.2	6.8	8.0			9.0	
	1976	10.2	31.8	42.0			15.3	
Sudan (millions of pounds)	1960	31	307	338	..	..	42	..
	1974	208	1,171	1,379	..	..	214	..
Syria (billions of pounds)	1963	0.6	2.9	3.5	..	..	0.5	..
	1976	5.0	14.3	19.3	..	..	7.8	..
Tunisia (millions of dinars)	1960	56	253	309	..	..	60	..
	1972	156	626	782	137	79	216	29
Turkey (billions of liras)	1960	5.0	(35.0)	40	..	..	7.5	..
	1976	(86)	(446)	(532)	(74)	(63)	(137)	24
North Yemen (millions of rials)	1969	83	2,192		..	..	178	..
	1973	370	3,586		..	..	384	..

[a] Including 7.3 billion in oil sector, regarded as 60 percent government-owned in estimating government share.
Source: United Nations, *Yearbook of National Accounts Statistics, 1978*; unpublished national accounts.

notably Iraq—the share of the private sector was far larger than that of the government, but in the 1960s the proportions were reversed. The public sector came to provide 90 percent or more of total investment in such countries as Egypt and South Yemen and is also very high in the oil countries, now including Iran. Only in Saudi Arabia, the United Arab Emirates, and Kuwait among the major oil producers are private investments significant. Of the other countries, in Jordan, Syria, Oman, Tunisia, and Morocco the private share is large (about one-third to two-fifths). In Turkey and Israel it accounts for about half the total and in Lebanon over half (see table 9.1).

Total government expenditure as a proportion of GNP also shows a sharp rise. In the 1950s in all countries except Israel and the Arabian oil producers, the share was below 20 percent, and in several it was closer to 10. By the mid-60s, however, the figure had everywhere reached 20 percent and in some countries (Egypt, Israel, Kuwait, Libya, Saudi Arabia, and Syria) it was 40 percent or more. More recent figures are shown in table 9.1; they are high compared to either advanced countries, where they usually range from 30 to 40 percent, or less developed countries, where they are much lower.

As regards taxation, in most countries in 1972–76 taxes accounted for 15 to 20 percent of GNP, but the figure was distinctly higher in Israel and the oil-producing states. This ratio is above the average for developing countries, though far below that of advanced ones. Adjustments to take account of various factors affecting tax capacity (such as the foreign trade ratio, the sectoral composition of the economy, and the size of industrial and commercial units) reinforce this conclusion: over half the countries for which calculations were made had high ITC (international tax comparison) indices, and only one-fifth had low ones.[31]

The huge expansion of the public sector has brought with it many problems. In all countries four or five year plans have been drawn up, and over the last two decades the planning process has improved somewhat. But, as in other parts of the world, the government machinery is not equipped to handle the immense sums involved— which in all countries run into many billion dollars and in several into the tens of billions.[32] Again as in other places, with the great expansion of the bureaucracies their quality has deteriorated, the energy provided by the few highly qualified, dedicated men at the top being dissipated by their subordinates. With the growth of government expenditure and intervention, corruption has flourished. And the concentration of economic, social, and cultural activity in the government has further undermined the foundations of democratic self-government, which at their best were weak.[33]

Yet is seems clear that the present system is here to stay, and that the Middle East is unlikely to move in the direction of free enterprise. Capitalism is alien to the region; it did not spring from native soil, worked over by feudalism, as in Europe and Japan, but came as part of Western domination, gave a disproportionately small share of the fruits of progress to Muslims and was never accepted as the natural order of things. The present rule by army and bureaucracy conforms to age-old traditions. It is also an adequate instrument for carrying out the basic objectives desired by the peoples of the region, along with those of most of the Third World. These are, first and foremost, nationalism, the determination to be masters in their own house and to exclude foreigners, or minority groups, from any significant share of power or wealth. Second is socialism, defined as state control over the means of production and the absence of large inequalities of wealth. Third is Islam, the application of some of the basic injunctions of that religion, such as aiding the poor and avoiding ostentation. Only a minority of middle-class intellectuals is troubled by the absence of liberty in the form of individual rights safeguarded by constitutional provisions, since this was not part of the region's heritage and was enjoyed only in the brief period of Western influence. Moreover, much of what passes for liberty in the West, particularly in personal conduct and family life, is profoundly offensive to Middle Easterners and is regarded as a threat to cherished values and institutions. This has been made very clear by recent events in Iran, and will probably receive further confirmation elsewhere. Next to national independence, justice and equality are most desired, and many would agree with the Persian saying, "Equality in injustice is justice."

Money and Prices

In the early modern period, the region's currency consisted mainly of silver coins—the Ottoman *akche*, Iranian *tuman*, Egyptian *para*, Moroccan *dirham*, etc.—supplemented by various Spanish, Italian, French, Indian, Austrian (Maria Theresa thalers), and other coins, also mainly silver. For several centuries the value of the native coins had depreciated, partly because of the influx of bullion from the New World but mainly because of steady debasement; in Turkey this had begun in the middle of the 15th century and in Iran during the 16th century, if not before. Consequently, by the end of the 18th century, the price level was many times as high as it had been 300 years earlier. Nevertheless, both travelers' accounts and the available data for the first half of the 19th century show that prices of foodstuffs and wages were far below those prevailing in Europe.[34]

The integration of the region into the world market in the 19th century had mixed effects on price levels. On the one hand, the price of imports, especially colonial goods such as sugar, textiles, and fuels, went down considerably. And if, as available figures and contemporary accounts indicate, an import surplus generally prevailed (chapter 2), that too must have exerted a downward pressure. But the price of foodstuffs and other export goods shot up toward the levels of the industrial countries. The large growth in population also presumably pushed up prices, and that of urban population was accompanied by a severalfold increase in rents. However, far outweighing all these factors, for a long time, was the continued depreciation of the currency. In the Ottoman Empire the exchange rate, which had fallen from 5–7 *kurush* to the pound sterling in 1740 to 12 in 1800, continued to decline sharply to around 100 by 1840; contributing factors were the debasement of the silver coins and, after 1840, the issue of paper money in the form of treasury bonds (*kaimeh*). In Iran, the *kran* fell from 11 to the pound sterling in 1800 to 50 by the 1890s; until around 1860 the main factor was the reduction in weight and fineness of the coins, and after that the rapid fall in the price of silver relative to gold. Egypt also suffered, to a lesser extent, from currency depreciation in the first two-thirds of the century. As for Morocco, the Spanish doubloon (or dollar) rose from 10 ounces (one *mithqal*) in 1800 to 13 in 1828, 18 in 1848, 50 in 1873, and over 100 in 1881. In the 1880s, in an attempt to stop the decline, a new currency, the *douro hasani*, was issued, but it too depreciated heavily until the eve of the First World War. However, exchange rates eventually stabilized—in the Ottoman Empire and Egypt, except for brief intervals, after around 1850, in Iran after 1890, and in Morocco after 1911. This was no doubt aided largely by the influx of capital into the region (chapter 4) but also by some reform of the currency. Both Egypt, in 1835, and the Ottoman Empire in 1844 adopted the bimetallic standard, but it was disrupted by the fall in the price of silver and overissue of silver, paper, or base-metal money. The Ottoman currency was shifted to the gold standard in 1880 but remained highly unsatisfactory; there were a wide range of internal exchange rates for both native and foreign coins until the First World War. Egypt adopted the gold standard in 1885; since, however, few Egyptian gold pounds were issued, the least undervalued foreign currency, the pound sterling, came to account for practically the whole monetary stock. Iran kept its silver currency, which showed greater stability than before. In North Africa, Algeria adopted the French franc in 1851 and Tunisia in 1891.[35]

Prices rose everywhere. Col. Patrick Campbell reported an "extraordinary augmentation in the price of . . . produce" between 1800 and 1840; between 1800 and 1882, prices at a rough average tripled, doubling again by 1907, the peak of the strongest speculative boom experienced by Egypt. A consumer price index compiled by Hansen shows an increase of about 40 percent between 1902 and 1913. In Turkey, scattered data suggest a tripling of food prices between 1800 and the 1840s; after that, except for the rise in the 1850s during the Crimean War, which was followed by a roughly equal decline, there was little change until the 1890s, when prices started to rise again, about doubling by 1914. Available figures on Syria show a comparable movement. In Iran, between the 1840s and 1870s the price of foodstuffs may have more than doubled; between the late 1870s and 1913, a rough price index for Tehran tripled.[36]

During the first World War overissue of paper money, the disruption of production and transport, the decline in imports, and, in Egypt, heavy expenditure by the Allied armies led to a sharp rise in prices. In Turkey in 1919, the price of consumer goods was about 22 times as high as in 1913. In Egypt the cost-of-living index (1913 = 100) peaked at 237 in 1920, and in Tunisia (for Muslims, 1914 = 100) at 311. Prices also rose in Iran.[37]

After the First World War there were two important developments in the monetary system. First, most countries either used the metropolitan currency (franc in Algeria and Tunisia, peseta in Spanish Morocco, lira in Libya—to which one might, without impropriety, add the Indian rupee in Aden and the sheikhdoms of the Gulf) or were on an exchange standard: sterling in Egypt, Sudan, Palestine, Transjordan, and Iraq, and franc in Morocco, Lebanon, and Syria. Only Iran and Turkey had their own currency, which soon came to consist almost entirely of paper, protected in the 1930s by exchange control, while Saudi Arabia used the silver riyal. Second, banking developed and deposits began appreciably to supplement currency. Thus most of the region was even more closely tied to Europe than before, and its price levels moved with world trends, being fairly stable in the 1920s and falling during the depression. In Iran, however, high government expenditure and investment, and in Palestine, Libya, and Morocco large-scale immigration and influx of funds exerted an upward pressure in the 1930s.

During the Second World War the region experienced strong inflationary pressures. In a large part of North Africa there was much fighting, which disrupted production and transport, and troop expenditures were a strong inflationary force. The Middle East was spared the hostilities, but the presence of large Allied armies,—which spent hundreds of millions of pounds,—raised incomes, increased the money supply, and pushed prices up (chapter 2). In Turkey, which did not have foreign troops, preemptive purchases by the Axis and Allies resulted in a large net export and a corresponding increase in incomes. The effect of this rise was reinforced by the sharp drop in imports. Local production increased somewhat, investment declined greatly, and some measures were taken by the governments to dampen inflation, but the combined result of these factors was small. The cost-of-living index (1939 = 100) rose to a peak, in 1944 or 1945, of 293 in Egypt, 756 in Iran, about 600 in Iraq, 253 in Palestine, 607 in Lebanon, and 350 in Turkey. In Algeria, the index for foodstuffs (1938 = 100) rose to 539 by 1945 and 2,160 in 1949, and in Tunisia to 512 and 2,124.[38]

During the war practically all countries imposed exchange controls; almost everywhere these have been retained. With the achievement of independence and rising nationalism, the links between local currencies and sterling, the franc, or other currencies have been severed. Central banks have been established, with large powers over the commercial banks. In other words, the Middle Eastern governments now have much control over their monetary and banking system, and also over other financial institutions. Care was taken, however, not to increase the money supply unduly, and except in Israel and Turkey prices remained reasonably stable through the 1960s. But in the 1970s the region was engulfed in the worldwide inflation, and some countries have seen a steep increase in prices.[39]

Savings and Investment

Data on savings and investment up to the First World War are almost nonexistent and remain scarce and unreliable until the 1950s. However, a few general observations may be hazarded.

In Egypt, under Muhammad Ali there was a large amount of capital formation in such schemes as the Mahmudiya canal, the port of Alexandria, the Suez road, irrigation works, factories, shipyards, shipping, and residential buildings in Cairo and Alexandria. In the 1820s–30s gross investment may conceivably have been as high as 10 percent of GNP, and since there was practically no inflow of foreign capital, the domestic savings rate was equally high. There was also much investment in the 1860s, in the Suez Canal, railways, ports, irrigation, housing, cotton gins, and sugar refineries (chaper 4), but this was probably covered or more than covered by foreign capital, implying no significant rise in the savings rate.

The period of the late 1870s and 1880s was one of liquidation and retrenchment. Around 1890, however, both government investment in irrigation and transport and foreign investment in banks, public utilities, mining, and industry rose shaply. There was also much investment, both foreign and domestic, in urban real estate. In constant (1960) prices, annual net fixed capital formation in agriculture rose from an average of £E 1.6 million in 1883–86 to £E 2.8 million in 1897–1900, and, after a sharp advance to £E 10.2 million in the 1901–7 boom, stood at £E 2.3 million in 1911–14. In industry, the corresponding series averaged £E 5.2 million in 1900–3, rose to £E 8.6 million in 1904–7, and stood at £E 2.7 million in 1910–14.[40] For the period 1903–13, Hansen estimates total net investment at about 7 percent of national income and net domestic savings at about 3.5 percent; a little over half the saving was generated by the governement.[41] Since Egypt already had a relatively large capital stock, in irrigation, transport, and utilities, the gross investment rate may have been as high as 9 percent.

In Algeria after about 1850 and in Tunisia starting in the 1880s, there was a large amount of investment in ports, roads, railways (chapter 3), vineyards, olive groves (chapter 7), residential buildings, and public utilities, and a significant amount in mining and industry; this also applies to Morocco after 1912. However, in all these countries practically all the capital was foreign, and there is no reason to believe that the domestic savings rate rose significantly. The same is broadly true of the Ottoman Empire, which saw considerable investment in railways, roads, ports, and public utilities in Turkey and Syria, in mining and industry in Turkey, in irrigation in Turkey and Iraq, and in urban construction in all the major towns. The bulk of this was covered by foreign capital, but domestic investment in industry, agriculture, shipping, and residential buildings seems to have risen appreciably in the twenty-five years or so preceding the First World War. One can surmise that the domestic savings rate, though small, was significant— perhaps on the order of 3–4 percent of GNP. Iran also saw considerable investment in the same period, in the form of roads, ports, oil and other mining, and urban development. Bharier estimates that gross domestic fixed capital formation amounted to 8–9 percent of GNP, which seems rather high; the bulk of this, however, must have been accounted for by Russian and British capital, and the savings rate was probably quite low.[42]

During the First World War investment fell off sharply everywhere, owing to the shortage of machinery and materials and the inability to make up for depreciation. In some countries—notably Turkey and Iran, but also Egypt and perhaps elsewhere—there was considerable disinvestment.[43] In Egypt, this was accompanied by a steep rise in savings, which took the form of large sterling balances, caused by the rise in incomes due to large expenditures by the British army on the one hand, and the shortage of imported and domestic consumer goods on the other.

The interwar period saw much higher rates of investment. In Libya, Morocco, and Palestine this came along with large immigration, and the rise in investment was due solely to the influx of foreign funds. For Palestine, Nathan, put gross investment at 30 percent of national income. Of this over 80 percent was from Jewish sources (half going to building and over one-third to manufacturing) and the balance from Arab sources and the government sector, giving investment rates of 47 and 12 percent, for Jewish and non-Jewish investment. However, Jewish investment was more than covered by capital inflow, and in the interwar period savings were negative.[44]

In Iran and Iraq, oil revenues provided funds. Iran used most of its oil revenues for purchase of armaments, but through indirect taxes and monopoly profits the government was able to invest some $750 million in 1925–41, of which $260 went to the Trans-Iranian Railway and other transport, and about $130 million to manufacturing. Another $130 million was invested by private individuals in manufacturing, and there was also considerable private investment in residential construction and transport. All this was financed from domestic sources.[45] In Iraq, oil revenues pushed annual gross investment (excluding private buildings) from £800,000 in 1922–30 to £2.1 million in 1931–39; of the latter 55 percent went to transport and 22 percent to agriculture.[46] This represents a savings and investment rate of perhaps 7–8 percent.

Turkey had a low investment rate in the 1920s, but in 1933–39 state investment alone (mainly in industry and railways) averaged 4 1/2 to 5 percent of national income, and the private sector may have contributed an equal amount. Since net foreign capital inflow was small, the savings rate must have risen correspondingly.[47] The same was broadly true of Egypt: in the 1920s investment was not much higher than in the prewar period, but it shot up in the 1930s. Radwan's series show an average of £E 16.6 million in agriculture in 1929–39 and £E8.2 million in industry.[48] Nevertheless, it seems unlikely that either the savings or the investment rate was much above 5 percent.

During the Second World War, Allied army expenditures, inflation, and the shortage of goods led to a great increase in savings, which took the form of foreign exchange reserves (chapter 2). According to Anis, in Egypt the savings rate rose from 5 percent in 1939 to 23 in 1942 and a peak of 29 in 1944, after which it declined to 13 percent in 1950.[49] In Palestine savings equaled 17 percent of national income in 1942 and 14 in 1943.[50] In the other countries, the rise was probably smaller, but nonetheless substantial. Investment, on the other hand, probably declined everywhere, owing to shortages of machinery and materials; indeed, the extra wear and tear on the roads, railways, and industrial machinery and the failure to carry out replacement probably resulted in negative investment rates in some years.[51]

In the postwar period these trends were reversed. Investment rates rose to unprecedentedly high levels, but, except in the oil countries, savings failed to increase proportionately. The gap was filled by foreign resources of various kinds: the drawing down of sterling, franc, and other balances in the immediate postwar years; German reparations and Jewish contributions to Israel; United States and Soviet aid to almost every country in the region and British and French aid to former dependencies; grants and loans from the Arab oil countries to the other Arab states.

In Egypt, gross investment in 1950 amounted to 12 percent of GNP and savings to 11, and in 1954 to 14 and 13.[52] In Iraq, in 1949 gross capital investment amounted to 10–15 percent of GNP, the savings rate being somewhat lower; both figures rose sharply with the increase of oil revenues, the investment rate to about 27 percent in 1956 and the savings rate to over 30.[53] In Israel, in 1950 gross capital formation was 31 percent of GNP; savings amounted to only 5 percent, and the balance was covered by outside aid. In 1954, the figures were 30 and 5 percent, respectively.[54] In Turkey, the gross capital formation rate rose from 9 percent in 1950 to 14 in 1954 and the savings rate from 9 to 11.[55] In Syria, fixed investment formed 7.5–8.5 percent of GNP in 1936–38, 6–7.5 in 1946–47, and rose to 14 percent in 1953–57, of which 11 percentage points came from domestic savings.[56]

In Iran, the spurt of the late 1920s and 30s, when investment may have equaled some 15 percent of GNP and savings nearly as much, was followed by a sharp drop during the war, a recovery in the late 1940s to nearly the prewar level, and, after a disruption during the nationalization crisis, a rapid rise from the mid- 1950s to 1978.[57]

Table 9.2 gives more recent figures covering the period before the great increase in oil revenues in 1974. The countries fall into four groups. First are the small, oil-rich countries, whose savings rate was well over half the GDP; the bulk of these savings was invested abroad. Second are the larger oil countries, whose high investment rates were, more or less,

Table 9.2
Gross Saving and Investment Ratios
(percent of gross domestic product)

	1957 or 1958[a]		1960–62		1966–68		1973	
	I	S	I	S	I	S	I	S
Kuwait	20	45	12	84	18	73	7	72
Libya	19	10	49	12	20	42	30	50
Saudi Arabia	—	—	15	30	16	36	12	68
Algeria	—	—	24	11	18	17	39	31
Iran	17	16	15	15	19	19	20	29
Iraq	23	27	19	18	16	22	11	29
Egypt	14	12	17	13	19	18	12	7
Morocco	—	—	11	10	14	12	15	14
Sudan	9	9	16	13	10	11	11	13
Syria	20	20	17	11	17	17	20	18
Tunisia	—	—	19	8	22	11	23	18
Turkey	13	13	15	11	17	16	20	19
Israel	29	13	26	12	19	5	31	7
Jordan	13	0	17	9	16	4	27	8
Lebanon	16	15	22	15	23	8	22	12

[a]Percent of GNP

Source: United Nations, *World Economic Survey, 1969–1970* (New York 1970), pp. 209–10; World Bank, *World Tables*, 1976.

covered by high savings rates. Third are the large countries that did not have substantial oil revenues and that accounted for the bulk of the region's population; their high investments were generally not matched by corresponding savings, the gap being filled by outside resources. Last are three small countries with very high investment and very low savings rates; in them the bulk of investment was met by outside resources.[58] The investment pattern of the region has been profoundly transformed, but saving habits have changed much less.

CHAPTER X

Petroleum:
Transformation or Explosion?

The literature on both the history of the Middle Eastern petroleum industry and its place in the world economy is voluminous.[1] Hence, this chapter will concentrate mainly on two aspects: the peculiar characteristics of the industry and its impact on the economy of the region. But first a few words are necessary on the framework in which the industry developed.

Concessions, Costs, Production, and Investment

Oil seepages have been known in various parts of the Middle East from remote antiquity, and have been put to a variety of uses—from the caulking of Noah's Ark to the rubbing of camel sores. In at least two spots in Iraq in the 1870s crude oil was extracted and refined by primitive methods.[2] But the modern industry began just before the First World War, and developed in the next four decades, within a framework marked by two outstanding features: British hegemony in the Middle East (and French in North Africa) and control of the world oil market (outside the United States and the Soviet Union) by five American and two British companies, plus one French firm (Esso, Mobil, Standard of California, Gulf, Texaco; Shell and British Petroleum; the Compagnie Française des Pétroles).[3] In all the Middle Eastern countries—and in contrast to, for example, Venezuela, Indonesia, and later Libya—oil concessions were not obtained under a general mining law but were granted by the government, which meant in practice the ruler or the colonial authorities. Only one concession was submitted for discussion

In this chapter I have incorporated a few passages from Issawi 1972 and Issawi and Yeganeh 1962. Throughout, the term "Middle East" refers to the area around the Gulf, in accordance with industry usage.

to a parliament—in Iraq in 1924; it was passed by 37 votes to 24, with 41 absent or abstaining. This situation was long accepted, but when resentment began to grow, many Middle Easterners came to believe that the oil concessions had been tainted from the start. The provisions of these concessions lent credence to this suspicion.[4]

First, all were for long durations—generally 60–75 years. Second, they covered huge areas: nearly 1.2 million square kilometers in Iran, i.e., all but the five northern provinces; the whole of Iraq (about 450,000 square kilometers) under three concessions all granted to the same group; over 900,000 square kilometers in Saudi Arabia; the whole country in Bahrain, Kuwait, and Qatar; and the whole of Musqat and Oman except Dhofar province. This contrasts with the relatively small areas conceded in other producing countries and the tiny plots in the United States. Within these areas the companies enjoyed exclusive rights, including eminent domain. Third, they had the right to pursue all operations connected with the industry, i.e., exploration, production, refining, transport, and marketing. Fourth, with the single proviso that they observe "good practices" in production, the companies had a free hand as regards quantity of output and location of wells; they could also sell where and to whom they wished, at prices set by themselves, and keep all the foreign exchange earned. Finally, they were exempt from all taxes or duties, national or local, except as stipulated and were to pay no export duties on petroleum or import duties on capital, intermediate, and other goods brought in from abroad. Many of these provisions were modeled on the railway concessions that had been granted earlier in the region.

In return, the companies had certain obligations. First, they were to undertake exploration and drilling within a stipulated period. They had to pay the specified royalties or taxes to the host government. They were to employ local workers wherever possible and to train them for higher responsibilities. Finally, they were to supply the local markets with petroleum products at world prices or below. Thus the main benefits accruing to the national economies were: the royalties and taxes paid to the governments; the foreign exchange sold to the national monetary authorities for local payments such as wages and supplies; and the employment of nationals. All these will be discussed more fully later.

The industry that grew within this legal framework proved to be extremely productive, low cost, and profitable. This was because of an unusual combination of favorable geological conditions, Muslim law, and the technology and efficiency of one of the world's most dynamic industries.

As regards natural conditions, with the exception of the northern

Iraqi fields, almost all the Middle Eastern oil deposits that are under exploitation are close to the coast, which means economy in pipeline and pumping costs. Most of them are not too far beneath the surface and have not necessitated very deep drilling—generally about 5,000 to 6,000 feet. Above all, the bulk of the oil lies in the world's largest discovered pools. In 1969, it was estimated that of 71 fields in the world outside the Soviet bloc and China with over 1 billion barrels of oil, 38 were in the Middle East and 7 in North Africa. The largest, the Burgan field in Kuwait, was estimated to hold 62 billion barrels, Ghawar in Saudi Arabia 45 billion, Safaniya, also in Saudi Arabia, 25 billion, and Kirkuk and Rumaila in Iraq 15 and 14 billion, respectively. By contrast, the biggest field yet developed in the United States, East Texas, is estimated to have originally contained only 6 billion. Finally, the porousness of the rock formations and the great gas pressure make it possible to extract oil far more cheaply than in most other parts of the world.

Three important consequences follow. First, there has been a great saving in capital costs because of the much smaller number of wells drilled; thus it was calculated that in 1959 gross fixed assets per barrel of daily crude oil capacity amounted to only $290 in the Middle East, compared with $1,340 in Venezuela and $3,190 in the United States. Second, owing in part to the favorable geological conditions mentioned above, output per well was much greater—about 6,500 barrels a day in the Middle East in 1971 compared to under 400 in Venezuela and 19 in the United States. Moreover, almost all the oil produced in the Middle East has come from "free-flowing" wells, i.e, the oil is forced up by gas pressure; by contrast, some nine-tenths of U.S. wells, three-fifths of Venezuelan, and a substantial proportion of Soviet wells require pumping, which naturally adds to cost. Finally, it may be presumed that unitization (see below) will result in the ultimate recovery of a larger proportion of the "oil in place" than in the United States.

The situation in Libya and Algeria is less favorable than that in the Middle East but distinctly better than in other regions. For one thing, the fields are smaller: Sarir, Zelten, and Gialo in Libya have estimated reserves of 8 billion, 2.2 billion, and 2 billion barrels respectively, and Hassi Messoud in Algeria, 2.7 billion. The relatively large number of concessions granted to foreign companies—which has had great financial advantages for the governments—and the desire of some companies to secure maximum possible output may have led to less than optimal operations. At any rate, the number of producing wells is relatively greater and daily output per well—2,800 barrels in Libya and 1,200 in Algeria in 1971—is distinctly lower. About one-third of the oil produced in Libya is pumped, but in Algeria the bulk comes from free-flowing wells.

Under Muslim as under civil law, and in contrast with Anglo-Saxon law, the subsoil and its minerals belong to the state, not to the owner of the land. This meant that, unlike the United States, where millions of wells have been sunk by tens of thousands of operators each of whom tried to extract as much as possible from the small concession area he had obtained from the owner of the land, Middle Eastern oil companies with their vast long-term concessions and their huge financial resources had a long time horizon and were untrammeled by individual property rights or other legal impediments. Unlike American producers, they could "unitize production," i.e., develop a field as a whole, instead of attempting to extract the maximum from the particular plot they owned on its surface. They therefore sank only the number of wells required for optimum operation. An illustration may be given: although they are different in certain respects, Abqaiq field in Saudi Arabia and East Texas are approximately equal in surface area (though Abqaiq has distinctly larger reserves); yet, even after attempts had been made to "unitize" its production in 1952, East Texas had no less than 26,000 producing wells, compared to 62 in Abqaiq.[5]

One more, minor, point may be mentioned: labor costs. Oil is one of the most capital-intensive industries, and labor costs usually account for little more than 5–10 percent of the total. In the Middle East and North Africa local labor (but not expatriate labor) was at first cheap, although wages in the oil industry were well above those in other branches of the economy, but gradually rose to high levels (see below).

The result of all these factors has been extraordinarily low costs of production. Adelman's careful calculations gave the following figures for total costs per barrel (including both developing and operating costs) in the 1960s: Middle East less than 10 cents, Libya 16 cents, Algeria 28, Nigeria 16, Venezuela 46, and United States $1.22.[6] No comparable figure is available for the Soviet Union, but it can safely be said that, in Western equivalent terms, it would not have been below $1.

Since oil is a bulky commodity, freight is a significant component of price on delivery. East of Suez the Middle East had a great advantage over all major producers except for Indonesia, but for the European and American markets its freight was distinctly higher than those of North Africa, Venezuela, and Nigeria. However, this handicap was greatly reduced by the downward trend of freights, owing to greater competition and the vast increase in size which has reduced unit costs of construction and operation. Thus, whereas in 1952 freight from the Gulf to the East

Coast of the United States was $1.25 to $1.30 per barrel, by 1966 it was 25–60 cents.

Since Middle Eastern, and later North African, oil was controlled by the large oil companies which also owned and operated the fields of other major producing areas, such as Venezuela and Indonesia, its price was set by them at a level that made it just competitive with other oils in the main markets—first Western Europe and then the East Coast of the United States.[7] By 1949 posted prices in the Gulf had come down to about $1.80 a barrel and, with minor fluctuations, stayed at that level through the 1960s.[8] This enabled Middle Eastern—and later North African—oil to capture the whole, or the greater part, of the European, Japanese, Indian Ocean, and African markets and to make serious inroads in North and South America as well. The result was a severalfold increase in output, shown in table 10.1. For a long time Iran—and on a much smaller scale Egypt—were the sole producers. They were joined by Bahrain in 1932 and Iraq in 1934, but the output of the latter was limited by the capacity of the pipelines carrying its oil to the Mediterranean and did not expand until the 1950s. The Arabian Peninsula countries started significant production after the Second World War and North Africa in the 1960s. By 1975 the Middle East was accounting for 35.9 percent of world output and North Africa for 5.0 percent, but their share has declined since then.

This enormous expansion would not have been possible without an even larger rise in reserves. In 1976 the Middle East and North Africa held over 60 percent of world "published proved" reserves; the leading countries were Saudi Arabia with 152 billion barrels, Kuwait 72 billion, Iran 65, Iraq 34, United Arab Emirates 32, and Libya 26. The discovery of these reserves, the development of production, the laying of pipelines such as the ones from Iraq and Saudi Arabia to the Mediterranean, and the building of some of the world's largest refineries demanded a huge investment. Table 10.2 shows the evolution of investment. It may be added that the original capital brought into the Middle East was about $500 million and the rest came from reinvestment of profits; and that the replacement value of the installations was distinctly greater than the historical costs shown in the table.

Rent, Royalties, and OPEC

Minimal production costs combined with sales at world prices resulted in a huge surplus, or economic rent, in the Middle Eastern oil

Table 10.1
Production of Petroleum
(millions of barrels)

	1914	1930	1940	1950	1960	1970	1975	1978	1980
Iran	3	46	66	242	391	1,398	1,953	1,913	565
Iraq	—	1	20	51	356	565	826	935	989
Saudi Arabia[a]	—	—	5	200	481	1,387	2,583	3,030	3,634
Kuwait[a]	—	—	—	126	619	1,091	761	778	596
Qatar	—	—	—	12	64	132	160	178	128
United Arab Emirates	—	—	—	—	—	285	607	688	624
Oman	—	—	—	—	—	97	125	115	104
Other Middle East[b]	—	—	7	11	20	114	122	100	103
Total Middle East	3	48	98	642	1,931	5,069	7,137	7,737	6,743
Egypt	1	2	7	16	24	169	84	169	225
Libya	—	—	—	—	—	1,211	540	724	654
Algeria	—	—	—	—	66	376	359	424	344
Total North Africa[c]	1	2	7	17	91	1,756	1,018	1,354	1,262
Total region	4	50	105	659	2,022	6,825	8,155	9,091	8,005
World	408	1,412	2,150	3,803	7,674	16,628	19,485	21,948	22,820
Middle East as percent of world	1	3	5	17	25	30	37	35	30
North Africa as percent of world	—	—	—	—	1	11	5	6	6
Region as percent of world	1	3	5	17	26	41	42	41	35

[a]Including half of production of neutral zone.
[b]Including Bahrain, Israel, Syria, and Turkey.
[c]Including Morocco and Tunisia.
Source: Organization of the Petroleum Exporting Countries, *Annual Statistical Bulletin,* 1978; *Petroleum Economist,* January, July 1981.

Table 10.2
Historical Costs of Investment in the Middle East and North Africa
(millions of dollars)

	1926	1935	1947	1951	1960	1971	1975	1977
Gross fixed assets, Middle East	100	350	900	2,000	4,125	7,450	14,050	25,400
Of which: British[a]	100	300	430	..	1,450	..	..	..
American	—	..	400	..	2,450	..	..	..
French	—	50	70	..	250	..	..	..
Net fixed assets	..	..	525	1,390	2,375	3,685	7,830	17,670
Net fixed and liquid assets	..	..	630	1,670	2,850	4,300	..	..
Share in Iran (percent)	100	(80)	50	33	(25)	..	..	..
Libya		—	—	—	..	..	(2,000)	..
Algeria		—	—	—	..	..	(over 1,000)	..
Free world	..	..	25,000	..	97,000	..	333,625	427,480

[a] Including Anglo-Dutch.
Sources: Issawi and Yeganeh 1962: chap. 2; Chase Manhattan Bank, *Investment Patterns in the World Petroleum Industry* (New York), various issues.

industry. Until the 1950s this was largely absorbed by the companies. Then the governments' share grew rapidly, and after the 1973 OPEC price revolution the rent expanded severalfold and the governments' share increased greatly.

It has been calculated that in 1948 just over 65 percent of gross receipts remained in the hands of the companies for depreciation, reinvestment or distribution to stockholders, the remainder consisting of operating costs and various payments to governments. For 1958 the corresponding figure was 55 percent. These percentages were almost twice as high as in Venezuela and three times as high as in the United States. And in 1948–60, the annual net income derived from Middle Eastern petroleum operations by the companies averaged about 67 percent of their Middle Eastern assets, compared to 21 percent in Venezuela and 11 percent on domestic operations in the United States.[9]

The governments' share consisted of receipts from royalties, taxes, and bonuses. The terms varied slightly among concessions, but one common feature was a fixed royalty of around 4 gold shillings per ton, or say 20–25 cents a barrel. On average Middle Eastern governments received 21 cents a barrel, a figure close to the Venezuelan one of 23 cents.

These arrangements may have been fair enough at a time when demand was growing slowly and prices were fluctuating or sagging, when the prospects of striking oil seemed uncertain, and when huge capital investments had to be made. But the sharp rise in prices, including that of oil, during and after the Second World War reduced both the purchasing power of the fixed royalty and the governments' share of the value of each barrel of oil—in Iran, for example, according to a government estimate, the government's share went from one-eighth before the war to one-sixteenth in 1947.

The growing discontent first came to a head in Venezuela in 1943, when taxes were imposed which eventually gave the government half the net income earned by the industry, thus raising company payments per barrel to 70–80 cents. In the Middle East, a similar arrangement was concluded with Saudi Arabia at the end of 1950; still earlier, in 1948 and 1949, concessions had been granted in the Neutral Zone lying between Saudi Arabia and Kuwait which offered royalties more than twice the current level. In the meantime, negotiations had been initiated in Iran for revision of the existing agreement. The explosiveness of Persian politics together with the rigidity of the company led to the crisis of 1951, when the industry was nationalized and production brought to a standstill. This crisis alerted the other companies, and by the end of 1952 the so-called fifty-fifty arrangement had been extended to all producing countries and was also applied to Iran when the dispute was finally settled in 1954. The result was to raise payments per barrel to 70-80 cents.[10]

The acceptance of the profit-sharing principle introduced a new element into the picture: it made the governments keenly interested in the pricing of oil. Hitherto their revenues had varied solely with volume of output; now revenues depended on price as well, since the sum that was split was the difference between the posted selling price of oil and its cost of production.

Hence, when in 1959 and 1960 the companies, faced with a glut in the world market, slightly reduced the price of oil, Iran, Iraq, Saudi Arabia, and Venezuela reacted by forming the Organization of Petroleum Exporting Countries, on September 14, 1960. Over the next ten years OPEC—acting like a new labor union—consolidated its position, accustomed its members to working together, and by persistent bargaining secured small but cumulatively significant concessions from the companies that raised the governments' take to some 85 cents a barrel in 1969.[11] When, in 1970, Libya started a new chapter in oil history by demanding higher revenues, OPEC was able to take advantage of the situation, and by 1973 the average take per barrel of its members had risen to $2.12, from 95 cents in 1970, and the price of oil had advanced to $3.00 a barrel. The "price revolution" of 1973 raised the posted price of oil in the Gulf to $11.65, and by 1980 it had reached $30.00 or more; of this all but at most $1.00 remained in the hands of the governments (see table 10.3). As an example, by 1980 Aramco was producing Saudi Arabian oil under a service contract, for which it received 21 cents a barrel.[12]

Impact of the Oil Industry
on the Economies

Until quite recently, the impact of the oil industry on the economies of the producing countries was limited in depth and extent, owing to the nature of the industry, the state of the surrounding economy and society, and the relatively small amount of oil revenues. In the last few years revenues have multiplied and the impact has become shattering.[13]

Oil is one of the most capital-intensive and self-contained industries. Hence, although for decades it was the largest private employer in the producing countries, and in most by far the largest, it absorbed only a small proportion of the total labor force—about 1 percent in Iran and Iraq in the late 1950s and 2 percent in Saudi Arabia. In the small

Table 10.3
Direct Payments by Petroleum Companies to Governments
(millions of dollars)

	1913–47	1950	1961	1970	1975	1979
Iran	326	91	301	1,136	19,900	17,300
Iraq	115	19	266	521	7,600	22,200
Kuwait	1	12	464	895	7,900	17,300
Saudi Arabia	43	113	400	1,200	26,700	59,400
Qatar	1	1	53	122	1,700	3,600
United Arab Emirates	—	—	—	(283)	6,500[b]	13,000
Others[a]	14	2	13	(100)	1,180	2,800
Total Middle East	500	238	1,498	4,257	71,480	135,600
Egypt	..	2	..	..	700	2,400
Libya	—	—	3	1,295	5,200	15,200
Algeria	—	—	—	325	3,400	8,800
Total North Africa	..	2	3	1,620	(9,500)	(27,000)
Grand total	500	240	1,500	(5,900)	(81,000)	(162,600)

[a] Bahrain and Oman (beginning 1967).
[b] Includes Dubay and Sharjah.
Sources: Issawi and Yeganeh 1962:129; *Petroleum Economist*; Exxon Background Series, *Middle East Oil* (September 1980).

countries, however, such as Kuwait, Bahrain, Qatar, and the United Arab Emirates, the percentage ranged from 20 to 50 percent. At that time total employment in oil in the producing countries was around 140,000, a figure only slightly larger than that of the Egyptian textile industry. Employment in the countries through which the oil passed in pipelines—Syria, Lebanon, and Jordan—was also quite small. It should be added that, after the initial development was completed, the huge expansion in production was usually achieved with a constant or even declining labor force.

For several decades the industry relied heavily on foreigners for managerial, technical, and clerical staff and even for skilled labor. With time, however, nationals of the respective countries took over more and more of the jobs, and today only a few of the very highest posts are filled by foreigners. The record of the companies in training their workers is mixed, Aramco in Saudi Arabia contrasting favorably with Anglo-Iranian and the Iraq Petroleum Company; in 1959, over 6,000 Saudi Arabs, or half the total employed, were enrolled in training programs organized by Aramco. But all the companies sent scores of young men abroad each year for advanced training. This made it possible in the 1950s, when government pressure increased, to replace many foreign technicians and administrators. Thus, in Iran, the number of foreigners in the industry (80 percent of whom were in the "staff" category) fell from 4,503 in 1950 to 572 in 1959 and continued to decline. In Iraq the percentage of foreign staff workers dropped from over 90 in the early 1950s to 51 in 1960 and was tiny by the late 1970s.

But in one important respect these figures understate the impact. The industry has exerted a large "indirect" effect on the labor markets through those of its employees who have moved on to other jobs. By 1960 some 100,000 Saudis had been employed by Aramco and most had left it for other industrial employment, many establishing their own firms with company encouragement. Similarly, many contractors and merchants supplying the company often branched out into other lines of business. The pattern was similar in the other countries.

Wages in the Middle Eastern oil industry were long far below those in more advanced oil-producing countries, but were above the level prevailing in other Middle Eastern industries—thus the *minimum* daily wage in 1950 was about $1.00 a day, a figure equal to the *average* wage in other industries.[14] But both money and real wages rose rapidly after that: e.g., the average annual income of Saudi workers and employees doubled between 1953 and 1959, reaching $1,888, and rose to over $3,500 by 1971. Similar developments took place in the other countries.

As regards the self-contained nature of the industry, it may be pointed out that it not only supplies its own fuel and generates its electricity but also carries its oil by pipeline and loads it onto tankers by submarine pipelines, forms of transport that cannot be used for any other purpose and that do not create external economies. The location of the oil fields, in inhospitable and largely uninhabited areas, has further insulated the industry from surrounding economies and societies. This was reinforced by the backward state of those economies and societies, which greatly reduced the linkages between them and the industry. This situation forms a sharp contrast to the one in developed countries, where petroleum has tight linkages, forward and backward, with the rest of the economy.[15]

On the input side, the industry had to import not only machinery and complex chemicals, but even construction materials. Thus, in the late 1940s, cement was brought to Abadan from England not only because it was cheaper but because the Iranian factories could only just meet the demands of Tehran and other nearby towns. Similarly, fresh fruits and vegetables were flown into the Gulf from Lebanon, Eritrea, and elsewhere, and most of the consumer goods used by company employees came from abroad. On the output side, the only linkage was long the supply of petroleum products to the local economy. For decades all the gas generated in the process of production was flared, because it could not be used by the local economy even when offered free of charge, owing to the high cost of all the complementary factors of production. It is significant that the first petrochemical industries in the region were set up in Egypt and Israel, neither of which was a large producer but in which industry was sufficiently advanced to absorb the refinery gases at Suez and Haifa. A plan to supply Tehran with natural gas from the oil fields in the late 1940s was abandoned because the market was too small to cover the cost of the pipelines. Concurrently a project for a gas pipeline from the Gulf to Paris was pronounced economical, though it was abandoned for obvious political reasons. In the 1960s, however, first in Iran and then in the other countries, various ways of using the gas were devised, including a pipeline to the Soviet Union, with branches to the main Iranian cities, plants for making fertilizers, plastics, and other materials, and aluminum and steel mills. The Gulf has emerged as one of the world's leading centers of petrochemical industry.[16]

Given these tenuous linkages, the main contribution of the industry was in the form of payments to governments and supplies of foreign exchange. At first these were quite small (table 10.3), but in the 1950s they expanded, and with them the share of oil in the economy. As late as

1948, it was estimated that the value added by the oil industry amounted to 10 percent of GNP in Iran and Iraq, 20 in Saudi Arabia, 70 in Kuwait, and 90 in Qatar. Over the next two decades the rise in revenues appreciably raised the share of oil (appendix table A.3). In addition, around 1958, oil contributed 2–4 percent to the GNP of the transit countries—Syria, Lebanon, Jordan, and Egypt (in the form of Suez Canal dues on tankers).[17]

By other criteria, the contribution of oil was much higher. In 1948 its share in foreign exchange receipts was 65 percent in Iran, 64 in Saudi Arabia, 34 in Iraq, and nearly 100 percent in the sheikhdoms; for the transit countries it was, around 1958, 18 percent in Jordan, 13 in Syria, 12 in Egypt, and 6 in Lebanon. After that these figures rose sharply in the producing countries, among which only Iran and Algeria have any significant exports other than oil.

Oil played a still larger role in public finance. Already in 1937 direct payments by the companies constituted 13 percent of government revenues in Iran and 26 in Iraq. By 1959 the figures had risen to 41 percent in Iran, 61 in Iraq, and 81 in Saudi Arabia, and in the sheikhdoms, and a little later Libya, it was almost 100. Around 1960 the figures for the transit countries were: Syria 25 percent, Jordan 15, and Egypt and Lebanon 10.

Oil has also made a large contribution, direct and indirect, to capital formation. In Iran in 1958 gross fixed investment by the oil companies was around 3 percent of GNP, and government investment (financed by oil revenues) 6 percent; together those two sources amounted to about half of gross investment. In Iraq in 1956–58 company investment was about 3 percent of GNP (compared to 10 percent in 1948–50) and government investment nearly 20 percent; those two sources accounted for the bulk of investment. In Saudi Arabia in 1956–58 company investment was over 10 percent of GNP and government investment about 10 percent; in Kuwait the figures were about the same, to which should be added investment abroad. In these two countries, the sheikhdoms, and later Libya, almost all capital formation came, directly or indirectly, from oil.

Finally, it may be mentioned that Aramco has greatly helped the Saudi government, both by supplying managerial and technical assistance and by building many non-oil projects on government account. Some other companies have performed similar services.

This brings us back to a central feature of the region's oil industry. Since the oil was owned by the state, and used practically no domestic resources except labor, first the bulk of that part of the value added in the industry which was domestically retained and then the greater part of the total value added accrued to the state, as an economic rent paid in the form of royalties and income taxes. This meant that the rentier oil-producing states acquired a vast amount of income, and an abundance of foreign exchange, which had no counterpart in the private sector. Therefore it put an enormous pressure on the governments to indulge in vast, insufficiently studied, and unsuitable development plans. It also gave them a strong bias toward highly capital-intensive technologies, since it could be plausibly, but erroneously, argued that their countries had an abundance of capital and a shortage of labor. It also reinforced the tendency, common to almost all underdeveloped countries, of putting the investible funds in manufacturing, infrastructure, and modern services, to the neglect of agriculture and the traditional handicrafts, which did not lend themselves to rapid transformation. The result has been highly distorted and unbalanced development.

Still more serious have been the moral effects of this sudden acquisition of unearned wealth. Appetites were whetted and expectations raised above the possibility of satisfying them. Corruption increased. And the abundance of money bred the belief that anything could be imported—from electronic defense systems staffed by foreign mercenaries to garbage collectors—and that the lucky inhabitants of these countries did not have to do any work but could live abundantly on handouts from the oil-rich state.

All this was not too harmful as long as oil revenues constituted only a small fraction of national product. But the OPEC price revolution of 1973 led to a drastic change in the situation. As table 10.4 shows, oil revenues in 1974 were almost everywhere greater than the GNP of 1972. In 1974–78 the oil producers received some $500 billion, a staggering sum. Clearly no comparable increment in income has ever occurred, not even in 16th-century Spain, not even in California during the gold rush.

The greater part of these funds streamed back to the developed countries from which they had come.[18] Tens of billions of dollars were spent on armaments, and a still larger amount was invested in the money markets of Western Europe and the United States, both by the monetary agencies and by private individuals. But that still left two flows that had a major impact on the local economies: the huge expansion in imports of goods and services and the enormous increase in money incomes. Between 1973 and 1977 imports of goods into the region increased fourfold, and aggregate imports in those five years exceeded $300 billion; services absorbed another $100 to $150 billion. As for money incomes, the rise in nominal GNPs was unprecedented, except in countries that

Table 10.4.
Impact of Oil Revenues, 1974

	(1) GNP 1972 (million)	(2) GNP 1973 (million)	(3) Oil revenues 1974 (million)	Ratio 3:1	Ratio 3:2	Oil revenues per capita
Algeria	$ 6,120	$ 8,340	$ 3,700	0.60	0.44	$ 250
Egypt	8,340	8,820	700[a]	0.08	0.08	20
Libya	3,820	7,620	6,000	1.57	0.79	2,200
Bahrain	150	210	280[a]	1.87	1.33	1,200
Iran	15,200	27,830	17,500	1.15	0.63	600
Iraq	3,730	8,880	5,700	1.53	0.65	700
Kuwait	3,440	10,610	7,000	2.03	0.66	8,000
Oman	320	610	900[a]	2.81	1.50	1,200
Qatar	330	1,090	1,600	4.85	1.47	10,000
Saudi Arabia	4,160	12,470	22,600	5.43	1.81	3,800
United Arab Emirates	830	3,720	5,500	6.63	1.48	9,900

[a] 1975.
Source: World Bank. *World Atlas, 1974 and 1975; Petroleum Economist,* July 1977; Exxon Background series. *Middle East Oil.*

had experienced galloping inflation. But real GNP also rose sharply—
by 20 or 30 percent a year in the oil-producing countries. Existing
development plans, which already had ambitious goals, were replaced
by far larger ones, and investment rates shot up drastically.[19]

A considerable advance in infrastructure, housing, manufacturing,
and social services was achieved. But agriculture grew only slowly, a fact
that aggravated inflation. Shortages and bottlenecks ensued, since
neither the transport systems nor the construction and other industries
could cope with the huge demands made on them and the supply of
nontradeable goods could not be expanded fast enough to meet demand.
Income inequality also increased sharply. The resulting convulsions
overthrew the government in Iran, and similar tensions are building
elsewhere.

Clearly, oil has been a mixed blessing. Until about 1970 its net effect
was surely positive.[20] It had helped the most backward part of the region
to develop its natural and human resources, generate industrial skills,
build an infrastructure, and lay the basis of a modern industry. The
impact of oil was large enough to move the society without shattering it.
More recently, however, the region has come increasingly to resemble
Midas, and its golden touch threatens to become fatal. A great
opportunity has been presented, but one fraught with even greater
danger.

In the meantime much income generated by oil has flowed to
nonproducing Arab countries. In addition to purchases of goods and
services and various official joint ventures (chapter 2), the remittances of
emigrant workers (chapter 5), and private investments in countries like
Egypt and Lebanon, there are the grants and loans made either
bilaterally or through the various Arab funds. These include the
national Kuwait Fund for Arab Economic Development founded in 1961
and followed in the 1970s by the Abu Dhabi Fund, the Iraqi Fund, the
Saudi Fund and the multilateral funds such as the Arab Fund and the
Islamic Development Bank. In 1973–77 they disbursed some $24.2
billion, over two-thirds of which went to Arab states.[21] Further amounts
were given by Libya and Iran. The impact of these flows has been
considerable.

CHAPTER XI

The Balance Sheets

This chapter deals with two related topics; it discusses the economic costs and benefits to the European powers of their political control of the Middle East, and attempts to assess the evolution of the region itself since 1800.[1] The purpose of this inquiry is limited. It does not seek to evaluate the gain to the "center" of the formation of a world market, nor does it discuss "neocolonialism," but it does deal with such types of "informal imperialism" as foreign influence in the Ottoman Empire and Iran. As far as the metropolitan powers are concerned, it seeks to ascertain their gains and losses, direct and indirect, from *political* control over the greater part of the Middle East, a process that has ended and may now be seen in perspective. For this purpose, as in national accounting, the unit of accounting taken here is the country (Britain, France, etc.) and not the government (as a taxing and spending unit) or the capitalist class. As noted below, this procedure fails to explain the *dynamics* of imperialism, but the analysis is still meaningful. For the region itself a broader approach has been used.

Even so, it is impossible to draw even a rough balance sheet. For one thing, almost no work has been done on the subject, and data on some of the most important items in the balance sheet are lacking. Perhaps more important, the basic concepts of gain and loss that should be used in such an analysis are far from clear, and the imponderable elements are numerous and important. Not only the magnitudes but even the signs of some items have to be constantly revised in the light of current events; for example, an assessment of Iran's experience made in 1970 would be very different from one in 1980. In addition, there were several sets of books, kept by many agents; not only were the balances in these accounts different, but the perceived items probably differed greatly from the real ones. Finally, the flow of costs and benefits over time was far from even; most costs were incurred at the beginning of the occupation whereas the benefits came much later—indeed oil, by far the largest credit item, did not become substantial until 1946.

Direct Economic Gains and Losses to
the Metropolitan Powers

This study is concerned with economics, but some mention must also be made of noneconomic costs and benefits. First, a distinction must be drawn between direct and indirect costs and benefits. For the imperial powers, the most obvious *direct cost* is in lives lost during the conquest of the various parts of the region. In North Africa, the number of French soldiers killed in Algeria in 1830–71 has been put at 100,000 to 200,000, and, according to official figures, in 1954–62 17,500 were killed and 65,000 wounded.[2] The "pacification" of Morocco in 1907–26 cost over 25,000 Spanish and over 10,000 French (and colonial) casualties. Italian losses in Libya were smaller, but quite significant.[3] And it may be assumed that in all these wars Arab casualties were far greater than European. Most Middle Eastern countries were subjugated with much smaller losses in life, European and local. Both Russian and Persian casualties in the campaigns of 1813 and 1828 may have been fairly high, since the two armies were not too unevenly matched, and Russian and Turkish losses in the numerous wars since the 17th century must have run into the hundreds of thousands. But the British conquered Egypt in 1882 and Sudan in 1896–98 with losses of only a few hundred lives, and the occupation of Aden and "pacification" of the Trucial Coast were achieved with virtually no casualties; it may be added that both Egyptian and South and East Arabian casualties were light but Sudanese were heavy.[4] The huge British (and Indian) losses in Iraq and Palestine in 1914–18 may be debited to the general cost of the First World War, and the suppression of the Iraqi revolt of 1920 and Palestinian revolt of 1936 took only a few hundred British but many more Arab lives.[5] The French lost several hundred soldiers during the Syrian revolt of 1925–26, and one may presume that Syrian casualties were much higher.[6]

At this point it may be noted that European losses in the region were high by colonial standards, i.e., compared to those incurred in India, Indonesia, Subsaharan Africa, and earlier Latin America.

The second direct cost was that part of the military and civilian costs of occupation and development borne by the metropolitan treasury. Here again data are lacking, though they may presumably be obtained by careful study of British, French, and other budgets. Even more important is the question of the allocation of indirect military costs. For example, what share of the British navy's budget should be attributed to the defense of the colonies and what share to that of Britain? Conversely, what share of that part of the costs of the Indian Army borne by India should be allocated to the defense of India and what part to the serving of British imperial interests in the Indian Ocean area, including the Middle East?

This having been said, a few indicative figures may be given. The Iraqi revolt of 1920 cost Britain some £40 million (about $150 million).[7] In Morocco, "By the 21st October [1925] the total cost of the Moroccan campaign for the current year had risen to 950,000,000 francs ($50 million), together with 400,000,000 francs' worth of war material borrowed from the home forces,"[8] and the French government continued thereafter to bear the cost of the occupation forces. In 1912, France's cumulative military expenditure in and subsidies to Algeria were put at about 4 billion francs ($800 million), and as late as 1939 "grants and subsidies" ran at 160 million francs ($4 million) out of Algeria's total "ordinary revenues" of 1,917 million. The Algerian War of Independence is estimated to have cost France some $10 to $11 billion.[9] The conquest of Tunisia cost France 100 million francs and budget support 20 million a year for 20 years, a total of 500 million francs ($100 million).[10] As for Syria, by 1938 it was estimated to have resulted in some 14 billion francs (roughly £120 million) "of expenditure from the French Treasury alone on the military services of the mandate." This figure may be too high, but the official estimate was that by 1936 the Mandate had cost France 4.3 billion francs, or say $150-200 million in military expenses and 543 million francs in civil. According to another source, the cost of the Armée du Levant ranged between 160 and 325 million francs per annum (say $6.5 million to $13 million) and "until 1937 an additional annual subsidy of 15 million francs was paid to the Troupes Spéciales."[11] In Libya Italian military expenditure was heavy. In Palestine military expenditure amounted to £2,226,000 in 1922–38 and about £10,500,000 in 1939–46.[12] One may also presume that the cost of the British garrison at Aden was borne by the imperial, or Indian, treasury. The cost of the army of occupation in Tunisia was relatively small and so was that of Egypt. The Sudan's military expenditure was met by Egypt, which in 1899–1940 contributed £17 million.[13]

Before 1945 the imperial powers made far smaller contributions for civilian expenditure, including development. Italy was the major exception; between 1913 and 1942 direct state expenditure on roads, ports, railways, public buildings, and agriculture was $159 million, and indirect state expenditure $71 million; in addition $35 million was granted in loans (chapter 4). Italy also subsidized Libya's administrative budget. Between 1942 and its independence in 1951, Libya received £10 million (about $35 million) in grants in aid from Britain, and after that large amounts of aid from Britain and the United States; in 1956–59 these averaged some £14 million a year, or about one-third of GDP.[14] Until 1939 French North Africa contracted large loans, on commercial terms, in the French market. After 1945 the French government advanced long-term, low-interest loans (25 years at 1.5 percent) and gave small grants for development; in 1947–55 the total for Algeria was 208 billion francs (about $600 million), for Morocco 110 billion ($300 million) and for Tunisia 82 billion ($250 million).[15]

Spain also heavily subsidized its portion of Morocco. In 1920, the territory's own revenues amounted to 5.6 million pesetas and its expenditures to 14.1 million, in 1930 to 22.8 and 62.7 million, respectively, and in 1931–36 averaged 26 and about 60 million. During the Spanish Civil war the gap widened greatly, and in 1941 the figures were 52.2 and 218.7 million and in 1951 193.4 and 318.6 million ($20 and $30 million), respectively.[16] These totals do not include the large amounts spent during the 1925–26 war, or the earlier expeditions of 1859–60 and 1909.

Britain was more parsimonious in its expenditure. As far as can be ascertained, no money was loaned or granted for civilian expenditure in Egypt, Iraq, or Sudan, but Sudan received £2.8 million in budget support from Egypt in 1899–1912. In Aden "during the 89 years that India was responsible for the Protectorate not one single penny was made available for any form of development or for the provision of any form of social service. Since 1928 . . . [Colonial Office] average annual subvention would amount to £90,000,"[17] or say £2 million in all. In Palestine, by 1944 British grants-in-aid for development totaled £192,000.[18]

The *direct benefits* of imperialism are loot, tribute, and indemnities. In 19th-century European empires loot played an insignificant part compared to the one it had in earlier imperialisms—Persian, Macedonian, Roman, Arab, Turkish—or in the previous centuries, e.g., the Spanish in America, the British in India, Nadir Shah's booty of £60–70 million in India, or the French revolutionary armies' pillaging of the art treasures of Italy. Nor, of course, does it compare with the Nazi and Soviet looting of both personal property and machinery in Europe and Manchuria in 1939–45. The only noteworthy exception is the French in Algiers, who in 1830 took an estimated 100 million francs ($20 million), of which 45 million was appropriated from the dey's treasury by the French government and the rest raised by private enterprise.[19]

Egypt paid a tribute to Istanbul from the time of the Ottoman conquest to 1914. It may be noted that the amount, £500,000 per annum, was almost exactly equal to the estimated value of the grain levy sent to

Rome under Augustus.[20] No European power levied tribute in the Middle East.

Indemnities were more substantial, though far smaller (in absolute, not relative terms) than the more than $500 million imposed on China between 1842 and 1901 by the Europeans and Japanese—not to mention the transfer to Germany of 20 percent of France's national income in 1941 and 1942 and 36 percent in 1943.[21] In 1828 the Russians levied on Iran an indemnity of 20 million rubles or 5 million tomans (about $13 million), which was partly offset by a British subsidy; in 1829 they imposed on the Ottoman Empire an indemnity of 200 million kurush ($15 million) and in 1879 one of 802.5 million francs ($160 million).[22] At the other end of the region. Morocco had to pay indemnities of 105 million francs ($20 million) to Spain in 1860 and another 20 million francs in 1894; in 1910 Spain exacted another 65 million francs and France 70 million.[23] Following the 1871 revolt in Algeria, the French imposed an indemnity of 36.5 million francs on Kabylia, in addition to sequestrating vast areas of land, part of which was repurchased for 63 million francs by the original owners.[24]

Making allowances for inaccuracy, the above figures and statements suggest that for every single country the direct economic costs of empire far outweighed the direct economic benefits.

Indirect Gains and Losses

These may accrue from five fields of activity: capital investment, migration, trade, shipping, and finance.

Capital Investment. Here the gain may be measured by:

a. The extent to which political domination or influence made possible certain investments that otherwise would not have taken place and that yielded a "normal" return. Clearly, every European country attempted to reserve certain fields for its own nationals, and some of the railway, mining, and other enterprises—though by no means all, or perhaps most (chapters 3 and 4)—proved profitable. One example may be given: when Nile dam construction projects were implemented in Egypt in 1933, the Egyptian government was not allowed to consider any non-British tenders.[25]

b. The extent to which some investments in the area under political control or influence yielded "supernormal" profits. In the Middle East oil, and perhaps the Suez Canal, spring to mind in this connection. It may be noted that the British government was a shareholder in the canal and Anglo-Iranian (BP) and the French government in Compagnie Française des Pétroles. However, one must ask whether in the prevailing circumstances investment could have come from any other source. For example, in oil in 1920–60 (though not necessarily before or after) there does not seem to have been any alternative to the British and American companies that actually carried out operations.

Foreign investment, however, carries costs as well as benefits. First, there are the huge losses borne by investors in various parts of the world through default or confiscation. In the Middle East hundreds of millions of dollars worth was lost after the First World War and in the 1950s–70s.

Second, there is the opportunity cost of the capital sent abroad. Keynes has argued persuasively that British industry was crippled by the fact that such a large proportion of savings was invested abroad rather than at home, and the same may well apply, to a lesser extent, to the United States today. This thesis has been disputed by Cairncross and others, and the debate is inconclusive. What is worth noting, however, is that the rate of return on British foreign investment was not much higher than at home. A careful study by Edelstein puts "the average annual realized rate of return on overseas equity wealth, 1870–1913, at 8.6% and on home equity wealth 6.61%"; in alternate decades home and overseas investment was the more profitable. For the United States, comparable figures for 1897–1914 are 6.75 and 4.2 percent, respectively.[26] This may be compared with W. A. Lewis' statement: "Neither was foreign investment that profitable—most of it was on fixed interest terms. One could lend to the British government at 3 per cent or to a fairly reputable foreign government at 5 per cent (less reputable ones or doubtful railways at perhaps 8 per cent). Investment in mortgages at home might bring 5 per cent; in commerce and industry perhaps 8 to 10 per cent."[27]

The record of many railways, mines, and public utilities in the region was rather poor. But, thanks mainly to oil, the overall return on capital invested in the region was high, and a marked net gain is shown under this heading.

Migration. As with capital, labor has an opportunity cost, measured by the contribution that emigrants would have made to their own country. The *net* gain of empire is the extent to which the citizens of the metropolitan powers earn, thanks to the political protection they enjoy, incomes (less hardship allowance) higher than those they would have had at home. They may do this as advisers, officials, industrialists, landowners, experts, business employees, farmers, or skilled laborers.

In the Middle East, the numbers involved were small. There were a few thousand British officials and experts in Egypt, Sudan, Iraq, Palestine, and southern Arabia and of French in Syria and Lebanon. A few hundred British and American employees of the oil companies may, questionably, be added to this list. But in North Africa Europeans were much more numerous, though their average incomes were much lower than those of their counterparts in the Middle East: nearly 100,000 Spaniards in Spanish Morocco, over 100,000 Italians in Libya and some 1.7 million "Frenchmen"—most of whom were Italians, Spaniards, and Maltese (chapter 5).[28] Over all, there was surely a net gain under this heading, but its magnitude was not very large.

Trade. Benefits may accrue from both imports and exports.

a. A metropolitan country can make an "imperialist" gain if it buys the products of its colonies or dependencies at prices below those of the world market. No example of this can be found in the region, though there are a few products, e.g., Algerian wine in France, which received a price *higher* than world levels. Of course, in such cases the beneficiaries were the foreign settlers in the dependency.

It may be argued that although the products of the Middle East were sold at world prices they were in some sense "unfairly low," i.e., that the factoral terms of trade of the region were artificially depressed. This may well have been so, but the operative forces are to be sought outside the region. Neither coerced labor nor compulsory deliveries were imposed by the foreign rulers of the Middle East, in contrast to those of Indonesia and parts of Africa; on the contrary, existing systems of *corvée* and deliveries were abolished in Egypt and elsewhere under British influence. Nor were wages depressed by the importation of cheap foreign labor, e.g., from India or China, which had such a marked impact on the tropics.[29] As noted earlier (chapter 6), rapid population growth supplied the necessary labor and prevented wages from rising. The course of the barter terms of trade was discussed in chapter 2.

b. In export trade the gain was much more substantial. By having access to a protected market, a metropolitan power can sell at higher prices than elsewhere. Still more important, it can keep out the goods of competing countries by preventing the dependency from buying better or cheaper products elsewhere. This can be done by tariffs and other legislation, by administrative pressure, or by monopolizing government contracts. It is surely not a coincidence that, before the First World War or even later, such a large share of imports (from 50 to 90 percent) was derived from Britain, France, Russia, or Italy in countries like Egypt, Iraq, Algeria, Tunisia, Iran, and Libya.[30]

There seems little doubt that considerable benefits accrued under this heading. But to judge their magnitude would demand careful analysis, item by item. For example, Britain's exports to the Middle East were high until the 1950s—including exports to countries over which it had no influence, such as Turkey and Syria. But so was its share of world trade—indeed, for many decades it was the sole or main supplier of some of the most important articles traded. One may assume that it protected its markets in its dependencies while other markets were shrinking, but a meaningful analysis would require much disaggregation. In addition, the magnitude of colonial markets can easily be exaggerated. In 1901-13, France's trade with its colonies, including Algeria and Tunisia, increased by 68 percent, while its total trade rose by 84 percent; in 1904-13 colonial trade formed only 12 percent of the total; and the colonies had a trade deficit with the rest of the world, which had to be covered by the French balance of payments. However, during the depression of the 1930s France was able to use its political power to advantage: between 1929 and 1936 French exports to foreign countries dropped by 76 percent but exports to its empire dropped by only 50 percent, and the share of the empire in overall trade rose to about 30 percent. The colonies still had a deficit in their trade with the rest of the world.[31] In 1934, the total trade of all Italy's colonies, including Libya, was 500 million lire (385 million for imports and 114 million for exports), of which 60 percent was with Italy. But, on the one hand, this represented only 2.3 percent of total Italian trade, and on the other, Italy's support for colonial budgets ran at 400 to 500 million lire.[32]

Shipping. There is little to say on this subject. The 1889 law declaring trade between France and Algeria to be "coastal," and therefore reserved for ships carrying the French flag, gave France a monopoly; it had been preceded by periods of restriction, as in 1835, and of opening up, as in 1861. One result was high freight rates: in 1900 freights per ton from Marseilles to Algiers were "50 or even 60 francs, whereas in Antwerp one can find space for the same destination at 20 or even 10 francs."[33] In 1913, shipping a ton of vegetables from Algiers to Marseilles cost 64 francs, i.e., more than the corresponding Melbourne-London freight, and a ton of cereals from Algiers to Rouen 15 francs, compared to 7 from New York to Le Havre.[34] The resulting shipping profits must be credited to French control over Algeria.

There was nothing similar in the other parts of the region. Navigation, including coastal shipping, was open to all flags. Rates to the region followed the downward trend in world freights (chapter 3). The leading British lines formed combines to arrest this decline, but their action is obviously not related to political control over any particular region.

Finance. London was the main banking center for the Middle East and

Paris for North Africa, but this was due more to the fact that they were the world's leading money markets than to political factors. On the other hand, the fact that the British zone (Egypt, Sudan, Iraq, Palestine, South Arabia) was on the sterling exchange standard and the French (North Africa, Syria, and Lebanon) on the franc exchange standard meant that those regions kept large reserves in London and Paris, respectively. This assumed great importance in wartime: Egypt accumulated sterling balances of over £100 million in the First World War and £400 million in the Second, Iraq £70 million in the Second World War and Palestine £116 million.[35] Franc balances were also large. In the postwar period those countries either withdrew from the sterling area or drastically brought down their balances, but this was more than offset by the accumulation of funds from the Gulf oil countries, which have continued to play an important part in the London money market. Here again it is difficult to disentangle the political from the purely economic element: after all, at various times, many countries over which Britain had no control, including South American and Scandinavian states, formed part of the sterling area, and it is surely not political considerations that account for the present large holdings of sterling by various Middle Eastern and other governments and nationals. This having been said, at least part of earnings on such funds and from financial services must be counted among the gains of empire.

One more, quite important indirect gain may be mentioned. Peoples subjected to foreign rule or influence develop a taste for metropolitan goods that usually long outlives the political ties. Thus Persians and Arabs from the Gulf flock to Britain as tourists and students, buy British consumer goods and machinery, place large orders with British construction firms, and hire British military and civilian experts. The same is even truer of the North Africans, who have had a long-lasting love affair with French culture; the Libyans have also developed a taste for things Italian. Such relations may make a significant contribution to the balance of payments and improve the terms of trade. And if the gains under the previous headings be added, the total, for the region as a whole, is substantial and almost certainly outweighs the high direct costs. This differentiates the Middle East from some other cases of "uneconomic imperalism."[36]

Moreover, certain noneconomic gains for the metropolitan powers should be added to the balance sheet. The diplomatic stature of both Britain and France was enhanced by their positions in the region. North Africans made a substantial addition to French military manpower from 1830 to the 1950s. Although neither Britain nor France used Middle

Eastern manpower on any significant scale, their military bases in that region played an important part in the two World Wars. As against that, without his Moroccan base Franco would probably not have been able to establish himself in Spain—presumably an unfortunate development not only for that country but for Europe. More generally, overseas possessions tend to strengthen nationalist and conservative forces, a good or bad thing according to one's opinions. Psychological considerations are also important, and "painting the map red" has yielded much psychic income.* Colonial possessions serve as outlets for the more restless elements of society, to the great comfort of their peaceful neighbors. Finally, such possessions may stimulate certain branches of learning, such as oriental studies, anthropology, and tropical medicine; it is worth noting, however, that in these fields Germany and Austria have done as well, without benefit of empire, as Britain and France. It may well be that such considerations are far more important in assessing both the motive forces and the costs and benefits of imperialism than all the economic factors mentioned above. Taken altogether, the non-economic gains definitely seem to exceed the losses.

Thus for the European powers, in the region as a whole, the balance sheet, including direct and indirect, economic and noneconomic, costs and benefits most probably shows a surplus. But, except for the oil bonanza of 1945–73, the cost-benefit ratio was probably much less favorable than in such areas as India, Indonesia, Zaire, and in earlier centuries Mexico and Peru. However, there are striking differences when the record of the individual Powers is examined.

For Spain a large loss must be recorded. The heavy casualties and occupation costs must surely have outweighed any conceivable benefits accruing to less than 100,000 settlers living modestly in Morocco or the profits on a volume of trade (imports and exports) amounting, in 1933, to $7 million, in 1938 to $24 million, and in 1946 to $54 million, and an investment in companies totaling, in 1940, 229 million pesetas (say $25–30 million).[37]

The same is true of Italy in Libya. The high military casualties and costs and the relatively large investments made by the state must have greatly exceeded the benefits accruing to the 100,000 Italian small farmers or urban workers and employees *plus* profits on a total trade of some $9 million in 1922, $17 million in 1933, $52 million in 1938 (the

---

*In 1971 I saw, plastered in the streets of Lisbon, maps of Europe showing Portugal with its colonies superimposed beside it, in red and stretching all the way to Poland. "This," the caption read, "is the true size of Portugal." But the war in those colonies was the undoing of the government that had put up the posters.

peak), and on private investments of $109 million. Of course, if oil had been discovered during the Italian occupation, the balance sheet would have looked different.

Germany was another heavy economic loser in the Middle East. Its investments in the Ottoman debt, railways, and other enterprises amounted to $250 million, practically all of which was a dead loss. In addition, during the First World War the German government extended aid totaling 5 billion marks, or about $1.2 billion.[38] The gains from trade or other economic activities could not possibly have offset these amounts. Germany did, however, derive a large noneconomic gain from the Turkish alliance, measured in terms of the opportunity cost of the hundreds of thousands of British, Russian, and other Allied troops pinned down in the Caucasus, Dardanelles, Iraq, and Palestine. Turkey's decision to join Germany was motivated mainly by political factors, but the investments may have played a part in the final decision.

Russia's balance sheet on its earliest Middle Eastern colony, Azerbaijan, is, however, strongly positive. The value of the billions of barrels of oil that have flowed from the wells of Baku far exceeds the costs of conquest and occupation. As for the casualties, both the Tsarist and Soviet governments would have readily subscribed to the dictum attributed to Clemenceau: "a drop of oil is worth a drop of blood." The Soviet Union's more recent balance sheet is discussed below.

For France a distinction must be made between the Levant and North Africa. In Syria and Lebanon there was no settlement, and at most a few thousand French officials and businessmen benefited from the Mandate. The combined trade of the two countries was small, averaging $57 million in 1937–38, and French investments were of the order of $50 million. The indirect economic gains must have fallen far short of the direct economic costs.

For North Africa the picture was different. Direct costs, as shown earlier, were high. But there were some 1.7 million settlers and a total investment (including the plowing-back of profits over several generations) that must have exceeded $10 billion. The trade of Algeria, Morocco, and Tunisia averaged some $500 million a year in the interwar period and much more after the Second World War. Such magnitudes suggest large indirect gains, which probably offset the direct costs. It is worth noting, however, that France's largest and most profitable investments were made in regions outside its political control: the Suez Canal in Egypt and the oilfields in Iraq and the Gulf.

For Britain, one can state with confidence that the balance sheet shows a large surplus. For one thing, direct costs were low; this was partly because of luck or good judgment (Britain got the less mountainous and more manageable parts of the region),[39] partly because of frugality (few subsidies were given), and partly because of Britain's skill in swiftly withdrawing from embarrassing situations, as in Iraq in 1920. On the other hand, returns on investments in oil were huge (chapter 10) and on trade not insignificant. The combined imports and exports in Egypt, Iraq, Palestine, and Sudan averaged over $500 million in the interwar period, of which well over a quarter was with Britain; and until 1914 Egypt was the richest economic unit in the region.

Although they have not, so far, exercised direct political control, the position of the Superpowers may also be examined. Neither the United States nor the Soviet Union (except as heir of the Tsarist conquests in Transcaucasia) has exercised direct rule in the region, but both have had military bases. Both have extended vast amounts of aid. Economic grants and credits from the United States to the Middle East in 1945–78 totaled $18,415 million, and military assistance has also been high. In addition, substantial sums have been disbursed by private philanthropy. On the assets side, net U.S. investment in the Middle East (excluding former French North Africa) and Libya at the end of 1966 was officially estimated at $2.2 billion and rose somewhat in subsequent years, the bulk being in oil. Returns on investment in oil rose to well over $500 million a year in the 1950s and approached $1.5 billion by the late 1960s. In addition, U.S. trade with the region has expanded greatly. In 1966 exports were about $2 billion or 5 percent of total U.S. exports, and imports $600 million, or 2 percent of the total. By 1977 figures were $12,850 million, or 10.7 percent, and $21,700 million, or 13.8 percent.

The Soviet record is not so good. The Soviet Union's economic credits to the region in 1954–76 were about $5.5 billion, and military assistance was several times as great. But there are no Soviet investments in the region, and trade (evenly divided between imports and exports) in 1977 was about $1.5 billion, or 4.5 percent of total Soviet trade.[40] Of course, neither the U.S. nor the Soviet account has been finally closed.

One more point may be made. The overall balance sheet does not explain the dynamics of economic expansion, much less imperialism in general. One must ask who pays the cost and to whom the benefits accrue, a question that is closely tied to the social and political structure and institutions of the country concerned. The fact that costs are borne, in a diffused way, by the taxpayers while the benefits go to small organized and articulate groups means that the forces making for expansion are far more effective. An example given by the President of the Puerto Rican Independence Party is suggestive: gross U.S. federal disbursements in Puerto Rico in 1976 amounted to $2,740 million, and net to $1,980 million; but the profits made by U.S. corporations—partly at the expense of American consumers—were $1,610 million.[41]

Costs and Benefits for the Region

It is difficult enough to draw a balance sheet for the Powers, but for the countries of the Middle East it is almost impossible. For the former, the imperial relation was peripheral, but it reached the center of the latter's being. To attempt to assess the costs and benefits to them of this relation would be tantamount to evaluating their historical development during the last 150 to 200 years, a task that should deter the boldest. Nor does it help much to engage in counterfactual history and reconstruct alternative scenarios. Most of those that have been attempted are highly implausible.

The first scenario is of total isolation accompanied by complete immobility. In other words, one could suppose that the region would have remained untouched by European economic, political, and cultural influence and entered the 20th century in the state it had been in during the 18th. This is almost inconceivable, given its weakness and its proximity to Europe. Moreover, isolation and immobility would have been no guarantee of bliss, as the examples of Afghanistan, Yemen, and Tibet show. But the region's prospects would certainly look much brighter if it could face today's problems with its 18th century population size.

Almost as unlikely is a variant, namely that the Middle East would have been left alone to an extent sufficient to allow its indigenous seeds of development to grow into a viable tree. Several authors have discerned such seeds. The Egyptian historian Shayyal states: "Towards the close of the eighteenth century we detect the first signs of a spontaneous cultural revival. It was an internal movement which emerged from within Egypt away from any outside influence whether from the east or from the west."[42] A Soviet scholar discerns the beginnings of capitalist forms in the Egyptian workshops at the end of the 18th century.[43] More recently, it has been argued that "internal forces were pushing the country [Egypt] toward a capitalist transformation long before the advent of the Western entrepreneur," and that intellectual developments reflected and prepared the way for such a change.[44]

It is conceivable that, if the region had been left alone, it would have evolved, slowly and gradually, a pattern of development more suited to its character and needs and more responsive to its factor mix. But in fact the region was subjected to a double pressure—that of European political expansionists, starting with Napoleon, and economic expansionists spearheaded by Britain and that of Middle Eastern modernizers such as Selim III, Muhammad Ali, and their followers or imitators. There was little likelihood of its being left alone.

A third variant is the Japanese model: the region could have modernized its society along lines similar to those of Japan. The only trouble with this suggestion is that in fact there was, in the whole non-Western world, only one Japan. And the more it is studied, the clearer it becomes that, except for technology, Japan had become a "modernized" society at an early date. One can mention such aspects as rigid population control, resulting in low growth from around 1700 to 1860; a high degree of urbanization; the publication of books in editions of 10,000 in the 18th century; a keen interest in Western science leading to the acceptance, around 1800, of the Copernican theory and the circulation of the blood; a male literacy rate of about 50 percent by 1850; a constant urge to increase output, exemplified by the steady rise in rice yields and by the printing of a book on improved farm methods, in an edition of 3,000, at the end of the 18th century; a low-cost transport system based on coastal navigation; an active trading class; and a relatively developed monetary and banking system, with extensive use of paper money and credit. Add to this Japan's remoteness, which gave it much protection from European aggression, its ethnic and cultural homogeneity, and the unrivaled discipline of its people, and one can easily see why its success has not been repeated elsewhere—except, very recently, in the East Asian fringe subject to its influence.[45]

A fourth unlikely possibility is what might be called "benevolent and enlightened tutelage." This scenario presupposes, in effect, that the metropolitan powers, equipped with the kind of knowledge that was not available until much later and guided solely by the interests of the governed peoples, would have led the region along the optimum path of economic and social development. Such knowledge and such disinterestedness have not been encountered in history.

Before we attempt to assess gains and losses, a closer look at the pattern of development in 1800–1939 is necessary. For this it is helpful to divide the region into three parts: the Mediterranean Middle East, the Indian Ocean Middle East, and North Africa. In the Mediterranean Middle East, population grew at a rate well above the world average of about 0.6 percent per annum and much higher than that of Asia and Africa. Foreign trade expanded rapidly; except in Egypt, its rate of increase was somewhat below the world average, but the per capita foreign trade figure in 1913 was well above those of Asia (specifically, Japan and India) and Africa, and the ratio of foreign trade to GNP was distinctly higher than in those regions. Foreign debt was exceptionally large, and little of it was put to productive use. Transport development was roughly in line with world trends, except in Egypt, where it was far above. Industrial development was negligible, compared not only to Europe, North America, Russia, and Japan but also to Latin America and India, and, except in Egypt, there was little improvement of agricultural methods. Finally, social development in the area had a peculiar and most unfortunate characteristic: the agents of economic change were either foreigners or members of minorities, and, partly as a consequence, it was possible to exploit the region's natural resources without correspondingly developing its human resources. Hence, in education and cultural activity this area lagged far behind countries that were much poorer and far less economically developed, such as Burma, Ceylon, and the Philippines—not to mention the Balkans.[46]

By contrast, the Indian Ocean Middle East (Iran, Iraq, Arabia, and Sudan) showed little development. Population growth was low; foreign trade grew slowly; except in Sudan (and, for a short while, the Hijaz line) there were no railways; there was no modern industry until oil was discovered in Iran, in 1908; agriculture remained untouched by progress; foreign capital investment was negligible; and educational and social progress was minimal.

In North Africa the pattern was largely determined by the influx of European settlers. This resulted in much more intensive development of resources, specifically agriculture and mining; in the building of a fine infrastructure of railways, roads, and ports; in the establishment of a good financial and commercial network; in a rather rapid growth of foreign trade; and in the investment of a huge amount of French and other capital. But human resources were developed even less than in the Mediterranean Middle East, since all the factors of production, other than land and unskilled labor, were supplied by the settlers.

Passing on to costs and benefits, the first debit item is the direct military losses suffered by the peoples of the region in their struggle against the foreign intruders. For the Algerians in 1830–71 and 1954–62, for the Moroccans in 1907–26, for the Libyans in 1912–41, and for the Sudanese in 1881–98, these costs were high. They have also not been negligible for the Iraqis, Syrians, and Palestinians. But it should be mentioned that conditions in the region before the advent of the West were not Arcadian; wars and insecurity had taken their toll and, more important, famines and epidemics periodically decimated the population. The fact is that the death rate dropped from well over 3 percent to 2 percent or less, presenting the region with perhaps its most severe problem. For today, as a result of 150 years of hygiene and security, the land ratio per capita is far lower than it was around 1800. For most countries, the growth of various sectors of the economy has more than compensated for this deterioration, but in some an almost insoluble problem has been created (see below).

The next possible loss is in the level of living. Here, unfortunately, little data are available, but it is necessary to make a distinction between the poorest 80 and the top 20 percent. It has been maintained that the level of living of the masses in the world declined during the period under review, and this may well have been true of some parts of this region. But in other parts there is clear evidence of improvement (chapter 6). And it should be noted that starvation, which was so common up to the 18th century, was overcome by the combination of peace, greater production, and mechanical transport, and that life expectancies have risen—in recent years sharply. As regards the upper 20 percent (to all intents and purposes the town dwellers, excluding the lowest strata)—there seems little doubt that their level of living— measured by such indicators as food, clothing, clean water and sewage, access to education and entertainment, and in more recent years durable consumer goods—has appreciably risen. This upper fifth included foreigners, in relatively small numbers in the Middle East but not in North Africa, and minority groups. In the last three decades or so, the figure for those who are better off may have risen to 30 percent or more, and its foreign and minority component has almost disappeared.

A third, important but unmeasurable cost is the alternatives that were forgone because of the presence of Western imperialism—for example, industrialization. One may speculate that, at least for some countries, these costs have been substantial. Closely connected with them are certain political costs, for example, the highly artificial European- designed frontiers in the Levant.

As for the gains, the first is the building up of the rudiments of a modern economic structure. A transport network has been laid down, large power plants have been erected, factory industry has been expanded enormously, a big mining sector (including oil) has been developed. Some of the world's greatest dams have been built and agriculture is slowly being improved. A commercial and banking system has been developed. In other words, both wealth and income have vastly increased. It is true that the most rapid expansion in these fields has taken place after the respective countries achieved independence, but some of the groundwork was laid during the period of European dominance.

No less important has been the educational and cultural progress achieved. The intellectual condition of the region in the 17th and 18th centuries was abysmal and quite unworthy of a culture that had produced al-Razi, al-Bayruni, Ibn Sina, al-Ghazali, and Ibn Khaldun, to mention only a few. Perhaps the best indicator of its backwardness is the fact that when Muhammad Ali started his modernization program, there was not a single Egyptian who knew a European language, and no one in the Middle East or North Africa had a glimmering of Western science (chapter 6).[47] The development of the region's human resources is the most important single achievement of the last 150 years. Again, one must be careful not to attribute too much credit for this to the metropolitan powers. It seems clear that independent Turkey, or Egypt until 1882, made far more intellectual progress than Algeria under French rule or Libya under Italian. But whatever the causes and channels, the peoples of the Middle East have entered on their human heritage and begun once more to participate in and make a contribution to world culture.

One more remark is in order. In some ways the Middle East (but not North Africa) had the worst of both worlds. It did not enjoy the independence that allowed Japan to carry out its modernization in a way that suited its national interests and character. Nor was it subjected to the kind of control that led to much development by the British in India, the Russians in Azerbaijan, the Japanese in Taiwan, or the Americans in the Philippines. Instead, most often, there was the influence of rival powers, which jealously watched and checked each other, preventing railway building in the Ottoman Empire and Iran and thwarting other schemes. Even in Egypt the Caisse de la Dette obstructed many British reforms. Of course, the experience of North Africa shows that direct foreign control can lead to much development of resources with very little benefit to the native peoples.

A closer, though summary, breakdown is desirable. For the oil countries (Iran, Iraq, Libya, Algeria, Saudi Arabia, and the smaller Arabian states) the increase in wealth has been quite out of proportion to the costs incurred. Of course, much of this wealth has been dissipated, especially in the last few years, and equally obviously such a vast accretion of riches is a mixed blessing, as the example of Iran has already shown; but there are few countries that would not gladly change places with the oil producers. For a second group, with little or no oil production but fairly abundant resources, prospects are reasonably good: Turkey, Syria, Lebanon, Sudan, Tunisia, and Morocco. The clearest hardship cases are Egypt, where early development and huge population growth have created an extremely difficult situation, and Palestine, where collision with a stronger intruding nationalism has caused much suffering. But, taken as a whole, the Middle East is in a far better position than most parts of Asia and Africa.

However, like other regions, it faces certain basic contradictions which almost ensure that the coming decades will be highly turbulent. More specifically, its peoples, like those of the rest of the world, are seeking to achieve incompatible aims: economic growth, higher levels of living, national power, equality, a greater sense of community and cultural identity, and political liberty. A few illustrations of the ensuing contradictions may be given. Growth tends to enhance national power and, at least after a while, to raise levels of living; but it also tends initially to increase inequality and, by opening the door to foreign technology and personnel, to pose a threat to the sense of community and identity, and thus arouse popular revulsion. Equality, perhaps not necessarily but almost always in practice, tends to impede growth and therefore prevent a rise in levels of living and an increase in national power. An excessive stress on community and national, cultural, or religious identity tends to weaken the springs of growth by impeding the inflow of foreign technology and personnel, and also to impede the development of political liberty. Liberty may—or may not— promote growth, but it tends to act against equality and to facilitate the introduction of foreign ideas and practices that are seen as a threat to community, identity, and national power. And so on. In addition, more than perhaps any part of the Third World, the Middle East is subject to the highly unsettling effects of constant interference and manipulation by the Powers.

These difficulties the region shares with the rest of the human race. However, the opportunities it enjoys, as a result of the developments described above, are unique. The use it makes of them in the coming decades will determine whether the balance sheet of the last two centuries will be judged to have been positive or negative.

Statistical Appendix

To study fully the economic development of the Middle East and North Africa since the First World War would require another book. Fortunately, the reader can be referred to a voluminous literature. For the Middle East in the interwar period there are the works of Bonné, Ducruet, Gaitskell, Hershlag, Himadeh, Issawi, Tezel, Webster, and Yaganegi, and the epilogues in EHME, EHI, and EHT. For more recent developments, in addition to numerous books on the individual countries, there are those of Aliboni, Galal Amin, Askeri and Cummings, Beaumont, Bharier, Clarke and Fisher, Clawson, Cooper and Alexander, Edens, Hershlag, Issawi and Yeganeh, Sayigh, Schurr and Homan, Udovitch, and the annual reports of the United Nations and the United Nations Economic Commission for Western Asia. North Africa has received much less attention, and the reader is referred to the reports of the United Nations Economic Commission on Africa and the works of Samir Amin, Chevalier, and Robana.

However, it has seemed useful to include a set of statistical tables in this appendix. They provide data on the main aspects of the economy at the end of the 1970s. In addition to indicating the current state of the region, they form a benchmark from which the development described in this book can be more accurately measured.

Table A.1
Economic and Social Indicators

	Population (million) 1977	Population growth (% p.a.) 1970-77	GNP per capita ($) 1977	GNP growth per capita (%) 1960-77	Adult literacy rate (%) 1975	Life expectancy at birth 1977	Index of per capita food production (1969-71 = 100) Average 1975-77
Sudan	17	2.6	290	0.1	20	46	106
Egypt	38	2.2	320	2.1	44	54	97
S. Yemen	2	1.9	340	-4.8	27	47	107
N. Yemen	5	1.9	430		13	47	100
Morocco	18	2.8	550	2.2	28	55	78
Jordan	3	3.3	710	1.8	59	56	71
Tunisia	6	2.0	860	4.3	38	57	130
Syria	8	3.3	910	2.3	53	57	146
Algeria	17	3.5	1,110	2.1	35	56	87
Turkey	42	2.5	1,110	4.1	60	61	107
Lebanon	3	2.5				65	87
Iraq	12	3.4	1,550	3.8		55	78
Iran	35	3.0	2,160	7.9	50	52	109
Israel	4	2.8	2,850	4.8	88	72	114
Saudi Arabia	8	3.0	6,040	6.7		48	92
Libya	3	4.1	6,680	6.6	45	55	149
Kuwait	1	6.1	12,270	-3.1	60	69	
India	632	2.1	150	1.3	36	51	99
Mexico	63	3.3	1,120	2.8	76	65	97
Greece	9	0.7	2,810	6.2		73	122
United States	220	0.8	8,520	2.4	99	73	112

Note: Countries are listed in ascending order of GNP per capita.
Source: World Bank, *World Development Report, 1979.*

Table A.2
Employment by Sector, 1970
(percent)

	Agriculture	Manufacturing, oil, mining, construction	Services
Algeria	50	16	34
Libya	37	16	47
Morocco	50	15	35
Tunisia	53	19	28
Egypt	53	16	31
Iran	41	24	35
Iraq	59	18	23
Israel	9	34	57
Jordan	29	26	45
Lebanon	19	24	57
Kuwait	2	34	64
Saudi Arabia	61	10	29
Sudan	80	6	14
Syria	54	20	26
Turkey	67	12	21

Source: World Bank, *World Tables 1976.*

Table A.3
Composition of Gross Domestic Product
(percent)

	1950				1971			
	A	M	O	S	A	M	O	S
Algeria (1950, 1970)	33	24	—	43	12	26	18	44
Libya (1960, 1971)	10	14	23	53	2	9	61	28
Morocco	30	24	—	46	31	28	—	41
Tunisia (1960, 1971)	25	25	—	50	17	22	—	61
Egypt (1953, 1970)	35	13	—	52	25	25	—	50
Iran (1960, 1971)	31	14	17	38	15	20	28	37
Iraq (1953, 1970)	22	10	40	28	21	15	32	32
Israel	11	30	—	59	6	30	—	64
Jordan (1960, 1971)	16	14	—	70	17	13	—	70
Kuwait	. .	. .	. .	. .	—	6	67	27
Lebanon	20	18	—	62	8	21	—	71
Saudi Arabia (1963, 1969)	9	8	54	29	6	12	48	34
Sudan (1956, 1970)	61	11	—	28	35	16	—	49
Syria (1953, 1971)	44	15	—	41	22	24	—	54
Turkey	49	16	—	35	28	28	—	44

A—Agriculture, forestry, fishing.
M—Manufacturing, mining, power, construction.
O—Oil.
S—Services.
Sources: IBRD, *World Tables*, Table 4; United Nations, *Statistical Yearbook*, 1973; other sources.

Table A.4
Income Distribution
(percent of national income received)

	1960		1970		
	Lowest 20	Highest 5	Lowest 20	Highest 5	Gini coefficient
Sudan	5	21			0.4376[a]
Egypt	4	20			0.4043[b]
Iraq	2	34			0.3615[c]
Turkey	4	33	3	32	0.5100[d]
Iran	4	32	5	25	0.4228[e]
Lebanon	7	35	4	26	0.5370[f]
Israel	7	13	8	13	0.3346[g]
Tunisia[h]	4	22			0.4436
India	4	27	5	25	0.4475[i]
Colombia	3	36	4	33	0.5615[j]
Brazil	5	23	5	27	0.5244[j]
Tanzania			5	34	0.5973[k]
Yugoslavia	7	17	7	15	0.3225[l]
United Kingdom	6	16	6	15	0.3385[l]
United States	4	16	7	13	0.4042[m]
Japan	5	20	4	20	0.4223[m]
Sweden	4	18	5	17	0.3872[j]
Germany	5	36	6	18	0.3939[j]
Algeria			27[n]	25°	

Sources: IBRD, *World Tables* 1976; Jain 1975.
[a] 1963, urban.
[b] 1974; Tignor and Abdel-Khalek 1981.
[c] 1971; Kelidar 1979:134.
[d] 1973; Ozbudun and Ulusan 1980:101.
[e] 1972; Pesaran 1976:280.
[f] 1955–60.
[g] 1975, urban; Ginor 1979:92.
[h] 1961, urban.
[i] 1967.
[j] 1970.
[k] 1961.
[l] 1968.
[m] 1971.
[n] 1975, lowest 50 percent, excluding Greater Algiers; Benissad 1979:272.
° 1975, highest 10 percent, excluding Greater Algiers; *ibid.*

Table A.5 Foreign Trade ($ million)   (Rounded to nearest $100 million after 1938)

	Imports					Exports				
	1938	1948	1963	1970	1977	1938	1948	1963	1970	1977
Algeria	140	500	700	1,300	7,100	160	400	800	1,000	5,800
Libya	50	20	200	600	5,100	6	10	300	2,400	10,100
Morocco	60	400	400	700	3,200	40	200	400	500	1,300
Tunisia	50	200	200	300	900	40	60	100	300	900
Egypt	190	700	900	800	4,800	150	600	500	800	1,700
Sudan	30	100	100	300	400	30	100	200	400	600
North Africa	500	1,900	2,500	4,000	21,200	400	1,400	2,400	5,100	20,400
Bahrain	..	..	..	300[a]	2,000	..	..	..	300[a]	1,800
Iran	..	200	500	1,700	13,800	..	500	900	2,600	24,200
Iraq	50	..	300	500	3,900	..	..	800	1,100	9,700
Israel/Palestine	56	300[b]	700	1,400	4,700	29	40[b]	300	700	3,000
Jordan	6	50	100	200	700	3	10	20	30	200
Kuwait	..	..	300	600	4,500	..	..	1,100	1,900	9,800
Lebanon	40	200	400	600	..	20	40	60	200	..
Syria	..	200	200	400	2,700	..	..	200	200	1,100
Oman	..	..	..	30[a]	900	..	..	..	100[a]	1,600
Qatar	..	..	..	100[a]	1,200	..	..	..	300[a]	2,100
Saudi Arabia	..	..	..	700	14,700	..	300	1,100	2,400	43,500
Turkey	119	300	700	900	5,700	115	200	400	600	1,800
United Arab Emirates	..	..	20[c]	300[a]	4,600	..	..	5[c]	900[a]	9,500
North Yemen	..	..	..	100	1,000	..	..	..	13	11
South Yemen	30	110	300	300	200	..	..	200	100	200
Asian ME	(400)	(1,500)	(4,300)	8,000	58,500	400	1,500	5,700	11,300	(109,000)
Asian ME excluding petroleum						300		1,300	2,400	5,500
Total region	900	3,400	6,800	12,000	79,800	800	2,900	8,100	16,400	(129,400)
World	25,400	63,500	162,900	328,900	1,154,600	23,500	57,500	154,500	313,200	1,124,500
Region as percent of World	3.5	5.4	4.2	3.6	6.9	3.4	5.0	5.2	5.2	11.5

[a] 1971   [b] 1949   [c] 1964   *Source:* United Nations Statistical Yearbook.

Table A.6
Land and Population, 1977
(thousand hectares and persons)

	Cultivated land	Irrigated land	Agricultural population	Percent of active population in agriculture
Algeria	7,542	285	9,124	52
Libya	2,544	135	479	18
Morocco	7,840	470	10,020	52
Tunisia	4,410	130	2,629	42
Egypt	2,831	2,831	19,941	51
Sudan	7,495	1,550	13,011	78
Iran	15,950	5,840	13,244	40
Iraq	5,290	1,160	5,091	42
Israel	430	192	274	7
Jordan	1,365	69	589	27
Lebanon	348	85	364	12
Oman	36	. .	530	63
Saudi Arabia	1,110	390	4,822	61
Syria	5,509	531	3,852	48
Turkey	27,929	2,050	24,631	57
North Yemen	1,570	230	4,400	76
South Yemen	265	58	1,087	60
Pakistan[a]	28,358	12,043	92,584	70
France[a]	19,265	2,500	7,255	14
Greece[a]	3,631	730	4,134	46
Italy[a]	14,932	2,444	9,735	21
Japan[a]	5,510	2,836	21,329	21
Mexico[a]	23,817	4,200	23,617	47
Philippines[a]	8,977	826	26,752	70
United States	176,440	14,996	8,216	4

[a] 1970.
Source: Food and Agricultural Organization, *FAO Production Yearbook*, 1959 and 1978.

Table A.7
Structure (1960) and Progress of Agriculture

	Agricultural output per farm worker ($)	Arable land per farm worker (ha)	Fertilizer per ha arable land (kg.)	Agricultural output per ha arable land ($)	Growth in output per farm person (% p.a.) (1950–68)
Morocco	295	2.0	1	144	. .
Tunisia	341	1.0	1	. .	(−0.8)
Egypt	365	0.6	87	643	0.2
Israel	1,825	3.0	81	557	7.1
Turkey	326	2.6	2	127	0.6
Iran	581[a]	3.0	1	187[a]	(1.4)
Syria	580[a]	10[a]	2	60	. .
Iraq	480	7	1	70	. .
Lebanon	360	0.8	60	450	. .
Japan	402	0.4	304	961	7.8
Chile	547	9.3	17	59	. .
Mexico	369	4.1	9	110	1.4
India	114	1.2	2	91	(−0.8)

[a]These figures seem too high.
Source: IBRD, *Agriculture*, June 1972; *ibid.*, *Land Reform*, May 1975; Syria, Iraq, and Lebanon from Clawson et al. 1971 and refer to 1964/65.

Table A.8
Index of Agricultural Production
(1961–65 = 100)

	Prewar	1948–52	1976–78
Algeria	113	106	108
Libya	. .	. .	195
Morocco	83	92	97
Tunisia	95	92	146
Egypt	67	76	104
Sudan	. .	. .	116
Iran	(60)	77	137
Iraq	(90)	93	105
Israel	. .	47	143
Jordan	. .	. .	71
Lebanon	. .	. .	129
Saudi Arabia	. .	. .	131
Syria	(40)	72	171
Turkey	62	75	119
North Yemen	. .	. .	112
South Yemen	. .	. .	121

Note: FAO index for 1948–52 is spliced on that for 1961–65, and prewar on that for 1948–52; figures in parentheses are rough estimates.
Source: Food and Agricultural Organization, *FAO Production Yearbook*.

Table A.9
Public Debt and Interest Charges

	External public debt ($ billion)		Interest payment on external public debt ($ million)		Debt service as % export of goods and services	
	1970	1978	1970	1978	1970	1978
Algeria	0.9	13.2	10	561	3	21
Morocco	0.7	5.1	23	252	8	19
Tunisia	0.5	2.4	18	95	18	12
Egypt	1.6	9.9	38	386	29	22
Sudan	0.3	2.1	13	36	11	9
Iran	2.2	8.3	85	391	12	3
Iraq	0.3	0.9	9	37	2	1
Israel	2.3	9.2	41	248	12	8
Jordan	0.1	0.8	2	24	4	4
Lebanon	0.1	0.1	1	4	. .	1
Syria	0.2	2.1	6	58	11	15
Turkey	1.9	6.2	42	182	16	11
North Yemen	0.1	0.5	. .	3	. .	1
South Yemen	—	0.3	—	1	—	2
	11.2	61.1	288	2,278		

Source: World Bank, *World Development Report,* 1980

Table A.10
Merchant Shipping Fleets, 1969–1978
(thousands of gross registered tons)

	1969		1978	
	Tankers	*Total*	*Tankers*	*Total*
Algeria	. .	19	643	1,152
Libya	. .	4	. .	885
Morocco	. .	72	341	
Egypt	75	239	131	456
Sudan	. .	20	. .	43
Iran	42	106	598	1,195
Iraq	1	37	1,141	1,306
Israel	. .	769	. .	421
Kuwait	316	441	1,219	2,240
Lebanon	. .	295	. .	278
Saudi Arabia	. .	51	1,022	1,246
Turkey	169	651	357	1,359
United Arab Emirates	. .	2	. .	156
Total	603	2,706	5,452	10,737
World	77,392	211,661	175,035	406,002
Region as % world	0.8	1.3	3.1	2.6

Source: United Nations, *Statistical Yearbook*, 1978.

Notes

I. CHALLENGE AND RESPONSE, 1800-1980

1. The end of the 18th century marked a low point in the long history of the region; this question is discussed in Issawi 1970, 1977, and 1980a; Ashtor 1978; Owen 1977. Stagnation or retrogression from Roman, early medieval, or, in Turkey and Iran, early modern periods is shown by such indicators as population, cultivated area, quality of handicrafts, and intellectual and cultural levels.

2. See Myint 1964:chap. 3.

3. See Berg 1965.

4. See the penetrating remarks of Lord Cromer (1910). Cromer was keenly aware that modern European imperialism (British, French, Dutch, and Russian) in Asia and Africa would prove to be far more ephemeral than Roman, and pointed out clearly its main weaknesses: differences of race, religion, and culture, religious and social barriers to intermarrige, and lack of knowledge of the local vernaculars, on the part of the rulers, preventing easy social intercourse. Moreover, unlike the Romans (except in the latter's dealings with the Jews and, one might perhaps add, the Egyptians) the Europeans were faced with powerful national feelings, largely based on religion. As regards North Africa, Cromer quotes (p. 89) M. Morand, Director of the School of Law at Algiers, who states: "Plus les indigènes musulmans nous connaissent, et mieux ils nous connaissent, plus ils s'éloignent de nous" and describes their revulsion at many aspects of Western civilization and their increased conviction of the superiority of Islam.

5. EHT:168, 174; EHFC.

6. "The Dissolution of the Village Community, in Baer 1969; Baer 1964, 1970a; Issawi 1965; Lewis 1961:82-125; EHME:244-47; EHI:284-92; EHT:13-15.

7. For Egypt, EHME:449-51; for Iran, EHI:339-42; for Turkey, EHT:332-38; for Iraq and Syria, EHFC and Gerber and Gross 1980.

8. For the rising cost of ships see EHT:163.

9. EHT: 55-56.

10. Berque 1972:190.

11. Eliot 1965:153.

12. EHT:23-24; R. Ricoux cited in Nouschi 1961:744.

13. Cromer 1910:113.

14. For Egypt see Issawi 1963:46-62; for Turkey EHT:366-69; for the more general trend toward nationalization and socialization, and its driving forces, see Johnson 1967 and Gouldner 1970:60-62 and passim.

15. See EI2, s.v. "Imtiyazat."

II. EXPANSION OF FOREIGN TRADE

1. MacGregor 1844: 2:13.
2. CEHE: 3:399-400.
3. *Ibid.*: 3:281-361, 408-19, 4:566-75.
4. Miège 1961: 2:82-84.
5. Urquhart 1833:188.
6. See texts in Hurewitz 1975: 1:1-49.
7. Text in EHME:39-40 and Hurewitz 1975: 1:265-66; details and documents in EHT:85-100 and Issawi 1980c. Europeans were not the only ones to complain; in 1801 the Imam of Musqat protested against the arbitrariness of the Basra customs. Seton to Bombay, 18 February 1801, IO PS 381/20.
8. Texts in Hurewitz 1975: 1:197-99, 231-37, 280-81; EHI:72-82.
9. Text in Hurewitz 1975: 1:324-36; Miège 1961: 2:261-347; Ponasik 1977.
10. Douin 1927:88; for details on commercial policy see Crouchley 1937; idem 1938:85-90; Owen 1969:19-88; Rivlin 1961:171-90.
11. See EHT:75-76.
12. Hunter 1877:89.
13. Demontès 1930a:98; Levasseur 1911:477.
14. *Tunisie 1900*:85, Donon 1920:passim; Piquet 1912:418, Isaac 1906:passim; Bloch-Lainé 1956:432-33.
15. Knight 1937:passim; Hoffherr 1932:passim; Bloch-Lainé 1956:432-33.
16. *Rinascita* 1926:255, 474.
17. Gordon 1932:162-70; Hershlag 1968:21-22.
18. For Iraq see Jamil 1949:194-201; for the eastern Arab countries, Musrey 1969:passim.
19. EHFC.
20. Musrey 1969:passim; Himadeh 1936:229-59, 1938a:432-39, 1938b:421-28; Burns 1933:passim; Saba 1960.
21. Wilmington 1971:passim.
22. See Issawi 1980d; Musrey 1969; Sayigh 1978:691-710; United Nations 1980:104-7.
23. Rostow 1978:67; Imlah 1958:97-98, 189.
24. Aden's trade was purely entrepot; if the land trade of Iraq and Syria, which may actually have declined during this period and at best grew slowly, be included, the overall rate of increase of those two countries would be greatly reduced. See EHFC.
25. W. A. Lewis 1978:196-217; Lewis' figures show real growth and should therefore be increased by some 20 percent to reflect the rise in the prices of primary products in 1880-1913.
26. Rostow 1978:67.
27. See memorandum by Chamber of Commerce of Marseilles, 1784, EHME:31-37; for Egypt, Raymond 1973: 1:107-305; for Ottoman Empire, Mantran 1970.
28. Furber 1976:230-34, 332.

29. EHME:270–73, 301–3; EHT:76–77.

30. Miège 1961: 4:417; Chevallier 1968:214–15.

31. Crouchley 1938:267–68; Pamuk 1978:appendix A; EHI:128–35; Bharier 1971:114–17; Hasan n.d.:appendixes 2 and 3; EHFC.

32. For figures on the Middle East, see United Nations 1951:76–77; for North Africa, Bloch-Lainé 1956.

33. For details see Issawi 1970b.

34. EHME:30–37; EHT:3; Raymond 1973:182–84; Masson 1896, 1903, 1911:passim; Paris 1957;passim.

35. In 1913 per capita exports *plus* imports were $24.30 in Egypt, $39.60 in Algeria, $15.00 in Syria, $31.00 in Tunisia, $15.20 in Turkey, and $10.30 in Iran; except for Iran these figures rank rather high in the international scale (see Issawi 1968:384). The ratio of exports to GNP in Egypt was about 32 percent and of imports 28; in the Ottoman Empire 14 and 19, respectively, again high figures; in Algeria and Tunisia they were probably still higher.

36. EHME:359–74, 446–48; Owen 1969:passim, Issawi 1963:224–26.

37. EHME:472; Gaitskell 1959:160–63.

38. Hasan n.d.:118–27; EHFC.

39. EHFC; Huvelin 1921:passim; Ruppin 1916:421–30.

40. Pamuk 1978:53–56.

41. For details see EHT:chap. 3; Krueger 1974:181–86.

42. EHI:135–42, 231–52; Jamalzadeh 1335:12–16.

43. EHME:293–349; Winder 1965:214–17; Lorimer 1908: 1:2, 220–93.

44. Mollard 1950:passim; Isnard 1954:passim; Demontès 1930a; Saint-Germès 1955; Benissad 1979.

45. *Tunisie 1900:*67; MacGregor 1844: 2:292.

46. *Initiation à la Tunisie* 1950:315–61; Piquet 1912:434–35.

47. Romanus 1934:10–40; F. Bernard 1917:61; Stewart 1964:197–203.

48. Rushdy 1953:108; Lindberg 1952:12–14; Segrè 1974:222.

49. Myint 1954.

50. *Ibid.*

51. Robinson 1954.

52. See table, EHI:135.

53. United Nations 1951:70.

54. Miège 1961: 2:73–74, 135, 4:387–89.

55. Jamalzadeh 1335:12.

56. EHT:77; Bharier 1971:107; Hasan n.d.:240–52; Ruppin 1916:421–30; Levasseur 1911:202.

57. United Nations 1951:71.

58. Raymond 1973: 1:107–202; EHI:263–67; EHFC; Miège 1961: 2:123–51; EHT:78–79.

59. EHME:37.

60. Levasseur 1911:335; *Etudes et Conjoncture*, February 1947; Benissad 1979:173–82.

61. *Tunisie 1900*: 2:66; MacGregor 1844: 2:292; Ganiage 1959:465.

62. MacGregor 1844: 2:284; Donon 1920:46; Miège 1961: 2:506, 3:427, 4:202; Barlow 1940:34–41.
63. Ruppin 1916:371; Huvelin 1921:40; Himadeh 1936:235–41.
64. Eldem 1970:181–83.
65. EHI: 71–72, 142–46.
66. See Egypt's *Annuaire Statistique*, various issues.
67. Hasan n.d.:128–37, 253–61.
68. Imlah and Board of Trade Indices, Mitchell and Deane 1962:331–32.
69. Pamuk 1978:279–82, 285.
70. See prices in EHME:373, 447–48.
71. EHME:373; Issawi 1963:230–31; Hansen and Lucas 1978; Girgis 1977:177.
72. Krueger 1974:241.
73. Kalla 1969:68–84; Nowshirvani 1981:554.
74. Issawi and Yeganeh 1962:64–70, 126–36; Issawi 1978a; *Petroleum Economist*, various issues; International Monetary Fund, *IMF Survey*, various issues.
75. Hanson 1980; EHME:446–48.
76. For the distinction between growth and development, see Flammang 1979.
77. Walton and Shepherd 1979:101 and passim.
78. W. A. Lewis 1978:162; Lockwood 1954:338–39.
79. *Ibid.*:318.

III. DEVELOPMENT OF TRANSPORT

1. Thistlethwaite 1955:203.
2. Cook 1974:218.
3. Braudel 1973:317; idem 1972: 1:295–312; see also CEHE: 5:530–33.
4. Raymond 1973: 1:168.
5. For earlier figures see Braudel 1973: 1:355–71; Udovitch 1978.
6. Ainslie to Carmarthen, 26 July 1788, FO 78/9.
7. Raymond 1973: 1:168.
8. Valensi 1969a:104.
9. CC Beyrouth vol. I, Report of 31 December 1825; CC Constantinople, vol. 74, Brune to Talleyrand, 26 Germinal, an 11 (1804). In the first half of the 19th century Istanbul was probably the leading Mediterranean port, followed by Marseilles, Trieste, and Leghorn; Alexandria was the 11th and Smyrna the 12th. Crawley 1960:419.
10. Report on Trade Smyrna, FO 78/195.
11. Raymond 1973: 1:111–12.
12. CC Bagdad, vol. 10, Report of 10 February 1846.
13. MacGregor 1844: 2:110; EHI:160–65.
14. Valensi 1969a:63–65; Raymond 1973: 1:168–69; EHT:152–57.
15. EHME:36–37; Gibb 1950: 1:309.
16. Raymond 1973: 1:170–71; EHT:152–54.

17. For early developments in the Mediterranean and Red Sea, see EHME:297-300, 406-15; EHT:160-65; MacGregor 1844:vol. 4; Lindsay 1876:vol. 4; Colin 1901:passim; Hoskins 1928:passim; Cable 1937:passim; Farnie 1969:3-31.

18. Abu-Lughod 1965:431.

19. CC Constantinople, vol. 90, Report of 7 May 1844; EHT:163.

20. Farley 1862:209; for details, EHFC.

21. Crouchley 1938:142.

22. Colin 1901:283-86; Masson 1912:44; MacGregor 1844:395; *Tunisia 1954*:139.

23. Ganiage 1959:55.

24. Miège 1961: 2:415-53; Brackmann 1935:18-19; Résidence 1915-21:279.

25. EHI:160-70.

26. EHT:165-66; HHS, Türkei, 1836:vol. 6; Issawi 1970c.

27. See figures in EHT:163.

28. Braudel 1973:265.

29. See figures in EHT:162.

30. Chevallier 1971:184; CC Smyrne, vol. 51, Report on trade of Smyrna for 1871.

31. For comparable figures on other Mediterranean ports around 1850, see Crawley 1960:419-20.

32. al-Hitta 1957:224-39; al-Shaf'i n.d.:28-30, 65-66; Arminjon 1911:134-35.

33. Baeza 1924:17-40; Cazès 1921:24-28, 63; Pawera 1964:75-82; Billiard 1930:29, 43, 90, 103, 155.

34. Piquet 1912:278-79.

35. Miège 1961:passim; Eyquem 1933:passim; Stewart 1964:156-58; Résidence 1915-21: 2:70-72, 7:274-75.

36. Higgins 1953:17.

37. EHT:167-69; Kurmuş 1974:266-72; Thobie 1977:132-37, 161-64.

38. Monicault 1936:42; EHFC; Thobie 1977:172-77.

39. *Ibid.*:376-91.

40. For examples of strain, see Issawi 1980d:15; for more recent data, United Nations 1980:73-75.

41. Hansen and Tourk 1976:4.

42. Fletcher 1958.

43. Farnie 1969:99-101, 200; this book contains a wealth of information and a full bibliography. See also Hershlag 1980:129-39.

44. Farnie 1969:171, 306, 354-56. British shippers and traders favored the canal from the start, but the government was opposed on strategic grounds. Britain controlled the two entrances (the Cape and the Straits of Malacca) to the Indian Ocean, the center of the empire, and did not want another opening which might come under hostile control. For the same reason it was later to oppose the Baghdad Railway, which would have given Continental powers access to the Gulf and Indian Ocean.

45. For figures see EHT:170-171; see also several series in Isserlis 1938 and North 1958.

46. For an excellent discussion, Bulliet 1975. The Roman roads gradually deteriorated and "as early as the 10th century the last ancient bridge over the Tigris collapsed" (Singer 1957: 2:527), but other bridges and caravanserais were built by various governments.

47. Bulliet 1975:5: EHI:195: EHT:177–79.

48. Crouchley 1938:32; CC Damas, vol. 2; "Mémoire" translated in EHFC; EHI:97; EHT:177–79; Burckhardt 1822:466, 1819:276.

49. Braudel 1973:252.

50. Hoskins 1928:237–42; Arminjon 1911:122–33; Issawi 1947:100–2.

51. Hill 1959:99–101, 132, 1965:2–5, 57–66; Wiener 1932:627–30.

52. British Consul, 23 June 1903, FO 195/2138; Batatu 1979:238; see also EHME:146–53 and EHFC.

53. EHI:171–77.

54. Thomas 1957:184–87; *Initation* 1950:378; Great Britain, Naval Intelligence, 1944a:2:293–340; idem 1945a:364–87; Régence de Tunis 1931a:6–9.

55. Thobie 1977:164; Report on Lebanon, 5 May 1900, FO 195/2075; EHFC; EHI:157, 361; Arminjon 1911:119–21; EHT:150–51. See also the relevant sections in the Geographical Handbooks series listed in the bibliography under Great Britain, Naval Intelligence.

56. EHME:410–12; Arminjon 1911:113–19; Wiener 1932:passim.

57. Bernard 1913:passim; Thomas 1957:190–202; *Initiation* 1950:371–77; Bousser 1934:passim.

58. International Bank 1960:230.

59. Hill 1965:passim; Wiener 1932:588–635.

60. Verney and Dambman 1900:253–60; Ruppin 1916:486; Elefteriades 1944:passim; Thobie 1977:165–72, 318–31; EHFC.

61. EI2, s.v. "Hidjaz Railway"; Elefteriades 1944:passim; Huvelin 1921; EHFC.

62. Grant 1937:261–70; Hoskins 1928:154–290, 423–53; EHME:137–45; EHFC.

63. Kurmuş 1974a:passim; Thobie 1977:331–41; EHT:183–88.

64. EHT:147–50, 188–94 and sources; Earle 1923:passim; Trumpener 1968:7–8, 316; Williamson 1971:80–110; Tezel 1975:65–66.

65. United Nations 1951:17 and Working Paper no. 14.

66. *Ibid.*

67. For roads see World Bank 1972; for vehicles Issawi 1976:62–64 and recent issues of United Nations *Statistical Yearbook*.

68. EHT:177–79; Ibn Bishr 1391: 1:183–99, 294, 2:42–58. See also Winder 1965:89–90.

69. Farley 1862:254; dispatch in FO 78/621; Kalla 1969:135.

70. Curzon 1892:1:638; for figures on wheat, barley, and other staples in various towns, see EHI:340 and Nowshirvani 1981:553.

71. Gaitskell 1959:37.

72. Quataert 1977; EHT:180–81.

73. Report on Trade, 23 October 1883, CC Beyrouth, 9; EHFC; figures for 1835 in Bowring 1973:46, 85.

74. EHI:375.

75. Miège 1961:3:460; Bousser 1934:18-35.

76. Elefteriades 1944:38.

77. For a fuller discussion of all these points, in the Turkish context, see EHT:147-48.

78. EHME:410; EHT:167; Landes 1958:84, 103-4, 154-55; BESM 1951:519-44.

79. See also United Nations 1980:75-78.

IV. THE INFLUX OF FOREIGN CAPITAL

1. Baster 1929, 1935:passim; Landes 1958:passim; Biliotti 1909:passim; Blottière 1948:215-17.

2. Jenks 1927:293. For an account of the repercussions of the 1837 crash in Tabriz, see EHI:105-8; for Egypt, Owen 1969:40.

3. Jenks 1927:273 and, more generally, chap. 9.

4. EI2, s.v. "asham," "kaima"; EHT:327-28; EHI:chap. 8, Hamza 1944:1-3; Miège 1961:2:225-40.

5. EHT:324.

6. Hurewitz 1969:28-46; for warships see EHT:163.

7. EHME:431.

8. Suvla in EHME:100-1. Eldem 1970:260-61 gives figures that, adjusted for the 1877 loan, amount to LT 237.9 million and LT 135.1 million, respectively.

9. Suvla in EHME:105-6. These totals do not, however, tally with the itemized list given by the same author for 1886-1914; EHME:94-106.

10. For details, EHT:361-65 and sources cited therein; Morawitz 1902:passim; du Velay 1903:passim; Blaisdell 1929:passim; EI2, s.v. "Duyun-i Umumiyye"; Hershlag 1968:61-68; Ducruet 1964:77-121.

11. Fişek 1962.

12. Thobie 1977:305-8 discusses the various estimates. See also Eldem 1970:190-91; Hershlag 1964:65; Avcioglu 1968; Ducruet 1964:77-116; and EHT for other figures.

13. Crouchley 1934:17-20; Hamza 1944:278-81 puts the amount received at only £35.1 million; Landes 1958:passim; see also Ducruet 1964:21-65.

14. There are discrepancies between the figures in Crouchley 1938:22-25 and those given by Cromer; see EHME:444-45.

15. EHME:439-45; Crouchley 1934:139-40; idem 1938:appendix tables 6 and 10; Hershlag 1980:122.

16. EHI:370-72; Kazemzadeh 1968:passim.

17. Piquet 1912:401-3; *Tunisie 1900*: 2:71-75; Sebag 1951:46-48.

18. Ayache 1956:56-59; Donon 1920:53-87.

19. Théry 1922:163.

20. For details, EHT:passim.

21. Thobie 1977:476-82.

22. Crouchley 1934:27-74, 147.

23. *Ibid.*:149–50, 158–59; see also Fridman 1963:13.

24. For details, EHI:316–22, 356–61.

25. Longrigg 1953:59–66; EHFC.

26. EHME:210; EHFC; Thobie 1977:164–77, 189–92, 318–31, 377–84.

27. Staley 1954:67; Barlow 1940:33; Askew 1942:29–31.

28. Barlow 1940:32; Hofherr 1932:306.

29. Barlow 1940:33; Piquet 1912:405.

30. Piquet 1912:266–67.

31. Trumpener 1968:182–84; Ducruet 1964:116–21.

32. *Report of the Council of Foreign Bondholders* 1927; Hershlag 1960:23, 113; Blaisdell 1929:197–208; for developments in the debt of Turkey and the other successor states, Ducruet 1964:121–27.

33. Ducruet 1964:230–36; Rozaliev 1962:61.

34. United Nations 1951:20, 76.

35. For the earlier period, see Crouchley 1934:passim; for subsequent developments Issawi 1963:passim; Ducruet 1964:66–76.

36. Marzouk 1957.

37. Frankel 1938:158, 171.

38. Gaitskell 1959:267–74 and passim.

39. Marzouk 1957.

40. Hickinbotham 1958:203.

41. Issawi and Yeganeh 1962:42–59.

42. Chase Manhattan Bank 1971; Hickinbotham 1958:203–4.

43. Samman 1955:40; for the Ottoman debt, Himadeh 1936:394; Longrigg 1956:268; Ducruet 1964:127.

44. Ducruet 1964:236–54, 330–37.

45. Himadeh 1938:467–572; Nathan 1946:336–40; Kahn 1944.

46. United States Bureau of Census, *Statistical Abstract of the United States,* various issues.

47. Italy 1946.

48. Picquemal 1957; Lepidi 1955; Bloch-Lainé 1956:113–18.

49. Tlatli 1957:208.

50. Belal 1968:15–45; Marty 1952:37.

51. Picquemal 1957.

52. *Ibid.*

53. Benhouria 1980:338.

V. MIGRATION AND MINORITIES

1. Nuss 1955:317.

2. Himadeh 1936:23.

3. Longrigg 1953:passim; for information and figures on the minorities Hourani 1947:passim.

4. United Nations 1949:passim.

5. Roumani 1975:1:18.

6. International Monetary Fund, *IMF Survey*, 4 September 1978; Ecevit 1979.

7. For a case study of a North Yemeni village, see Swanson 1979; for Oman, see Birks and Sinclair 1979, which takes a more pessimistic view in general.

8. Karpat 1973; see also Shaw and Shaw 1977:2:116–17 for further figures.

9. Politis 1928:1:201–5.

10. *Statistique de l'Egypte* 1873; *Annuaire Statistique de l'Egypte* 1910.

11. Issawi 1963:88–90; Deeb 1978; Tignor 1980.

12. There were about 300 Europeans in Baghdad in 1904 (Saleh 1957:199); the 1957 census lists 5,600 Europeans and Americans in Iraq. Some 2,000 German "Templars" settled in Palestine from 1868 on (see EHFC) and remained until the Second World War. During the Mandates there were only a few hundred French and British officials, businessmen, and teachers. In Lebanon in 1954 there were some 8,500 Europeans and nearly 3,000 North and South Americans, many of the latter being returned Lebanese emigrants.

13. For figures on the 1950s, see Issawi and Yeganeh 1962:153–54.

14. Ecevit 1979.

15. For further details, see EHT:58–59

16. *Initiation* 1957:140–87.

17. Europeans represented 93 percent of "cadres supérieurs," 82 percent of "techniciens et agents de maîtrise," and 86 percent of officials; Ageron 1966:80. Of 2,000 high officials only 8 were Muslims; Jeanson and Jeanson 1955:167.

18. Ageron 1966:68.

19. See breakdowns in Maspetiol Report of 1955, quoted in Knight 1956. In 1909 Muslims paid 42 million francs out of a total of 94 million raised in taxes, including 18 million out of 26 in direct taxes, per capita the Muslim share was 12 francs and the European 77. Piquet 1912:234; Ageron, 1966:67–68.

20. United Nations 1961:12.

21. Miège 1961: 1:28, 474.

22. Ayache 1956:256–88 states that the French took 50 percent of GNP, suggesting a ratio of 19:1 within Morocco; this seems too high, but is in line with a breakdown for 1934. See BEM (January 1935).

23. See Figueras and Roda Jimenez 1955:1:70, 3:300 for details.

24. Rushdy 1953:113.

25. See Segrè 1974:83; in 1934 the total population of all Italian colonies was 70,000 and in 1941 well under 200,000; this may be compared with Italy's annual natural increase of about 500,000

26. Birot and Dresch 1953:2:456–58.

27. Ruppin 1916:192–96; EHME:272–73.

28. Halevi and Malul 1968:38.

29. *Survey* 1946:3:1272.

30. Sussman 1973.

31. *Survey* 1946: 1:508, 3:1277–78.

32. Sussman 1973.

33. Loftus 1948.

34. Lustick 1980:158–63; Zureik 1979:122–30; Ben-Porath 1966; Smooha 1978:140–41.

35. Van der Kroef 1954; Ingrams 1946:37.

36. Himadeh 1936:16; EHME:269–73; EHFC.

37. Safa 1960; Tu'meh n.d.; *Arabic-Speaking Americans* 1946; Aswad 1974. On West Africa, see Winder 1962; *Kronik* 1975.

38. Brown and Roucek 1945:241–57, 299–310; EHT:61–68.

39. Chevalier 1947:138–40; Ray 1938.

40. Bouhdiba in Aliboni 1979:138, following G. Tapinos. Figures differ: for 1970, Freeman 1979:23 has 918,000 immigrants in France (650,000 Algerians, 171,000 Moroccans, 97,000 Tunisians) and Trebous 1970 has 280,000–290,000 Algerian workers plus 260,000 dependents, 100,000 Moroccan workers, and 70,000 Tunisian workers; Granotier 1976:193–200, puts the number of Algerians in 1975 at 871,000, of Moroccans at 300,000, and of Tunisians at 160,000. For 1979 Miller 1979 gives a figure of 884,000 Algerians. For Morocco, see also Noin 1970:2:161–252.

41. Ottaway and Ottaway 1970:36; Trebous 1970:60; Ecevit 1979; Bouhidba, in Aliboni 1979:165; for earnings of Algerians in France, Aliboni 1979:152.

42. Trebous 1970:179, 194–95; see also Benissad 1979:258–65.

43. Abadan 1976:5–8.

44. Krane 1975:170–84; Abadan 1976:11, 156.

45. See estimates in Abadan 1976:147–72; Krane 1975:133–34.

46. Ecevit 1979.

47. Krane 1975:140–60.

48. *Ibid.*:95–123, 135–36; Abadan 1976:169–78.

49. Abadan 1976:185–86.

50. This section is based on Issawi 1981c, to which the reader is referred for fuller details and sources.

51. EHT:53–58.

52. EHT:13–14, 54–73; EHME:114–25.

53. Indzhikyan 1977:211–14.

54. EHI:57–65.

55. Hourani 1970.

56. Issawi 1977b.

57. EHFC; Bowring 1973:7, 25.

58. Tignor 1976, 1977, 1980; Deeb 1976.

VI. POPULATION, LEVEL OF LIVING, AND SOCIAL DEVELOPMENT

1. For country breakdowns and sources see Issawi 1981a; for a thorough study of the Black Death see Dols 1977, and of the pandemic of 541–749, Conrad 1981.

2. See Rostow 1978:7 for regional breakdowns.

3. Yacono 1954.

4. Valensi 1977:407–39; *Initiation* 1950; Ganiage 1959:130–31.

5. Evans-Pritchard 1949:39–40.

6. Noin 1970:1:24–28.

7. McCarthy 1976.

8. Holt 1958:172–74; Cromer 1908:2:545; Henderson 1946:13.

9. Antonius 1939:240–41; EHFC; Chevallier 1971:40–48.

10. EHI:20–22.

11. Issawi 1977a; EHT:17–19; McCarthy 1981.

12. Musallam 1981.

13. EHT:23–25.

14. Clarke and Fisher 1972:24; this presents a full study of the subject. See also the discussion and tables by Nadia Youssef in Beck and Keddie 1978:69–99, which contains valuable information on the position of women; a very good recent study is Allman 1980.

15. See list of wars, EHT:4.

16. Caillé 1949:108; Noin 1970:1:239; Valensi 1977:404–33; idem 1969a:20–23; Miège 1961:3:148; Nouschi 1961:338, 546. In Algiers in 1787, according to an enumeration at the gates, 14, 334 Muslims, 1,774 Jews, and 613 Christians died not including those who died "in the gardens of its territory." Masson 1911:579.

17. Raymond 1973: 1:83–104; idem 1972.

18. Volney 1825: 1:152.

19. McCarthy 1977; Lane 1908:3; Crouchley 1938:256; Cromer 1908: 2:513; see also Bowring 1840; it is surprising that Lane (1908) does not mention the 1831 epidemic.

20. Longrigg 1925:266; Batatu 1978:15; Haider 1942:112; EHFC.

21. EHI:21.

22. For Smyrna, Panzac 1973.

23. EHT:11–12.

24. Valensi 1977:471, 1969a:24; Nouschi 1961:198–205, 338–78.

25. Raymond 1973:83–104.

26. Haider 1942.

27. For Iran EHI:21; for Turkey EHT:12; for Egypt Tignor 1966:348–57; for Syria and Iraq, EHFC; for Morocco, Noin 1970: 2:103–10.

28. FO 198/11; Raymond 1973: 1:83–104; Valensi 1969a:24.

29. Chevalier 1947:33–34.

30. For Morocco, Bouy 1930:54–61, BEM (April 1934); for Sudan, United Kingdom, Parliament, *Accounts and Papers*, "Egypt No. 1," 1904, p. 80; for Turkey, EHT:24.

31. The following account is based on Issawi 1969; for fuller details and sources the reader is referred to it and to EHI:26–35, EHT:33–36, EHFC, and EI1 and EI2 entries on various towns.

32. Figures in EHME:300–2, 464–68.

33. For figures see Issawi 1969:107-11; EHME:54-62; EHI:26-34; EHT:33-36; EHFC; Baer 1969:133-48. Data on Algeria and Tunisia show similar trends.

34. For a discussion of Egypt, see Abu-Lughod 1965a.

35. Issawi 1969:115-19; see also the interesting remarks in Planhol 1972:1-41.

36. For figures see Issawi 1976.

37. Rivlin 1961:157-60, 211, 244, 68-71; see also O'Brien 1968:165; on the Mamluk period see Abd al-Rahim 1974.

38. Owen 1969:70-71, 175-76, 106-10, 147-52; Rifaat 1947:101-3.

39. Hershlag 1980:114-15; Hansen 1974, using O'Brien's data and calculating at both 1821 and 1913 prices.

40. Hansen 1974.

41. Hansen 1979a; Hansen and Wattleworth 1978; Craig and Abdel-Karim 1947; see also EHME:365 and Issawi 1947:54-55.

42. Issawi 1963:121-22, 1976:63-65.

43. EHT:7-8, 37-50, 99; Eldem 1970:308; Issawi 1980b.

44. Tezel 1975:380-82.

45. Hershlag 1968:214, 290-91, 355-56; Issawi 1976:63-65.

46. EHI:40-42.

47. Keddie 1950, quoted in ibid.:54.

48. Lambton 1953:129-77; Ansari 1974:232-34; Nowshirvani 1981:576-78.

49. EHI:22, 11; see also Lambton 1970.

50. EHI:373-90; Issawi 1976:63-65; idem 1978a; Hershlag 1980:216.

51. EHFC; for conditions in the 1830s, see Bowring 1973:25, 49-51.

52. EHME:226-47.

53. Chevallier 1968; Schatkowski-Schilcher 1975.

54. Himadeh 1936:passim; United Nations 1955:119-207; Issawi 1976:63-65; Halevi 1968:99-103.

55. Hasan n.d.:171-78; Himadeh 1938b:passim; United Nations 1955:92-118; Penrose 1978:163-96, 248-52; Issawi 1976:63-65.

56. Ageron 1968:376-90, 792-815; Nouschi 1961:passim; A. Berque 1948.

57. Ageron 1966:81-83.

58. Valensi 1977:448-79.

59. Poncet 1962:102-4, 248-56, 498-521; Initiation 1950:307-61; Birot and Dresch 1953:1:480-82; Tunisia 1954; Régence de Tunis 1931b:3-6; for case studies see Institut 1957.

60. Miège 1961: 3:375-459; Burke 1976:56-58; see also Hoffherr and Moris 1934:passim.

61. Ayache 1956:239-42, 288-91; Sabbagh 1980.

62. Despois 1935:44-62; Lindberg 1952:9-15.

63. For income distribution in Egypt and Turkey see two studies sponsored by Princeton University, Tignor and Abdel-Khalek 1981 and Ozbudun and Ulusan 1980. For Iran, Bank Markazi 1972; Pesaran 1976; Parvin and Zomani 1979; Issawi 1978a:144-46; for Iraq, Issa 1979; for Israel, Ginor 1979; for Morocco, Griffin 1975; for a short survey that covers most countries in the region, Tuma 1980.

64. See, for example, J. L. Burckhardt's remarks, in 1831, on the Arabian beduins, EHME:342–43.

65. Heyworth-Dunne 1939:41–65; al-Shayyal 1951:70–74.

66. On Turkey Berkes 1964:23–50, Lewis 1961:86–87; on Lebanon, Hourani 1962:55–60.

67. See Issawi 1980a.

68. al-Shayyal 1962, 1968; Gran 1979:57–110.

69. Breakdown in Mosharaffa 1947:54, reproduced in Issawi 1954:51; Heyworth-Dunne 1939:157–80.

70. EHT:13; Berkes 1964: 127–28, Lewis 1961:82, 339; Shaw and Shaw 1977: 2:47–48, 109–11; EHI:23–24; Nazhad and Shariaty 1352:3–10; Farman Farmayan 1968.

71. Heyworth-Dunne 1939:115–52; Berkes 1964:47–48, 59–60, 75–76; Shaw 1977: 2:48–49, 106–10, Lewis 1961:82–85.

72. al-Shayyal 1951:passim, Berkes 1964:49–50, 59–60, 118–21; Shaw and Shaw 1977: 1:236–38.

73. Arasteh 1962:29; Farman Farmayan 1968.

74. Lewis and Holt 1962:18.

75. Hourani 1962:passim; Khury 1943:passim; Mardin 1962:passim; Berkes 1964:289–430. For a detailed account of learned societies and periodicals in Lebanon see Haqqi 1334: 2:569–93.

76. Longrigg 1953:21; Notes on the city of Mosul, FO 195/2308.

77. Ageron 1968:962; Blottière 1948:90; Ray 1938:243.

78. Kettani 1974.

79. Hijab 1967; this article gives a good account of the development of scientific thought and institutions in the Arab countries. For more detailed studies on various countries, including Turkey, see Nader and Zahlan 1969; for the Arab countries, Zahlan 1980; United Nations 1980:85–90, 129–36.

80. For a discussion, see Issawi 1968.

81. Steppat 1968:281; Heyworth-Dunne 1939:38.

82. Ageron 1968:961, 318; see pp. 317–42, 923–62 for an excellent study of educational policy in Algeria. For Tunisia, Brown 1965; for the Ottoman Empire, Kazamias 1966; for Iran, Arasteh 1962; and for Egypt, 'Abd al-Karim 1938, Heyworth-Dunne 1939.

83. Shaw 1978; Issawi 1954:33, 50; Ageron 1968:950.

84. Shaw and Shaw 1977: 2:112–13; EHT:13.

85. Heyworth-Dunne 1939:385; Issawi 1954:51–52; Boktor 1936:117.

86. Ageron 1968:950.

87. Piquet 1912:381–89; Brown 1965; Lindberg 1952:9.

88. In 1932, for "Greater Lebanon," which had absorbed other, less educated districts, the figure was 53 percent and for Syria 37. Himadeh 1936:11.

89. Easterlin 1981.

90. Inalcik 1973:65–69, 89–118; Itzkowitz 1972:37–61; see also Gibb and Bowen 1950, vol. 1; Lambton 1953:passim; EI2, s.v. "Ikta."

91. EHT:201-4; Karpat 1973; McGowan (forthcoming).
92. Issawi 1955, 1965.
93. For the early years see EHT:50-51, 'Izz al-Din 1968:passim.

VII. AGRICULTURAL EXPANSION

1. Clawson 1971:66; Kebbaj 1963:passim.
2. For figures for various parts of the Ottoman Empire see EHT:214-16; for Europe, Blum 1978:144-45. In 1844 Egyptian wheat yields were estimated at over 1,000 kilograms; Rivlin 1961:262.
3. For present-day output see sources used in table 7.2; for earlier periods see, on Egypt, *Description* 1809-22, Rivlin 1961, al-Hitta 1950; on Algeria, Nouschi 1961; on Tunisia, Despois 1955 and Valensi 1977; on Libya, Despois 1935; on Iran, EHI:chap. 5 and Lambton 1953; on Turkey, EHT:chap. 5; on Syria and Iraq, Latron 1936 and EHFC; see also Gibb and Bowen 1950: 1:235-75. For more recent data, see Clawson 1971:74-81.
4. For figures on 1800, see EHME:378; on 1880-1910, Owen 1969:235; on the 1930s, Issawi 1947:64; on 1948-57, idem 1963:140.
5. Owen 1969:28-88.
6. *Ibid.*;89-121, 183-211; EHME:359-74.
7. For details see EHI:244-47.
8. For details see EHT:105-6, 132, and 233-46; Quataert 1973:278-95; Ozbudun and Ulusan 1980:247-66.
9. For details see EHFC; Himadeh 1936; International Bank 1955. In the 1830s, under Muhammad Ali, cotton output had risen sharply, but this proved only temporary; EHME:229.
10. United Nations 1958:176-77.
11. For details and sources, see EHI:231-38; for the earlier period, EI2, s.v. "Harir," and Glamann 1958:114-27.
12. For details and sources, EHT:253-59.
13. For details, Issawi 1973; Ducousso 1913; Haqqi 1334: 2:487-518; Fawaz 1979:152; EHFC.
14. For the change in one area, see Swanson 1979; for a more comprehensive account, World Bank 1979a:92-94; for the earlier period, EI2, s.v. "Kahwa," and Glamann 1958:183-211.
15. For details and sources, see EHT:249-53; EHME:60-64.
16. Verney and Dambmann 1900:183; Himadeh 1936:81-83; EHFC.
17. For details, see EHI:247-51; Keddie 1966.
18. Arminjon 1911:316.
19. For details and figures on output and exports, see EHI:238-41, EHT:261-63.
20. For details and figures, see EHT:264-68.
21. Isnard 1954:36-90.

22. See *ibid.*:220-21, for breakdown of labor functions and costs.

23. *Ibid.*:224, 245-350.

24. *Ibid.*:510-17.

25. *Algérie économique* 1930:75-79; *Initiation* 1957:376; see also Saint-Germès 1955:111-26.

26. *Initiation* 1950:323-27.

27. EHT:246-49.

28. Watson 1974.

29. "Report on Jaffa," United Kingdom, Parliament, *Accounts and Papers,* 1882, vol. 71; Ruppin 1916:421; for details, see EHFC.

30. EHT:129, 201.

31. Kebbaj 1963:66-68.

32. Hershlag 1968:164.

33. *Initiation* 1957:400, citing A. Berque.

34. See Linant de Bellefonds 1872; Willcocks and Craig 1913; Rivlin 1961; Owen 1969; Crouchley 1938; Hurst 1952; Shibl 1971; Benedick 1979.

35. EHME:191-97; Willcocks 1911; Sousa and Atkinson 1944-46; Juwaideh 1963; EHFC.

36. Demontès 1922-30:1:315-96; EHT:204, 229-33; EHI:207; Ansari 1974:8-9.

37. For Algeria, Blottière 1948:113-16; *Initiation* 1957:374-75; for Iraq, Longrigg 1953:211-14, 262-63, 370-72; Sousa 1944:passim; Himadeh 1938b:201-15; McLachlan 1979:passim; for Sudan, Gaitskell 1959:49, 93-95, 115-19; for Egypt, Waterbury 1979; Hurst 1952:passim; for Morocco, Stewart 1964:111-14.

38. Viktorov 1968:127.

39. Ministry of Information, *The Sudan Gezira Board* (Khartum, 1967), p. 4; Waterbury 1979:138-39; *Economist* Intelligence Unit, *Quarterly Review*, Egypt (1977) no. 4; Waterbury 1979:138-39.

40. See an unpublished study by M. Sherbini for the FAO and United Nations Economic Commission for West Asia, March 1977; for the effect of weather on wheat yields in Turkey, Ozbudun and Ulusan 1980:203-4 and sources cited.

41. FAO, *Monthly Bulletin of Statistics* (March 1978).

42. FAO 1967:112; Ozbudun and Ulusan 1980:255.

43. See table in Tezel 1975:268; for Syria, Latron 1936:106-12; for Egypt, Foaden and Fletcher 1910.

44. See figures in United Nations 1975:table 7.

45. For Turkey, EHT:97-99; for Egypt, Owen 1969:67-71.

46. Eldem 1970:79; see also Quataert 1973:186-226, 379-90; EHT:211-13.

47. Norman Lewis in EHME:267.

48. EHME:132, 171; EHFC.

49. For available figures, Gilbar 1978; for Khuzistan, Ansari 1974:225-29, 234-43; EHI:chap. 5.

50. Ageron 1968:380, 798; Saint-Germès 1955:96-154; Valensi 1977:467-72; *Initiation* 1950:308-21.

51. FAO 1965:98.

52. Unpublished paper for United Nations Economic Commission for West Asia (March 1977).

53. See EI2, s.v. "ikta"; Lokkegaard 1950:passim; Morimoto 1975; Ashtor 1976:36-41, 168-83, 213-15, 235-42, 261, 273-75, 285-88; Cahen 1953, 1956, 1960; Rabie 1972:passim; Poliak 1939:passim, Lambton 1953, 1965.

54. See EI2, s.v. "askari," "ayan," "çiftlik," and "derebey"; Lewis 1961:30-33; idem 1974; Inalcik 1973:104-18; idem 1953, 1970; Itzkowitz 1972:40-49; Gibb and Bowen 1950:1:235-75; MacGowan (forthcoming); Mehmet Genç, in La Révolution industriélle 1976:242-79.

55. For Egypt see Baer 1969:chaps. 2-4; for Iraq, Haider 1942:passim; for Syria Weulersse 1946:90-132; Latron 1936:49-84; more generally, Planhol 1972 and Harik 1972.

56. Knauerhase 1975:120-22; Survey of Palestine 1946:2:272-89; Benissad 1979:87; Issawi and Dabezies 1951; EHT:206-7; for labor inputs and yields of irrigated and dry lands in Israel, see Bonné 1957:141.

57. Pouyanne 1900:223, quoting Warnier report of 1873.

58. Preamble to Ordinance of 1844.

59. Levasseur 1911:317; Despois 1958:357; Hardy 1953:191; Ageron 1968:1:67-68; Piquet 1912:137-64.

60. Hardy 1953:198-99; Passeron 1926:passim, Piquet 1912:165-70.

61. Ageron 1968:1:34-36, 78-102, 2:166-67; Piquet 1912:171-208.

62. Birot and Dresch 1953:1:480; Ageron 1966:49-53, 78-79; Initiation 1957:379; Tiers Monde (1962); Piquet 1912:241; Vatin 1974:150, 288.

63. Clegg 1971:passim; Land Policy 1967:235-46;Benhouria 1980; Benissad 1979:76-111.

64. Piquet 1912:356-75; Poncet 1962:618-30 and passim; Passeron 1926:passim, Birot and Dresch 1953:1:481; Despois 1958:364; Initiation 1950:307-34; Tunisia 1954; Land Policy 1967:189-204; Simmons 1972.

65. Passeron 1926:290-93; Milleron 1954:116-26; Despois 1958:chap. 5; Birot and Dresch 1953:1:481-82; Ayache 1956:149-62; Morocco 1954; Land Policy 1967:247-56; Griffin 1975.

66. Birot and Dresch 1953.

67. International Labour Office 1960:57; Despois 1935:54-62; Evans-Pritchard 1949:222.

68. Italian Empire n.d.:60-63; International Bank 1960:428; Lindbergh 1952:9-11; Land Policy 1967:137-51.

69. See Survey of Palestine 1946:1:244-45, 372-86; Khalidi 1971:841-42; Granott 1952:278.

70. Himadeh 1938a; Halperin 1957; Darin-Drabkin 1962; Kanovsky 1966; Abarbanel 1974; Survey of Palestine 1946, vols. 1, 3, which also contain much information on Arab land tenure and agriculture; Peretz 1958:144-45, 165.

71. Munzer 1945:39; Arab Office 1947:117-19.

72. Literature is abundant and of high quality; see Barakat 1978; Baer 1962; idem in EHME:79-90; Rivlin 1961; Owen 1969.

73. See references in preceding note and table in Issawi 1947:73; idem, 1954:126; Owen 1981.

74. Hansen 1979b; see also Richards 1980.

75. Owen 1981; Issawi 1947:77–80; 1963:153–55; for details see Saab 1967; Warriner 1962; Mabro 1974; Abdel Fadil 1975; Richards 1980; Tignor and Abdel-Khalek 1981.

76. EHME:500–2; Gaitskell 1959; Barnett 1977; Waterbury 1979; reports of Gezira Board.

77. EHT:199–227; Warriner and Baer in EHME:71–90; Inalcik 1955; Quataert 1973:36–48; Mears 1924:238–64; land legislation in Fisher 1919; Tute 1927; Young 1905.

78. Figures in EHT:201–10; Mears 1924:295–96.

79. Yerasimos 1976:3:1463; Ozbudun and Ulusan 1980:142.

80. Longrigg 1925:306–11; EHME:163–78; EHFC; Warriner 1948:99–119, 1962:55–183; Haider 1942:passim; Dowson 1932:passim; Ali 1955; Alwan 1956; Adams 1958; *Land Policy* 1967:218–34.

81. Warriner 1962; Penrose and Penrose 1978:240–48, 452–60; Gabbay 1978:passim; Fernea 1969.

82. Warriner and Baer in EHME:71–90; EHFC; Himadeh 1936:51–69; Granott 1952:38; Latron 1936:passim; Weulersse 1946:passim; International Bank 1955:351–56; Warriner 1948:81–98; Moussly 1951; Klat 1957, 1958; FAO 1955; Firestone 1981.

83. Hammadi 1966; Viktorov 1968:118–22.

84. EHFC; Ismail 1958; Harik 1968:passim; Lebanon 1960.

85. *Survey of Palestine* 1946; 3:1197–1213.

86. Human Relations Area Files, *Jordan* 1957; Baer 1957.

87. For Khuzistan see Ansari 1974:259–63 and, more generally, Nowshirvani 1981.

88. Lambton 1953:passim; Denman 1978; EHI:206–31.

89. Denman 1978; Lambton 1969; Keddie 1972; Moghadam 1978.

VIII. DEINDUSTRIALIZATION AND REINDUSTRIALIZATION

1. Issawi 1970b; Raymond 1973:209–12. Ashtor 1977 claims that "most Near Eastern industries were [by the 14th century] no longer able to compete with Western manufactured goods, imported by Italian and other merchants." See also idem 1978.

2. Pennec 1964:211; Valensi 1969b; Venture du Paradis 1898.

3. Raymond 1973:170–82; Masson 1911:456; Davis 1967.

4. Mehmet Genç, in *Révolution* 1976; EI2, s.v. "Harir"; Cizakca 1980.

5. Stoianovich 1960.

6. *Ibid.*; Raymond 1973:206–7.

7. A. D. Novichev in EHT:300–3.

8. Chevallier 1971:200; Report on Aleppo, 1862, FO 195/741. Other, sometimes incompatible, figures have been given: "the number of Aleppo's textile looms, which had reached in the past a record of 40,000, diminished to about 5,500 in 1856 and rose back to only 10,000 in 1859. Similarly the number of looms

in Damascus fell from some 34,000 in the recent past to about 4,000 in the late 1850's"; Ma'oz 1968:179, citing British consular reports. According to the Russian consul, the number of looms in all Syrian cities fell from 50,000 in 1840 to 2,500 forty years later; Bazili 1962:243. In 1873 the American consul in Beirut stated that the number of looms in Damascus had fallen from 3,000 before the 1860 troubles to barely 1,300; US GR 84, Misc. Corr. Beirut, 1873 "Report on Syria."

9. Ömer Sarç, in EHME:50–51; various British consular reports, cited in EHT:298–99.

10. EHI:258–59.

11. Hasan n.d.:281–85.

12. Pennec 1964:211–24; Valensi 1969b; Fleury 1896.

13. Miège 1959; idem 1961:4:367, 394–96; for the crafts of Salé, Brown 1976.

14. EHT:299.

15. EHME:452–58; for details, see al-Khadim 1957:105–42 and several articles in EC (1910, 1911).

16. US GR 84, Misc. Corr. Beirut, 1875–80, reply to questionnaire, 21 July 1880.

17. Kalla 1969:203–4; Himadeh 1936:120–30; Grunwald and Ronall 1960:298; for Palestine, Himadeh 1938a:216–23.

18. Richardson to O'Conor, 6 January 1900, FO 195/2122.

19. Report on Handlooms, 15 August 1907, FO 195/2243.

20. United Nations 1955:65.

21. Pennec 1964:211–24; Stewart 1957; *Initiation* 1950:351; for figures on Tunisia around 1900, Mustapha n.d.:passim.

22. EHI:298–99.

23. For details and sources, see EHT:306–9 and Kurmuş 1974a:128–35.

24. EHI:301–5; United Nations 1955:65–66, 79.

25. Piquet 1912:299.

26. US GR, Misc. Corr. Beirut, 1881–84, "Report on Syria for year ending September 30, 1884."

27. *Ibid.*, 1873, "General Report on Syria," 30 September 1873. Figures for the 1830s were about the same; see Bowring 1973:51.

28. See table in EHT:42–43.

29. Clerget 1934:2:155–56. In 1872 weavers in Cairo earned 5 piasters a day and in Alexandria 3.50. In other branches wages were somewhat lower (except for skilled craftsmen like carpenters, who earned 8.75 piasters in Cairo) and in factories higher; see *Statistique de l'Egypte 1873*:206–24. In Fez in 1870 wages in the leading crafts averaged 4 to 6 d (8 to 12 cents) a day; British consul cited by Miège, *BESM* (December 1953).

30. EHI:41; table in dispatch of 17 October 1870, FO 83/337.

31. Ali Giritli, in EHME:389–402; Mabro and Radwan 1976:11–18. For details on the industries see Fahmy 1954:passim.

32. Baer 1964:136–37.

33. EHME:55–57; EHT:277–78; Clark 1974.

34. Adamiyyat, in EHI:292-97; Brown 1974:295-99; Martz 1897; Miège 1961:4:98-100, 123-25.

35. For example, whereas in 1860 there were almost no mechanical spindles in China, India, and Japan, by 1890 there were 3.2 million (300,000 of them in Japan) and in 1913 9.2 million (2.3 million in Japan), or 6.4 percent of the world total; Bairoch 1974. The steel and other industries had also developed in India and Japan. For a more general, concise, and recent discussion see W. A. Lewis 1978:194-224.

36. Maunier 1976; EHME:452-60; for data on 1872, see *Statistique de l' Egypte* 1873:202-26.

37. EHI:305-10; Bharier 1971:170-71; Ashraf and Hekmat 1981.

38. EHT:309-30; Himadeh 1938a:221.

39. Piquet 1912:299-300, 432-33; Martz 1897; Miège 1961:4:336-39; *Résidence* 1915-21:1:93, 2:53-56, 7:280-82; Caillé 1949:1:349.

40. For Syria, see al-Qasimi 1960, quoted in EHFC; for Egypt al-Khadim 1957 and Lord Cromer's report for 1905, quoted in EHME:454; for Iran, EHI:268-82 and *Jughrafiya-i Isfahan* 1342.

41. Clerget 1934:2:155-56; EHI:260; EHT:43; see also EHME:47.

42. Radwan 1974:236; for Iran in 1900-10, Bharier (1971:54) estimates that all imported capital goods accounted for only 6 percent of total gross domestic fixed capital formation, housing alone constituting 44 percent; this suggests a very low figure for industrial investment.

43. EHME:47, 452; EHI:275; but see Owen 1966. Earlier some governments had made feeble efforts to save the handicrafts; for Turkey in the 1790s and 1860s, see EHME:52-53; for Tunisia in the 1870s, Ganiage 1959:455.

Mehmet Genç has shown, in an unpublished paper, that in the 1720s the Ottoman government made unsuccessful attempts to develop a few industries by installing machinery imported from Europe.

One should add that, before the First World War, active government intervention in economic matters was rather unusual and fumbling; for India see Dewey 1979, where many points applicable to the Middle East are made. And, as pointed out by Owen, the Indian example strongly influenced the British rulers of Egypt.

44. For Harb see Tignor 1976, 1980; Deeb 1976; for Iran, Jamalzadeh 1335:passim; for Turkey, Ahmad 1980.

45. Ahmad 1980; EHT:318-20.

46. al-Gritly 1947; Deeb 1976; Tignor 1976, 1980.

47. Hershlag 1968:52-57.

48. For details on tariff protection in Egypt, see Mabro and Radwan 1976:50-62; for Palestine, Himadeh 1938a:432-39; for Syria, idem 1936:254-58; for Iraq, idem 1938b:421-28; for Turkey, Hershlag 1968:65-67, 115-17.

49. Mabro and Radwan 1976:26-29; Tignor 1976, 1980; Deeb 1976; for details, Issawi 1947:84-88.

50. Himadeh 1938a:230-80, 1938b:236-38, 1936:130-69.

51. EHI:377-79; Bharier 1971:172-81.

52. EHT:367-69; Hershlag 1968:80-84.

53. Stewart 1957:96-100; *Industrialisation* 1952; Evin 1934; Hoffherr and Mauchaussé 1933, 1935.

54. *Algérie économique* (1930):passim; Blottière 1948:178-87; *Initiation* 1950:253-57; *Industrialisation* 1952:21-27; Stewart 1957:passim.

55. United Nations 1958:16.

56. See tables in Himadeh 1938a:239-50.

57. Bharier 1971:172-81; United Nations 1955:58.

58. United Nations 1958:9-13.

59. See table in idem 1953:34.

60. Wilmington 1971:passim.

61. See tables in United Nations 1953:34-35; idem 1955:9-11; for Egypt, Mabro and Radwan 1976:82-84; for Turkey, Hershlag 1968:171-72; Singer 1977:30-39.

62. Leff 1979; for figures on the individual countries see Hershlag 1975:chap. 7 and idem 1979.

63. Bank Markazi, Iran, *Annual Report 2535* (1976/77) and various unpublished reports.

64. Hershlag 1979:66; see also Makdisi 1979 for details.

65. To take a striking example—by no means the worst—in Jordan's Input-Output Table for 1968 only 215 of the 1,500 entries were filled; for Algeria see Benissad 1979:142-46.

66. For details and analysis see Turner and Bedore 1979:passim. In 1977 it was estimated that the region's 1975-80 plans for oil refineries and petrochemicals would aggregate $74 billion, i.e., two and one-half times the projected investments of North America and Western Europe combined; these plans have since been drastically reduced. *Petroleum Economist* (January 1977).

67. Harbison and Ibrahim 1958:136. United Nations 1953:48, which gives other examples; Central Bank of Egypt, *Economic Review* (1972), no. 2.

68. Stucken 1963:179, Continental Allied Co 1960:3; for Syria in the 1970s, Carr 1980.

69. See figures in United Nations 1958:70-71, 85. An extreme example is the car industry; in Egypt in the late 1970s output was about 1 car per worker per year, compared to 6 in Britain and 30-50 in leading Japanese firms. Another is the Turkish state-owned mill at Iskenderun, where a ton of steel takes 72 man-hours, compared to 5 in the United States and 7 in Europe.

70. United Nations 1974.

71. In this respect latecomers to industrialization, who enjoy certain other important advantages, are under a handicap. To take an extreme example, when Japan started its petrochemical industry in the 1950s, an ethylene plant of optimum size produced about 20,000 tons a year. Today, when the Middle Eastern countries are building their plants, the corresponding figure is around 400,000 tons: Turner and Bedore 1979:155.

72. In Egypt in 1965-66 a study showed that "at least 25 percent of the productive capacity of the nationalized industries was idle"; *al-Ahram al-*

iqtisadi, January 1, 1968. In Israel in 1966, excess capacity "even if narrowly defined" was about 40 percent of output—this was partly because of the recession; United Nations, *Industrialization and Productivity,* no. 15. In Syria in the 1960s the textile industry was working at 59 percent of capacity and the sugar industry at 75–80 percent; United Nations 1967:55–57. In Sudan over a stretch of years in the late 1960s, a date factory averaged 27 percent of capacity; a sugar factory 35 percent, because of inadequate supply of cane; a cardboard factory 6 percent, because of inadequate preliminary survey and the failure to produce the kinds needed by the market; and an onion dehydrating plant 25 percent, because of the failure to provide the right kind of onions in sufficient quantity at the right time; Republic of Sudan, *Economic Survey* (1969):68–80, where other examples are given. Turkish industry has also been working well below capacity, mainly because of shortage of raw materials and power.

73. Thornburg, et al. 1949; for a discussion of Iraq, see Penrose and Penrose 1979; of Algeria, Benissad 1979.

74. In the late 1940s, in many Turkish industries the annual turnover was around 50 percent or more of the work force, and in Egypt and Iraq 20 percent. United Nations 1953:46–47, 1958:84–85. These ratios have been sharply reduced by providing workers with seniority benefits, housing, etc. A similar trend is observable in the oil industry; see Issawi and Yeganeh 1962:96–97.

75. For examples see Hansen and Nashashibi 1975; Krueger 1974; Michaely 1975; and M. Avramovic in *Tahqiqat-e Eqtesadi,* Tehran (Spring 1970). There are also examples of formerly efficient industries that have deteriorated, e.g., the Egyptian fertilizer industry; see Central Bank of Egypt, *Economic Review* (1979) no. 1.

IX. INSTITUTIONS AND POLICY, MONEY AND PRICES, SAVINGS AND INVESTMENT

1. On this and other topics discussed in this section see Issawi 1980a, which gives bibliographic references for both Europe and the Middle East.

2. Cook 1974:224. This is somewhat overstated: by threatening to cut off credit, bankers often influenced policy, at least in the negative sense of preventing certain obnoxious measures, or securing their repeal; Mottahedeh 1980:117–20.

3. See EI2, s.v. "Karimi" and references cited therein.

4. Schumpeter 1950:160–61.

5. See the perceptive observations by Hodgson 1975: 1:340–44 on European and Muslim family types.

On the Karimis, see EI2, s.v. "Karimi," and Labib 1969; on Cairo, Raymond 1973:2:412–15; on Fez, Le Tourneau 1949:487–93; on Tunis, Brown 1974:83–91; on 16th-century Turkey, Inalcik 1969; on the 18th-century Ottoman Empire, Gibb and Bowen 1950: 1:137–234; on 19th-century Iran, Ashraf and Hekmat 1981.

6. See Mazrui 1967:159–78.

7. For examples and references see Issawi 1980a.

8. Watson 1974; Ashtor 1976:155-58.

9. Issawi 1980a, EHME:4-7, Issawi 1970b, and references cited; Ashtor 1976:242-48, 308-10.

10. For the Ottoman Empire see Inalcik 1969; for 17th century Turkey, Jennings 1973; for 18th-century Egypt, Shaw 1962:56-57; for 17th-century Iran, John Chardin, quoted in Rodinson 1966:57; for Syria, Poliak 1939:68-69, Rafeq 1981:663, 674-75.

11. For excellent accounts of these partnerships see Udovitch 1970:passim and Goitein 1967:169-79.

12. See the interesting discussion in Rodinson 1966; Ashtor 1976:109-14; Labib 1969.

13. See Planhol 1959:1-70; Weulersse 1946:60-71; Ashtor 1976:36-70. The classical indictment of the beduins is Ibn Khaldun's *Muqaddimah*; see Issawi translation, *An Arab Philosophy of History* (London: John Murray, 1950), pp. 54-60; Rosenthal translation, *The Muqaddimah* (3 vols.; New York: Bollingen, 1958) 1:302-8.

14. For examples, Issawi 1980a.

15. Goitein 1967:266-72; Ashtor 1976:chaps. 2-4.

16. Ashtor 1976:247 and chaps. 7-8.

17. Itzkowitz 1972:37-61; Inalcik 1973:121-66, 1969; Kortepeter 1966.

18. Issawi 1980a; Mantran 1962:214, 287, 423.

19. MacGowan (forthcoming).

20. EHT:24-35; for Mamluk Egypt, see Shoshan 1980.

21. For examples see Issawi 1981c.

22. See Baster 1929, 1935; EHT:339-43; EHI:346-56; Forte 1938.

23. For Egypt, see Crouchley 1938:274-78; Rivlin 1961:53-60, 105-36; Hamza 1944:33; EHME:439-45; Hershlag 1980:97-107; for Turkey, EHT:353-55; Hershlag 1980:55-61; Shaw 1975; Akarli 1976; for Iran, EHI:336-38, 361-70; Jamalzadeh 1335:118-19; for Tunisia, Brown 1974:137, 340; Ganiage 1959:397, 426, 452; Piquet 1912:401-2.

24. See EHT:353-55 and EHME:107-13.

25. EHME:439-45; Shaw 1978; EHI:367-69; Akarli 1976:202-5.

26. For the Ottoman agricultural bureaucracy, see Quataert 1973:64-91 and, more generally, Findley 1980:passim.

27. EHT:passim; Ahmad 1980.

28. Wilmington 1971:passim.

29. United States 1980.

30. Amin 1974:84; Halevi and Klinot-Malul 1968:162.

31. Tait et al. 1979.

32. For figures see Issawi 1980d.

33. Issawi 1956.

34. For details and figures on the Ottoman Empire, see EHT:321-26 and Barkan 1975; for Iran, EHI:339-45, 387-39 and Gilbar (forthcoming); for Egypt, Crouchley 1938:96-98; EHME:446-51, 520-24; for Tunisia, Valensi 1977:448-58;

for Syria, EHFC and Gerber and Gross 1980; see also E12, s.v. "Akçe," "Dinar," "Dirham."

35. For the Ottoman Empire see EHT:328-32; Biliotti 1909:passim Kolerkiliç 1958;passim; for Egypt, Crouchley 1938.96-101, 174-77; Rifaat 1938:47-55; Sultan 1914:passim; for Iran, EHI:339-56; Yaganegi 1934:passim; Bharier 1971:45-49; for Syria, Himadeh 1935:passim; for Morocco, Miège 1961:3:97-106, 428-36, 4:113-23; Ayache 1956:104-6; Marty 1951:passim; for Tunisia, De Candia 1932-35.

36. For figures on Egypt see Artin 1908, reprinted in part in EHME:450-51; Campbell, appendix A to Bowring 1840; Hansen 1979b; for Turkey, EHT:335-36; for Syria, EHFC; Gerber and Gross 1980; Bowring 1973; for Iran, EHI:340-42; Nowshirvani 1977, Gilbar (forthcoming).

37. EHT:366; EHI:373; League of Nations *Statistical Yearbook*; Tunisia, *Statistisque générale*, 1929.

38. United Nations 1951:19-21, 84; idem, *Statistical Yearbook*, 1949-50; Prest 1948:passim.

39. See United Nations, *Statistical Yearbook*, and International Monetary Fund, *International Financial Statistics*.

40. Radwan 1974; tables on 63 and 98 and passim.

41. Hansen 1979c.

42. Bharier 1971:49-56.

43. Radwan 1974:63, 98.

44. Nathan et al. 1946:147-55; Halevi 1968:21-22; Gruenbaum 1941.

45. United Nations 1955:58-59; EHI:374-79.

46. Abu El-Haj 1961.

47. Hershlag 1968:94-95; Tezel 1975:146.

48. Radwan 1974:63, 98.

49. Anis 1950.

50. Nathan 1946:159.

51. See figures for Egypt in Radwan 1974 and Iraq in Abu El-Haj 1961.

52. Mead 1967:216-17.

53. Abu El-Haj 1961; United Nations 1955:101.

54. Halevi and Klinot-Malul 1968:284-85.

55. United Nations 1958:20; Hershlag 1968:154-55; Tezel 1975:341.

56. Makdisi 1963; for more recent figures, see Carr 1980.

57. See series in Bharier 1971:49-56.

58. For recent data on savings and investments, the latter broken down, for the Asian Arab countries see United Nations 1980:18-31; for Algeria, Benhouria 1980:299-359.

X. PETROLEUM: TRANSFORMATION OR EXPLOSION?

1. Mention may be made of Longrigg 1968, Shwadran 1974, Issawi and Yeganeh 1962, Kent 1976, Rustow and Mugno 1976, Chisholm 1976, and the sources cited in those works.

2. Report on Petroleum of Mendeli and Kifri, 30 August 1871, CC Baghdad, vol. 13, translated in EHFC.

3. For details see the sources cited above; before the First World War Germans had sought a concession in Iraq, and the 1914 agreement gave them a 25 percent interest in the Turkish Petroleum Company; this was lost as a result of the war. See Kent 1976:passim and EHFC.

4. For details, Issawi and Yeganeh 1962:24–39, 175–81.

5. The paragraphs above in the text have been taken from Issawi 1972:23–28, where sources are given.

6. Adelman 1972:chap. 2.

7. There is a large literature on the pricing of oil; see Adelman 1972:passim; Issawi and Yeganeh 1962:chap. 3; and sources cited.

8. For 1948–61 see table in Issawi and Yeganeh 1962:68.

9. Issawi and Yeganeh 1962:103–13.

10. For details, *ibid.*:chap. 6.

11. For details, Rouhani 1971, Mikdashi 1972, and Rustow and Mugno 1976.

12. *Petroleum Economist* (October 1980):428; for an analysis of the 1973 events, Rustow and Mugno 1976 and Issawi 1980.

13. For more details see Issawi and Yeganeh 1962:chap. 7, and sources cited.

14. *Ibid.*:96–99; United Nations 1953:48.

15. Hirschman 1958:105–7.

16. Turner and Bedore 1979:passim.

17. For this and the following topics see Issawi and Yeganeh 1962:chap. 7.

18. For a much fuller discussion of the topics covered in the following paragraphs see Issawi 1980d.

19. See tables 3, 7, and text in *ibid.*

20. Kuwait, the first oil-producing country to reach affluence and the one that has most effectively used its oil wealth to raise the economic and social level of its inhabitants (appendix table A.1) provides an example. On September 6, 1903 the British consul in Basra reported (FO 195/2139) that the ruler, Sheikh Mubarak al-Sabah, had transferred to his nephews all portions of the estates of his father and grandfather: his grandfather's house worth $1,400, his father's house worth $4,000, another small house worth $200, and 18 shops worth $1,800, or a total of $7,400. Further correspondence (FO 195/2163) showed other assets totaling £T 8,000 but, since the sheikh had no ready cash, he was asking for a British loan of 100,000 rupees. One can presume that sheikhs were among the wealthiest people in Kuwait. As late as 1945, the GNP of Kuwait was under $5 million, or $50 per capita; see Khouja and Sadler 1979:passim. Saudi Arabia stood at a comparable level and the other Arabian countries at a lower one. As late as 1950, Libya's per capita income was put at only $35.

21. For details, see United Nations 1980b:37–62.

XI. THE BALANCE SHEETS

1. This chapter has benefited from criticism and comments made in 1981, at the seminar on Comparative Colonialism, Institute for Advanced Study, a

seminar at the Department of Near Eastern Studies, Princeton University, and the Economic History Seminar, Columbia University. The economic costs and benefits of imperialism are discussed in Clark 1936, Knight 1937, Leduc 1969, and Wesseling 1980, and in the works cited by them.

2. Egretaud 1961:56; Horne 1977:538. The earlier figures seem too high; Headrick 1981:92 states that by 1857 "France had lost 23,787 men in action, and thousands more from disease."

3. Toynbee 1927:101-3, 115-51; Ziyadeh 1958:81-82, 109-11.

4. Cromer 1908: 1:300-330, 2:79-110.

5. Longrigg 1953:123. The number of British killed in Palestine from 1936 to 1939 was about 200 and wounded 500-600; about twice as many casualties were suffered by Arabs, Jews, and others in the armed forces and police. *Survey* 1946:1:38-41. Estimates of Arabs killed range between 3,000 and 5,000 and of wounded between 1,000 (*sic*) and 20,000 Khalidi 1971:846-49.

6. Toynbee 1927:424-39.

7. Longrigg 1953:123. Compare the following: "The annual cost of the army of occupation prior to mid-1920 amounted to £ 24,000,000 and after that date was expected, on account of the need for reinforcements, to rise to £ 28,250,000"; Batatu 1979:88-89.

8. Toynbee 1927:149-50. In 1907-13, French expenditure on troops in Morocco totaled $237 million; Stewart 1964:56.

9. Piquet 1912:267; Knight 1937:16; Great Britain 1944a:286-87; Horne 1977:538.

10. Piquet 1912:405.

11. Antonius 1939:386; Hourani 1946:155; Longrigg 1958:260.

12. Nathan et al. 1946:340; *Survey* 1946:536, supplement p. 72.

13. Marzouk 1957.

14. Lindberg 1952:22, 36; International Bank 1960:45; see also Bank of Libya 1965:53-54.

15. Bloch-Lainé 1956:113-18.

16. Figueras and Jimenez 1953:284-86.

17. Hickinbotham 1958:153.

18. Nathan et al. 1946:340.

19. Abun Nasr 1971:238.

20. Cromer 1910:42.

21. For details see Fairbank et al. 1965:chaps. 2 and 5; Caron 1979:269.

22. EHI:370; EHT:13.

23. Ayache 1956:50, and 69; Miège 1961:2:369.

24. Abun-Nasr 197:255.

25. U.S. Department of State 1933:2:320-26. The initial cost of the British locomotives used by the Egyptian State Railways was slightly higher than that of German or Austrian and their delivery time longer; on the other hand, their running costs were slightly lower and their finish better. UK Parliament, *Accounts and Papers*, 1906, "Egypt No. 1."

26. Edelstein 1976; Lebergott 1980; A. K. Cairncross, *Home and Foreign Investment 1870-1913* (Cambridge: Cambridge University Press, 1953).

27. W. A. Lewis 1978:116.

28. "We have despoiled, pursued and hunted down the Arabs in order to populate Algeria with Italians and Spaniards"; Anatole France, quoted by Horne 1977:32.

29. W. A. Lewis 1978:188-93.

30. I witnessed a case in point. In 1938 Britain, worried by Japanese competition in cotton textiles, sent a delegation to Egypt which persuaded the Egyptian government to impose an import quota, tying purchases of textiles to exports of cotton, with safeguards for Egyptian industry. Approval of this scheme was delayed in Parliament and the outbreak of war rendered it superfluous.

31. Kemp 1971:295; Knight 1937:184-98; Clark 1936:64.

32. Segrè 1974:83, Clark 1936:67.

33. Colin 1901:287; see also Piquet 1912:280-81.

34. Cazès 1921:69; to this may be added Blottière's (1948:185) judgment that but for the monopoly it enjoyed French shipping between Algeria and France would not have been able to face foreign competition, which would "certainly supplant it in this traffic."

35. Issawi 1954:204; Penrose 1978:151; *Survey* 1946.

36. For example, the German colonies, which in 1914 "contained in all 5,000 German inhabitants and which cost the German taxpayers in subsidies six times what the German merchants and investors made out of them in profits." Taylor 1961:151. The colonies accounted for only 0.5 percent of Germany's trade and provided only 1.6 percent of its raw material imports; see also Clark 1936:43. The same was true of Portugal's empire; see Hammond 1966:passim.

37. Figueras and Jimenez 1955:3:274.

38. Trumpener 1968:182-84.

39. British garrisons in Egypt consisted of a few thousand men. I have been informed by Lord Caradon that when the 1929 troubles broke out there was not a single British soldier in Palestine; following a telephone call by him to London some troops were sent by sea from Malta. No troops were kept in the Gulf and only tiny garrisons in Aden and Sudan.

40. Central Intelligence Agency, *Communist Aid to the Less Developed Countries of the Free World* (Washington, D.C., August 1977); IMF, *Direction of Trade.*

41. Ruben Berrios Martinez in *Foreign Affairs* (July 1977).

42. al-Sayyal 1962:403.

43. Atsamba 1959:6.

44. A. Marot in Gran 1979:vii and Gran passim.

45. Black et al. 1975; Keene 1969; Smith 1959; see also Owen 1969:356-64.

46. This matter is discussed more fully in Issawi 1965, 1968, and 1970a; for world figures see Rostow 1978.

47. See Issawi 1980a.

Selected Bibliography

ARCHIVES

Austria, Haus-Hof und Staatsarchiv, Vienna.
France, Ministère des Affaires étrangères, Correspondence commerciale, Paris.
Turkey, Başbakanlik Arşivi, Bab-i Ali Evrak Odasi, Istanbul.
Turkish Embassy, London, Archives.
United Kingdom, Board of Trade Series, London.
—— Foreign Office Series, London.
—— India Office Series, London.
United States National Archives, Dispatches to Department of State, Washington, D.C.

GOVERNMENTAL PUBLICATIONS

Austria, *Ausweise über den Handel von Oesterreiche.*
Egypt, Ministère de l'Interieur, *Statistique de l'Egypte, 1873.*
—— Ministère des Finances, *Annuaire Statistique.*
—— *Rapport de la Commission du Commerce et de l'Industrie*, 1918.
France, Ministère des Affaires étrangères, *Bulletin Consulaire.*
Prussia, *Preussisches Handelsarchiv.*
Turkey, Nezaret umumi ticaret ve nafia. *Istatistik umumi idaresi 1316.*
—— Office central de Statistique, *Annuaire Statistique.*
United Kingdom, Parliament, *Accounts and Papers.*
United States, Department of State, *Foreign Relations of the United States.*

BOOKS, ARTICLES, DISSERTATIONS

(For additional references see bibliographies in EHME, EHI, EHT, and EHFC, Ageron 1968, Ganiage 1959, Valensi 1977, Miège 1961, Noin 1970; Batatu 1978)

Abadan, Nermin, ed. 1976. *Turkish Workers in Europe, 1960–1975*. Leiden: Brill.

Abarbanel, Jay. 1974. *The Co-operative Farmer and the Welfare State*. Manchester: University of Manchester Press.

'Abd al-Karim, 'Izzat. 1938. *Tarikh al-ta'lim fi 'asr Muhammad 'Ali*. Cairo.

'Abd al-Rahim, 'Abd al-Rahim. 1974. *Al-rif al-misri fi-al qarn al-thamin 'ashar*. Cairo.

Abdel Fadil, Mahmoud. 1975. *Development, Income Distribution, and Social Change in Rural Egypt*. Cambridge: Cambridge University Press.

Abrahamian, E. 1974. "Oriental Despotism: The Case of Qajar Iran." IJMES (January).

Abu El-Haj, Rabhi. 1961. "Capital Formation in Iraq, 1922–1957." EDCC (July).

Abu-Lughod, Janet. 1965a. "Urbanization in Egypt." EDCC (April).

—— 1965b. "A Tale of Two Cities." *Comparative Studies in Society and History* (July).

——1971. *Cairo*. Princeton, N.J.: Princeton University Press.

Abun-Nasr, Jamil. 1971. *A History of the Maghrib*. Cambridge: Cambridge University Press.

Adamiyyat, Feridun. 1324 [1945]. *Amir-i Kabir wa Iran*. Tehran.

Adams, Doris. 1958. *Iraq's People and Resources*. Berkeley: University of California Press.

Adelman, M. A. 1972. *The World Petroleum Market*. Baltimore: Johns Hopkins University Press.

Ageron, Charles-Robert. 1966. *Histoire de l'Algérie contemporaine, 1830–1966*. Paris: Presses Universitaires de France.

—— 1968. *Les Algeriens musulmans et la France, 1871–1919*. 2 vols. Paris: Presses Universitaires de France.

Ahmad, Feroz. 1980. "Vanguard of a Nascent Bourgeoisie: The Social and Economic Policy of the Young Turks." In Osman Okyar and Halil Inalcik, eds. *Social and Economic History of Turkey*. Ankara.

Akarli, Engin. 1976. "The Problems of External Pressures, Power Struggles, and Budgetary Deficits in Ottoman Politics under Abdulhamid II. . . ." Ph.D. dissertation, Princeton University.

L' Algérie, 1954. (*Encyclopédie mensuelle d'outre mer*, special issue).

L' Algérie économique en 1930. Algiers. 1930.

Ali, Hasan Mohammad. 1955. *Land Reclamation and Settlement in Iraq*. Baghdad.

Aliboni, Roberto. 1979. *Arab Industrialization and Economic Integration*. London: St. Martin's Press.

Allman, James. 1980. "The demographic transition in the Middle East and North Africa." IJMES (November).

Alwan, Abdul Salih. 1956. "The Process of Economic Development in Iraq with Special References to Land Problems and Policies." Ph.D. dissertation, University of Wisconsin.

Amin, Galal. 1974. *The Modernization of Poverty*. Leiden: Brill.

Amin, Samir. 1966. *L'économie du Maghreb*. Paris: Éditions de Minuit.

—— 1970. *The Maghreb in the Modern World*. London: Penguin.

Anis, M. A. 1950. "The National Income of Egypt." EC, special issue.

Ansari, Mostafa. 1974. "A History of Khuzistan, 1878–1925." Ph.D. dissertation, University of Chicago.

Antonius, George. 1939. *The Arab Awakening*. Philadelphia: Lippincott.

Antoun, Richard and Iliya Harik, eds. 1972. *Rural Politics and Social Change in the Middle East*. Bloomington: Indiana University Press.

Apelt, Fritz. 1929. *Aden*. Grossenhain.

Arab Office, London. 1947. *The Future of Palestine*. Geneva: Imprimerie Centrale.

Arabic-Speaking Americans. 1946. New York: Institute of Arab American Affairs.

Arasteh, Reza. 1962. *Education and Social Awakening in Iran*. Leiden: E. J. Brill.

Arminjon, Pierre. 1911. *Situation économique et financière de l'Egypte*. Paris: Pichon.

Artin, Yacub. 1883. *La propriété foncière en Egypte*. Cairo.

—— 1908. *Essai sur les causes de renchérissement*. Cairo.

Ashraf, A. and H. Hekmat. 1981 "Merchants and Artisans in the Development Process of Nineteenth-Century Iran." In Udovitch, ed., *The Islamic Middle East* (q.v.)

Ashtor, E. 1976. *A Social and Economic History of the Near East in the Middle Ages*. Berkeley and Los Angeles: University of California Press.

—— 1977. "L'apogée du commerce vénitien." In Hans-Georg Beck et al., eds. *Venezia, Centro di Mediazone*. Florence.

—— 1978. "Underdevelopment in the Pre-Industrial Era." JEEH 7, nos. 2–3.

Askari, Hossain and J. T. Cummings. 1976. *The Middle East Economies in the 1970s*. New York: Praeger.

Askew, William. 1942. *Europe and Italy's Acquisition of Libya.* Durham: Duke University.

Aswad, Barbara, ed. 1974. *Arabic Speaking Communities in American Cities.* New York: Center for Migration Studies.

Atsamba, F. M. 1959. "Sostoyanie promyshlennosti. . . ." In *Ocherki po Istoriya Arabskikh Stran.* Moscow.

Avcioglu, Dogan. 1968. *Türkiyenin Düzeni.* Ankara.

Ayache, Albert. 1956. *Le Maroc.* Paris: Éditions Sociales.

'Azzawi, 'Abbas. 1958. *Tarikh al-nuqud al-'Iraqiyah.* Baghdad.

—— 1958. *Tarikh al-daraib al-'Iraqiya.* Baghdad.

Baer, Gabriel. 1957. "Land Tenure in the Hashimite Kingdom of Jordan." *Land Economics* (August).

—— 1962. *A History of Landownership in Modern Egypt.* London: Oxford University Press.

—— 1964. *Egyptian Guilds in Modern Times.* Jerusalem.

—— 1969. *Studies in the Social History of Modern Egypt.* Chicago: Chicago University Press.

—— 1970a. "The Administrative, Economic, and Social Functions of Turkish Guilds." IJMES (January).

—— 1970b. "Monopolies and Restrictive Practices of Turkish Guilds." JESHO (April).

—— 1981. "Village and City in Egypt and Syria." In Udovitch, ed., *The Islamic Middle East* (q.v.)

Baeza, Hubert-Louis. 1924. *Le rôle économique du Port d'Alger.* Algiers.

Bairoch, Paul. 1974. "Geographical Structure and Trade Balance of European Foreign Trade from 1800 to 1970." JEEH (Winter).

Balloui, Jean. 1939. "L'artisanat marocain à la croisée des chemins." *Federation des Sociétés savantes de l'Afrique du nord, Quatrième Congrès,* 2:895–900. Algiers.

Bank Markazi, Iran. 1972. *National Income of Iran, 1959–72.* Tehran.

Barakat, 'Ali. 1978. *Tatawwur al-milkiyya al-zira'ia fi misr.* Cairo.

Barkan, Omer. 1975. "The Price Revolution of the Sixteenth Century." IJMES (January).

Barlow, Ima 1940. *The Agadir Crisis.* Chapel Hill: University of North Carolina Press.

Barnett, Tony. 1977. *The Gezira Sudan Scheme: An Illusion of Development.* London: F. Cass.

Barsoumian, Hagop. 1980. "The Armenian Amira Class of Istanbul." Ph.D. dissertation. Columbia University.

Baster, A. S. J. 1929. *The Imperial Banks*. London: P. S. King.

—— 1935. *The International Banks*. London: P. S. King

Batatu, Hanna. 1978. *The Old Social Classes and the Revolutionary Movements of Iraq*. Princeton, N.J.: Princeton University Press.

Bazili, Konstantin. 1835. *Ocherki Konstantinopolya*. 2 vols. St. Petersburg.

—— 1962. *Sirya i Palestina*. Moscow, reprint.

Beaumont, Peter et al. 1976. *The Middle East: A Geographical Study*. London: Wiley.

Beck, Lois and Nikki Keddie. 1978. *Women in the Muslim World*. Cambridge: Harvard University Press.

Belal, Abdel-Aziz. 1968. *L'investissement au Maroc (1912–64)*. Paris: Mouton.

Bémont, Fredy. 1969. *Les Villes de l'Iran*. Paris: privately printed.

Ben-Arieh. 1970. *The Population of the Large Towns in Palestine*. Jerusalem.

Benedick, Richard. 1979. "The High Dam and the Transformation of the Nile." MEJ (Spring).

Benhouria, Tahar. 1980. *L'Economie de l'Algérie*. Paris: Maspéro.

Benissad, Mohammed. 1979. *Economie du Développement de l'Algérie*. Paris: Economica.

Ben-Porath, Yoram. 1966. *The Arab Labor Force in Israel*. Jerusalem.

Berg, Elliot. 1965. "The Development of a Labor Force in Sub-Saharan Africa." EDCC (July).

Berkes, Niyazi. 1964. *The Development of Secularism in Turkey*. Montreal: McGill University Press.

Bernard, F. 1917. *Le Maroc économique et agricole*. Paris: Masson.

Bernard, M. A. 1913. *Les chemins de fer algériens*. Algiers.

Berque, Augustin. 1948. "La bourgeoisie algérienne.", *Hesp*. 35.

Berque, Jacques. 1965. "Trois stades de l'economie proche-orientale." In George Makdisi, ed. *Arabic and Islamic Studies in Honor of Hamilton A. R. Gibb*. Cambridge, Mass.: Harvard University Press.

—— 1972. *Egypt: Imperialism and Revolution*. London: Faber.

Beshai, Adel. 1976. *Export Performance and Economic Development in the Sudan*. London: Ithaca Press.

Bharier, Julian. 1971. *Economic Development in Iran*. London: Oxford University Press.

Biliotti, A. 1909. *La Banque Ottomane*. Paris. Jouve.

Billiard, Louis. 1930. *Les ports et la navigation de l'Algérie*. Paris: Larose.

Birks, J. S. and C. A. Sinclair. 1979. "Migration and Development: The Changing Perspectives of the Poor Arab Countries." *Journal of International Affairs.* (Fall/Winter).

Birot, Pierre and Jean Dresch. 1953. *La Méditerranée et le Moyen-Orient.* 2 vols. Paris: Presses Universitaires de France.

Black, Cyril et al., eds. 1975. *The Modernization of Japan and Russia.* New York: Free Press.

Blaisdell, Donald. 1929. *European Financial Control in the Ottoman Empire.* New York: Columbia University Press.

Bloch-Lainé, F. 1956. *La zone franc.* Paris: Presses Universitaires de France.

Blottière, Jean. 1948. *L'Algérie.* Paris: Sociéte d'éditions geographiques.

Blum, Jerome. 1978. *The End of the Old Order in Europe.* Princeton, N.J.: Princeton University Press.

Boktor, Amir. 1936. *School and Society in the Valley of the Nile.* Cairo.

Bonine, Michael. 1980. "Urbanization of the Persian Gulf Nations." In Cottrell, *The Persian Gulf States* (q.v.)

Bonné, Alfred. 1945. *The Economic Development of the Middle East.* London: Oxford University Press.

—— 1955. *State and Economics in the Middle East.* 2d ed. London: Routledge.

—— 1957. *Studies in Economic Development.* London: Routledge.

Bousser, Marcel. 1934. *Le problème des transports au Maroc.* Paris.

Bouy, Ernest. 1930. *Le problème de la main d'oeuvre et la législation du travail au Maroc.* Paris.

Bowring, John. 1840. "Report on Egypt and Candia." *British Parliamentary Papers,* vol.21.

—— 1973. *Report on the Commercial Statistics of Syria.* Reprint. New York: Arno Press.

Brackmann, Karl. 1935. *Fünfzig Jahre deutscher Afrikaschiffart.* Berlin

Braudel, Fernand. 1972. *The Mediterranean and the Mediterranean World in the Age of Philip II.* 2 vols. New York: Harper.

—— 1973. *Capitalism and Material Life, 1400–1800.* London: Weidenfeld.

Brown, Francis and Joseph Roucek. 1945. *One America.* New York: Prentice-Hall.

Brown, Kenneth. 1976. *People of Sale. . . .* Cambridge, Mass.: Harvard University Press.

Brown, L. Carl. 1965. "Tunisia." In James Coleman, ed. *Education and Political Development.* Princeton, N.J.: Princeton University Press.

—— 1974. *The Tunisia of Ahmad Bey.* Princeton, N.J.: Princeton University Press.

Buhuth al-'id ai-Khamsiny. 1960. Cairo (EC).

Bulliet, Richard. 1975. *The Camel and the Wheel.* Cambridge: Harvard University Press.

Burckhardt, John Lewis. 1819. *Travels in Nubia.* London.

—— 1822. *Travels in Syria and the Holy Land.* London.

—— 1829. *Travels in Arabia.* London.

—— 1831. *Notes on the Bedouins and Wahabys.* 2 vols. London.

Burke, Edmund. 1976. *Prelude to Protectorate in Morocco.* Chicago: University of Chicago Press.

Burns, Norman. 1933. *The Tariff of Syria.* Beirut.

Butler, H. 1932. *Report on Labour Conditions in Egypt.* Cairo.

Cable, Boyd. 1937. *A Hundred Year History of the P & O.* London.

Cahen, Claude. 1953. "L'évolution de l'iqta." *Annales* (January–March).

—— 1956. "Le régime des impôts dans le Fayyum ayyubide." *Arabica* (January).

—— 1960. "Féodalité." JESHO (April).

Caillé, Jacques. 1949. *La ville de Rabat jusqu'au Protectorat.* 2 vols. Paris: Vanoest.

Caponera, Dante. 1954. *Water Laws in Moslem Countries.* Rome: Food and Agricultural Organization (March).

Caron, François. 1979. *An Economic History of Modern France.* New York: Columbia University Press.

Carr, David. 1980. "Capital Flows and Development in Syria." MEJ (Autumn).

Cazès, Maurice. 1921. *Le Port d'Oran.* Mascara.

Chase Manhattan Bank. 1956 and 1971. *Investment Patterns in the World Petroleum Industry.* New York.

Chevalier, Louis. 1947. *Le problème démographique nord-african.* Paris: Presses Universitaires de France.

Chevallier, Dominique. 1968. "Western Development and Eastern Crisis." In Polk and Chambers, *Beginnings of Modernization in the Middle East* (q.v.)

—— 1971. *La Société du Mont Liban.* Paris: P. Geuthner.

Chisolm, A.H.T. 1976. *The First Kuwait Oil Concession Agreement.* London: Cass.

Chouraqui, André. 1952. *Les Juifs de l'Afrique du Nord.* Paris: Presses Universitaires de France.

Cizakca, Murat. 1980. "Price History and the Bursa Silk Industry." JEH (September).

Clark, E.C. 1974. "The Ottoman Industrial Revolution." IJMES (January).

Clark, Grover. 1936. *The Balance Sheets of Imperialism*. New York: Columbia University Press.

Clark, J. I. and W. B. Fisher. 1972. *Populations of the Middle East and North Africa*. New York: Africana.

Clawson, Marion et al. 1971. *The Agricultural Potential of the Middle East*. New York: American Elsevier.

Clegg, Ian. 1971. *Workers' Self-Management in Algeria*. London: Allen Lane.

Clerget, Marcel. 1934. *Le Caire*. 2 vols. Cairo.

Clot, A. 1840. *Aperçu génerál sur l'Egypte*. 2 vols. Paris.

Cohen, Stuart. 1976. *British Policy in Mesopotamia*. London: Ithaca Press for Middle East Centre.

Colin, Ambroise. 1901. *La Navigation commerciale au XIXe siècle*. Paris: Rousseau.

Conrad, Lawrence. 1981. "The Plague in the Early Medieval Near East." Ph. D. dissertation, Princeton University.

Continental Allied Co. 1960. "An Economic Strategy for Morocco." Washington, D. C.

Cook, M. A., ed. 1970. *Studies in the Economic History of the Middle East*. London: Oxford University Press.

—— 1972. *Population Pressure in Rural Anatolia*. London: Oxford University Press.

—— 1974. "Economic Developments." In Schacht, *The Legacy of Islam* (q.v.)

Cooper, Charles and Sidney Alexander. 1972. *Economic Development and Population Growth in the Middle East*. New York: American Elsevier.

Cottrell, Alvin. 1980. *The Persian Gulf States*. Baltimore: Johns Hopkins University Press.

Crabitès, Pierre. 1933. *Ismail, the Maligned Khedive*. London: Routledge.

Craig, J. I. and Mahmoud Abdel-Karim. 1947. *Cereals Consumption in Egypt*. Cairo.

Crawley, C. W. 1960. "The Mediterranean." *The New Cambridge Modern History*, vol. 10. Cambridge: Cambridge University Press.

Cressaty, Comte de. 1912. *L'Egypte d'Aujourd'hui*. Paris: M. Rivière.

Cromer, Earl of. 1908. *Modern Egypt*. 2 vols. New York: Macmillan.

—— 1910. *Ancient and Modern Imperialism*. New York: Longmans.

Crouchley, A. E. 1934. *The Investment of Foreign Capital in Egyptian Companies and Public Debt*. Cairo.

—— 1937. "The Commercial Policy of Muhammad Ali." EC (February–March).

—— 1938. *The Economic Development of Modern Egypt.* London: Longmans.

Cuinet, V. 1892. *La Turquie d'Asie.* 4 vols. Paris: Leroux.

Cunningham, A., ed. 1966. *The Early Correspondence of Richard Wood.* London: Royal Historical Society.

Curzon, George. 1892. *Persia and the Persian Question.* 2 vols. London: Longmans, Green.

al-Dajjany, 'Ali. 1954. *Iqtisadiyyat al-Urdun.* Cairo.

Darin-Drabkin, H. 1962. *The Other Society.* New York: Harcourt, Brace & World.

Davis, Ralph. 1967. *Aleppo and Devonshire Square.* London: Macmillan.

De Candia, Farrugia, 1932–35. "Monnaies husseinites." RT.

Deeb, Marius. 1976. "Bank Misr and the Emergence of the Local Bourgeoisie in Egypt." In Kedourie, ed. *The Middle Eastern Economy* (q.v.)

—— 1978. "The Socioeconomic Role of the Local Foreign Minorities in Modern Egypt." IJMES (February).

Demontès, Victor. 1922–30. *L'Algérie économique.* 6 vols. Algiers.

—— 1930a. *L'Algérie industrielle et commerçante.* Paris: Larose.

—— 1930b. *L'Algérie agricole.* Paris: Larose.

Denman, D. 1978. "Land Reforms." in Lenczowski, ed., *Iran Under the Pahlavis* (q.v.)

Description de l'Egypte, état moderne. 1809–22. Paris: Commission des monuments d'Égypte.

Despois, Jean. 1935. *La Colonisation italienne en Libye.* Paris: Presses Universitaires de France.

—— 1955. *La Tunisie Orientale.* Paris: Presses Universitaires de France.

—— 1958. *L'Afrique du nord.* Paris: Presses Universitaires de France.

Dewey, Clive. 1979. "The Government of India's 'New Industrial Policy', 1900–1925." In K. N. Chaudhuri and Clive Dewey, *Economy and Society: Essays in Indian Economic and Social History.* Delhi.

Dols, Michael. 1977. *The Black Death in the Middle East.* Princeton, N.J.: Princeton University Press.

Donon, J. 1920. *Le régime douanier au Maroc et le développement du commerce morocain.* Paris: Larose.

Douin, Georges. 1927. *La mission du Baron de Boislecomte.* Cairo.

Dowson, Ernest. 1932. *An Inquiry into Land Tenure.* Letchworth, England: Garden City Press.

Dresch, Jean, et al. 1963. *Réforme agraire au Maghreb.* Paris: Maspero.

Ducousso, Gaston. 1913 *L'industrie de la soie en Syrie*. Paris.

Ducruet, Jean. 1964. *Les capitaux européens au Proche-Orient*. Paris: Presses Universitaries de France.

Earle, Edward. 1923. *Turkey, the Great Powers and the Baghdad Railway*. New York: Macmillan.

Easterlin, Richard. 1981. "Why isn't the whole world developed?" JEH (March).

Ecevit, Zafer. 1979. "International Labor Migration in the Middle East and North Africa." Unpublished paper. World Bank (June 4, 1979).

Edelstein, Michael. 1976. "Realized Rates of Return on U.K. Home and Over-Seas Portfolio." *Explorations in Economic History* (March).

Edens, David. 1979. *Oil and Development in the Middle East*. New York: Praeger.

Egretaud, Marcel. 1961. *Réalité de la Nation algérienne*. Paris: Éditions sociales.

Eldem, Vedat. 1970. *Osmanli Imparatorlugunun iktisadi*. . . . Ankara.

Elefteriades, Eleuthère. 1944. *Les chemins de fer en Syrie et au Liban*. Beirut.

Eliot, Sir Charles. 1965. *Turkey in Europe*. New York (reprint).

Evans-Pritchard, E. E. 1949. *The Sanusi of Cyrenaica*. Oxford: Clarendon Press.

Evin, Guy. 1934. *L'industrie au Maroc et ses problèmes*. Paris.

Eyquem, Jean. 1933. *Les ports de la zone française du Maroc*. Algiers.

Fahmy, Moustafa. 1954. *La révolution de l'industrie en Egypte*. Leiden: E. J. Brill.

Fairbank, John, Edwin Reischauer and Albert Craig. 1965. *East Asia: The Modern Transformation*. Boston: Houghton Mifflin.

Farley, J. L. 1862. *The Resources of Turkey*. London.

Farman Farmayan, Hafez. 1968. "The Forces of Modernization in Nineteenth Century Iran." In Polk and Chambers, *Beginnings of Modernization in the Middle East* (q.v.)

Farnie, D. A. 1969. *East and West of Suez*. Oxford: Clarendon Press.

Fawaz, Leila. 1979. "Urbanization and Change: The Population of Beirut in the 19th Century." Ph.D. dissertation, Harvard University.

Feis, H. 1930. *Europe, The World's Banker*. New Haven, Conn: Yale University Press.

Fernea, Robert. 1969. "Land Reform and Ecology in Post-Revolutionary Iraq." EDCC (April).

Figueras, Tomas Garcia and Rafael de Roda Jimenez. 1955. *Economia Social de Marruecos*. 3 vols. Madrid: Instituto do Estudios Africanos.

Findley, Carter. 1980. *Bureaucratic Reform in the Ottoman Empire*. Princeton: Princeton University Press.

Firestone, Y. 1981. "Faddan and Musha." In Udovitch, *The Islamic Middle East.* (q.v.)

Fişek, K. 1962. "Osmanli Diş Borçlari Üstüne." *Siyasal Bilgiler Fakültesi Dergisi* (June).

Fisher, S., ed. 1919. *Ottoman Land Laws.* London: Oxford University Press.

Flammang, Robert. 1979. "Growth and Development." EDCC (October).

Fleury, V. 1896. "Les industries indigènes de la Régence." RT.

Fletcher, Max. 1958. "The Suez Canal and World Shipping." JEH (December).

Foaden, G. P. and F. Fletcher. 1910. *Egyptian Agriculture.* Cairo.

Food and Agricultural Organization. 1955. Center on Land Problems in the Near East. Salahuddin, Iraq. (October). Reports.

—— 1965. *The State of Food and Agriculture.*

—— 1967. *The State of Food and Agriculture.*

Forte, Albert. 1938. *Les Banques en Egypte.* Paris.

Frankel, Sally, 1938. *Capital Investment in Africa.* London: Oxford University Press.

Freeman, Gary. 1979. *Immigrant Labor and Racial Conflict in Industrial Societies.* Princeton, N.J.: Princeton University Press.

Fridman, L. A. 1963. *Kapitalisticheskoye razvitiye Yegipta.* Moscow.

Furber, Holden. 1976. *Rival Empires of Trade in the Orient.* St. Paul, University of Minnesota Press.

Gabbay, Rony. 1978. *Communism and Agrarian Reform in Iraq.* London: Croom Helm.

Gaitskell, Arthur. 1959. *Gezira: A Story of Development in the Sudan.* London: Faber.

Ganiage, Jean. 1959. *Les origines du Protectorat français en Tunisie.* Paris: Presses Universitaire de France.

Gerber, Haim and Nachum Gross. 1980. "Inflation or Deflation in Nineteenth Century Syria and Palestine." JEH (June).

Gibb, H. A. R. and H. Bowen. 1950. *Islamic Society and the West.* 2 vols. London: Oxford University Press.

Gilbar, Gad. 1976. "Demographic Development in Late Qajar Persia." *Asian and African Studies.* 11 (2).

—— 1978. "Persian Agriculture in the Late Qajar Period." *Asian and African Studies.* 12 (3).

—— (forthcoming). "Trends in the development of prices in late Qajar Persia, 1870–1906." *Iran Studies.*

Ginor, Fanny. 1979. *Socio-Economic Disparities in Israel.* Tel Aviv.

Girgis, Maurice. 1977. *Industrialization and Trade Patterns in Egypt.* Tübingen: Mohr.

Glamann, Kristof. 1958. *Dutch-Asiatic Trade, 1620–1740*. Copenhagen: Danish Science Press.

Goitein, S. D. 1967. *A Mediterranean Society*. Vol. 1, *Economic Foundations*. Berkeley and Los Angeles: University of California Press.

Gordon, Leland. 1932. *American Relations with Turkey*. Philadelphia: University of Pennsylvania.

Gouldner, Alvin. 1979. *The Future of Intellectuals and the Rise of the New Class*. New York: Seabury Press.

Gran, Peter. 1979. *Islamic Roots of Capitalism: Egypt 1760–1840*. Austin: University of Texas Press.

Grandchamp, Pierre. 1920–33. *La France en Tunisie*. 10 vols. Tunis.

Granotier, Bernard. 1976. *Les travailleurs immigrés en France*. 3d ed. Paris: F. Maspéro.

Granott, A. 1952. *The Land System of Palestine*. London: Eyre and Spottiswoode.

Grant, Christina. 1937. *The Syrian Desert*. London: Black.

Great Britain, Admiralty War Staff. 1916. *A Handbook of Arabia*. London.

Great Britain, Naval Intelligence, Geographical Handbook Series.
—— 1943a. *Syria*. (April).
—— 1943b. *Palestine and Transjordan*. (December).
—— 1944a. *Algeria*. 2 vols. (May).
—— 1944b. *Iraq and the Persian Gulf*. (September).
—— 1945a. *Tunisia*. (February).
—— 1945b. *Persia*. (September).
—— 1946. *Western Arabia and the Red Sea*. (June).

Griffin, K. 1975. "Income Inequality and Land Redistribution in Morocco." *Bangladesh Development Studies*, vol. 3.

al-Gritly, Ali. 1947. "The Structure of Modern Industry in Egypt." EC.
—— n.d. *Tarikh al-sina'a fi 'ahd Muhammad 'Ali*. Cairo.

Gruenbaum, L. (Gaathon) 1941. *National Income and Outlay in Palestine, 1936*. Jerusalem.

Grunwald, Kurt and Joachim Ronall. 1960. *Industrialization in the Middle East*. New York: Council for Middle Eastern Affairs Press.

Haider, Saleh. 1942. "Land Problems of Iraq." Thesis, London University.

Halevi, Nadav and Ruth Klinot-Malul. 1968. *The Economic Development of Israel*. New York: Praeger.

Halperin, Haim. 1957. *Changing Patterns in Israel Agriculture*. London: Routledge.

Hammadi, Sadoon. 1966. "Comments on the Results of the Agrarian Reform in Syria." Planning Institute. Damascus (July).

Hammond, R. J. 1966. *Portugal and Africa, 1815–1910: A Study in Uneconomic Imperialism.* London: Stanford University Press.

Hamont, Pierre. 1843. *L'Egypte sous Mehemet-Ali.* 2 vols. Paris.

Hamza, Abdel Maqsud. 1944. *The Public Debt of Egypt, 1854–1867.* Cairo.

Hansen, Bent. 1974. "Preliminary Report on an Attempt to estimate National Product and Income for Egypt, ca. 1880 to 1913." University of California, Berkeley. (March 25, 1974).

—— 1979a. "Income and Consumption in Egypt, 1886/7 to 1937." IJMES (February).

—— 1979b. "Prices, Wages and Land Rents, Egypt, 1895–1913." Department of Economics, University of California, Berkeley.

—— 1979c. "Savings and Investments, Flow of Funds Egypt, 1884–1914." Department of Economics, University of California, Berkeley.

Hansen, Bent and Edward Lucas. 1978. "A New Set of Foreign Trade Indices for Egypt, 1885–1961." JEH, 7, (2–3).

Hansen, Bent and Karim Nashashibi. 1979. *Egypt.* New York: Columbia University Press.

Hansen, Bent and Khairy Tourk, 1976. "The Profitability of the Suez Canal." Working Papers in Economics, No. 5. University of California, Berkeley.

Hansen, Bent and Michael Wattleworth. 1978. "Agricultural Output and Consumption of Basic Foods." IJMES (November).

Hanson, John. 1980. "Export Instability in Historical Perspective." JEH (March).

Haqqi, Ismail, 1334 [1918]. *Lubnan, mabahith 'ilmiyya wa ijtima'iyya.* Reprint, 1970. 2 vols. Beirut.

Harbison, Frederick and Ibrahim Ibrahim. 1958. *Human Resources for Egyptian Enterprise.* New York: McGraw-Hill.

Hardy, G. 1953. *Histoire sociale de la colonisation française,* Paris: Larose

Harik, Iliya. 1968. *Politics and Change in Traditional Society, Lebanon.* Princeton, N.J.: Princeton University Press.

—— 1972. "The Impact of the Domestic Market on Rural-Urban Relations in the Middle East." In Antoun and Harik, *Rural Politics and Social Change in the Middle East* (q.v.).

Hasan, Muhammad Salman. 1958. "Growth and Structure of Iraq's Population," *Bulletin of the Oxford University Institute of Statistics,* vol. 20.

Hasan, Muhammad Salman. *Al-tatawwur al-iqtisadi fi al-Iraq*. Beirut.

Headrick, Daniel. 1981. *The Tools of Empire*. Oxford: Oxford University Press.

Hecker, M. 1914. "Die Eisenbahnen in der asiatischen Türkei." *Archiv für Eisenbahnwesen* (Berlin).

Henderson, K. D. 1946. *Survey of the Anglo-Egyptian, Sudan*. London: Longmans, Green.

Hershlag, Z. Y. 1960. *Turkey: An Economy in Transition*. Leiden: E. J. Brill.

—— 1968. *Turkey: The Challenge of Growth*. Leiden: E. J. Brill.

—— 1975. *The Economic Structure of the Middle East*. Leiden: E. J. Brill.

—— 1979. "Industrialization of Arab Countries." In Aliboni, *Arab Industrialization and Economic Integration* (q.v.)

—— 1980. *Introduction to the Modern Economic History of the Middle East*, 2d. ed. Leiden: E. J. Brill.

Heyworth-Dunne, J. 1939. *An Introduction to the History of Education in Modern Egypt*. London: Luzac.

Hickinbotham, Sir Tom. 1958. *Aden*. London: Constable.

Higgins, Benjamin. 1953. *The Economic and Social Development of Libya*. New York: United Nations.

Hijab, Wasfi. 1967. "Al-fikr al-'arabi fi maah sana—al-fikr al 'ilmi." *Al-fikr al-'arabi* (Publications of Centenary, American University, Beirut).

Hill, Richard. 1959. *Egypt in the Sudan*. London: Oxford University Press.

—— 1965. *Sudan Transport*. London: Oxford University Press.

Himadeh, Said. 1935. *Monetary and Banking System of Syria*. Beirut.

—— 1936. *The Economic Organization of Syria and Lebanon*. Beirut.

—— 1938a. *Economic Organization of Palestine*. Beirut.

—— 1938b. *Al-nizam al-iqtisadi fi al 'Iraq*. Beirut.

Hirsch, Eva. 1970. *Poverty and Plenty on the Turkish Farm*. New York: Columbia University Press.

Hirschman, Albert. 1958. *The Strategy of Economic Development*. New Haven: Yale University Press.

al-Hitta, Ahmad. 1950. *Tarikh al zira'a al-misriyya fi 'ahd Muhammad 'Ali*. Cairo.

—— 1957. *Tarikh Misr al-iqtisadi*. Cairo.

Hodgson, Marshall. 1975. *The Venture of Islam*. 3 vols. Chicago: University of Chicago Press.

Hoffherr, René. 1932. *L'économie marocaine*. Paris: Sirey.

Hoffherr, René and Paul Mauchaussé. 1933. *Formules modernes d'organisation minière africaine*. Paris: Sirey.

—— 1935. *Charbon et pétrole dans L'Afrique du Nord*. Paris: Sirey.

Hoffherr, René and Roger Moris. 1934, *Revenus et niveaux de vie indigènes au Maroc*. Paris: Sirey.

Holt, P. M. 1958. *The Mahdist State in the Sudan*. London: Oxford University Press.

Horne, Alistair. 1977. *A Savage War of Peace*. London: Macmillan.

Hoskins, Halford. 1928. *British Routes to India*. New York: Longmans, Green.

Hourani, Albert. 1946. *Syria and Lebanon*. London: Oxford University Press.

—— 1947. *Minorities in the Arab World*. London: Oxford University Press.

—— 1962. *Arabic Thought in the Liberal Age*. London: Oxford University Press.

—— 1970. "The Syrians in Egypt in the Eighteenth and Nineteenth Centuries." In *Colloque sur l'histoire du Caire*. Cairo.

Human Relations Area Files, *Jordan*. 1957. New Haven: HRAF. See also recent country studies, covering all parts of the Middle East and North Africa.

Hunter, F. M. 1877. *An Account of the British Settlement of Aden*. London: Trübner.

Hurewitz, J. C. 1969. *Middle East Politics: The Military Dimension*. New York: Praeger.

—— 1975–81. *The Middle East and North Africa in World Politics*. 3 vols. New Haven: Yale University Press.

Hurst, H. E. 1952. *The Nile*. London: Constable.

Huvelin, Paul. 1921. "Que vaut la Syrie." *L'Asie française* (December).

Ibish, Yusif, tr. 1967. "Elias Qudsi's Sketch of the Guilds of Damascus in the Nineteenth Century." *MEEP*.

Ibn Bishr, 'Uthman. 1391 [1971]. *'Unwan al-majd fi tarikh Najd*. 'Abd al-Rahman ibn'Abd al-Latif, ed. Mecca.

Imlah, Albert. 1958. *Economic Elements in the Pax Britannica*. Cambridge, Mass.: Harvard University Press.

Inalcik, Halil. 1955. "Land Problems in Turkish History." *Muslim World*.

—— 1969. "Capital Formation in the Ottoman Empire." *JEH* (March).

—— 1970. "The Ottoman Decline and Its Effect on the Reaya." Association internationale des études du Sud-est Européan, IIᵉ Congrès. Athens, May 7–13, 1970.

—— 1973. *The Ottoman Empire*. London: Weidenfeld.

L'Industrialisation de l'Afrique du Nord. 1952. Centre d'études de politique étrangère. Paris: A. Colin.

Indzhikyan, O. G. 1977. *Burzhuaziya osmanskoi imperii.* Yerevan.

Ingrams, Doreen, 1946. *A Survey of Social and Economic Conditions in the Aden Protectorate.* Eritrea.

Initiation à l'Algerie. 1957. Paris: Maisonneuve.

Initiation à la Tunisie. 1950. Paris: Maisonneuve.

Institut des Hautes Études de Tunis. 1957. *Niveaux de vie liés à l'agriculture.* Paris: Presses Universitaires de France.

International Bank for Reconstruction and Development (IBRD), Washington, D.C. (See also World Bank)

—— 1951. *The Economy of Turkey.*

—— 1952. *The Economic Development of Iraq.*

—— 1955. *The Economic Development of Syria.*

—— 1960. *The Economic Development of Libya.*

—— 1965a. *The Economic Development of Kuwait.*

—— 1965b. *The Economic Development of Morocco.*

International Labour Office. 1960. *Labour Survey of North Africa.* Geneva.

Isaac, Maurice. 1906. *Étude sur le régime douanier de la Tunisie,* Paris: Kapp.

Ismail, Adel. 1958. *Histoire du Liban.* Vol. 4. Beirut.

Isnard, H. 1954. *La vigne en Algérie.* Paris.

—— n.d. *La réorganisation de la propriété rurale dans la Mitidja.* Algiers.

Issa, Shakir. 1979. "The Distribution of Income in Iraq, 1971." In Kelidar, ed. *The Integration of Modern Iraq* (q.v.)

Issawi, Charles. 1947. *Egypt: An Economic and Social Analysis.* London: Oxford University Press.

—— 1954. *Egypt at Mid-Century.* London: Oxford University Press.

—— 1955. "The Entrepreneur Class." In Sydney Fisher, ed., *Social Forces in the Middle East.* Ithaca, N.Y.: Cornell University Press. (Reprinted in Issawi 1981b).

—— 1956. "The Economic and Social Foundations of Democracy in the Middle East." *International Affairs* (January). (Reprinted in Issawi 1981b.)

—— 1963. *Egypt in Revolution.* London: Oxford University Press.

—— 1965. "The Arab World's Heavy Legacy." *Foreign Affairs* (April). (Reprinted in Issawi 1981b.)

—— 1968. "Asymmetrical Development and Transport in Egypt." In Polk and Chambers, eds. *Beginnings of Modernization in the Middle East* (q.v.) (Reprinted in Issawi 1981b.)

—— 1969. "Economic Change and Urbanization in the Middle East." In Ira Lapidus, ed. *Middle Eastern Cities.* Berkeley and Los Angeles: University of California Press. (Reprinted in Issawi 1981b.)

—— 1970a. "Middle East Economic Development, 1815-1914." In M. A. Cook, ed. *Studies in the Economic History of the Middle East* (q.v.)

—— 1970b. "The Decline of Middle Eastern Trade." In D. S. Richards, ed. *Islam and the Trade of Asia* (q.v.) (Reprinted in Issawi 1981b.)

—— 1970c. "The Tabriz-Trabzon Trade, 1830-1900." IJMES (January).

—— 1972. *Oil, The Middle East and the World.* New York: Library Press.

—— 1973. "Lebanese Agriculture in the 1850's." *The American Journal of Arabic Studies* 1(1). Leiden

—— 1976. "The Economy of the Middle East and North Africa: An Overview." Avrom Udovitch, *The Middle East* (q.v.)

—— 1977a. "Population and Resources in the Ottoman Empire and Iran." In Naff and Owen, *Studies in the Eighteenth Century* (q.v.)

—— 1977b. "British Trade and the Rise of Beyrut, 1830-1860." IJMES (January).

—— 1978a. "The Iranian Economy, 1925-1975." In George Lencowski, ed. *Iran under the Pahlavis.* Stanford, Calif.: Hoover Institution.

—— 1978b. "The 1973 Oil Crisis and After." *Journal of Post Keynesian Economics* (Winter 1978-79).

—— 1980a. "Europe, the Middle East and the Shift in Power." *Comparative Studies in Society and History* (October 1980). (Reprinted in Issawi 1981b.)

—— 1980b. "Wages in Turkey, 1850-1914." In Osman Okyar and Halil Inalcik, eds. *Social and Economic History of Turkey.* Ankara.

—— 1980c. "Notes on the Negotiations leading to the Anglo-Turkish Commercial Convention of 1838." In *Mémorial Ömer Lûtfi Barkan.* Paris: Maisonneuve.

—— 1980d. "Economic Trends in the Middle East and Future Prospects." In U.S., 96th Cong., 2d sess., Joint Economic Committee, *The Political Economy of the Middle East, 1973-78.*

—— 1981a. "Area and Population of the Arab Empire." In A. L. Udovitch, ed., *The Islamic Middle East, 700-1900.* Princeton: Princeton University Press. (Reprinted in Issawi 1981b.)

—— 1981b. *The Arab World's Legacy.* Princeton: Darwin Press.

—— 1981c. "The Transformation of the Economic Position of the Millets." In Bernard Lewis and Benjamin Braude, eds. *Christians and Jews in the Ottoman Empire.* New York: Holmes and Meier.

Issawi, Charles and Carlos Dabezies. 1951. "Population Movements and Population Pressure in Jordan, Lebanon and Syria." *Milbank Memorial Fund Quarterly* (October).

Issawi, Charles and Mohammed Yeganeh. 1962. *The Economics of Middle Eastern Oil*. New York: Praeger.

Isserlis, L. 1938. "Tramp Shipping, Cargoes and Freights." *Journal of the Royal Statistical Society*. Part 1.

The Italian Empire of Libya. n.d. Rome.

Italy, 1946. *Memorandum on the Economic and Financial Situation of the Italian Colonies in Africa*. Rome (July).

Itzkowitz, Norman. 1972. *Ottoman Empire and Islamic Tradition*. New York: Knopf.

'Izz al-Din, Amin. 1968. *Tarikh al-tabaqa al-'amilah al-misriyya*. Cairo.

Jacqz, Jane, ed. 1976. *Iran: Past, Present, and Future*. New York: Aspen Institute.

Jain, Shail. 1975. *Size Distribution of Income*. Washington, D.C.: World Bank.

Jalal, F. 1972. *The Role of Government in the Industrialization of Iraq*. London: F. Cass.

Jamalzadeh, Muhammad Ali. 1335[1916]. *Ganj-i Shaigan*. Berlin.

Jamil, Muzaffar Husayn. 1949. *Siyasat al Iraq al-tijariyya*. Cairo.

Jeanson, Colette and Francis Jeanson. 1955. *L'Algérie hors la loi*. Paris: Éditions du seuil.

Jenks, Leland. 1927. *The Migration of British Capital*. New York: Knopf.

Jennings, Ronald. 1973. "Loans and Credit in the Early Seventeenth Century Ottoman Judicial Records." *JESHO* (April).

Johnson, Harry, ed. 1967. *Economic Nationalism in Old and New States*. Chicago: University of Chicago Press.

Jughrafiya-i Isfahan. 1342[1963]. Tehran.

Juwaideh, A. 1963. "Midhat Pasha and the Land System of Lower Iraq." *St. Antony's Papers* 16. (London.)

Kahn, Alfred. 1944. "Palestine: A Problem in Economic Valuation." *American Economic Review* (September).

Kalla, M. S. 1969. "Role of Foreign Trade in the Economic Development of Syria, 1831–1914." Ph.D. dissertation, American University, Washington, D.C.

Kanovsky, Eliyahu. 1966. *The Economy of the Israeli Kibbutz*. Cambridge: Harvard University Press.

Karal, Enver. 1943. *Osmanli imparatorlugunda ilk nufus sayimi*. Ankara.

Karkar, Yaqub. 1972. *Railway Development in the Ottoman Empire, 1856–1914*. New York: Vantage.

Karpat, Kemal. 1973. "An Inquiry into the Social Foundations of

Nationalism in the Ottoman State." Unpublished paper, Woodrow Wilson School, Princeton University.

Kazamias, Andreas. 1966. *Education and the Quest for Modernity in Turkey*. London: Allen and Unwin.

Kazemzadeh, Firuz. 1968. *Russia and Britain and Persia, 1864–1914*. New Haven, Conn.: Yale University Press.

Kebbaj, Abd el Khalek. 1963. *L'économie céréalière au Maroc*. Rabat.

Keddie, Nikki. 1950. *Historical Obstacles to Agrarian Change in Iran*. Claremont, Calif.

—— 1966. *Religion and Rebellion in Iran: The Tobacco Protest of 1891–1892*. London: Cass.

—— 1972. "Stratification, Social Control, and Capitalism in Iranian Villages." In Antoun and Harik, *Rural Politics and Social Change in the Middle East* (q.v.)

Kedourie, Elie, ed. 1977. *The Middle Eastern Economy*. London: Cass.

Keene, Donald. 1969. *The Japanese Discovery of Europe*. Stanford, Calif.: Stanford University Press.

Kelidar, Abbas, ed. 1979. *The Integration of Modern Iraq*. London: St. Martins Press.

Kemp, Tom. 1971. *Economic Forces in French History, 1760–1914*. London: Dobson.

Kent, Marian. 1976. *Oil and Empire: British Policy and Mesopotamian Oil, 1900–1920*. London: Macmillan.

Kerr, Malcolm. 1959. *Lebanon in the Last Years of Feudalism*. Beirut.

Kettani, M. A. 1974. "Engineering Education in the Arab World." MEJ (Autumn).

al-Khadim, Sa'd. 1957. *Al-sina'at al-Sha'biya fi misr*. Cairo.

Khalidi, Walid. 1971. *From Haven to Conquest*. Beirut.

Khouja, M. W. and P. G. Sadler, 1979. *The Economy of Kuwait*. London: Macmillan.

Khury, Raif. 1943. *Al-fikr al-'arabi al-hadith*. Beirut.

Klat, Paul. 1957. "Musha Holdings and Land Fragmentations in Syria." MEEP.

—— 1958. "The Origins of Landownership in Syria." MEEP.

Knauerhase, Ramon. 1975. *The Saudi Arabian Economy*. New York: Praeger.

Knight, Melvin. 1937. *Morocco as a French Economic Venture*. New York: Appleton-Century.

—— 1956. "The Algerian Revolt" MEJ (Autumn).

Kolerkiliç, E. 1958. *Osmanli imparatorlugunda para*. Ankara.

Kortepeter, Carl. 1966. "Ottoman Imperial Policy and the Economy of the Black Sea Region." *Journal of the American Oriental Society* (April–June).

Krane, R. E., ed. 1975. *Manpower Mobility Across Cultural Boundaries.* Leiden: E. J. Brill.

Kronik van Afrika. 1975. Special Issue on Asian Minorities in Africa. The Hague: Mouton.

Krueger, Anne. 1974. *Turkey.* New York: Columbia University Press.

Kurmuş, Orhan. 1974a. "The Role of British Capital in the Economic Development of Western Anaotolia, 1850–1913." Ph.D. dissertation, London University.

—— 1974b. *Emperyalizm Türkiyeye Girişi.* Istanbul.

Labib, Subhi. 1965. *Handelsgeschichte Aegyptens im Spätmittelalter.* Wiesbaden.

—— 1969. "Capitalism in Islam." JEH (March).

Lambton, A. K. S. 1953. *Landlord and Peasant in Persia: A Study of Land Tenure and Land Revenue Administration.* London: Oxford University Press.

— 1965. "Reflections on the Iqta'." In George Makdisi, ed. *Arabic and Islamic Studies in Honor of Hamilton A. R. Gibb.* Cambridge: Harvard University Press.

—— 1969. *Persian Land Reform, 1962–1966.* London: Oxford University Press.

—— 1970. "Persian Trade Under the Early Qajars." In Richards, *Islam and the Trade of Asia* (q.v.)

Landes, David. 1958. *Bankers and Pashas.* Cambridge, Mass.: Harvard University Press.

Land Policy in the Near East. 1967. Published for the Government of Libya by *the FAO.* Rome.

Lane, Edward. 1908. *The Modern Egyptians.* London: J. M. Dent.

Langley, Kathleen. 1961. *The Industrialization of Iraq.* Cambridge, Mass.: Harvard University Press.

Latron, A. 1936. *La vie rurale en Syrie et au Liban.* Beirut.

Lebanon. Ministère de l'Agriculture. 1960. *Aspect Général de l'agriculture libanaise.* Beirut.

Lebergott, Stanley. 1980. "The Returns to U.S. Imperialism. 1890–1929." JEH (June).

Leduc, Gaston. 1969. "The Economic Balance Sheet of Colonisation." *Journal of Contemporary History.*

Lees, Francis and Hugh Brooks. 1977. *The Economic and Political Development of the Sudan.* London: Macmillan.

Lenczowski, George, ed. 1978. *Iran Under the Pahlavis.* Stanford, Calif: Hoover Institution.

Lepidi, Jules. 1955. *L'économie tunisienne*. Tunis.

Leroy-Beaulieu, Paul. 1897. *L'Algérie et la Tunisie*. Paris: Guillaumin.

Lespès, R. 1930. *Alger*. Paris: F. Alcan.

—— 1938. *Oran*. Paris: F. Alcan.

Le Tourneau, Roger. 1949. *Fès avant le Protectorat*. Casablanca.

Levasseur, Emile. 1911.*Histoire du commerce de la France*. 2 vols. Paris: A. Rousseau.

Lewis, Bernard. 1961. *The Emergence of Modern Turkey*. London: Oxford University Press.

—— 1974. "Ottoman Land Tenure and Taxation in the Syrian Lands." Paper presented to Colloquium on History of Syria, Amman, April.

Lewis, Bernard and Benjamin Braude, eds. 1981. *Christians and Jews in the Ottoman Empire*. New York: Holmes and Meier.

Lewis, Bernard and P. M. Holt, eds. 1962 *Historians of the Middle East*. London: Oxford University Press.

Lewis, W. A. 1978. *Growth and Fluctuations, 1870-1913*. London: Allen and Unwin.

Libya, Bank of. 1965. *The Development of Public Finance in Libya, 1944-1963*. Tripoli.

Linant de Bellefonds. 1872.*Mémoire sur les principaux travaux d'utilité publique exécutés en Egypte*. Paris: Bertrand.

Lindberg, John. 1952. *A General Economic Appraisal of Libya*. New York: United Nations.

Lindsay, W. S. 1876. *History of Merchant Shipping*. 4 vols. London: Low, Marston, Low, and Searle.

Lockwood, William. 1954. *The Economic Development of Japan*. Princeton, N.J.: Princeton University Press.

Loftus, Patrick. 1948. *National Income of Palestine, 1945*. Jerusalem.

Lokkegaard, Frede. 1950. *Islamic Taxation in the Classic Period*. Copenhagen.

Longrigg, Stephen. 1925. *Four Centuries of Modern Iraq*. Oxford: Oxford University Press.

—— 1953. *Iraq, 1900 to 1950*. London: Oxford University Press.

—— 1958. *Syria and Lebanon Under French Mandate*. London: Oxford University Press.

—— 1968. *Oil in the Middle East*. 3d ed. London: Oxford University Press.

Lorimer, J. G. 1908-15. *Gazetteer of the Persian Gulf*. Calcutta.

Lustick, Ian. 1980.*Arabs in the Jewish State*. Austin: University of Texas Press.

Mabro, Robert. 1974. *The Egyptian Economy, 1952-1972*. Oxford: Clarendon.

Mabro, Robert and Samir Radwan. 1976. *The Industrialization of Egypt: Policy and Performance.* Oxford: Clarendon.

McCarthy, Justin. 1976. "Ottoman Sources on Arabian Population." First International Symposium Studies in the History of Arabia, University of Riyad.

—— 1977. "Nineteenth Century Egyptian Population." In Kedourie, ed. *The Middle Eastern Economy* (q.v.)

—— 1980. "Population of the Ottoman Fertile Crescent." Paper presented to Haifa Conference (December).

—— 1981. *International Historical Statistics: The Late Ottoman Empire.* Boston.

McCoan, J. C. 1877. *Egypt As It Is.* London.

—— 1880. *Egypt Under Ismail.* London.

MacGowan, Bruce. (forthcoming) *South Eastern Europe in the Seventeenth and Eighteenth Centuries.*

MacGregor, John. 1844. *Commercial Statistics.* 4 vols. London: Nott.

McLachlan, Keith. 1979. "Iraq: Problems of Regional Development." In Kelidar, ed., *The Integration of Modern Iraq* (q.v.)

Makdisi, Samir. 1961. "Some Aspects of Syrian Economic Growth 1945–1957." MEEP.

—— 1963. "Fixed Capital Formation in Syria, 1936–1957." MEEP.

—— 1979. "Arab Economic Cooperation." In Aliboni, *Arab Industrialization and Economic Integration* (q.v.)

Mantran, Robert. 1962. *Istanbul dans la seconde moitié du XVIIe siècle.* Paris: Maisonneuve.

—— 1970. "L'empire ottoman et le commerce asiatique aux 16e et 17e siècles." In D. S. Richards, *Islam and the Trade of Asia* (q.v.)

Ma'oz, Moshe. 1968. *Ottoman Reform in Syria and Palestine.* Oxford: Oxford University Press.

—— ed. 1975. *Studies in Palestine during the Ottoman Period.* Jerusalem.

Mardin, Şerif. 1962. *The Genesis of Young Ottoman Thought.* Princeton, N.J.: Princeton University Press.

Marty, André. 1951. *Le franc marocain, monnaie satellite.* Paris: Librarie generale de droit et de jurisprudence.

—— 1952. *Le problème de la solidarité monétaire franco-marocaine.* Paris.

Martz. 1897. "L'industrie européene en Tunisie." RT 4.

Marzouk, G. 1957. "The Economic Background of the Currency Reform in the Sudan." MEEP.

Masson, Paul. 1896. *Histoire du commerce français dans le Levant au XVIIe siècle.* Paris: Hachette.

—— 1903. *Histoire des établissements et du commerce français dans l'Afrique barbaresque.* Paris: Hachette.

—— 1911. *Histoire du commerce français dans le Levant au XVIIIe siècle.* Paris: Hachette.

—— 1912. *Marseille et la colonisation française.* Paris.

Maunier, René. 1916. "L'exposition des industries égyptiennes." EC (November).

Mazrui, Ali. 1967. *On Heroes and Uhuru Worship: Essays on Independent Africa.* London: Longmans.

Mead, Donald. 1967. *Growth and Structural Change in the Egyptian Economy.* Homewood, Ill: Irwin.

Mears, Eliot. 1924. *Modern Turkey.* New York: Macmillan.

Michaely, Michael. 1975. *Israel.* New York: Columbia University Press.

Miège, Jean-Louis. 1959. "Coton et cotonnades au Maroc au XIXe siècle." *Hesp.* 47.

—— 1961. *Le Maroc et l'Europe.* 4 vols. Paris: Presses Universitaires de France.

Mikdashi, Zuhayr. 1972. *The Community of Oil Exporting Countries.* Ithaca, N.Y.: Cornell University Press.

Miller, Mark. 1979. "Reluctant Partnership: Foreign Workers in Franco-Algerian Relations 1962-1979." *Journal of International Affairs.* Fall/Winter.

Milleron, Jacques. 1954. *Regards sur l'économie marocaine.* Rabat.

Mitchell, B. R. and P. Deane. 1962. *Abstract of British Historical Statistics.* Cambridge: Cambridge University Press.

Moghadam. Fatemeh. 1978. "The Effect on Productivity of Farm Size and Management Systems in Iran." Thesis, Oxford University.

Mollard, Ghislaine, 1950. *L'évolution de la culture et de la production du blé en Algérie.* Algiers.

Mommsen, Wolfgang, ed. 1975. "Imperialismus im Nahen und Mittleren Osten." *Geschichte und Gesellschaft* 1 (4) Göttingen.

Monicault, J. de. 1936. *Le port de Beyrouth.* Paris.

Morawitz, Charles. 1902. *Les Finances de Turquie.* Paris.

Morimoto, Kosei. 1975. "Land Tenure in Egypt During the Early Islamic Period." *Orient.*

Morocco. 1954 (*Encyclopédie mensuelle d'outre-mer*, special issue.)

Mosharaffa, M. M. 1947. *Cultural Survey of Modern Egypt.* London: Longmans, Green.

Mottahedeh, Roy. 1980. *Loyalty and Leadership in an Early Islamic Society.* Princeton, N.J.: Princeton University Press.

Moussly, Nazim. 1951. *Le problème de l'eau en Syrie.* Paris.

Munzer, G. 1945. *Jewish Labour, Economy*. London.

Musallam, Basim. 1981. "Birth Control and Middle Eastern History." In Udovitch. *The Islamic Middle East* (q.v.).

Musrey, Alfred. 1969. *An Arab Common Market: A Study in Inter-Arab Trade Relations*. New York: Praeger.

Mustapha, Ahmed Ben. n.d. *Déplacement des richesses*. Tunis.

Myint, Hla. 1954. "An interpretation of Economic Backwardness." *Oxford Economic Papers*.

—— 1958. "The Classical Theory of International Trade and the Underdeveloped Countries." *Economic Journal* (June).

—— 1964. *The Economics of the Developing Countries*. London: Hutchinson.

Nader, Claire and A. B. Zahlan. 1969. *Science and Technology in Developing Countries*. Cambridge: Cambridge University Press.

Naff, T. and E. R. J. Owen. 1977. *Studies in the Eighteenth Century*. Carbondale: Southern Illinois University Press.

Nathan, Robert et al. 1946. *Palestine: Problem and Promise*. Washington, D.C.

Nazhad, Husayn and Parviz Shariaty. 1352[1973]. *Naqsh wa athar tahsil Kardegan.* . . . Tehran University, Tehran.

Nezarat umuri tijaret ve nafia. *Istatistik umumi idaresi*. 1316 [1898]. Istanbul.

Noin, Daniel. 1970. *La Population rurale du Maroc*. 2 vols. Paris: Presses Universitaires de France.

North, Douglass. 1958. "Ocean Freights and Economic Development." JEH (December).

Nouschi, André. 1961. *Enquête sur le niveau de vie des populations rurales constantinoises*. Paris: Presses Universitaires de France.

Novichev, A. D. 1935. *Ekonomika Turtsii v period mirovoi voiny*. Leningrad.

—— 1937. *Ocherki ekonomiki Turtsii*. Moscow and Leningrad.

Nowshirvani, Vahid. 1981. "The Commercialization of Agriculture in Iran, 1800–1925." In Udovitch, ed., *The Islamic Middle East* (q.v.)

Nuss, Izzat. 1955. *Ahwal al-sukkan fi al-'alam al-Arabi*. Cairo.

O'Brien, P. 1962. "Industrial Development and the Employment Problem in Egypt, 1945–1965." MEEP.

—— 1968. "The Long-Term Growth of Agricultural Production in Egypt, 1821–1962." In P. M. Holt, ed., *Political and Social Change in Modern Egypt: Historical Studies from the Ottoman Conquest to the United Arab Republic*. London: Oxford University Press.

Osmanli Sanayii 1913, 1915. 1970. A. Günduz Ökçun, ed. Ankara.

Ottaway, David and Marina Ottaway. 1970. *Algeria: The Politics of a Socialist Revolution.* Berkeley and Los Angeles: University of California Press.

Owen, E.R.J. 1966. "Lord Cromer and the Development of Egyptian Industry." *Middle Eastern Studies* 2 (4).

—— 1969. *Cotton and the Egyptian Economy.* Oxford: Oxford University Press.

—— 1970. "The Attitudes of British Officials to the Development of the Egyptian Economy." In Cook, ed., *Studies in the Economic History of the Middle East* (q.v.)

—— 1977. "Introduction." In Naff and Owen, *Studies in the Eighteenth Century* (q.v.)

—— 1981a. "The Development of Agricultural Production in Nineteenth Century Egypt." In Udovitch, *The Islamic Middle East* (q.v.)

—— 1981b. *The Middle East in the World Economy, 1800–1914.* London: Methuen.

Ozbudun, Ergun and Aydin Ulusan. 1980. *The Political Economy of Income Distribution in Turkey.* New York: Holmes and Meier.

Pack, Howard. 1971. *Structural Change and Economic Policy in Israel.* New Haven: Yale University Press.

Palgrave, William. 1865. *Narrative of a Year's Journey Through Central and Eastern Arabia.* London: Macmillan.

Pamuk, Şevket. 1978. "Foreign Trade, Foreign Capital, and the Peripheralization of the Ottoman Empire." Ph.D. dissertation, University of California, Berkeley.

Panzac, D. 1973. "La peste à Smyrne au XVIIIᵉ siècle." *Annales* (July–August).

Paris, Robert. 1957. *Histoire du Commerce de Marseille: De 1660 à 1789, le Levant.* Paris.

Parry, V. J. and M. E. Yapp, eds. 1975. *War, Technology, and Society in the Middle East.* London: Oxford University Press.

Parvin, Manoucher and Amir Zamani. 1979. "Political Economy of Growth and Destruction." *Iranian Studies* (Winter–Spring).

Passeron, René. 1926. *Les grandes sociétés et la colonisation dans l'Afrique du Nord.* Algiers.

Pawera, John. 1964. *Algeria's Infrastructure.* New York: Praeger.

Pennec, Pierre. 1964. *Les transformations des corps de métier de Tunis.* Tunis.

Penrose, Edith and E. F. Penrose. 1978. *Iraq.* London: Westview Press.

—— 1979. "Industrial Policy and Performance in Iraq." In Kelidar, *The Integration of Modern Iraq* (q.v.)

Peretz, Don. 1958. *Israel and the Palestine Arabs*. Washington, D.C.: Middle East Institute.

Pesaran, M. H. 1976. "Income Distribution and Its Major Determinants in Iran." In Jacqz, *Iran* (q.v.)

Peyamiras, Parviz. 1944. *Méthodes d'interventionnisme en Iran*. Geneva.

Peyerimhoff, M. de. 1906. *Enquête sur les résultats de la colonisation officielle*. 2 vols. Algiers.

Picquemal. Marcel. 1957. "Les exportations de capitaux français dans les Colonies." *Economie et Politique* (August–September).

Piquet, V. 1912. *La colonisation française dans l'Afrique du Nord*. Paris.

—— 1920. *Le Maroc*. Paris.

Planhol, Xavier de. 1959. *The World of Islam*. Ithaca, N. Y.: Cornell University Press.

—— 1972. "Regional Diversification and Social Structure." In Antoun and Harik, *Rural Politics and Social Change in the Middle East* (q.v.)

Poliak, A. N. 1939. *Feudalism in Egypt, Syria, Palestine, and Lebanon*. London: Royal Asiatic Society.

Politis, Athanase. 1928 *L'Hellénisme et l'Egypte Moderne*. 2 vols. Paris: Alcan.

Polk, William. 1963. *The Opening of South Lebanon, 1788–1840*. Cambridge: Harvard University Press.

Polk, William and Richard Chambers. 1968. *Beginnings of Modernization in the Middle East*. Chicago: University of Chicago Press.

Ponasik, Diane. 1977. "The System of Administered Trade as a Defense Mechanism in Preprotectorate Morocco." IJMES (April).

Poncet, Jean. 1962. *La Colonisation et l'Agriculture européenes en Tunisie*. Paris: Mouton.

Pouyanne, H. 1900. *La Propriété foncière en Algérie*. Algiers.

Prest, A. R. 1948. *War Economics of Primary Producing Countries*. Cambridge: Cambridge University Press.

al-Qasimi, Muhammad Sa'id. 1960. *Qamus al-Sina 'at al-shamiyya*. Zafir al-Qasimi, ed. Paris.

Quataert, Donald. 1973. "Ottoman Reform and Agriculture in Anatolia." Ph.D. dissertation, University of California, Los Angeles.

—— 1977. "Limited Revolution." *Business History Review* (Summer).

Rabie, Hassanein. 1972. *The Financial System of Egypt*. London: Oxford University Press.

Radwan, Samir. 1974. *Capital Formation in Egyptian Industry and Agriculture, 1882–1967*. London: Ithaca Press.

Rafeq, Abdul Karim. 1981. "Economic Relations between Damascus and The Dependent Countryside." In Udovitch, ed, *The Islamic Middle East* (q.v.)

Ray, Joanny. 1938. *Les marocains en France*. Paris.

Raymond, André. 1972. "Les grandes épidémies de peste au Caire aux XVIIᵉ et XVIII siècles." *Bulletin d'Études Orientales* 25. Damascus.

—— 1973. *Artisans et Commerçants au Caire*. 2 vols. Damascus.

Régence de Tunis. Direction générale des Travaux Publics.

—— 1931a. *Note sur le réseau routier*. Bourg.

—— 1931b. *Le Commerce et le Travail en Tunisie*. Bourg.

Report of the Council of Foreign Bondholders. 1927. London.

Résidence générale de la République française au Maroc. 1915–21. *Villes et tribus du Maroc*. 7 vols. Paris: Leroux.

La Révolution industrielle dans le Sud-est européen, XIXᵉ siècle. 1976. Sofia.

Richards, Alan. 1980. "Agricultural Technology and Rural Social Classes." *Middle Eastern Studies* (May).

Richards, D. S. 1970. *Islam and the Trade of Asia*. Oxford: B. Cassirer.

Rifaat, M. 1947. *The Awakening of Modern Egypt*. London: Longman.

Rifaat, M. A. 1935. *The Monetary System of Egypt*. London: Allen.

La. Rinascita della Tripolitana. 1926. Milan: Mondadori.

Rivlin, Helen. 1961. *The Agricultural Policy of Muhammad Ali in Egypt*. Cambridge: Harvard University Press.

Robana, A. 1973. *The Prospects for an Economic Community in North Africa*. New York: Praeger.

Roberts, Stephen H. 1963. *The History of French Colonial Policy, 1870–1925*. London: Cass.

Robinson, E. A. 1954. "The Changing Structure of the British Economy." EJ (September).

Rodinson, Maxime. 1966. *Islam et Capitalisme*. Paris: Seuil.

Romanus, Herbert. 1934. *Eine Wirtschaftgeographische Darstellung der Nordafrikanisch-französischen Protektorate Marokkos und Tunesiens*. Königsberg.

Rostow, W. W. 1978. *The World Economy*. Austin: University of Texas Press.

Rouhani, Fuad. 1971. *A History of OPEC*. New York: Praeger.

Roumani, Maurice. 1975. 2 vols. *The Case of the Jews from Arab Countries*. Jerusalem.

Rozaliev, Yu. N. 1962. *Osobennosti razvitiya kapitalizma v Turtsii*. Moscow.

Ruppin. A. 1916. *Syrien als wirtschaftsgebiet*. Berlin.

Rushdy, Rasim. 1953. *Tarablus, al-gharb*. Tripoli.

Rustow, Dankwart and John Mugno. 1976. *OPEC: Success and Prospects*. New York: New York University Press.

Saab, Gabriel. 1967. *The Egyptian Agrarian Reform*. London: Oxford University Press.

Saba, Elias. 1960. "The Syro-Lebanese Customs Union." MEEP.

Sabbagh, Georges. 1980. "Population and Economic Development in Morocco." *Journal of South Asian and Middle Eastern Studies* (Fall).

Safa, Elie. 1960. *L'Emigration libanaise*. Beirut.

Saint-Germès, J. 1955. *Economie algérienne*. Algiers.

St. John, James. 1834. *Egypt and Mohammad Ali*. 2 vols. London.

Saleh, Zaki. 1957. *Mesopotamia (Iraq) 1600–1914*. Baghdad.

Samman, Ahmad. 1955. *Muhadarat fi-iqtisadiyat Suriya*. Cairo.

Sayigh, Yusif. 1978. *The Economies of the Arab World*. New York: St. Martins Press.

Schacht, Joseph. 1974. *The Legacy of Islam*. 2nd ed. Oxford: Clarendon.

Schander, Albert. 1902. "Die Eisenbahnpolitik Frankreichs in Nordafrika." *Probleme der Weltwirtschaft*. No. 12. Kiel.

Schatkowski-Schilcher. 1975. "Ein Modellfall indirekter wirtschaftlicher Durchdringung, Das Beispiel Syrien," *Geschichte und Gesellschaft* 1 (4). Göttingen.

Schumpetér, Joseph. 1950. *Capitalism, Socialism, and Democracy*. New York:

Schurr, Sam and P. Homan. 1971. *Middle Eastern Oil and the Western World*. New York: Elsevier.

Sebag, Paul. 1951. *La Tunisie*. Paris: Editions sociales.

Segrè, Claudio. 1974. *Fourth Shore: The Italian Colonization of Libya*. Chicago: University of Chicago Press.

al-Shaf'i. n.d. *Al-ashghal al-'amma al-Kubra fi 'ahd Muhammad Ali*. Cairo.

Shaler, William. 1826. *Sketches of Algiers*. Boston: Hilliard.

Shaw, Stanford. 1962. *The Financial and Administrative Organization and Development of Ottoman Egypt, 1517–1798*. Princeton, N. J.: Princeton University Press.

—— 1975. "Nineteenth-Century Ottoman Tax Reforms." IJMES (October).

—— 1978. "Ottoman Expenditures and Budgets." IJMES (August).

Shaw, Stanford and Ezel Shaw. 1977. *History of the Ottoman Empire and Modern Turkey*. 2 vols. Cambridge: Cambridge University Press.

al-Shayyal, Jamal al-Din, R. 1951. *Tarikh al-Tarjama wa al-haraka al-thaqafiyya fi 'asr Muhammad 'Ali*. Cairo.

—— 1962. "Historiography in Egypt in the Nineteenth Century." In Bernard Lewis and P. M. Holt, eds., *Historians of the Middle East* (q.v.)

—— 1968. "Some Aspects of Intellectual Life in Eighteenth-Century Egypt." In P. M. Holt, ed., *Political and Social Change in Modern Egypt* (q.v.)

Shibl, Yusuf. 1971. *The Aswan High Dam*. Beirut.

Shoshan, Boaz. 1980. "Grain Riots and the 'Moral Economy': Cairo." *Journal of Interdisciplinary History*, (Winter).

Shwadran, Benjamin. 1974. *The Middle East, Oil and the Great Powers*. 3d ed. New York: Wiley.

Simmons, John. 1972. "The Political Economy of Land Use: Tunisian Private Forces." In Antoun and Harik, *Rural Politics and Social Change in the Middle East* (q.v.)

Singer, Charles, ed. 1957. *A History of Technology*. 5 vols. Oxford: Oxford University Press.

Singer, Morris. 1977. *The Economic Advance of Turkey*. Ankara.

Smith, Thomas. 1959. *Agrarian Origins of Modern Japan*. Stanford, Calif.: Stanford University Press.

Smooha, Sammy. 1978. *Israel: Pluralism and Conflict*. Berkeley and Los Angeles: University of California Press.

Sousa, Ahmad and J. D. Atkinson. 1944–46. *Iraq Irrigation Handbook*. Baghdad.

Staley, Eugene. 1954. *The Future of Underdeveloped Countries*. New York: Harper.

Statistical Yearbook for 1909. Cairo.

Statistique de l'Egypte, 1873. Cairo.

Steppat, Fritz. 1968. "National Education Projects in Egypt before the British Occupation." In Polk and Chambers, *Beginnings of Modernization in the Middle East* (q.v.)

Stewart, Charles. 1964. *The Economy of Morocco, 1912–1962*. Cambridge: Harvard University Press.

—— 1957. "Industrialization in Morocco." MEEP.

Stoianovich, Traian. 1960. "The Conquering Balkan Orthodox Merchant." JEH (June).

Stucken, Rudolf. 1963. *Entwicklungsbedingungen und Entwicklungschancen der Republik Sudan*. Berlin: Duncker.

Sultan, Fouad. 1914. *La monnaie égyptienne*. Paris: Rousseau.

A Survey of Palestine, 1946. Prepared by the Government of Palestine. 4 vols. Jerusalem.

Sussman, Zvi. 1973. "The Determination of Wages for Unskilled Labor in the Advanced Sector of the Dual Economy of Palestine." EDCC (October).

Swanson, Jon. 1979. "Some Consequences of Emigration for Rural Economic Development in the Yemen Arab Republic," MEJ (Winter).

Tait, Alan et al. 1979. "International Comparisons of Taxation for Selected Developing Countries." International Monetary Fund. *Staff Papers* (March).

Taylor, A. J. P. 1961. *The Course of German History*. London: Putnam.

Tezel, Yahya. 1975. "Turkish Economic Development. 1923–1950." Thesis, Cambridge University.

Théry, Edmond. 1922. *Conséquences économiques de la Guerre pour la France*. Paris: Bolin.

Thistlethwaite, Frank. 1955. *The Great Experiment*. Cambridge: Cambridge University Press.

Thobie, Jacques. 1977. *Intérêts et impérialisme français dans l'empire ottoman*. Paris: Imprimerie nationale.

Thomas, Benjamin. 1957. *Trade Routes of Algeria and the Sahara*. Berkeley and Los Angeles: University of California Press.

Thornburg, Max et al. 1949. *Turkey: An Economic Appraisal*. New York: Twentieth Century Fund.

Tignor, Robert. 1966. *Modernization and British Colonial Rule in Egypt*. Princeton, N. J.: Princeton University Press.

—— 1976. "The Egyptian Revolution of 1919: New Directions in the Egyptian Economy." In Kedourie. *The Middle Eastern Economy* (q.v.)

—— 1977. "Bank Misr and Foreign Capitalism." IJMES (April).

—— 1980. "Economic Activities of Foreigners in Egypt, 1920–1950." CSSH (July).

Tignor, Robert and Gouda Abdel-Khalek. 1981. *The Political Economy of Income Distribution in Egypt*. New York: Holmes and Meier.

Tlatli, Salah Eddine. 1957. *Tunisie Nouvelle*. Tunis.

Toynbee, Arnold. 1927. *Survey of International Affairs, 1925*. London: Oxford University Press.

Trebous, M. 1970. *Migration and Development: The Case of Algeria*. Paris: OECD.

Trumpener, Ulrich. 1968. *Germany and the Ottoman Empire*. Princeton, N. J.: Princeton University Press.

Tuma, Elias. 1980. "The Rich and the Poor in the Middle East." MEJ (Autumn).

Tu'meh, George, n.d. *Al-mughtaribun al-'arab fi Amerika al-shimaliyya*. Damascus.

Tunisia, 1954. (Encyclopédie mensuelle d'outre-mer, special issue) Paris.

La Tunisie: Agriculture, industrie, commerce, 1900. 2 vols. Paris: Berger-Levrault.

Turner, Louis and James Bedore. 1979. *Middle East Industrialisation.* Fainborough, Eng.: Saxon House.

Tute, R. C. 1927. *The Ottoman Land Laws.* Jerusalem.

Udovitch, Avram. 1970. *Partnership and Profit in Medieval Islam.* Princeton. N. J.: Princeton University Press.

—— 1976. *The Middle East: Oil, Conflict and Hope.* Lexington, Mass.: Lexington Books.

—— 1978. "Time, the Sea, and Society." *La navigazzione mediterranea nell'alto medioevo.* Spoleto.

—— 1981. *The Islamic Middle East, 700–1900.* Princeton, N.J.: Darwin Press.

United Nations. 1949. *Final Report of the United Nations Survey Mission for the Middle East.* New York.

—— 1951. *Review of Economic Conditions in the Middle East.* New York.

—— 1953. *Review of Economic Conditions in the Middle East, 1951–1952.* New York.

—— 1954. *Progress in Land Reform.* New York.

—— 1955. *Economic Developments in the Middle East, 1945 to 1954.* New York.

—— 1958. *Structure and Growth of Selected African Economies.* New York.

—— 1961. *Perspectives de Développement économique. . . .* TAO/TUN/3. New York.

—— 1966. *Progress in Land Reform.* Fourth Report. New York.

—— 1967. *Industrial Development in the Arab Countries.* New York.

—— 1969. *Industrial Development Survey.* New York.

—— 1974. *The Growth of World Industry.* New York.

—— 1975. *World Economic Survey.* New York.

—— 1980a. *Survey of Economic and Social Development in the ECWA Region.* Beirut.

—— 1980b. *Studies on Development Problems. . . .* Beirut.

United States. Department of State. *Foreign Relations of the United States.*

—— 1933. *Diplomatic Papers.* Washington, D.C.

—— Arms Control and Disarmament Agency, 1980. *World Military Expenditures and Arms Transfers, 1969–1978.*

Urquhart, David. 1833. *Turkey and Its Resources.* London.

Valensi, Lucette. 1969a. *Le Maghreb avant la prise d'Alger*. Paris: Flammarion.

—— 1969b. "Islam et capitalisme: Production et commerce de chechias en Tunisie et en France." *Revue d'histoire moderne et contemporaine* 16.

—— 1977. *Fellahs tunisiens*. Paris: Mouton.

Vallet, J. 1911. *Les conditions des ouvriers au Caire*. Valence.

Van der Kroef, Justus. 1954. *Indonesia in the Modern World*. Bandung.

Vatin, Jean-Claude. 1974. *L'Algérie politique: histoire et société*. Paris: A. Colin.

Velay, A du. 1903. *Essai sur l'histore financière de la Turquie*. Paris.

Venture du Paradis. 1898. *Alger au XVIIIᵉ siècle*. E. Fagnan, ed. Algiers.

Verney, Noel and George Dambmann. 1900. *Les Puissances étrangéres dans le Levant*. Paris: Guillaumin.

Viktorov, V. P., 1968. *Ekonomika sovremennoi Sirii*. Moscow.

Volney, C. F. 1825. *Voyage en Egypte et en Syrie*. 2 vols. Paris.

Walton, Gary and James Shepherd. 1979. *The Economic Rise of Early America*. Cambridge; Cambridge University Press.

Walz, T. 1978. *Trade Between Egypt and Bilad as-Sudan, 1700–1820*. Cairo.

Warriner, Doreen. 1948. *Land and Poverty in the Middle East*. London: Oxford University Press.

—— 1962. *Land Reform and Development in the Middle East*. London: Oxford University Press.

Waterbury, John. 1979. *Hydropolitics of the Nile Valley*. Syracuse: Syracuse University Press.

Watson, Andrew. 1974. "The Arab Agricultural Revolution and Its Diffusion." JEH (March).

Webster, Donald. 1939. *The Turkey of Ataturk*. Philadelphia: American Academy of Political and Social Science.

Wesseling, Henk. 1980. "Post—Imperial Holland." *Journal of Contemporary History* (January).

Weulersse, Jacques. 1946. *Paysans de Syrie et du Proche-Orient*. Paris: Gallamard.

Wiener, Lionel. 1932. *L'Egypte et ses chemins de fer* Brussels: M. Weissenbruch.

Williamson, John. 1971. *Karl Helfferich*. Princeton, N.J.: Princeton University Press.

Willcocks, William, 1911. *The Irrigation of Mesopotamia*. London.

Willcocks, William and J. I. Craig. 1913. *Egyptian Irrigation*. London: Spon.

Wilmington, Martin. 1971. *The Middle East Supply Centre.* Lawrence Evans, ed. Albany: State University of New York.

Winder, R. Bayly. 1962. "The Lebanese in West Africa." CSSH 4 (3).

—— 1965. *Saudi Arabia in the Nineteenth Century.* London: Macmillan.

World Bank (see also International Bank). 1972. *Transportation.*

—— 1979a. *Yemen Arab Republic.* Washington, D.C.

—— 1979b. *People's Democratic Republic of Yemen.* Washington, D.C.

—— 1980. *World Development Report.* Washington, D.C.

Yacono, X. 1954. "Peut-on évaluer la population de l'Algérie vers 1830." RA.

Yaganegi, Esfandiar. 1934. *Recent Financial and Monetary History of Persia.* New York.

Yerasimos, Stefanos. 1976. *Azgelişmişlik Sürecinde Türkiye.* 3 vols Istanbul.

Young, G. 1905–6. *Corps de Droit Ottoman.* Oxford: Clarendon.

Zahlan, A. 1980. *Science and Science Policy in the Arab World.* New York: St. Martin's.

Ziyadeh, Niqula. 1958. *Libiya min al-isti 'mar al-Italiy ila al-istiqlal.* Cairo.

Ziwar-Daftari, May. 1980. *Issues in Development: The Arab Gulf States.* London.

Zureik, Elia. 1979. *The Palestinians in Israel.* London: Routledge.

Subject Index

Index of Principal
Names and Places